Folklife and Museums

T0294647

AMERICAN ASSOCIATION FOR STATE AND LOCAL HISTORY BOOK SERIES

SERIES EDITOR

Russell Lewis, Chicago History Museum

EDITORIAL ADVISORY BOARD

Anne W. Ackerson, Leading by Design
William Bomar, University of Alabama Museums
Jessica Dorman, The Historic New Orleans Collection
W. Eric Emerson, South Carolina Department of Archives and History
Tim Grove, National Air and Space Museum
Laura Koloski, Pew Center for Arts & Heritage
Jane Lindsey, Juneau-Douglas City Museum
Ann E. McCleary, University of West Georgia
Laurie Ossman, Preservation Society of Newport County
Sarah Pharaon, International Coalition of Sites of Conscience
Laura Roberts, Roberts Consulting
Sandra Smith, Heinz History Center
Kimberly Springle, Charles Sumner School Museum and Archives
Will Ticknor, New Mexico Department of Cultural Affairs
William S. Walker, Cooperstown Graduate Program, SUNY Oneonta

STAFF

Bob Beatty, AASLH
Charles Harmon, Rowman & Littlefield Publishers

ABOUT THE SERIES

The American Association for State and Local History Book Series addresses issues critical to the field of state and local history through interpretive, intellectual, scholarly, and educational texts. To submit a proposal or manuscript to the series, please request proposal guidelines from AASLH headquarters: AASLH Editorial Board, 1717 Church St., Nashville, Tennessee 37203. Telephone: (615) 320-3203. Website: www.aaslh.org.

ABOUT THE ORGANIZATION

The American Association for State and Local History (AASLH) is a national history membership association headquartered in Nashville, Tennessee. AASLH provides leadership and support for its members who preserve and interpret state and local history in order to make the past more meaningful to all Americans. AASLH members are leaders in preserving, researching, and interpreting traces of the American past to connect the people, thoughts, and events of yesterday with the creative memories and abiding concerns of people, communities, and our nation today. In addition to sponsorship of this book series, AASLH publishes *History News* magazine, a newsletter, technical leaflets and reports, and other materials; confers prizes and awards in recognition of outstanding achievement in the field; supports a broad education program and other activities designed to help members work more effectively; and advocates on behalf of the discipline of history. To join AASLH, go to www.aaslh.org or contact Membership Services, AASLH, 1717 Church St., Nashville, TN 37203.

Folklife and Museums

Twenty-First-Century Perspectives

EDITED BY
C. KURT DEWHURST, PATRICIA HALL,
AND CHARLIE SEEMANN

ROWMAN & LITTLEFIELD
Lanham • Boulder • New York • London

Published by Rowman & Littlefield
A wholly owned subsidiary of The Rowman & Littlefield Publishing Group, Inc.
4501 Forbes Boulevard, Suite 200, Lanham, Maryland 20706
www.rowman.com

Unit A, Whitacre Mews, 26-34 Stannary Street, London SE11 4AB

Copyright © 2017 by Rowman & Littlefield

All rights reserved. No part of this book may be reproduced in any form or by any electronic or mechanical means, including information storage and retrieval systems, without written permission from the publisher, except by a reviewer who may quote passages in a review.

British Library Cataloguing in Publication Information Available

Library of Congress Cataloging-in-Publication Data

Names: Dewhurst, C. Kurt., editor. | Hall, Patricia, 1948– editor. | Seemann, Charlie, editor.
Title: Folklife and museums : selected readings / edited by Kurst Dewhurst, Patricia Hall, and Charles H. Seemann Jr.
Description: Second edition. | Lanham : Rowman & Littlefield, [2017] | Series: American association for state and local history | Includes bibliographical references and index.
Identifiers: LCCN 2016032751 (print) | LCCN 2016033935 (ebook) | ISBN 9781442272910 (cloth : alk. paper) | ISBN 9781442272927 (pbk. : alk. paper) | ISBN 9781442272934 (electronic)
Subjects: LCSH: Ethnological museums and collections—United States. | Historical museums—United States. | Material culture—Collection and preservation—United States. | Folklore—United States.
Classification: LCC GN36.U6 F65 2017 (print) | LCC GN36.U6 (ebook) | DDC 306.0973/074—dc23
LC record available at https://lccn.loc.gov/2016032751

∞™ The paper used in this publication meets the minimum requirements of American National Standard for Information Sciences—Permanence of Paper for Printed Library Materials, ANSI/NISO Z39.48-1992.

Printed in the United States of America

This volume is dedicated to all those pioneers and colleagues who have contributed to the presence of folklife in museum theory and practice.

Contents

Foreword

Bill Ivey

In 1987 the book *Folklife and Museums: Selected Readings* was published. This collection was timely; the institutional capacity of American museums had matured, and the field of folklore (or folklife) had widened its view of both career opportunities and appropriate venues for the dissemination of folklore knowledge—museums and folklife seemed a good fit. But over the past three decades new trends—some barely visible in the 1980s—have reconfigured the relationships between museums and folklife studies, and it is time to revisit assumptions and conclusions. By revising and updating essays from the first edition, and by adding articles on recent developments that affect the interconnections between folklore and museums, this new book stands as a worthy successor to the 1987 volume—it is both a fresh assessment of how folklife studies can work with and in museums and a valuable resource for any folklorist interested in museum work.

Folklore denotes a multidimensional arena of human activity—one that has spawned an equally complex discipline. The field encompasses huge swaths of expressive life—songs and tales, myths, legends, religious beliefs, traditional practices, and material culture—all connected through the shared fabric of community. Further, folklore is dynamic, created and continually re-created through a process of transmission in social networks. As museums have gained the capacity to feature both objects and performance, institutional practice has become increasingly compatible with folklore's complexity.

The modern museum has its origins in "cabinets of curiosities," which featured startling, beautiful, or exotic objects. Artifacts extracted from peasant and tribal societies, admired for their beauty and exotic character, displayed for the amusement and enlightenment of sophisticated observers, were often featured in early collections. This object-centered excursion into the exhibition of folk culture paralleled the nineteenth-century display of fine art—crowded, floor-to-ceiling clusters of paintings that eased comparison of one artist with another.

By the early twentieth century, inspired in part by Vienna-based designers intent on using galleries as spaces to display graphs and pictorial statistics, museums had become big schoolbooks in which visitors could not only admire objects but also absorb related text and charts during a gallery stroll. Open-air facilities added another dimension, enabling museums to employ craftspeople or actors to demonstrate historical or traditional practices and techniques in agriculture, manufacture, and homemaking.

In the last two decades of the twentieth century, it was possible to view the character of museums as fully formed. Institutions were primarily focused on the preservation of objects, on displaying selected examples in meaningful arrangements explained by captions or presentations by docents. Although twentieth-century media were difficult to maintain in continually accessible public settings, sound recording, film, and videotape had begun to provide museums with the opportunity to demonstrate process. It was easy for observers to see the character of the modern museum as evolved and fixed, but change was on the way. In fact, no category of cultural institution has undergone more change over the past three decades than has the museum.

Technology has transformed museums, offering opportunities to capture, preserve, and demonstrate the richness of folklife in ways barely imaginable in the 1980s. Museums (like libraries) were quick to embrace computers; after all, collections inevitably hold more items than can be interpreted or displayed, and digital technology offered an exciting opportunity to aggregate and share collection data with the public and across institutional boundaries. By the 1980s the Smithsonian had developed its SELGEM and GRIPHOS systems, accommodating and controlling large quantities of information. But the most important impact of digital technology would be in the easy capture of process and the dependable use of moving images, even virtual reality, as display techniques linking museum with visitor.

Digital technology has connected museums with folk culture to audiences in new ways, but the relationship between museums and geographical, ethnic, and virtual communities has grown more complex. Museums featuring folklife bring the stories of minorities, tribes, ethnic and religious minorities to the world. And as never before these tribes, nationalities, and ethnic groups have questioned the way museums speak for them. Human remains were moved from burial grounds to museum, ceremonial objects were displayed. No surprise, provenance and ownership rights have been challenged as never before. By the late twentieth century, repatriation of both fine art objects and tribal treasures had become a major concern for museum leadership. Curators in general, and folklife specialists in particular, found themselves caught in the middle as museums, auction houses, collectors, and communities struggled to determine both ownership rights and the nature of representation.

But even as the content of museum collections and the nature of museum narratives triggered community sensitivities, museums themselves were increasingly drawn into the center of institutionalized civic life. The influence of amusement park storytelling, the capacity of technology to make artifacts and traditional processes come alive, and the marriage of ambitious construction projects with the talents of groundbreaking architects and designers placed museums at the center of civic pride and ambition. Architect Frank Gehry's design for the Guggenheim Museum, Bilbao (1997), created an international sensation, cementing the idea of museum as centerpiece for cultural tourism. The United States Holocaust Memorial Museum, opened in 1993 in Washington, DC, documented a tragic historical episode that, by its very nature, left few artifacts. But by combining mood-setting architecture with excellent exhibit design and media, the Holocaust Museum disseminated a horrific story of permanent significance to the global Jewish community. Plans for institutions dedicated to the stories of African American and Hispanic American populations followed, carrying the narrative function of museums to a new level.

Museums further extended community service to include festivals, live performances, and demonstrations, even using collections to develop services not directly connected to exhibitions. Folklore festivals had existed from the 1930s forward, but the Smithsonian Institution's Festival of American

Folklife (now the Smithsonian Folklife Festival), launched in 1976, specifically linked the intellectual gravitas of museum curatorial expertise with public performance. The National Cowboy Poetry Gathering in Elko, Nevada (1985), reversed the museum-to-festival idea by first initiating a successful live performance event, then building a program of historic-site preservation, collection, and exhibition on that curatorial foundation. By acquiring historic Folkways Records (1987), the Smithsonian Institution Center for Folklife and Cultural Heritage successfully made an active record label a part of the Smithsonian's commitment to education and outreach.

Over the past thirty years the term "folk art" has emerged as an especially insistent example of the ways museums and galleries deploy some of the materials and much of the terminology of the folklore field in a manner quite contrary to discipline theories and practices. The Museum of American Folk Art (now known as the American Folk Art Museum), chartered in 1966 but only open to the public in the mid-1980s, eschews the key concepts of traditionality and community context in order to celebrate humble artmaking as singular artifact. The approach of what can be called the "folk arts movement" is in many ways a throwback to the nineteenth-century view of folklife as a source of "curiosities" to be gathered, organized, admired, bought, and sold. For the folklife specialist, folk art means traditional expressive life—quilts, log cabins, carved decoys, to be sure, but also intangible forms like song, storytelling, and dance. Drawing inspiration from fine art galleries, museum collections, and exhibitions, the American folk arts phenomenon treats each object as unique, imposing the individualistic model of the solo painter or sculptor on traditional, community-based art forms like quilting, woodcarving, or Native American beadwork. Further, this collector-driven movement conflates traditional art with the work of self-taught painters and sculptors and exhibits a special affection for idiosyncratic "outsider" or "visionary" artists inspired by dreams, religion, and sometimes mental illness. While the modern folklife specialist can often comment smartly on the character and significance of this kind of art and these creative practitioners, folklorists have only occasionally found ways to connect with this influential but distorting exploitation of folklife terminology.

The field of folklore, framed through much of the past century as an academic discipline, has itself changed over the past three decades. The creation of multiple folklore positions at all levels of government and with many nonprofit organizations opened career opportunities scarcely visible in the 1980s. Today, half of the membership of the American Folklore Society works outside the academy; many folklorists are employed by museums, either as full-time staff or as independent curators. But the museum field has also changed; an increasing proportion of leaders in the field hold degrees in museum studies. Folklorists seeking a museum career must frequently acquire additional graduate-level training.

In his foreword to the first edition of this collection, folklorist Alan Jabbour wondered "what museums can offer folklife, and what folklife can offer museums." Jabbour's hope for a "happy and compatible match" has in many ways been realized. But digital technology, an intensifying engagement between museums and communities of all kinds, and nagging issues of understanding and definition suggest that there remains work to be done before the marriage of folklife and museums is fulfilled. This new and expanded collection will help.

Introduction

In 1987, the American Association for State and Local History published *Folklife and Museums: Selected Readings*, edited by Patricia Hall and Charlie Seemann. The book, now out of print for a number of years, included fourteen essays by scholars and practitioners representing both academic and public sectors in the fields of folklife studies, museology, anthropology, history, and art history. It was widely used as a textbook in both folklore and museum studies classes. In 2011, American Folklore Society (AFS) president C. Kurt Dewhurst delivered a presidential address titled "Folklife and Museum Practice: An Intertwined History and Emerging Convergences" at the society's annual meeting. In conversations after that address, a number of colleagues asked if we had considered producing a new, updated version of the 1987 book. Dewhurst offered to join the original two editors as a third editor, and planning began to revise and enlarge the 1987 volume. The result eventually became a new book, *Folklife and Museums: Twenty-First-Century Perspectives*, including some seminal pieces from the 1987 book but comprising mostly new articles. Another parallel development arising from Dewhurst's presidential address was the creation of an AFS Public Policy Working Group on Folklore and Museums, comprising a group of folklorists working in various museum situations around the country, by Marsha Bol,

C. Kurt Dewhurst, Carrie Hertz, Jason Baird Jackson, Marsha MacDowell, Charlie Seemann, Suzy Seriff, and Dan Sheehy. The working group produced a white paper, "Rethinking the Role of Folklore in Museums: Exploring New Directions for Folklore in Museum Policy and Practice." Eventually, all of the members of the working group contributed chapters to the new *Folklife and Museums* book and were joined by a distinguished group of additional authors to arrive at a total of nineteen new and revised chapters. It is the purpose of this proposed forum to discuss the context that gave rise to the 1987 volume, the rationale for the scope and content of the new book, its purpose, and its hoped-for impact.

The contributors to this volume capture the growing contributions to the museum field by the discipline of folklife in the twenty-first century. Attention is also given to the emergence of folklife as an intellectual approach to museum studies at the end of the twentieth century. Contributors address the way that folklife and folk art have been featured and integrated into museums of different disciplines—be they fine art, history, anthropology, natural history, outdoor and farm, children's and youth, or culturally specific museums—and tackle issues of "what is heritage" and the importance of connecting the tangible artifact to the intangible cultural heritage approach of folklore.

A growing number of folklorists are serving as museum professionals as staff members or board members or are working closely with museums as contract staff, research fieldworkers, or consultants. They include the full range of roles from administration to curation, collection management, exhibition, education, community engagement, digital asset management, and communication and marketing.

Graduate students in folklore and related fields are choosing to pursue museum-based careers in growing numbers—as their training enables them to work effectively in innovative ways in museums today that are deeply committed to collaborative research, educational outreach, and using digital tools to provide greater access to museum programs, collections, and resources. Progressive museum theory and practice today has embraced the sharing of authority in all areas of museum operations with the communities they serve. Folklorists bring to museum work an ethical approach that values deep community collaboration, respect for local traditional culture, a trained lens for reading community assets, and building trust with community members and partners.

This collection of essays conveys the evolving role of folklife in museums today. Some of the most compelling issues of today include "what is heritage" and how we document and meaningfully connect the intangible cultural heritage to the tangible museum object or artifact. Folklorists in the twenty-first century are now working in and with museums in ever more creative ways to respond to the pressing societal issues museums are facing. They are contributing significantly by expanding the deep participation of community members in all of the daily operation of many museums. They are assisting museums by striving to include community voice and actual involvement—to enhance the broader representation of communities in museums. The results include the following: expanded collaborative interpretive strategies, reenvisioned collecting practices, more democratic community approaches to exhibition development, expanded sharing of curatorial authority, more community-centered educational programming, redefinition of the power relationships between museums and communities, and remarkable innovative use of technology to foster access.

In the process of developing this book, we have found ourselves not only impressed with the entrepreneurial but highly inspired by the work of folklorists working in the museum field today in the United States. Clearly, museum work today is a collaborative act, so we are not suggesting that folklorists are doing this innovative practice on their own; rather they have used their training to work effectively as team members with their museum colleagues from other disciplines. However, their perspectives are playing an increasingly important role in this century for their museums. Whether it be through appreciation for oral history, collected stories, documentary fieldwork, expressive material culture, or a more inclusive view of expressive culture, folklorists are especially helping foreground the community voice in museum exhibitions, collection development/access, and educational programming. The field of folklife is now truly enriching the visitor experience at museums of all kinds across the country. We hope this volume fosters an increased appreciation for, and application of lessons shared here about, the field of folklore and the growing role of folklorists in the museum world.

1

Folklife and Museum Practice

An Intertwined History and Emerging Convergences

C. Kurt Dewhurst

C. Kurt Dewhurst traces the history of the contributions of the field of folklore to museum theory and practice. In discussing the early role that museum-based folklorists played in the establishment of the American Folklore Society (AFS), he makes the case that folklorists have played a significant role in reenvisioning the relationship between museums and the communities they serve. The chapter stresses the role folklorists have played in the documentation, protection, collection development, and presentation of not only tangible cultural heritage but, perhaps even more important in the twenty-first century, intangible cultural heritage. He emphasizes that current folklore training and a more community-centered approach to engaged scholarly work are timely and enrich the twenty-first-century museum. He provides a valuable overview of some recent innovative museum movements and the folklorist's capacity for deep documentation, commitment to community voice, and a participatory ethos. This chapter is based on Dewhurst's 2011 presidential address at the American Folklore Society's annual meeting.

Folklore and museums have had a long and intertwined history. Among those responsible for the founding of the American Folklore Society in 1888 were museum-based anthropologists, curators, and collection managers. Since that time, folklorists have worked in and with museums in a variety of ways—work that has reflected intellectual and political shifts in folklore studies as well as changes in museum practice. As cultural heritage work in the twenty-first century seeks simultaneously to document, interpret, present, preserve, and protect tangible and intangible heritage, while at the same time addressing the needs of civil society, the logical interfaces between folklore and museum work have increased. As an individual who has spent almost forty years as a folklorist and museum professional, I have had many opportunities to reflect on that work and how it mirrors, supports, or even contests what I have seen in the fields of folklore and museum practice. In this presentation today, I hope to elucidate some of my own reflections set in the context of a review of American folklore and museum professional practice since the late nineteenth century. My comments in today's presentation will also reflect the insights of a group of folklorists whom I have interviewed over the past two years in preparation for this address; I am deeply indebted to them for the insights they have shared. Therefore, this presentation today will provide a brief history of the intersections of museum and folklore practice, highlight some of the significant global shifts in museum practice, examine some of the challenges and opportunities folklorists have encountered in museum practice, and finally suggest ways in which more interaction between folklorists and museums can advance the respective work of each domain. I want to note that the emphasis in this chapter will be on shifts in museum theory and practice as well as on shifts in folklore practice in more applied contexts; I will not be providing a parallel examination of folklore theory and practice.

MUSEUMS AND THE AMERICAN FOLKLORE SOCIETY: HISTORICAL AND PHILOSOPHICAL CONNECTIONS

I would like to begin by reviewing some historical and philosophical connections between museums and the American Folklore Society. The American Folklore Society was founded in 1888, an era in which private individuals were amassing collections of objects, books, specimens, and—for folklorists—information about traditions. Of the folklore collecting of that period, Simon J. Bronner has written, "The collection of traditions was similar to the methods of natural history, with specimens gathered through fieldwork and compared to specimens from other locales."[1] Like other learned societies that were established during the 1880s, the American Folklore Society attracted "not only faculty but also writers and museum curators."[2] Among those who founded the AFS were Francis James Child, William Wells Newell, Daniel Garrison Brinton, Stewart Culin, and Franz Boas—all were collectors, and the latter three held significant museum-based positions. Bronner has also noted that Culin once called "for museums to form collections that would convey the ideas of folklore to the public. As folklore deals with ideas, so it would be the mission of the folklore museums to collect, arrange, and classify the objects associated with them."[3]

As the society moved into the twentieth century, the numbers of AFS members whose research focused on the object began to dwindle. Bronner has also observed, "Where many museum professionals with a natural interest in artifact collection joined the American Folklore Society in the early years, more academics with less concern for objects later took up the rolls."[4] Folklorist John Michael Vlach speculates the reason for this shift is that "scholars of oral forms, being generally employed in English departments, found tales, lyrics to be compatible with their academic homes. . . . Material culture scholars, by contrast, were connected to museums where they had little access to students and hence little opportunity to instill an appreciation of artifacts in subsequent generations of potential folklorists."[5]

Although the numbers of AFS members who pursued material culture studies and/or were employed in museums were not robust in the early twentieth century, the numbers began to increase again during the latter part of the century and continue to do so today. I believe this increase in numbers, as well as the expansion and deepening of the ways in which folklorists and museums mesh, can be attributed to some significant changes in museum practice and theories and, on the folklore side, to a number of key activities in both academic and public-sector folklore training and practice.

MUSEUM SHIFTS: DEVELOPING A CLIMATE FOR EXPANSION OF MUSEUMS AND FOLKLORE INTERSECTIONS

Now I want to move to share some museum shifts that have developed a climate for the expansion of museums and folklore intersections.[6] Museums in the United States and around the world certainly predated the formation of the American Folklore Society. In western European and American contexts, museums were generally built upon collections of art objects and natural specimens assembled by scholars and collectors of personal, religious, and civic means. Generally these collections were primarily intended to support scholarly work, to provide private enjoyment, or, as in the case of collections owned by church or state, to demonstrate the power and influence of their institutions. The collections did not include the material culture of everyday life unless an object was deemed an artifact of curiosity or considered to represent the culture of the "other," and "cabinets of curiosities" were the mainstay technique of displaying collections.

Beginning in the late nineteenth century, changes began to occur within the museum world that impacted what was collected, why it was collected, who did the collecting, and how collections were interpreted and used. I'd like to provide a sampling of the changes I believe have created a fertile landscape in folklore and museum practices. The first development was the emergence and growth of open-air museums and living history programming. In 1872, Swedish teacher, scholar, and folklorist Artur Hazelius established a museum in Stockholm for Swedish ethnography, now called Nordiska Museet, to house the peasant life materials he bought or managed to get donated from all over Sweden and the other Nordic countries. Inspired by the open-air display of the collection of buildings owned by Norway's king Oscar II near Oslo, Hazelius began to collect entire buildings and farmsteads. In 1891, he opened the open-air museum Skansen in Stockholm. Skansen became the prototype for a movement of creating model open-air museums first in northern Europe and then around the world.[7] In the United States, the Skansen model informed the development of the Henry Ford Museum and Greenfield Village, Old Sturbridge Village, Williamsburg, and scores of other museums. In each iteration, the open-air museum typically consisted of "traditional homes, farmsteads, and community buildings relocated into a unified setting where regional differences were contrasted."[8]

In an effort to animate the buildings and enhance understanding of the cultures, time periods, and experiences associated with the individuals who lived in the buildings, these open-air museums began to use "living history" techniques to re-create the historical work and daily life associated with the buildings. The buildings became a virtual theatrical set for demonstrations and presentations of traditional lifeways and expressive culture.[9] "The open-air museums were real laboratories for the development of new strategies for interpretation and they led to the growth of living farm museums and living history museums in the years that followed."[10] The Association for Living History, Farm and Agricultural Museums explicitly includes folklife in its mission statement, that is, "to serve those involved in living historical farms, agricultural museums and outdoor museums of history and folklife."[11]

Another, more recent development has been the eco-museum movement that began to emerge in the closing decades of the twentieth century.[12] The concept of an eco-museum is one more of process than a type of museum; it relies on an agreement with the community to preserve, interpret, and manage its heritage resources for "sustainable development." The goal is to foster a dynamic process for broader community involvement and shared responsibilities, for heritage becomes closer to the idea of "place"—where the history of the inhabitants and the physical objects, buildings, and environment are infused with intangible memories and aspirations. It is a strategy for place-based development that honors local networks/relationships, and it plays a role in fostering social capital at the local level.[13] Eco-museums have been developed around specific immigrant groups, ethnicities, occupational cultures, and regional traditions: many serve as centers of community activity. Eco-museums in western Europe have become a hospitable work setting for some folklorists.[14] Perhaps the most widespread shift in museum practice has been the call for museums to be more active forces for civil society. Museums in America have been challenged by cultural activists, community members, the American Association of Museums, and funding agencies to become more engaged in civic life. Cultural researcher Ellen Hirzy describes this engagement:

> Civic engagement occurs when museum and community intersect—in subtle and overt ways, over time, and as an accepted and natural way of doing business. The museum becomes a center where people gather to meet and converse, a place that celebrates the richness of individual and collective experience, and a participant in collaborative problem solving. It is an active player in civic life, a safe haven, and a trusted incubator of change. These are among the possibilities inherent in each museum's own definition and expression of community. Across professions and institutions throughout society, a vigorous exploration and reinvention of civic roles is underway. Power and decision making are shared more broadly than ever before, giving citizens both expanded obligations and unparalleled opportunities.[15]

Museums are increasingly being expected to proactively use their facilities, collections, and staff skills to address the needs of their communities and thus build a civil society. For instance, the Institute of Museum and Library Services—a federal agency—in 2009 issued a report titled *Museums, Libraries, and 21st Century Skills* that identifies the skills necessary to develop twenty-first-century communities, citizens, and workers and calls for museums and libraries to take a more active role in helping members of their communities to attain those skills.[16] Historian Robert Archibald also believes that museums face unprecedented opportunities to exert even greater influence in society. We are becoming places of dialog, advocates for inclusion, places of values, and incubators of community. Without straying from our foundations, we can become places where consensus evolves around fundamental questions faced by people in every age. How can we work differently in order to reach our potential?[17] Despite the perceptions and realities of museums as sites of authoritative knowledge, their reservoir of social capital, and their potential to be agents and sites of civic engagement, museums are rarely at the center of community life. Maria Rosario Jackson, a researcher specializing in studies of community cultural assets, has analyzed the potential and challenges of museums' increasing connections to and playing more meaningful roles in civic life. She argues, "Too often, they are on the sidelines of civic life. . . . [The museum field faces] a noble challenge—to stretch its boundaries, step away from the sidelines, come to the center of civic life, and become a more active participant and even a leader in social-capital and community-building processes."[18]

Folklorists, especially those working in the public sector, have the skill sets to conduct community cultural asset inventories, to map and describe those assets, to develop strategies to present those assets in public contexts, and to engage community members and facilitate dialog. Folklorists who work in and with museums often serve as critical bridge builders between museums and communities. Folklore training enables one to acquire a deep understanding of how to work with diverse communities in an equitable, respectful, and informed way. Folklorists can also assist libraries and museums in their new mission to cultivate a twenty-first-century workforce especially by lending their expertise in visual literacy, cross-disciplinary thinking, and social and cross-cultural skills. One example of the ways in which folklorists based in museums are helping their institutions become active forces for convening, community building, and social cohesion can be seen in the new uses that were made of Smithsonian facilities for the inauguration of President Barack Obama in 2009. Since the inauguration of President Abraham Lincoln, the Smithsonian has served as a host site for many official presidential inauguration activities—which were typically reserved for an exclusive set of attendees. In 2009, folklorist Richard Kurin, then the Smithsonian's acting undersecretary for history, art, and culture, decided that all of the museums on the National Mall should be open for all individuals coming to Washington for the inauguration, thus fostering a greater sense of inclusion among those who wanted to be part of the historic event. Some buildings were even open through the night to provide shelter from the bitter cold for those who came to the "nation's front lawn" for the historic inauguration. For many, it was their first time in a museum—let alone the Smithsonian. The Smithsonian also offered free exhibitions, programs, and support for the overflow crowds of visitors. The Smithsonian Folklife Festival staff was even enlisted to provide extra support and equipment to help facilitate the official swearing-in ceremony.[19] It was an inspiring moment in which many folklorists and museum workers took action, putting their training, perspective, and values to work.

MUSEUMS AS SITES OF HISTORIC CONSCIENCE AND PUBLIC MEMORY

One of the most powerful new museum movements is the development of museums that preserve and use sites of historic conscience as places of healing and education, as places where public memory is made more visible, and especially as realms of memory dealing with difficult histories and issues. Corinne Kratz and Ivan Karp have stated that museums in general need to become sites for exploring the social challenges and issues that often divide communities and for museums to become sites of dialog, critical discourse, and the forging of community well-being. They state,

> Museum work is not without strife and conflict. Many in our field seek to avoid engaging in the issues that occupy their community and choose to be sites of only reflection and reverence. While museums do play a valuable role in these ways, today, museums are finding themselves more marginalized due to global forces and we are just beginning to understand the intensity of the challenge that lies ahead if indeed we want to be players in our civic landscapes and to be a central force in the cultural commons of our communities.[20]

In 1999, the International Coalition of Sites of Conscience was established; its more than 260 member organizations are "specifically dedicated to remembering past struggles for justice and addressing contemporary legacies."[21] These museums aim to "assist the public in drawing connections between the history of our sites and the contemporary implications. We view stimulating dialogue on pressing social issues and promoting humanitarian and democratic values as a primary function."[22] There is a growing number of folklorists who strive to give voice to those individuals whose stories and life experiences are underrepresented in the scholarly record or public discourse. Their interests and skills are especially suited for advancing the mission of the sites of historic conscience.

It is not surprising that American museums where folklorists have long been employed have been places that are bringing difficult issues and memories into the public discourse. The Michigan State University (MSU) Museum, for instance, has developed a number of exhibitions on human rights and social justice, at least one in tandem with the Vermont Folklife Center and City Lore. Another example is the Museum of International Folk Art in Santa Fe, New Mexico, which now has a dedicated Gallery of Conscience. And, of course, the Smithsonian Institution's Center for Folklife and Cultural Heritage, which has had one of the largest museum-based concentrations of folklorists, has, particularly through its festival programs and Folkways recordings, brought to public attention many previously untold and difficult histories. Let me just mention here that one of MSU Museum's exhibitions is the "Quilts of Human Rights" exhibition—a portion was shown at the Mathers Museum of World Cultures as part of the AFS conference theme "Peace, War, Folklore," to coincide with Indiana University Themester 2012, "Making War, Making Peace."

GLOBAL INTEREST OF MUSEUMS IN TANGIBLE AND INTANGIBLE HERITAGE PRESERVATION AND PROTECTION

Much has been made by folklorists in recent years—including at the annual meetings of the American Folklore Society—of the growing global awareness of the critical importance of the documentation and preservation of our intangible as well as our tangible cultural heritage. In 1989, the General Conference of the United Nations Educational, Scientific, and Cultural Organization (UNESCO) adopted the *Recommendation on the Safeguarding of Traditional*

Culture and Folklore.[23] A little more than a decade later, on May 16, 2001, the *Report on the Preliminary Study on the Advisability of Regulating Internationally, through a New Standard-Setting Instrument, the Protection of Traditional Culture and Folklore* significantly shifted the terms of the 1989 document. First, rather than emphasize the role of the professional folklorists and folklore institutions in documenting and preserving the records of endangered traditions, it focused on sustaining the traditions themselves by supporting the practitioners. This entailed a shift from artifacts (tales, songs, customs) to people (performers, artisans, healers), their knowledge, and their skills.[24] Barbara Kirshenblatt-Gimblett has written of the emerging opportunity to understand the tangible object from the perspective of a folklorist. She asks a central question: "Under what circumstances does the substance of the object matter? The conception of intangible heritage guiding UNESCO's preservation program is directed to supporting practitioners and the transmission of what they know—so that what is preserved is the ability to continue to make and do things in ways that continue to be meaningful and valued."[25]

Museums are also coming to grips with the need to document, collect, provide stewardship for, and present intangible heritage—along with, for them, the more familiar focus on the tangible. As intangible heritage becomes a stronger focus of cultural heritage work, and as museums increasingly address intangible heritage needs, it becomes even more evident that folklorists can play vital roles in museums to elevate the standing of intangible heritage.

Museums, Sense of Place, and Cultural Tourism

Museums are now considered critical to cultural tourism and cultural economic development, movements that inherently depend on identifying, marketing, and connecting local cultural assets to more global audiences. In this realm of activity, folklorists have been active agents in not only identifying assets but also trying to triage the impacts of these larger movements in ways that are positive for traditional artists and their communities. Only a few years ago, a group of folklorists convened at an annual meeting to discuss reactions to Lucy R. Lippard's book *The Lure of the Local: Senses of Place in a Multicentered Society*, in which she states, "All places exist somewhere between the inside and the outside views of them, the ways in which they compare to, and contrast with, other places. A sense of place is a virtual immersion that depends on lived experience and a topographical intimacy that

FIGURE 1.1
Since 1982, the National Endowment for the Arts has annually awarded up to eight individuals with a National Heritage Fellowship recognizing their excellence and authenticity in contributing to the rich artistic and cultural legacies of America. In 2013, the Michigan State University Museum developed an exhibition, "Extraordinary/Ordinary People: American Masters of Traditional Arts," which featured deep content on selected recipients. The interpretation included photographs, video and listening stations, QR codes, visitor questions posed on text panels, and computer stations to access other media. Also, public programming included performances and demonstrations during the exhibition. This exhibition was cocurated by Marsha MacDowell and Alan Govenar. (Photo: Pearl Yee Wong, Michigan State University Museum.)

is rare today both in ordinary life and in the traditional educational fields." From Lippard's viewpoint, it demands extensive visual and historical research, a great deal of walking "in the field," contact with oral tradition, and intensive knowledge of both local multiculturalism and the broader context of multicenteredness.[26] Lippard's concepts resonate soundly with our field's deep interest in describing and understanding what defines the local and a sense of belonging to place.

Digital Preservation and Access to Collections

Museums, libraries, and archives are rapidly developing initiatives for digital preservation of and access to collections. Scholars now have unprecedented access to primary materials, including folklore collections. After years in which museum collections have been stored separately from fieldwork notes, oral recordings, and photographic documentation, today, with the advent of digital tools and a shift in philosophy, the tangible collections are being reunited or connected with the intangible resources in remarkable ways. Collaborations among folklorists and museum, library, and archive information and collection specialists are resulting in new digital tools such as the Ethnographic Thesaurus, digital projects such as the National Folklore Archives Project, Open Folklore, and Oral History in the Digital Age, as well as digital repositories of traditional material culture such as the Quilt Index. These resources are serving museums and the folklore field in ways we are just beginning to appreciate.

MUSEUM AND FOLKLORE INTERSECTIONS IN THE TWENTIETH CENTURY

Now I would like to share some notable shifts and intersections of museums and folklore in the twentieth century. Just as the landscape of museum work was shifting and becoming a place that was more hospitable to and needful of folklorists, there were also shifts in the world of folklore studies and practice that helped increase opportunities for folklore and museum intersections. I would like to point to four that I believe have been critical.

Linking of Folklore and Museum Graduate Training

The emergence of graduate programs that purposefully link folklore and museum studies has had a deep and lasting impact on the number of cultural heritage professionals who have been engaged in both folklore and museum work. "In the 1960s, [folklorist] Dr. Louis C. Jones, then Director of the New York State Historical Association, lamented the lack of training for museum professionals. He wondered who would staff the growing number of museums, and preserve the objects of our nation's heritage."[27] Jones hired folklorist Bruce Buckley as the first director of the Cooperstown Graduate Program, a program affiliated with the State University of New York at Oneonta, and the "two men set about the task of creating museum and folk culture programs that focused on community study, documentation, and cultural preservation."[28] Subsequent graduate programs at universities such as Western Kentucky University have also been able to bring together their folk studies, anthropology, and museum studies programs to foster graduate training for students who have entered the workforce in many museum and/or folklore positions.

The National Endowment for the Arts Folk and Traditional Arts Program

In 1974, the National Endowment for the Arts (NEA) established a folk arts program to underwrite grants to place folklorists in state arts councils and other state agencies across the country to conduct projects that would document and present traditional arts, increase public understanding of our country's folk and traditional arts, and, hopefully, encourage the arts council or agency to provide ongoing support for both a folklorist and a folk arts program.[29] Among the first grants awarded in this new program were grants to support statewide surveys of folklife/folk arts and then to present the collected data to the public in an accessible form. (In the spirit of full disclosure, I should note that Michigan was one of the first two NEA-funded state survey exhibit project grants.[30]) Barry Bergey, then director of the program, observed, "Early on when we began to fund state programs, surveys proved to be critical to the success of many programs. It helped identify the state folk assets, it provided folk arts coordinators the opportunity to do fieldwork and to be in the field building networks and linkages."[31] Many of the projects funded by the NEA program resulted in exhibitions accompanied by published catalogs and public programs in which traditional artists were brought into museums to do workshops, performances, and demonstrations. In the process of fieldwork and documentation, the folklorists working on these projects often also inventoried what historical materials were held in their state's public and private collections. As a result, the work of the folklorists brought new attention to collection holdings and helped to forge new interfaces between traditional artists and museums as well as between the grant's host institution—typically the state arts council—and other museums in the state.

Material Folk Culture Studies in Graduate Folklore Programs

The addition of material folk culture specialists to some of the major folklore graduate programs, such as Indiana University, the University of Pennsylvania, the University of California, Los Angeles, and Memorial University, helped foster an increased attention to the material culture forms of traditional expression. The impact of these university-based scholars of material folk culture has

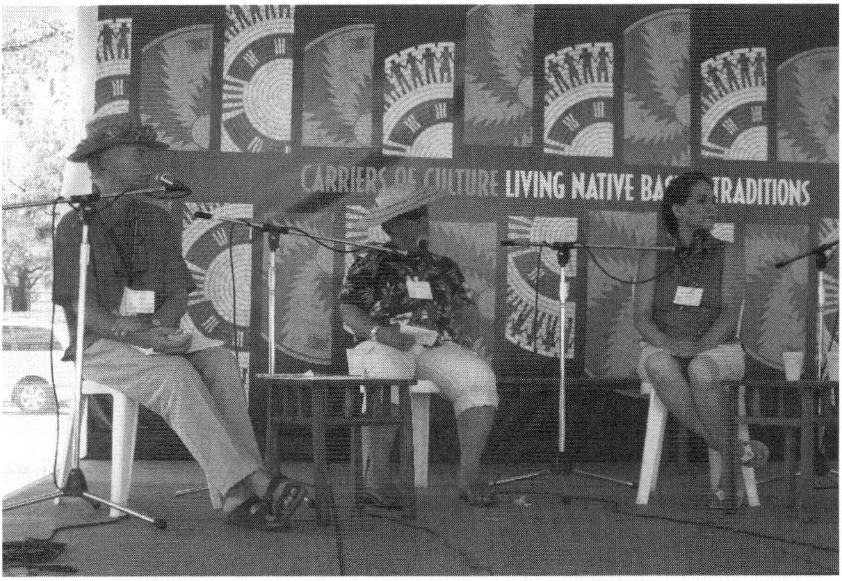

FIGURE 1.2
Native weavers participate in a narrative session at the "Carriers of Culture: Native Basket Traditions" program of the 2006 Smithsonian Folklife Festival on the National Mall in Washington, DC. This discussion format led by a folklorist or cultural specialist "gives voice" to the artists/tradition bearers in a public setting, and the sessions are recorded for archival use. The presenter, C. Kurt Dewhurst, is leading a discussion on how weavers learned to weave. The Native weavers are Harriet Soong and Bernadette Phillips. (Photo: Minnie Wabanimkee, Michigan State University Museum.)

been instrumental in expanding the numbers of students who have become interested in material folk culture studies and museum-based work.

The Smithsonian Folklife Festival

In 1976, the Smithsonian Institution staged its first folklife festival on the National Mall in Washington, DC. The sustained presence of the annual Smithsonian Folklife Festival has not only provided a high-profile annual living museum exhibition of traditional culture on America's front lawn, but it has also served as a field school/training experience for the presentation and interpretation of living traditional culture.[32] The planning and implementation stages of each festival program have drawn together folklorists and museum practitioners whose skill sets and expertise were meshed in producing

FIGURE 1.3
The American Folklore Society has an ongoing partnership with the Chinese Folklore Society, focusing on the safeguarding, documentation, and presentation of intangible cultural heritage. One of the initiatives is a partnership between three museums in the United States and China that has involved educational forums, publications, staff exchanges, fieldwork, and a collaborative exhibition. The first exhibition, "Quilts of Southwest China," opened at the Michigan State University Museum in 2015 and will travel to the partner and other museums in the United States. The exhibition was cocurated by Marsha MacDowell and Li Jun Zhang. (Photo: Pearl Yee Wong, Michigan State University Museum.)

groundbreaking interpretive programming, and that experience attracted some folklorists to pursue work with museums over their careers.

ASSESSING THE CONNECTIONS AND IMPACTS OF FOLKLORE AND MUSEUMS

So, let's assess the connection and impacts of folklore with museums. Today, folklorists are employed in American museums in a variety of staff and consultative capacities. Folklorists have helped build a body of published scholarship that has described and critiqued folklore and museum history, practice, and policy. Their engagement in museum work has helped museums meet the changes demanded of them by the society and by new international standards of practice. Folklorists have contributed to the growing expectation for a "proliferation of voices" in the reshaping of the museum experience in the twenty-first century.[33] Drawing on the interviews I've conducted with folklorists whose careers have been based wholly or primarily in museums, I would like to offer some observations of how folklore training has prepared them for this work, how the work of these individuals has augmented changes within their respective institutions, and, last, some of the challenges and unique opportunities that folklorists have faced in their museum-based careers.

Folklorists have helped museums expand their definition of what should be collected, how it should be collected, and how those collections should be presented. Folklorists, importantly, have built collections of material objects from cultural groups whose work was previously not represented in museums, as well as types of materials typically not collected. They have also added field documentation (taped interviews, photographic resources, and fieldwork reports) associated with those objects that allow museums to more authentically and deeply interpret collections. Folklorist and ethnomusicologist Stephen Stuempfle, who was a curator at the Museum of Southern Florida in Miami, points out,

> Folklorists focus on traditional arts but examine such arts as interrelated with all cultural domains, from economics and social structure to politics and religion. When collecting artifacts, for example, folklorists are concerned with how they are embedded in particular environments, social processes and cultural systems. Thus, their collecting projects typically involve substantial participant-observation, interviewing, sound recording, photography, and videography. This documentation, along with the artifacts themselves, greatly enriches museum collections. The artifacts and documentation are also a tremendous resource in developing multimedia exhibitions that engage museum visitors and offer meaningful interpretations of community life, past and present.[34]

Building collections that convey an authentic deep sense of place can also mean capturing place shaped by historic moments to be featured in museums. Folklorists demonstrated the understanding and trust they had cultivated within community networks, and the folklorist's concurrent understanding of the need to document tangible and intangible historic moments was clearly evidenced by the work of folklorists like Steve Zeitlin and Martha Cooper in the moments and days following 9/11. The powerful human stories and material expressive objects they collected were exhibited at the New York Historical Museum and will be featured in the forthcoming World Trade Center Memorial and Museum.[35]

Charlie Seemann is director of the Western Folklife Center (Elko, Nevada) and a former curator at the Country Music Hall of Fame Museum (Nashville, Tennessee); he coedited with Patricia Hall *Folklife and Museums: Selected Readings*.[36] Seemann believes that his folklore training gave him "a commitment to authenticity in the presentation of culture, both intangible and material. This served [him] well in designing museum programs and conceptualizing exhibitions."[37] Folklorist and ethnomusicologist Dan Sheehy, director of the Smithsonian Institution's Center for Folklife and Cultural Heritage, believes that folklorists build context into exhibits and connect objects with stories by "helping pull the curtain back."[38] He contends that folklorists should now think more broadly of "what museums can do using more technology to activate more of the senses to capture the totality of human expression."[39] Folklorists can and do play a role in creating a more "cultural democratic" museum when they are in positions of leadership—where fieldwork, collection development, exhibits, and educational outreach programs are shaped by shared decision making with the communities presented.[40]

The potential for folklorists finding work in museums is great, but those seeking to work in museums should consider gaining additional skills that might better position them for employment in museums. Stephen Stuempfle suggests that the skills most folklorists have acquired through their studies and field experience make them ideally suited to a variety of roles within a museum.

> While many museum curators, education specialists and administrators have somewhat limited networks of contacts and move within circumscribed channels, folklorists are willing to go anywhere and work with anyone. They know how to get people excited about the mission of a museum. Their ability to understand diverse cultural settings and connect with people means that they can be highly effective not only as curators but as exhibition developers/designers, education specialists, public relations and media specialists, fund-raisers and senior administrators. Moreover, their wide-ranging and holistic perspective facilitates employment in anthropology, history, art, or multi-disciplinary museums. Folklorists seeking jobs in museums might pay less attention to the content specializations listed in position ads and more to the types of research, communication, and project-building skills required. There are possibilities for folkloristic infiltration of all aspects of museum work in all kinds of museums.[41]

Charlie Seemann suggests, however, that folklorists would be well served to gain additional competencies.

> Folklore has always been a pretty marginalized field and I have always been an advocate of complementary training to increase employability. Not that often you can walk out of grad school and get employed as "a folklorist." Those who have gotten second degrees in areas like library science or museology armed themselves with powerful combinations of skills that make them employable in places other than the academy or the increasingly scarce state/local public folklorist arena.[42]

Folklorists are finding that museums provide sites for experimenting with new methodologies and research models. Diana N'Diaye, a curator at the Smithsonian Center for Folklife and Cultural Heritage, has been able to experiment with new models, including digital ones, in a variety of museum exhibition, festival, and education projects that have been developed in partnership with community scholars. The inclusion of community partners in developing museum projects has generated new relationships between the Smithsonian and the communities from which those projects were based, an important outcome that N'Diaye values:

> Working in the context of the museum with cultural practitioners has expanded the ways that the museum engages with living cultural communities and the way that research and cultural representation can be reciprocal, reflexive, and grounded. I am proud of the technologies of cultural heritage representation that we, as folklorists, have developed to facilitate and support living artists presenting themselves, their work, and interpreting their own culture within the context of the museum setting. I also believe that folklorists have influenced the role of museums as places of cultural conversation as well as cultural conservation. Going into collections with community experts, recognizing the value of community traditions and knowledge as regards museum collections.[43]

Folklorists working in museums have generally not been recognized as folklorists with a capital F, *but there is an increasing number of folklore-specific jobs in museums. These folklore-specific positions are having an impact on the ways in which the public, the museums, and other disciplines view folklore.* Carrie Hertz, a folklorist who recently became employed as a curator of folk art at the Castellani Art Museum at Niagara University (Lewiston, New York), spoke to this shift.

> I have worked in history, historical house, and anthropology museums, but this is the first time I have been openly labeled a folklorist, doing folklore. While I tried to draw upon my theoretical and methodological training as a folklorist at all of my positions, some institutions were more welcoming than others to my disciplinary principles of equity, multi-vocality, and diverse community engagement. Some were outright hostile. Now at an art museum, oddly enough, I feel the most at home, in part because I am leading a Folk Arts program modeled off of public folklore practice. It's a sort of hybrid, anchored by museum exhibitions and programming that are developed not through permanent collections, but through active ethnographic fieldwork with the local community.[44]

Moreover, Hertz hopes her new position and work can inform both the academic and public views of folklore, and her case, specifically folk arts.

> I also hope that my work can help re-define (both in practice at the museum and academically within the university) the idea of "folk arts" within the discipline of Art History. . . . By "infiltrating" other arenas like this, I think folklorists have a better chance of controlling and disseminating our disciplinary knowledge within the intellectual community, as well as the broader public.[45]

The work of folklorists in museums can enhance the museum's responsibility to be an agent to foster a civil society. Seemann's reflections on his own experience confirm this. "I think the folklorist's commitment to cultural diversity and equity can definitely contribute to the dialog about civil society. This dovetails with a healthy two-way engagement with the communities museums are working with."[46] Likewise, Seemann said that his work in museums "gave [him] an appreciation of the importance of community involvement in all aspects of program development and the obligation of the museum to serve the community."[47]

CONCLUSION

Today, according to the American Association of Museums, there are over 17,500 museums in the United States; the International Council of

Museums estimates there are 55,000 museums in 202 countries;[48] and the number and variety of museums continue to grow. This includes a dramatic growth of ethnically specific museums. Folklorists can and should be part of this phenomenon; they have made and can continue to make "a difference" in helping museums become more effective agents for creating a civil and inclusive society, sites of more effective informal learning for "birth to gray" audiences, as neutral places to explore differences, as institutions that embrace and take responsibility for both the tangible and intangible aspects of our cultural heritage, and as socially responsive forces that embrace the evolving diverse traditions and expressive culture in America.[49] Folklorists' capacity for deep documentation, commitment to community voice in educational programs and exhibitions, and participatory ethos are timely and critical assets for museums. Barry Bergey has observed that there is a need for a greater "curatorial presence" in these museums.[50] Given the vast number of museums, the opportunities for folklorists to be part of that "curatorial presence" are unprecedented.

Given that so many founding members of the AFS were "museum men," as John Vlach has observed, it is ironic that one of the hallmarks of folklore studies in the late twentieth century has been the discovery—or better—the rediscovery of the artifact.[51] I would suggest that it is also the rediscovery by folklorists of museums and, conversely, the emergence of museums of folklore that is ironic. Because our field is small, in order to forge new alliances between museums and folklore, perhaps it is especially timely now to formalize new connectivity and synergies between folklore and museum studies.

Perhaps folklorist and museum director Joyce Ice says it best: "Folklorists working in museums have made a real difference by 'just being there' through exhibits, collections, and programs . . . situating them in a contextual setting . . . giving space to a community of artists, their work, the time depth of their traditions, the cultural identity of their communities."[52] In conclusion, let me say that I hope that we will continue to see steady growth in the number of folklorists who, through "just being there" in museums, are helping both museums and folklore continue to advance knowledge of our diverse and rich cultural heritage, to meaningfully engage others in the pursuit and understanding of this knowledge, and to be responsive to the needs of the communities we study and serve.[53]

NOTES

1. Bronner 1988, 18.

2. Ibid., 19.

3. Ibid., 19.

4. Ibid., 40.

5. Vlach 1998, 19.

6. Ibid., 21.

7. A comprehensive history of the open-air museum as idea and institution can be found in Swedish museologist Sten Rentzhog's *Open Air Museums: The History and Future of a Visionary Idea*, trans. Skans Victoria Airey (Stockholm: Jamtli Förlag and Carlsson Bokförlag, 2007), distributed in the United States by the Association for Living History, Farm and Agricultural Museums (ALHFAM).

8. For more information, see "Living History," ALHFAM, http://www.alhfam.org/?cat_id=153&nav_tree=153.

9. See "Open Air Museums," Wikipedia, http://en.wikipedia.org/wiki/Open-air_museum (accessed October 11, 2011).

10. See "Living History."

11. See "The Mission of ALHFAM," ALHFAM, http://www.alhfam.org/index.php?cat_id=101&nav_tree=101.

12. The eco-museum idea has been credited to the French museum scholar Hugues de Varine. He defined the eco-museum in this way:

> The term "ecomuseum" came about in France in 1971. This period is marked by a will to reinvigorate the museum and redefine its relationship with the public. The concept of an ecomuseum thus reflects a concern with reinforcing the connection between the museum and its social surroundings and environment. An ecomuseum promotes the entirety of a culture and heritage related to a geographical territory and sphere of activity. This heritage can be material (artifacts, buildings) or immaterial (personal accounts, know-how).

For more, see "Definition of an Ecomuseum," L'Écomusée du Fier Monde, http://ecomusee.qc.ca/en/ecomuseum/definition-of-an-ecomuseum.

13. See Corsane et al. 2001, 101–6.

14. In 1999, the author participated along with three other folklorists/museum directors in one sponsored by the French-American Foundation in cooperation

with the National Endowment for the Arts that involved site visits to French eco-museums with the desire to share folklore expertise between the United States and France to foster academic and professional discourse on eco-museums. The other folklorists included Joyce Ice, then director of the Museum of International Folk Art; Tim Lloyd, then director of City Lore; and Hope Alswang, then director of the Shelburne Museum.

15. Hirzy 2002, 9.

16. This report, *Museums, Libraries, and 21st Century Skills*, has played a major role in the rethinking of the nature of the skills needed when hiring or training museum staff members to more effectively engage their communities. The Institute of Museum and Library Services website provides additional video and content related to the use of the report. Marsha L. Semmel, *Museums, Libraries, and 21st Century Skills* (Washington, DC: Institute of Museum and Library Services, 2009), http://www.imls.gov/assets/1/workflow_staging/AssetManager/293.PDF.

17. Archibald 2002, 5.

18. Jackson 2002, 29.

19. Author conversation with Richard Kurin, Smithsonian undersecretary for history, art, and culture, describing the shift in policy he helped lead to open the Smithsonian to the public in a variety of ways during the activities for the inauguration week of President Barack Obama.

20. Kratz and Karp 2006, 2.

21. See the International Coalition of Sites of Conscience website (http://www.sitesofconscience.org) for the history and growing role of this organization.

22. The District Six Museum (South Africa), Gulag Museum (Russia), Lower East Side Tenement Museum (United States), Maison des Esclaves (Spain), National Park Service (United States), Memoria Abierta (Argentina), Terezin Memorial (Czech Republic), and Work House (United Kingdom) founded the coalition in 1999 with the following statement: "It is the obligation of historic sites to assist the public in drawing connections between the history of our sites and the contemporary implications. We view stimulating dialogue on pressing social issues and promoting humanitarian and democratic values as a primary function." Currently, the coalition has seventeen "Accredited Sites of Conscience" and more than 260 individual and institutional members from around the world. The Sites of Conscience have expanded their focus to include other museums that are not historic sites of conscience but have a shared commitment to "using the lessons of history to spark conscience in people around the

world so that they can choose the actions that promote justice and lasting peace." To learn more, visit http://www.sitesofconscience.org.

23. See the UNESCO General Conference document *Recommendation on the Safeguarding of Traditional Culture and Folklore*, UNESCO, November 15, 1989, http://portal.unesco.org/en/ev.php-URL_ID=13141&URL_DO=DO_TOPIC&URL_SECTION=201.html.

24. See the UNESCO ICH Convention, "Towards the Convention," to learn more about the *Report on the Preliminary Study on the Advisability of Regulating Internationally, through a New Standard-Setting Instrument, the Protection of Traditional Culture and Folklore*, May 16, 2001, http://ichcap.org/eng/html/02_04_02_08.php.

25. Kirshenblatt-Gimblett 2006, 165.

26. Lippard 1997, 33.

27. The creation of these important digital repositories and resources has been developed through partnerships with state and federal agencies, professional organizations, and universities. The American Folklore Society has been lead partner in the National Folklore Archives Project with a number of regional folklore archives/museum collections; the AFS has also partnered on the Open Folklore Project with Indiana University; AFS collaborated on Oral History in the Digital Age with the Oral History Association, the American Folklife Center of the Library of Congress, the Smithsonian Center for Folklife and Cultural Heritage, and Michigan State University; and the Quilt Index was developed by the Michigan State University Museum and MATRIX: The Digital Humanities Center at MSU along with the Alliance of American Quilts. Many of these new research tools and repositories have benefited from major external grant funding from the National Endowment for the Humanities and the Institute of Museum and Library Services and other funding sources matched by local resources. These resources have become important models for digital access and research, and they are enhancing the way museums can assess collections resources for documentation, access for research, and public programming.

28. For more information on the Cooperstown Graduate Program, a leading museum studies program in the United States, go to http://www.oneonta.edu/academics/cgp.

29. Today the program is known as the Folk and Traditional Arts Program at the National Endowment for the Arts. This program has played a major role in

the funding of the documentation and presentation of the many forms of folk expression in the United States. For more information, see http://www.nea.gov.

30. In 1975, the NEA funded two state folk art surveys, one in Georgia and the other in Michigan. The Michigan survey was led by a team of folklorists hired by the Michigan State University Museum, working in concert with the Michigan Historical Museum. The folklorists were Marsha MacDowell and C. Kurt Dewhurst. This initial work led to the establishment of the ongoing Michigan Traditional Arts Program, based at the Michigan State University Museum.

31. Notes from an interview with Barry Bergey, director of the Folk and Traditional Arts Program, National Endowment for the Arts, on April 23, 2011.

32. To learn more about the festival, see Richard Kurin, *Smithsonian Folklife Festival: Culture of, by, and for the People* (Washington, DC: Smithsonian Center for Folklife and Cultural Heritage, Smithsonian Institution, 1998). Also see Dewhurst, N'Diaye, and MacDowell 2015, 1–18.

33. See *Museums for a New Century: A Report of the Commission on Museums for a New Century* (Washington, DC: American Alliance of Museums Press, 1984) for a discussion of one of the "forces of change" facing museums, characterized as a growing "proliferation of voices" in museum decision making that is reshaping all facets of museum governance, mission, collections, programs, and community engagement. This has evolved into ongoing discussions of the rethinking of the sharing of authority in museums.

34. Notes from interview and e-mail communications with Stephen Stuempfle, executive director, Society for Ethnomusicology, and adjunct associate professor, Department of Folklore and Ethnomusicology, Indiana University. "Museums and Folkloristic: Folklorists' Legacy and Future in Museum Theory and Practice," American Folklore Society, September 3, 2011.

35. Notes from conversation with Steve Zeitlin, director, City Lore, New York City, following the 9/11 events, October 20, 2003.

36. See the most comprehensive anthology of essays on the contributions of folklife to museums: Hall and Seemann 1987.

37. Notes and e-mail communication with Charlie Seemann, director, Western Folklife Center, Elko, Nevada, in preparation for a session titled "Museums and Folkloristic: Folklorists' Legacy and Future in Museum Theory and Practice," 2011 American Folklore Society Annual Meeting, Bloomington, Indiana, September 20, 2011.

38. Notes from an interview with Dr. Dan Sheehy, former director of the Folk and Traditional Arts Program at the NEA and director of folkways, Smithsonian Center for Folklife and Cultural Heritage, July 26, 2006.

39. Ibid.

40. Ibid.

41. Notes and e-mail communication with Stephen Stuempfle, in preparation for a session titled "Museums and Folkloristic: Folklorists' Legacy and Future in Museum Theory and Practice," 2011 American Folklore Society Annual Meeting, Bloomington, Indiana, September 3, 2011.

42. Notes and e-mail communication with Charlie Seemann, in preparation for a session titled "Museums and Folkloristic: Folklorists' Legacy and Future in Museum Theory and Practice," 2011 American Folklore Society Annual Meeting, Bloomington, Indiana, September 2011.

43. Notes from interview and e-mail communication with Diana N'Diaye, curator, Smithsonian Center for Folklife and Cultural Heritage, August 26, 2011.

44. Notes and e-mail communication with Carrie Hertz, curator of folk art, Castellani Art Museum, Niagara University, Lewiston, New York, August 21, 2011.

45. Ibid.

46. Notes and e-mail communication with Charlie Seemann, in preparation for a session titled "Museums and Folkloristic: Folklorists' Legacy and Future in Museum Theory and Practice," 2011 American Folklore Society Annual Meeting, Bloomington, Indiana, September 2011.

47. Ibid.

48. The International Council of Museums (ICOM) is not aware of the accurate number of museums in the world. However, in its seventeenth edition (2010), the most comprehensive directory *Museums of the World*, published by De Gruyter Saur, lists fifty-five thousand museums in 202 countries. See the ICOM website (http:// icom.museum, accessed October 10, 2011).

49. The museum field is experiencing a significant shift in its approach to working with communities, emphasizing inclusiveness and deeper civic engagement, which is creating significant tensions between past and emerging practice—especially around the move for more shared "authority" with communities. A notable collection of

essays that capture this "friction" is Karp et al. 2006. Also see C. Kurt Dewhurst and Marsha MacDowell, "Strategies for Creating and Sustaining Museum-Based International Collaborative Partnerships," *Practicing Anthropology* 37, no 3 (Summer 2015): 54–55, and Dewhurst and MacDowell 2013.

50. Notes from interview with Barry Bergey on April 23, 2011.

51. Vlach 1988, 21.

52. Notes from interview with Dr. Joyce Ice, director of the Museum of International Folk Art, Santa Fe, New Mexico, August 25, 2006 (Ice is currently director of the Art Museum, West Virginia University).

53. See Bol et al. 2015. See American Folklore Society website (http://www.afsnet.org, accessed April 14, 2016).

REFERENCES

Archibald, Robert R. 2002. Introduction to *Mastering Civic Engagement: A Challenge to Museums*, 1–8. Washington, DC: American Alliance of Museums.

Bol, Marsha, C. Kurt Dewhurst, Carrie Hertz, Jason Baird Jackson, Marsha MacDowell, Charlie Seemann, Suzy Seriff, and Dan Sheehy. 2015. *Rethinking the Role of Folklore in Museums: Exploring New Directions for Folklore in Museum Policy and Practice.* American Folklore Society Policy White Paper. American Folklore Society, http://www.afsnet.org (accessed April 14, 2016).

Bronner, Simon J., ed. 1987. *Folklife Studies from the Gilded Age: Object, Rite, and Custom in Victorian America.* Ann Arbor: University of Michigan Research Press.

———. 1988. "The Intellectual Climate of Nineteenth-Century American Folklore Studies." In *100 Years of American Folklore Studies: A Centennial Publication of the American Folklore Society, 1888–1988*, edited by William M. Clements, 6–7. Centennial Meeting, Cambridge, Massachutsetts, October 26–30, 1988.

Corsane, Gerard, Peter Davis, Sarah Elliott, Maurizio Maggi, Donatella Murtas, and Sally Rogers. 2001. "Ecomuseum Evaluation: Experience in Piemonte and Liguria, Italy." *International Journal of Heritage Studies* 13, no. 2: 101–6.

Dewhurst, C. Kurt, and Marsha MacDowell. 2013. "Going Public through International Museum Partnerships." In *Going Public: Civic and Community Engagement*, edited by Hiram Fitzgerald and Judy Primavera. East Lansing: Michigan State University Press.

———. 2015. "Strategies for Creating and Sustaining Museum-Based International Collaborative Partnerships." *Practicing Anthropology* 37, no 3 (Summer): 54–55.

Dewhurst, C. Kurt, Diana Baird N'Diaye, and Marsha MacDowell. 2015. "Cultivating Connectivity: Moving Toward Inclusive Excellence in Museums." *Curator: The Museum Journal* 57, no. 4: 1–18.

Hall, Patricia, and Charlie Seemann, eds. 1987. *Folklife and Museums: Selected Readings*. Nashville, TN: AASLH.

Hirzy, Ellen. 2002. "Mastering Civic Engagement: A Report from the American Association of Museums." In *Mastering Civic Engagement: A Challenge to Museums*, 9–20. Washington, DC: American Alliance of Museums.

Jackson, Maria Rosario. 2002. "Coming to the Center of Community Life." In *Mastering Civic Engagement: A Challenge to Museums*, 29–38. Washington, DC: American Alliance of Museums.

Karp, Ivan, Corinne A. Kratz, Lynn Szwaja, and Tomas Ybarra-Frausto, eds. 2006. *Museum Frictions: Public Cultures/Global Transformations*. Durham, NC: Duke University Press.

Kirshenblatt-Gimblett, Barbara. 2006. "World Heritage and Cultural Economics." In *Museum Frictions: Public Cultures/Global Transformations*, edited by Ivan Karp, Corinne A. Kratz, Lynn Szwaja, and Tomas Ybarra-Frausto, 35–45. Durham, NC: Duke University Press.

Kratz, Corinne A., and Ivan Karp. 2006. Introduction to *Museum Frictions: Public Cultures/Global Transformations*, edited by Ivan Karp, Corinne A. Kratz, Lynn Szwaja, and Tomas Ybarra-Frausto. Durham, NC: Duke University Press.

Lippard, Lucy R. 1997. *The Lure of the Local: Senses of Place in a Multicentered Society*. New York: The New Press.

Vlach, John Michael. 1988. "Folklore and the Tangible Text." In *100 Years of American Folklore Studies: A Centennial Publication of the American Folklore Society, 1888–1988*, edited by William M. Clements, 18–20. Centennial Meeting, Cambridge, MA, October 26–30, 1988.

SPECIAL ACKNOWLEDGMENT

I want to acknowledge the contributions of Marsha MacDowell, my colleague and life partner, for her thoughtful reading, editorial assistance, and counsel in preparing this chapter. We have shared much of our professional journey as folklorists and curators together—including many of the projects and experiences cited here.

2

Folklife and the American Museum

Retrospective Reflections and Reimaginings

ROBERT BARON

First published in 1981, "Folklife and the American Museum" provides a historical overview and examines contemporary practices of incorporating folklife within exhibitions, public programs, and collections for various types of museums. It contends that folklife provides alternatives for elitist, decontextualized, and overaestheticized approaches. Emphasizing the value of field research, it illustrates how it can provide a foundation for multiple dimensions of museums. A reprinting here of the 1987 publication of this essay is preceded by "Retrospective Reflections and Reimaginings," discussing developments in museums and public folklore in the past three decades. It points to how folklife can have a greater impact upon museums and suggests what folklorists can learn from current museological practice and discourse. These developments include new approaches to mutual engagement, shared authority, community curation, participatory programming, relational aesthetics, and social practice.

RETROSPECTIVE REFLECTIONS AND REIMAGININGS

"Folklife and the American Museum" first saw life at a session I organized on folklife and museums at the 1979 American Association of Museums[1] annual meeting and as a 1981 article in the association's magazine, *Museum News*.[2] Addressing the nation's largest organization of museum professionals, I made a case for including folklife objects, programming, methodologies, and interpretive approaches in museums. The expanded 1987 version of the article that appears here was published in *Folklife and Museums: Selected Readings*.[3] Rereading it after almost three decades, I see now that my rhetorical strategy incorporated both critiques of elitist, decontextualized, and overaestheticized museum practices and the missionary zeal of a young folklorist seeking to convince the museum field that folklife and folklorists could remedy many of its shortcomings. The several iterations of the article embodied the optimism and fresh contributions of the rapidly expanding field of public folklore during its decade of greatest growth. Many more examples of folklife exhibitions and programs were available to include in 1987 than in the 1979 and 1981 versions.

In the years since this article was published, critical museological scholarship proliferated, and communities widely challenged how they are represented and engaged by museums. Elitist dichotomies of high and low continued to erode as museums broadened their collections to include previously overlooked cultural expressions. New approaches for visitor participation emerged. Nevertheless, critical discourse about museums recognizes that they still have a long way to go in addressing chronic problems of elitism and exclusion.

Three decades ago folklife anticipated issues and practices now more widespread among museums. As the chapters in this volume demonstrate, folklorists working with museums continue to deeply engage communities, present cultural forms and practices of neglected groups, and dynamically engage visitor participation. While folklore and folklife is a small discipline with an outsize impact, much larger disciplines are now involved with the same matters. The museum field remains largely unaware of what folklife can offer museums. Folklife approaches and practices need to be more widely communicated and better articulated with the museum field as a whole. Rather than revise this article yet again to deal with folklife and museums today, I feel that it should remain here as published in 1987, with the exception of a few small corrections. It can serve as both historical document and baseline for contemporary analysis and practice. Toward the latter end, my discussion here is meant to be suggestive of how the 1987 article might be reimagined today. Following this initial section, we will step back three decades for the reprinting of the 1987 article.

I have long found the term "outreach" deeply problematic, connoting a top-down, missionary reaching out to communities, a *service* provided largely or entirely on a museum's own terms.[4] I pointed out in the 1987 article that the late-nineteenth-century charter principles of many museums emphasized service to the poor and working man and enlightenment of the masses, reflecting a concern for social usefulness and relevance. This sense of mission and service continues, reinterpreted with more inclusive and egalitarian approaches in some museums and persisting as noblesse oblige in others. The service dimension of museums is fueled by pressure from communities of color for inclusion, the financial and political benefits of expanding audiences, and the requirements of foundations and public funding agencies.

I prefer to think that the relationship of museums to communities needs to consist of *mutual engagement*. This relationship should entail shared authority for curation, programming, and interpretation. During the late twentieth century, anthropology, history, and folklore (among other disciplines) experienced a paradigm shift in how scholars view their research subjects and collaborate with those they study. This shift was concurrent with a changing view of how communities engage with museums. Indigenous groups and a wide variety of other communities asserted control over whether they would be studied and how they would be represented, challenging the epistemological authority of the anthropologist. What James Clifford called anthropology's "dialogic turn" generated jointly authored ethnographies, with anthropological subjects thought of as *collaborators* rather than *informants*. Ethnography became, according to Clifford, "a dialogical enterprise in which both researchers and natives are both active creators or, to stretch a term, authors of cultural representations."[5] The academic history discipline was transformed as social history increasingly focused upon the historical experience of subalterns, shifting from concentration upon the more extensively documented study of prominent white men. Both lay and scholarly involvement with oral history proliferated, supplementing the written record with oral testimony of those largely excluded from the historical record. In oral history, Michael Frisch developed the concept of "a shared authority," involving the mutual construction of meaning by historian and interviewee in the course of the oral history interview and the creation of oral histories.[6]

In the 1980s, "public folklore" replaced "applied folklore" as the term most widely used for folklore practiced outside the academy. The new term reflected a conceptual and ideological change from an applied folklore of the time that applied and disseminated expertise in a unidirectional manner, to a dialogism involving ongoing collaboration and community cultural self-determination, emphasizing representation and interpretation on a community's own terms.[7] Public folklore programs are frequently designed to diminish the authority of the folklorist as the community assumes responsibility for shaping and directing presentations. Folklorists are reflexive about the impact of their intervention in cultures, which notwithstanding the sharing and yielding of authority continues to maintain power asymmetries between folklorist and community.[8]

During the 1980s and 1990s, museums experienced what Ivan Karp characterized as "political contests over who has the right to speak for whom," occurring as an "inevitable result of the emergence of new communities that make claims on museums."[9] Museums increasingly became arenas of contestation about the lack of diversity in collections, among professional staff, and on boards; repatriation of sacred and funerary indigenous objects; and exhibitionary practices that excluded diverse communities. There has been a wide range of responses to these concerns. They range from obliviousness and cursory top-down "outreach" gestures to successful diversification of the institution at every level and the development of innovative methods for involving community members in shaping how they are represented in collections, exhibitions, and programming.

Community curation long practiced by museums serving specific local constituencies and cultural groups is providing a model for current museum participation initiatives that serve multiple constituencies. Initially developed in the 1960s and 1970s by ecomuseums in Europe[10] and such community museums as the Anacostia Community Museum,[11] important approaches to community curation were developed in subsequent decades by the Japanese American National Museum and the Museum of Chinese in the Americas (MOCA), which was founded as a dialogic museum. MOCA sees a dialogic museum as involving the shared authority for conceiving, developing, and interpreting exhibitions with community members, thereby realigning traditional museum authority structures.[12]

Folklorists are experimenting with new approaches for collaboratively developing museum programs and exhibitions, such as the Gallery of Conscience at the Museum of International Folk Art. Through the gallery, "project goals and exhibition development" installations about social issues are generated through "interactions with artists, community advisors, and partnering organizations." They are "prototyped as 'works in progress' and revised throughout their run based on community feedback."[13] Community-driven exhibitions are an idea whose time has come again, whether prototyped like the ones proposed by visitors to the Museum of International Folk Art or entirely community initiated and curated. Deborah Schwartz notes that there have been "versions of community-driven galleries in museums for decades," although "there haven't been more of them recently," because, she thinks, "this work is largely being done on the internet these days."[14] In 2006, Schwartz's Brooklyn Historical Society revived the community gallery idea through community-curated exhibits in its Public Perspectives exhibition series. Communities proposed exhibitions, which were evaluated by a committee that included a folklorist. Once an exhibition was approved, the community organizing the exhibition had complete autonomy for designing and curating it in this museum's Independence Community Gallery.[15]

Folklife stands out as a field grounded in field research, valorization of the local, close collaboration with communities, and facilitation of greater voice and agency for neglected and marginalized cultural groups. However, when collaborating with communities, folklorists need to reflexively recognize their shaping role and ongoing authority. Community curation and the dialogic museum are generating provocative discourse about professional expertise in activities designed to share authority with community members. In discussing such roles in *Letting Go: Sharing Historical Authority in a User-Generated World*, folklorist Steve Zeitlin and historians Michael Frisch and John Kuo Wei Tchen, who have developed highly influential dialogic initiatives, acknowledge the curatorial and interpretive authority they maintain based upon their professional expertise. At the same time, their projects incorporate the knowledge and perspectives of community members. Discussing the "tension between curation and participation [that] played out in a number of key decisions we made in constructing the *City of Memory*" website of stories about New York neighborhoods, Zeitlin indicated that "from the start, we

[City Lore] distinguished between contributed stories and curated stories." They were "guided by an artful vision and committed to accuracy and contextualization."[16] Frisch writes of the importance of "genuine dialogue" between "vernacular understandings and professional scholarship."[17] Tchen, who first conceived of the dialogic museum as a founder of the Museum of Chinese in the Americas, underscores the need for articulating perspectives of both historian and community:

> I think historians have an important role to play in contextualizing individual stories; in helping to parse out what likely happened, what's the difference between a mythical recounting of an event or a policy and something that is more complex and more accurate. But it's not simply the historians who have the authority here. It's also people who have lived the experience. And what about those communities of people who did not have that power to document and archive their perspectives, to develop historians and institutions that would then represent their point of view?
>
> This is the foundational question of authority and trust: what's the basic stuff that historical explanations and meaning can be made from? And when you have two very different perspectives and two very different parts of the power struggle, how do we, in a dialogic context, sort these questions out? Can there be a trusted public venue? This is particularly challenging online, where anyone can blog about anything.[18]

Since my article was last published in 1987, technology has vastly opened up new opportunities to communities for discourse about and documentation of their histories and traditional cultures, providing information once limited to institutions like museums and academic disciplines. Now we can find local video documentation of folk culture in seconds on YouTube, along with a once-unimaginable variety of scholarly and lay materials about traditions, their makers, and their communities on the Internet. Museums are but one of many kinds of venues for experiencing cultures, and they are less immediately accessible than the Internet at our fingertips. As they attempt to utilize technology on their own terms, museums seek to reach new audiences while maintaining their authority. Digital media is now widespread in museums. In recent years, museums have "attempt[ed] to embrace a participatory culture facilitated by new digital technologies," which, as the Humanities, Arts, Science and Technology Alliance and Conservatory indicates, challenges their "expertise and authority as guardians of our culture and heritage." These modes of participation include "crowdsourcing curating" and social media like Twitter and Facebook, along with the "internet and mobile devices to disseminate their digitized collections, interactive kiosks, iPads and multimedia headsets."[19]

Folklorists working with museums utilize social media and digital interactivity both within and outside the museum's walls. In "Digital Practices in Museum Ethnography," Jason Baird Jackson and Marsha MacDowell mention digital exhibitions organized by folklorists about Native American communities and multi-institutional collections databases such as the Quilt Index developed by MacDowell.[20] Crowdsourced exhibitions organized by folklorists could also be developed. Since the professional community of folklorists is highly networked on local, regional, and national planes, crowdsourcing involving folklorists and the communities with which they work in multiple locations could contribute to broadening the scope, reach, and inclusiveness of folklife in museums.

The most original and significant contribution of folklife for museum mediation remains the public presentation of traditional practitioners. The Aditi program of the Smithsonian Folklife Festival discussed in the 1987 article was exemplary in its presentation of performances both within the Smithsonian National Museum of Natural History and on the National Mall. In such presentations, practitioners perform, demonstrate, and discuss material culture, narrative, and folk presenting traditions in dialog with audience members, curators, and presenters. They are more interactive and immediate than conventional museum public programs, with audience members trying their hand at a craft being demonstrated, dancing in response to featured musicians, and discussing traditions and issues of significance to the communities whose folklife is being represented.

Since the 1990s, *participation* has become a major thrust in museums as well as a widespread movement among contemporary visual artists. The movement toward participation provides an alternative to audiences acting as passive cultural consumers. Participation in museums entails creating performance and programming structures that interactively engage audiences. Museums experimenting with participation share the same premise as folklorists, using what Nina Simon sees as "the institution as meeting grounds for dialogue around the content presented." In her influential book *The Par-*

ticipatory Museum, Simon shows how museums engender participation in multifaceted and often highly sophisticated ways. Museums are providing "diverse visitor co-produced experiences," with the institution serving "as a 'platform' that connects different users who act as content creators, distributors, consumers, critics and collaborators."[21] In her contribution to *Letting Go: Sharing Historical Authority in a User-Generated World*, Simon lists among the features of a "truly participatory museum" activities that include "putting visitors' objects on display . . . featuring a story or artifact that online visitors love to discuss . . . working with [local people] to develop programming . . . responding to visitors' comments." For Simon, the participatory museum "adapts and changes based on the contributions of all stakeholders—staff, trustees, visitors and community members alike."[22]

Simon's distinction between two categories of collaboration parallels two common types of folklife practice: In "*consultative* projects," "institutions engage experts or community representatives to provide advice and guidance to staff members as they develop new exhibitions, programs or publications." In "*co-development projects* . . . staff members work together with producers to produce new exhibitions and programs," helping to "create them" rather than guide their development.[23] *The Participatory Museum* and Simon's essay in *Letting Go* mention a large number of participatory and collaborative projects within and outside museums, but none of them are folklife projects. New modalities of museum participation could be both informed by folklife practice for presenting traditional practitioners and adapted by folklorists for a broader range of kinds of engagement with museums. While the contemporary participatory projects she describes advance the institutional needs for community engagement of museums, folklife projects tend to give greater primacy to the needs of a community. Unlike projects in non-community-based museums, folklife projects are often designed to equip communities to develop the skills and resources to present their traditions on their own, progressively disempowering the folklorist.

Relational aesthetics, *social practice*, and *participatory art* are major trends in contemporary art that also bear similarities to public folklore but incorporate distinctively different motivations, objectives, and community relationships. Identifying relational aesthetics during the 1990s as a transformative development in contemporary art, Nicolas Bourriaud characterized "*relational art*" as "an art taking as its theoretical horizons the realm of human interactions and its social context, rather than the assertion of an independent and *private* symbolic space."[24] In contrast, with the "object closed in on itself by the intervention of a style and a signature, present-day art shows that form only exists in the encounter and the dynamic relationship enjoyed by an artistic proposition with other formations, artistic and otherwise,"[25] and the artist "embarks upon a dialogue."[26] Writing in 2006, Claire Bishop discussed a "social turn" in the visual arts marked by a "surge of artistic interest in collectivity, collaboration and direct engagement with specific social constituencies"[27] in projects that "blur art and life."[28] Artists in the social turn, practicing what Bishop came to relabel "participatory art,"[29] are viewed with many of the same terms that can be used for public folklore, which is intrinsically collaborative, dialogic, collective, and embedded in social interactions. She discusses artists who see themselves as "mediators" "between groups of people who normally don't have contact with one another."[30] The audience, "previously conceived as a 'viewer' or 'beholder,' is now repositioned as a collaborator and producer of *situations*."[31] Folklorists stress the functionality and social grounding of works of art, and "relational art works insist upon *use* rather than contemplation."[32]

Much of contemporary art arises out of the artist's alienation, with social practice an effort to engage art functionally within the lived reality of everyday life. The social engagement of contemporary art is often experienced within a limited sphere by audiences predisposed to attend contemporary art events. As an example, Bishop relates that a work of noted participatory artist Rirkrit Tiravanija generated "networking among a group of art dealers and like-minded art lovers" who have a "common interest in art."[33] Folklife, in contrast, lives in local communities and among the practitioners who maintain traditions expressive of the shared aesthetics and values of groups of people quite unlike contemporary art cognoscenti. Writing of the work of public folklorist Pat Jasper, contemporary art curator Nancy Zastudil relates that Jasper "sees the work of public folklorists concentrating in the arts as having anticipated 'relational aesthetics' and 'social practice,' but done so on its own terms and by privileging the voice of the artistic tradition-bearer rather than the curator or artist/interpreter."[34]

Jasper's comments represent a rare example of a folklorist speaking to these major trends in contemporary art. For their part, contemporary art historians and artists are unaware of public folklore practices with far more grounding in community life than are generally found in the work these artists create. Jasper, like other public folklorists, "works to utilize some of the existing standard presentational formats (gallery or museum exhibitions, staged performances, etc.) when and if appropriate, for sharing artistic traditions with a larger public." Greater penetration of the museum world by folklorists depends upon such dual approaches of utilizing standard modes of arts presentation and articulating their work with museum and contemporary arts discourse.

Art museums, in principle, should be more receptive to folklife projects now than they were when I wrote the 1981 and 1987 versions of this article. Hierarchies of *high* and *low* in the arts have eroded, and a wider variety of kinds of artistic production is now accepted by scholars and presented in museums. James Elkins indicates that the new discipline of visual studies is "founded on the denial that differences between high art and low art are a relevant starting place or reference point for interpretation, or on the more drastic claim that high art and low art have become mixed and are effectively inseparable." Such "revaluation or rejection of the modernist distinction between high art and low art creates a relativized field of art in which the act of privileging one work over another cannot be justified by appealing to values that are taken to be normative. This relativism is compounded by the pluralism of the contemporary art world."[35]

As I indicated in the 1987 version of this article, folklife can contribute substantially to all types of museums. It can provide new dimensions for art, anthropology, history, children's, science, and, of course, folk art museums. I noted that folklife activities in museums have consisted of both special initiatives constituting episodic involvement with uncertain long-term impact and institutionalized folklife programs. While ongoing, institutionalized folklife programs were beginning to be developed at the time, three decades later few such programs have been created. Most of the projects described in the 1987 article occurred at museums that now rarely or never present projects initiated by folklorists, although other museums have since developed important programs, such as those described in the essays in this volume. It is much more likely that greater involvement of folklorists with museums will occur episodically within a museum primarily devoted to other disciplines than through folklife curatorial departments.

Having looked at current museological and contemporary art practice of the past several decades with a retrospective and reflective gaze, it's time now to dial back to the reprinted "Folklife and the American Museum," reprinted as it appeared in 1987 with only a few minor changes.

FOLKLIFE AND THE AMERICAN MUSEUM, 1987

What is the place of folklife in a museum? The exploration of this subject, which relates to virtually every kind of museum, begins with the recognition that it is an issue of central importance. In the spirit of nineteenth-century humanitarian ideals, many American museums were founded with a mission to serve the poor and working man and to enlighten the masses. Their charter principles reflect a basic concern for social usefulness and relevance.[36]

These ideals have been variously interpreted or ignored by our museums. The need for relevance and social usefulness and the value of attracting mass audiences are continually questioned. Although museums are repositories of objects that may be said to represent aspects of a common cultural heritage, the question "Whose cultural heritage?" is often neglected in the discussion of elitism versus populism, relevance, or community service. If museums are not to be exclusively the treasure houses of a royalist or aristocratic legacy—the "fine arts" in the art museum—or shrines devoted to the relics of great men in the history museum, then folklife must enter the picture.

The great museologist John Cotton Dana recognized the need for folklife studies. Dana spoke of the need for museums to be of practical use, contributing "to a more intelligent enjoyment of daily life by adding interest to the things of that life." He contrasted this notion with the tendency of museums to "arouse astonishment and a harmful reverence by means of objects rare, old, costly and of aristocratic history."[37] As director of the Newark Museum from 1902 to 1929, he organized exhibitions of the work of local artisans and a "homelands exhibit" in which immigrants to Newark from Italy, Germany, Russia, and Hungary demonstrated the weaving of cloth, the making of lace and embroidery, and the preparation of costumes and other objects of everyday life.[38] Dana also organized exhibitions of Hungarian peasant art and East Indian objects of daily use.

Dana's activities coincided with increasing recognition of the aesthetic value of folk and tribal arts on the part of modernist artists and collectors.

American folk art was "discovered" and exhibited during the 1920s at the Whitney Studio Club, the gallery shows of Isabel Carleton Wilde, and the museum of folk art on the estate of Elie Nadelman.[39] The emphasis that Dana and others placed upon the material basis of art and the arts of everyday life also helped to influence a spate of folk art exhibitions in the 1930s. Shortly after Dana's death, Holger Cahill organized an exhibition of American primitives at the Newark Museum and was instrumental in organizing an exhibition of American folk art the following year. Cahill would soon curate an exhibition at the Museum of Modern Art, "American Folk Art: The Art of the Common Man in America, 1750–1900." In the tradition of Dana, he called it "the expression of the common people made by them and intended for their use and enjoyment."[40] Interest in the sources of American art, the increasing influence of folk and tribal arts upon the work of modernist artists, and the heightened awareness of American culture during the Depression provided some of the impetus for a number of folk art exhibitions.

Such exhibitions greatly broadened the spectrum of artifacts presented in the art museum. Today, many art museums have permanent collections or temporary exhibitions of folk art. But the characteristic mode of presentation of folk art within museums is viewed with skepticism by many folklorists. To the folklorist, it is rarely clear what these frakturs, weathervanes, or other folk art objects are *doing* in the museum, for they are frequently presented as sorts of objets d'art, chosen according to a loosely defined standard of connoisseurship that manifests no true sense of the historical or social circumstances of their production. In the eyes of the folklorist, their presentation and interpretation suffer from their categorization as "folk," implicitly viewed as something to be compared to or contrasted with "fine" art. Folklorists are critical of romantic approaches according to which these works are the unique creations of untutored geniuses or the products of anonymous artists acting as the exemplars of an American heritage characterized by unspecified particulars of history and tradition.

Such criticisms by folklorists have provoked spirited controversy with folk art specialists, who disdain to view folk art primarily as "artifact" rather than as "art." Rather than approach folk art as a social document, as a dimension of material culture, or as the embodiment of the aesthetics and values of a particular culture, these individuals employ an approach that relies upon the application of formal aesthetic criteria similar to those used for the evaluation of European and American fine arts.[41]

Many of the traditional distinctions between "folk" and "fine" art are beginning to erode. Art historians such as Lee Baxandall and Svetlana Alpers speak of the "demystification of the notion of artistic invention," viewing processes once considered "mysterious" as a "task of fitting a work to a particular task, to a particular set of describable historical conditions."[42] They are calling into question the authority of an individual maker and the uniqueness of individual works in the process of dealing with the collaborative efforts of such workshop products as illuminated manuscripts or Renaissance frescoes—much as folklorists would consider the making of a quilt. In fact, Alpers speaks of a "modern blurring of the line between art and craft."[43] We can now see where the approaches of various disciplines begin to converge. When objects that may be called art are considered within the totality of all artifacts, all man-made objects may be viewed as part of the "designed world."[44]

Folklorists breathe more easily when art is more broadly construed, but it is also important not to view folklife solely as art. Folklife is the embodiment of traditional knowledge, belief, and values and exists as a communicative behavior with cultural specifications as to the time, place, and company in which it is performed. It can include oral literature, folk music, play, food, and ritual as well as folk arts and crafts. Folklife is generally learned orally, by example or in performance, and is maintained or perpetuated without formal means of instruction. It depends for its existence upon a structured group, which shares folklife on the basis of a common ethnic, geographical, generational, occupational, or gender identity.[45]

The many dimensions of folklife make it a challenge to select for folk art exhibitions objects that both satisfy aesthetic criteria and represent the traditional culture of a group of people. The challenge appears to have been met in the exhibition "Webfoots and Bunchgrassers: Folk Art of the Oregon Country." This exhibition was the first among a number in the early 1980s to explore the folk arts of a state, including diverse communities and offering a broad perspective on the historical and cultural experience of the state as a whole. The objects in this exhibition were viewed as the "expressions of a group of people who were responding to life situations in aesthetic ways . . . , objects which actually grew out of a complex of historical and geographic forces which determined the kinds of communities that eventually characterized the human dimension of the Pacific Northwest at a certain time in history."[46] In its organization, the exhibition reflects the cultural diversity of the area in a division that corresponds to four groups characteristic of the state during successive periods of settlement. The folk art of a culturally plural Oregon includes that of the original Native American inhabitants, pioneers and early settlers, "buckaroos" (cowboys), and ethnic groups that have arrived since the initial settlers from the eastern United States.

This exhibition expands on the notion of "American" folk art while illuminating the unique characteristics of the folk culture of one western state over time. Every state has its own particular mixture of ethnic, occupational, and regional identities that have shaped its folk arts; exhibited together they suggest an overarching view of the state's history and culture.

The excellent catalog for "Webfoots and Bunchgrassers" answers many of the questions that a folklorist asks of an object and its maker: How did a folk artist learn his or her craft? What materials and processes are used in the making of the object? How can its form be described? What are its functions? What makes an object exemplary in an aesthetic sense? What sort of meaning does a folk artist give to his or her work? How does the object manifest the ideas and values of the culture that produced it? Is there evidence of continuity and change in a tradition over time?

The buckaroo portion of the exhibition, for example, deals with the functional art of one of several highly distinctive occupational groups that have developed in Oregon. Oregon cowboys have artistically elaborated objects of everyday life in at times extraordinary ways. We see rancher Rankin Crow's silver-mounted headstalls, which were fashioned from table silver; learn that Lon Davis's spur making grew out of his work as a buckaroo and farrier; and view a belt buckle made by radio announcer Kenneth Hanson and inscribed with a rodeo association logo and a message seen on bumper stickers throughout the West in 1973: "I'm not a cowboy, I just found the hat."

"Webfoots and Bunchgrassers" also tried to address the vexing problem of how to show folk objects in the natural contexts of everyday life for which they were created. Information in text panels and photo murals (such as embroidered cloth set among plastic flowers in a home) was used so that a "live context may emerge." Of course, the need to restore a sense of context to objects hanging uneasily in a museum gallery is by no means unique to folk art exhibitions. André Malraux claimed in *The Voices of Silence* that museums are by their very nature artificial contexts, isolating objects loaded with particular cultural meanings in settings estranged from the original functions and meanings of the objects.[47]

As a result of the trend among folklorists to view folklife as a situated activity, folklorists have been developing folk performances in museum settings grounded in performance modes present in natural contexts. Adding a vital dimension to museums, such activities help restore to objects something of the associated behaviors and beliefs that constitute their cultural significance.

This approach to folk performance is of great value when performers from communities served by a museum are involved, as Dana recognized long ago. In preparing for the Haitian art exhibition at the Brooklyn Museum in 1978, I coordinated the Banboch! Festival of New York Haitian Folk Arts, which was based upon a survey of New York Haitian culture. The survey was conducted by folklorists and anthropologists together with nine interns, most of whom were Haitian New Yorkers.

For the festival's presentation of ritual arts, it would have been relatively simple to have a performance group present highly stylized, arranged, or choreographed material, which often passes for folklore in museums. Although we were in close contact with practitioners of the Vodoun religion known for their ritual dancing, we planned a presentation that selected from their repertoires ritual dances used in ceremonies rather than the "Voodoo dances" of theatrical performances. Ritual actions were presented in a "sacred space," separated from other areas devoted to children's play and games, the telling of folk tales, or performances of secular music.

The replication of traditional physical settings for these performance situations was undertaken with great care. Much of the festival site was embellished with the plastic strips that often adorn Haitian bars and social clubs. A *bel antre* (festival arch) framed the entrance to the festival site. Ritual arts for the festival took place in a large canopy erected to serve as a *tonnelle*, the traditional shelter for Vodoun worship activities. A decorated *poteau mitan* (center pole passageway for the gods), Vodoun altar, and other material culture functioned in an intimate relationship with ritual enactments rather than as static artifacts. That this setting and performance situation were appropriate was apparent from the absence of a sensational attitude among most festival goers, who, while mainly Haitians, included members of other

New York communities. Spirit possession was generally received as an event issuing naturally from the other events of the afternoon.

The shaping presence of folk performance was evident during other activities related to the exhibition, such as storytelling and the performance of ritual music in the galleries. Materials prepared for the exhibition, such as panel texts, dealt with folk culture in various ways. Folklife has obvious roles to play in the creation of didactic materials. Texts of songs or folk narratives on panels or slide presentations rendering a culture through visual images and sounds of folk culture can be highly effective in illustrating aspects of the historical period and cultural environment in which objects were created and used.

Folk performances can illuminate museum collections and special exhibitions in a number of ways, enhancing the museum experience for the visitor, but there are obvious limitations as well. The presence of culturally significant objects makes a museum what it is and provides its major means of communication. Folk music concerts or folk festivals presented as part of a museum's ongoing public programs are most valuable when they are tied to a special exhibition or to an aspect of the permanent collection.

The Smithsonian Festival of American Folklife,[48] the model for most of the best recent folk festivals, provides several examples of such effective uses of folk performance. While most of the festival's events have taken place on the National Mall in Washington, DC, in a sphere of activity distinct from the Smithsonian's museums, some unique festival activities have also occurred in the galleries of two of the museums along the Mall. During the 1978 festival, teachers and schoolchildren related narratives of school activities—games, practical jokes, and scholastic accomplishments—in a replica classroom in the National Museum of American History. Immigrant narratives were exchanged in the Ellis Island area of this museum. Elsewhere in the Museum of American History, traditional artisans demonstrated crafts such as saddle making alongside related historical artifacts.

Presentations of the traditional arts of India at the 1985 Festival of American Folklife were closely linked to the exhibition "Aditi: A Celebration of Life" at the National Museum of Natural History. This exhibition, which dealt with major stages of the life cycle from the perspective of a growing child, was animated by artists from India practicing traditional art forms relating to the themes of the exhibition.

This exhibition and the "Mela" (fair) held on the Mall presented an unusually close relationship between static museum objects and folk arts being practiced and performed. The coordinator of the exhibition indicated in the festival program booklet that "throughout the sections of the exhibition, objects associated with the particular stage of the life cycle are presented together with the folk artists who give them meaning—the dancers, singers, musicians, puppeteers, painters, jugglers and acrobats of India. The juxtaposition of artists from diverse regions of the country with objects of varied temporal and geographic provenance suggests thematic unities as well as continuities of form and function. Thus 'Aditi' views Indian culture, not as an atomistic collection of cataloged objects and traditions, but as an integrated and vital pattern for living."[49] "Aditi" was an extraordinary exhibition that imaginatively combined objects and performances.

At the Festival of American Folklife, established in 1967, folklife documentation has played a central role in providing a foundation for the presentation of folk arts, occupational traditions, and customary practices. Professional folklorists, ethnomusicologists, and other specialists with expertise regarding an aspect of folklife engage in short-term field research to identify exemplary folk artists and research traditional activities in preparation for the festival. Since the late 1970s, projects involving the original documentation of folklife traditions have proliferated in other museums and have resulted in temporary and permanent exhibitions, educational activities, and public programs.

The New York State Council on the Arts has been the catalyst for a number of these projects. It has emphasized folklife documentation in its program guidelines, has provided assistance by professional staff members for the conceptualization and planning of projects, and has awarded extensive funding support. These projects have brought tangible benefits both to the sponsoring cultural organizations and to the communities represented in the documentation projects. Successful documentation projects in museums in New York State have involved original research about communities represented in a museum's collections. Photographs and audio recordings made during the documentation process are, in themselves, culturally significant artifacts and may prove to be vital parts of the historical record about contemporary folk cultures. These folklife documentation projects involve the recording of traditions actively performed in communities, the collecting of artifacts maintained within communities, and research about what is known as "memory culture," traditions remembered within communities but not actively practiced.

The baymen of eastern Long Island were the subject of a documentation project of the East Hampton Historical Society. The "bubbies," or baymen of eastern Long Island, have maintained their traditional culture over three centuries, but their livelihoods are now threatened by pollution, environmental regulation, and a rapidly changing economy amid the boom in land values in their area, "the Hamptons," known at present more for its chic reputation as a resort than as the home of the working fishermen. The documentation project involved field research about maritime practices, the extensive photographing of these activities, and the recording of oral traditions relating to maritime folklife. The documentation project served as a vehicle to call attention to a threatened traditional culture, an endeavor demonstrating how a museum can contribute to the preservation of a culture through means beyond the acquisition and preservation of artifacts.

The Anglo-American families of a county and their descendants have frequently represented the dominant focus of county historical museums. At the DeWitt Historical Society of Tompkins County, New York, ongoing folklife documentation has provided a research foundation for an ethnic heritage program, which has helped to expand the purview of the society's museum dramatically so that it encompasses a variety of ethnic communities that have settled in the county throughout this century. The museum has mounted exhibitions and has engaged in educational programs on the county's Afro-American, Czech, Finnish, Greek, Italian, and Southeast Asian communities. The exhibitions have incorporated material culture related to such traditions as the Finnish sauna, Southeast Asian embroidery, and Afro-American quilting, folklife traditions viewed within the perspective of these groups' adaptations to changing cultural and historical circumstances and the perpetuation of their traditional cultural values.

Rural folklife documentation projects in New York State have occurred within a context of changing rural communities. The economic bases of communities in agriculture and manufacturing have been altered as a result of such factors as the rise of service industries, the development of public works projects, the decline of the family farm, and the advent of suburbanization. A folklife program at the Saratoga County (New York) Historical Society is exploring the traditions of rural communities, which have been in transition during this century, through ongoing documentation, public programs, and exhibitions. Narratives about the past in small communities that continue in oral traditions have been presented to the public in "old-time story nights," storytelling programs featuring elderly residents of these communities in transition. The institution of the rural social dance, which once played a central role in the social and cultural life of rural Saratoga County, has also been documented. It is being revitalized through the museum's sponsorship of dances featuring local callers and musicians and held in the traditional setting of a grange hall. These public programs were linked to an exhibition of the rural social dance over time.

A growing number of other folklife documentation projects leading to museum activities are under way in New York State at the time of this writing. These documentation projects often concern themes and cultural forms previously unexplored in museums. The development of temporary exhibitions arising from these projects, like others in New York State in recent years, frequently involves both the documentation of living folk traditions and research into the folklife of the past.

Past and present work practices, recreational activities, and oral traditions relating to ice on Lake Champlain will be explored in an exhibition to be organized by the Clinton-Essex-Franklin Library System in northern New York. An exhibition at the Roberson Museum and Science Center in Binghamton on East European embroidery will demonstrate the continuity of traditions through the exhibiting of nineteenth-century and early-twentieth-century East European embroideries as well as embroideries by contemporary local folk artists of East European heritage. The latter were documented through ongoing fieldwork on the folk cultures of New York State's Southern Tier carried out by this museum's curator of folklife. Contemporary urban play traditions documented over several years and the history of play in New York City are being addressed in a comprehensive project, "City Play," of the folklife organization City Lore. An exhibition planned for a museum in New York City in 1987 will include images of street games of the past in prints and photographs and such contemporary objects as a Korean game of chance currently played in New York City. The exhibition will include a re-created city block designed to reflect the various ways in which streets are transformed for play activities, a setting in which visitors will be able to engage in traditional play activities.

The 1980s have seen a flourishing of folklife documentation projects that have resulted in museum activities. These projects have varied in their impact upon the museums sponsoring the activities. For some museums, a folklife project is a special initiative, focusing attention upon a particular community or aspect of folklife for a limited period, an episodic involvement with folklife whose enduring impact upon the museum's ongoing activities and collections is often uncertain, where the spotlight placed upon a particular community rapidly fades after an exhibition closes.

Museums are now beginning to institutionalize folklife programs. A folkloristic perspective is incorporated into a variety of the museum's activities, and the museum commits itself to a tangible involvement with the folklife field and the traditional culture of the communities it serves. While in the United States we have few museums devoted primarily to folklife and engaged in the sort of systematic collecting that characterizes many European museums, the folklife programs that have recently emerged in American museums can be addressed to the core activities and concerns of the museums in which they exist.

An essential feature of a museum folklife program is the maintenance of a properly maintained and accessible archive, following the professional standards for the archiving of folk materials, standards that parallel those for maintaining other museum materials. Folklife museum programs can actively acquire folk artifacts for the museum's collections, something that these programs should do within the framework of the museum's general collections policies. These programs should also engage in long-range planning of their documentation and exhibition programs to ensure that activities are sustained and thorough and that they are not ad hoc. Folklife museum programs could also benefit from greater knowledge of the approaches of European folk museums and of American programs, like that of the Folk Arts Division of the Michigan State University Museum, which have been engaged in folklife collecting and exhibition programs for a number of years.

Folklife plays an integral role in the public programs of many outdoor historical museums. The re-creation of traditional crafts and agricultural or maritime practices is a central feature of outdoor museums employing a "living history" approach. In these museums the work of the folklorist can ideally complement that of the historian, helping to ensure a solid research foundation for the representation of an American region's ordinary rural life at a particular period in the past. The reconstructed cultural landscape of the outdoor museum can provide a laboratory for experimental folklife research and a setting for innovative interpretive activities.[50]

The results of folklife research are realized in such activities as demonstrations of traditional games, accurate reconstructions of food preparation, and use of traditional techniques of farming and technology. Visitors to these museums learn to understand the place of folklife objects and processes in the context of work, leisure, religion, or domestic life during a period in the past. In the most successful outdoor museums, folklife provides an accessible means by which visitors may learn about the background of their everyday life in such typical activities as the making of clothing or farming practices, presented much as they existed in the past.

Folklife in historical museums is easy prey to inauthentic and misleading interpretations. Folklorists and historians alike should be concerned about demonstrations of revived traditional crafts not grounded in activities that can be documented as having occurred in a particular region during a particular period of the past. Museums should determine whether their obligatory spinner or candle maker relates to a practice known to have existed in the community being represented. Museums should also be sensitive to the place of a folklife practice in the seasonal round of activity. Old Bethpage Restoration, for example, takes care to demonstrate sheepshearing and Indian corn planting during the planting season in May, the time of year when they occurred in early-nineteenth-century Long Island.

Folklorists and historians should also share a responsibility for discouraging the skewed historical perspective epitomized by the once popular "Age of Homespun" approach.[51] The persistence of traditional crafts and agricultural practices during the early and mid-nineteenth century may be misinterpreted as the mark of a self-sufficient agrarian society seemingly untouched by external influences. A more accurate historical perspective recognizes the influence of a burgeoning industrial society upon traditional folklife and places folklife within the framework of societies beginning to undergo rapid social and cultural change.

Along with an enhanced understanding of history and a broadened perspective on art in society and culture, folklife may suggest intriguing interpretive possibilities for science in museums. The presentation of material relating to traditional beliefs about healing, herbal remedies, and various unorthodox medical practices can give new dimensions to exhibitions dealing with botany or medicine.[52] Traditional ideas and beliefs about the cosmos and the solar system might be related to scientific astronomy in a planetarium. By presenting traditional modes of knowledge concerning the physical world, science museums can provide a more holistic perspective in relating science to culture.

John Cotton Dana recognized early in this century that both the objects and the processes of folk culture have a central role to play in the museum—they help place the museum in a living relationship to human creativity in all communities. Folklife can contribute to a fuller understanding of the cultural experience of classes and social groups often ignored in museums. Carefully planned folk performances in museums give a dynamism to museum activities by placing the context of the artifacts in a new light. Folklife can be related to traditional concerns of museums as well as to interdisciplinary areas that are just beginning to be developed. As museums continue to reevaluate themselves and explore new dimensions of their activities, the many ways to apply folklife presentations in museums must become apparent.

NOTES

1. The American Association of Museums is now known as the American Alliance of Museums.

2. Robert Baron, "Folklife and the American Museum," *Museum News* 59 (March/April 1981): 46–50, 58, 60, 64.

3. Robert Baron, "Folklife and the American Museum," in *Folklife and Museums: Selected Readings*, ed. Patricia Hall and Charlie Seemann (Nashville: American Association for State and Local History, 1987), 12–26.

4. When I served as director of the Museum Program of the New York State Council on the Arts from 1996 to 2000, I expunged the term "outreach" from the program's lexicon, as I indicated in a 2003 article in *Curator*. As I stated in the article, Robert Baron, "Reinventing a State Funding Program for Museums," *Curator* 46 (2003): 31, "Outreach suggests a top-down approach, characteristic of a one-way relationship with communities, rather than mutual engagement."

5. James Clifford, *The Predicament of Culture: Twentieth-Century Ethnography, Literature and Art* (Cambridge, MA: Harvard University Press, 1988), 84.

6. Michael Frisch, *A Shared Authority: Essays on the Craft and Meaning of Oral and Public History* (Albany: State University of New York Press, 1990).

7. Robert Baron, "Sins of Objectification? Agency, Mediation and Community Cultural Self-Determination in Public Folklore and Cultural Tourism Programming," *Journal of American Folklore* 122 (2010): 71.

8. Baron, "Sins of Objectification," 85; Robert Baron, "'All Power to the Periphery': The Public Folklore Thought of Alan Lomax," *Journal of Folklore Research* 49 (2012): 310.

9. Ivan Karp, "Introduction," in *Museums and Communities: The Politics of Public Culture*, ed. Ivan Karp, Christine Mullen Kreamer, and Steven D. Lavine (Washington, DC: Smithsonian Institution Press, 1992), 14.

10. For a history and overview of eco-museums, see Peter Davis, *Ecomuseums: A Sense of Place*, 2nd ed. (London: Continuum International Publishing Group, 2011).

11. History of the Anacostia Community Museum appears in Portia James, "Building a Community-Based Identity at Anacostia Museum," *Curator* 39 (1996): 19–44.

12. See John Kuo Wei Tchen, "Creating a Dialogic Museum: The Chinatown History Museum Experiment," in *Museums and Communities*, 285–326, and John Kuo Wei Tchen and Liz Ševčenko, "The 'Dialogic Museum' Revisited: A Collaborative Reflection," in *Letting Go: Sharing Historical Authority in a User-Generated World*, ed. Bill Adair, Benjamin Filene, and Laura Koloski (Philadelphia: Pew Center for Arts and Heritage, 2011), 80–97.

13. Carrie Hertz, "Curating Community Engagement," in *Rethinking the Role of Folklore in Museums: Exploring New Directions for Folklore in Museum Policy and Practice*, ed. Folklore and Public Policy Working Group (Bloomington, IN: American Folklore Society, 2015), 36 (https://c.ymcdn.com/sites/afsnet.site-ym.com/resource/resmgr/Folklore_and_Museum_Policy_a.pdf?_sm_au_=iVVVFN1Tn20sg617).

14. Deborah Schwartz and Bill Adair, "Community as Curator: A Case Study at the Brooklyn Historical Society," in Adair, Filene, and Koloski, *Letting Go*, 116.

15. Ibid., 112–23.

16. Steve Zeitlin, "Where Are the Best Stories? Where Is My Story?—Participation and Curation in a New Media Age," in Adair, Filene, and Koloski, *Letting Go*, 35.

17. Michael Frisch, "From *A Shared Authority* to the Digital Kitchen and Back," in Adair, Filene, and Koloski, *Letting Go*, 128.

18. Tchen and Ševčenko, "The 'Dialogic Museum' Revisited," 112.

19. "The Future of Museums," Humanities, Arts, Science and Technology Alliance and Collaboratory Scholars Program, 2012, https://www.hastac.org/initiatives/hastac-scholars/scholars-forums/future-museums.

20. Jason Baird Jackson and Marsha MacDowell, "Digital Practices in Museum Ethnography," in *Rethinking the Role of Folklore in Museums*, 40, 42.

21. Nina Simon, "Chapter 1: Principles of Participation," The Participatory Museum (Museum 2.0), 2010, http://www.participatorymuseum.org/chapter1.

22. Nina Simon, "Participatory Design and the Future of Museums," in Adair, Filene, and Koloski, *Letting Go*, 31.

23. Nina Simon, "Chapter 7: Collaborating with Visitors," The Participatory Museum, http://www.participatorymuseum.org/chapter7.

24. Nicolas Bourriaud, *Relational Aesthetics*, trans. Simon Pleasance and Fronza Woods with Mathieu Copeland (Paris: Les Presses du Réel, [1998] 2002), 14.

25. Ibid., 21.

26. Ibid., 22.

27. Claire Bishop, "The Social Turn," *Artforum* (February 2006): 178.

28. Ibid., 179.

29. Claire Bishop, *Artificial Hells: Participatory Art and the Politics of Spectatorship* (London: Verso, 2012), 1.

30. Bishop, "The Social Turn," 180.

31. Bishop, *Artificial Hells*, 2.

32. Claire Bishop, "Antagonism and Relational Aesthetics," *October* 110 (2004): 55.

33. Ibid.

34. Nancy Zastudil, "We Are All Folk: The Art of Everyday (Folk) Life," *Arts + Culture Texas*, November 29, 2015, http://artsandculturetx.com/we-are-all-folk-the-art-of-everyday-folk-life.

35. James Elkins, *Master Narratives and Their Discontents* (New York: Routledge, 2005), 148.

36. Susan Jane Frieband, "An Institution in Transition: A Case Study of Four Art Museums and Their Libraries" (PhD diss., Rutgers University, 1973), 18–19.

37. Richard Grove, "Pioneers in American Museums: John Cotton Dana," *Museum News* 56 (May–June 1978): 87.

38. The ideas for these exhibits originated at the Hull House Museum and at the John Herron Art Institute of Indianapolis several years before. See Alice W. Kendall, "Homelands Exhibit in Museums," *Museum* 1 (May 1917): 7–10.

39. Beatrix T. Rumford, "Uncommon Art of the Common People: A Review of Trends in the Collecting and Exhibiting of American Folk Art," in *Perspectives in American Folk Art*, ed. Ian M. G. Quimby and Scott T. Swank (New York: W. W. Norton for the Henry Francis du Pont Winterthur Museum, 1980), 13–26.

40. Holger Cahill, *American Folk Art: The Art of the Common Man in America, 1750–1900* (New York: Museum of Modern Art, 1932), 3.

41. These positions were debated throughout a conference on American folk art held at the Winterthur Museum in November 1977. See Quimby and Swank, *Perspectives in American Folk Art*.

42. Svetlana Alpers, "Is Art History?" *Daedalus* 106 (Summer 1977): 2.

43. Ibid., 3.

44. Kenneth L. Ames, *Beyond Necessity: Art in the Folk Tradition* (New York: W. W. Norton for the Henry Francis du Pont Winterthur Museum, 1980), 18. George Kubler has been greatly responsible for articulating this approach. See his *The Shape of Time* (New Haven, CT: Yale University Press, 1962).

45. Dan Ben-Amos, "Toward a Definition of Folklore in Context," in *Towards New Perspectives in Folklore*, ed. Américo Paredes and Richard Bauman (Austin: University of Texas Press, 1972), 3–15; American Folklife Preservation Act, Public Law 94-201.

46. Barre Toelken, "In the Stream of Life: An Essay on Oregon Folk Art," in *Webfoots and Bunchgrassers: Folk Art of the Oregon Country*, ed. Suzi Jones (Salem: Oregon Arts Commission, 1980), 19.

47. André Malraux, *The Voices of Silence*, trans. Stuart Gilbert (Garden City, NY: Doubleday, 1953).

48. The Smithsonian Festival of American Folklife is now known as the Smithsonian Folklife Festival.

49. Richard Kurin, "Aditi: A Celebration of Life," in *1985 Festival of American Folklife*, ed. Smithsonian Institution and National Park Service (Washington, DC: Smithsonian Institution and National Park Service, 1985), 95.

50. Howard Wight Marshall, "Folklife and the Rise of American Folk Museums," *Journal of American Folklore* 90 (October–December 1977): 391–413.

51. The term "Age of Homespun" comes from a book of the same name: Jared van Wagenen, *Age of Homespun* (New York: Hill and Wang, 1963). It should be noted that van Wagenen viewed the practices described as occurring at the eve of the industrialization of America.

52. The 1979 Festival of American Folklife included presentations by healers, herbalists, and curers in the medical sciences area of the National Museum of American History.

3

Folklore and Museum Artifacts

JOHN MICHAEL VLACH

In this chapter John Michael Vlach outlines the special ways folk artifacts can be used in museums to interpret history and culture. He contrasts prevailing definitions of the terms "folk" and "historical" and demonstrates the important ways folk artifacts can contribute to a better understanding of technological processes, social frameworks, and regional or cultural contexts. Making the point that a history based on a study of traditional artifacts is, by its very nature, a more democratic and detailed history, Vlach calls for an interdisciplinary alliance between the historian and the folklorist as they work to document and interpret past and present cultures. Vlach prepared the chapter especially for *Folklife and Museums: Selected Readings* (1987), drawing upon presentations he made at the 1979 American Association of Museums Annual Meeting and the 1980 Conference on Folklore and Local History sponsored by the American Association for State and Local History. It is reprinted here in its entirety, in conjunction with a new chapter by John Moe.

To speak of a link between folklore and museums will to many readers seem strange. The museum is often regarded as a "temple" where, under the diligent care of specialized technicians and knowledgeable curators, the treasures of civilization are preserved for posterity. Folklore, on the other hand, is generally considered as that curious old stuff that everyone already knows about, which thus needs no care. Moreover, it is often thought to consist mostly of old songs, sayings, and stories.[1] How would such ephemeral verbal and musical creations be captured for display? What place do they have in the museum? Folklore and museums would certainly seem to be strange, even unlikely, companions. Unless the image of folklore improves there will be few chances for a fruitful collaboration between folklorists and museum specialists.

The discipline of folklore in the United States is now nearing its hundredth anniversary. In its first decades it was mainly a special kind of literature study, and folklorists were sheltered mostly in English departments. While early students of culture, particularly those trained by anthropologist Franz Boas, saw folklore as a universal expression, not until the 1920s and 1930s did Boas's students exercise much control over the directions of the discipline. Folklore then became an adjunct of anthropology, caught somewhere between the study of art and the study of language. The split that developed between folklorists who saw themselves as humanists and those who considered themselves social scientists eventually promoted the development of a synthetic field of study, one concerned with specific forms (tales, proverbs, ballads) situated among broad social forces (ethnicity, politics, religion, economics, and so on).[2] By the mid-twentieth century the study of American folklore had begun to achieve maturity and a new confidence. The maturation process also entailed growth, for not only were new theoretical perspectives incorporated into folklore's view, but the subject matter was also expanded. In the 1960s folklore came to mean not only the verbal arts but all the products of traditional technology as well.[3] American folklore studies were coming closer to the European approach in which the object of study was labeled "folklife," the totality of cultural expression, including its verbal, material, and spiritual elements. Unfortunately the academic growth of folklore has not been accompanied by a concurrent improvement of its public perception. Most people continue to maintain a nineteenth-century view of folklore as story, as quaint survival, and worse, they see it as half-truth and unimportant. These attitudes are quite prevalent and, depressingly, frequently encountered in academic circles. Potential colleagues in history, American studies, ethnic studies, sociology, government, art history, and other fields fail to realize what folklorists actually study. They are unaware of the interdisciplinary nature of folkloristic inquiry, which demands constant cross-checking of findings and often results in extensive collaboration and cooperation.[4]

One of the key arenas for cooperation between folklorists and other fields should be the museum. Folklife research in Europe has a long tradition for museum enterprise. So-called folk parks sprang up all over the Continent, in the Scandinavian countries, and in the northwestern islands in the nineteenth century. These open-air museums contain examples of the local traditional architecture, primarily domestic buildings of all sorts that are furnished with representative examples of crafted items and decorative arts.[5] The museums employ large staffs of researchers, fieldworkers, curators, and technicians who locate, investigate, transport, restore, and explain the functions of these domestic structures. Hence in Europe folklorists are often seen as specialists who work in a museum, quite different from their American counterparts, whose work rarely has any impact beyond the walls of the academy. Since the mid-1960s American folklorists have become increasingly aware of and even competent with the principles of European folklife research.[6] In the 1980s more folklorists are ready to offer their services to museums, as their European colleagues have done for more than a century. Museums are, among other things, storehouses for objects. When it is understood that folklore consists of objects as well as words, of tangible products as well as verbal products, then museums should welcome the research of folklorists.

While folklorists could contribute to different kinds of museums, institutions devoted to the presentation of history would seem to have aims almost compatible with those of folklore. Folkloristic expressions are patently historical, since for something to be folklore it must have had a prior existence in either its form or its content. A story, for example, may change characters but retain the same plot; plots may change, but the familiar hero may still be present. In either case, an element from the past is preserved in the present. Folklorists, it might be argued, study both the historical record and the present. But because folklore is so positively shaped by precedent, a contemporary folk event is really history made vital or living history. The mark of time is heavily imprinted on the products of folklore, whether they are current or ancient in origin. It follows, then, that folkloristic expressions are indispensable for any historical analysis, particularly if one is concerned about the personal textures of history.[7]

No record of the past is comprehensible without some explanation of process. A list of facts has no power to reveal insight unless it is placed within a model of action, just as a dictionary cannot allow one to speak a language unless one already knows the rules of its grammar. Because folklore is as much a statement of the "here and now" as of the "over and done," folklorists are very much concerned with current performance, with social acts and processes. Working closely with contemporary chair makers, for example, a folklorist is likely to inquire about their source and manner of design selection, their modes of technology, their means of procuring raw materials, their choice of markets, their negotiation of prices, their customers' degree of satisfaction, and their sense of self-worth. All of these aspects of chair making taken together constitute a holistic view of the making of an artifact, moving from idea to action to object to personal and social context. Other chairs and their makers can be judged against this model of production, and informed speculations can be made about the nature of other, similar activities from different times and places.[8] It is standard operating procedure for a folklorist to direct ethnographic skills toward historical purposes. It is the folklorist's prime task to record the impact of history on the present and to use the present to gain insight into the past, particularly for those groups of people and individuals to whom conventional history has paid little attention.[9]

It should be evident, then, that folklorists as humanists and social scientists have a greater contribution to make than is generally realized. The materials they study, the methods they use, and their commitment to issues of popular concern qualify them for participation in many research domains. The museum is one area that, until quite recently, has not been generally used, and hence it holds great potential. After they are admitted into the museums, what specific contributions can folklorists expect to make? As I see it, they could play at least three roles. First, in the areas of museum planning and policy development, the folklorist can contribute a fresh point of view. The folklorist's outlook on history is decidedly focused on the normative and the popular. In the organization of a particular exhibit, a folklorist would encourage an inclusive program of research that incorporates themes that are often beyond the sight lines of "consensus" history. Recognizing that much of what people do day in and day out is never recorded by official statistic takers, they would remind curators of the deep and varied strata of human experience that lie below the surface of noteworthy events and of the noteworthy sentiments that are disguised by the placid surface of seemingly unremarkable occurrences. Folklorists can clarify the objectives of a museum.[10]

A second contribution involves the implementation of a folkloristic viewpoint. Folklorists by training are prepared to gather the information needed for museum presentations, whether it is from museum collections or from a natural setting in a home, a factory, a shop, or a barn. The study of an industry such as coalmining might require extensive interviewing of miners, both active and retired, for a close-up sense of the nature of their work. Mine owners might also be consulted for their viewpoint. These interviews would doubtless reveal not only attitudes essential for shaping the storyline of an exhibit but also much specific data about machinery, equipment, tools, protective gear, and physical conditions that an accurate museum exhibit on mining must include.[11] Folklorists not only gather information but also present it. Just as they might instruct dancers on proper steps for the re-creation of a traditional polka, so too they can direct museum installers on the position of artifacts, the kind of lighting, the choice of color, and other innumerable problematic details that impinge upon the effectiveness of a museum display. A museum can never totally replace or re-create the past or the context of a specific event or place, but it can come reasonably close if care is taken to present key details. Knowledge of just what constitutes a "key detail" stands at the center of folkloristic research, since the critical nub of folklore study is the appreciation and understanding of the traditional values a group considers central to its existence.

The third major contribution folklorists can make to museums derives from their work in the social arena. Certain museums, particularly those in urban areas, are finding that they are losing their audiences, that their direction or philosophy no longer has as much appeal. In such cases the elitist or exotic narrative maintained by the museum has little relevance to the citizens of the community. One solution to this problem lies in restoring popular interest by a shift or expansion in programming. But how does a museum make such a critical decision? On what should it base the new program? Here local fieldwork by a staff folklorist might pay off by uncovering a hidden interest in ethnic art or in local history or in family biography or in hometown ingenuity. Should the museum pick up on one of these topics, its actions would no doubt be perceived as a valuable public service. Of the many new people who might be induced to visit the museum, a large number would probably be attracted to other exhibits and would hence give the museum the chance to broaden the horizons of the community while, at the same time, deepening the community's appreciation of the museum.[12] Folklorists can give museums access to their public.

From the foregoing remarks some readers might realize that their museums and institutions already engage in folkloric research but under a different name. Indeed, there might be an impression that the folklorist is a Johnny-come-lately to the fields of history and museology (at least in the United States). It might then be helpful to clarify just what the materials of folklore are and specifically what place they might have in a museum.

A museum artifact, to state the obvious, is an object from a museum collection. What kind of object it is depends on the nature of the museum. Art museums collect paintings and sculptures; natural history museums collect specimens of animals and minerals; history museums collect the documents and objects associated with the great or near-great. Should any of these kinds of museums collect items of folk art, folk breeds of livestock, or traditional tools, then folk artifacts automatically become museum artifacts. The museum as storehouse provides a large classificatory umbrella for any material element of human experience. The overt concern for folk things in the United States, however, is quite underdeveloped in the museum world. Traditional items rarely find their way into museum collections on purpose. Folk artifacts in museums are usually seen exclusively as historical statements, as leftovers from faraway times and dead-and-gone people. To read folk artifacts in this way is to have only half the story. These objects do have a historical dimension because they are inextricably tied to the past. Oftentimes, however, they are still tied to the present either as relicts or as thriving traditions. Potters in Georgia and North Carolina still make their butter churns and crocks the way their nineteenth-century ancestors did.[13] To view their works solely as historical items is to deny their contemporary vitality. These people are not simply nineteenth-century throwbacks caught in a time warp. They are modern men and women, fully aware of current events, who have found a way to make sense of their lives with the means bequeathed to them by their families. To freeze them and their works in an exclusive historical perspective is to exile the actuality of their existence to an academic never-never land.

Folk artifacts are more than historical artifacts. As items, both the historic and the folk artifact might be the same object, but the interpretation one derives from a folk artifact can be quite different, yielding an alternative view of events. If one assumes that it is part of a dynamic social context (either of the past or of the present), the folk object represents more than itself. Historic artifacts are often treated as adjuncts to a literary narrative. They are treated as so many tidbits to spice up and decorate an account derived from documentary sources. They become sources for the reaffirmation of the myths of the already famous. Consider the impact of *the* sword of Washington, *the* first Edison lightbulb, *the* first Model T Ford. Folk artifacts debunk myths by portraying the typical, the rudimentary, the basic, the fundamental aspects of the lives of groups of people who had few pretentions to greatness. The glorious pioneers who opened the West come to be seen as poor people at work. Their material possessions honestly and accurately express what they did and give some insight into what they hoped for. One key difference between folk and historic artifacts lies in the intentions of an object's interpreter. Another more fundamental difference arises in the nature of the object. The material residues of elite culture are often one-of-a-kind items made precious by the kind of material or the reputation of the owner or maker. They are so special and specialized that they cannot represent anyone but single, isolated, nonrepresentative individuals.[14] The folk thing belongs to a class of objects and thus does not usually stand out as extraordinary or special. It is used by many, not just by a single person. The folk object is then extremely representative because it is so typical. It thus yields admittance to an extensive social segment.[15] Because of the conservatism of that segment, one simultaneously also gains access to a longer span of years than can be attained through the artifacts of so-called straight history.

An inventory of folk artifacts would touch every aspect of life, including its domestic, industrial, agricultural, economic, political, religious, and aesthetic realms. Material folk culture constitutes all the things people make that can be seen or touched. To date, American scholarship has focused on four major material topics in folklife: folk art, crafts, traditional architecture, and domestic and agricultural technology.[16] These four areas provide enough materials for the development of a folk museum. The major element would be architectural structures—houses, sheds, barns, and other outbuildings arranged according to traditional farm or town plans. The crafted items and artworks would provide the needed furnishings for an accurate restoration. The domestic technologies such as cooking, weaving, soap making, and candle making could be demonstrated in the houses to create a sense of the vitality of households, while displays of machinery maintenance, plowing, and animal husbandry would bring a sense of reality to the outdoor sector of the museum. A more conventional museum would probably find slots in its program for a display of domestic technology or an exhibit of works of folk art from a given place or period. The materials of folklife are distinctive enough for their difference either in kind or interpretation to make a significant addition to most museums.

A commitment to folk artifacts by a museum would direct attention to several themes that together constitute a worthy program of public education. First, there could be an increase in the general understanding of technical processes. Industrial technology is so complex that few people understand how it works or that it is even an extension of human effort and that mankind is ultimately accountable for it. Hand technologies are easier to comprehend and as such can provide a springboard for tackling more advanced systems of production. At the same time, appreciating the effort and skill required to throw a pot, turn a chair leg, weave a basket, embroider a pillow, frame a house, lay out a drainage ditch, and so forth is sure to stimulate a sense of respect that is well deserved by the practitioners of folk technology. From the example of the resourceful we learn that our seemingly insurmountable problems might also be conquered.

A second goal involves the presentation of outstanding artisans or performers. While folklore is a social phenomenon, one can learn a great deal about it through the in-depth study of society's individual members, particularly those individuals to whom a group looks for leadership or special services. An essential craftsman such as a blacksmith or a carpenter might be considered a local celebrity or hero. To review this person's career at length would give an opportunity to move beyond the obvious accomplishments attained by expert control over technology to the personal sense of achievement. The folk society might then be revealed in microcosm as communal knowledge is put to personal use.[17] The craftsman would be seen as a creator sorting out the demands of his community and his personality. That critical debate between self and others occurs repeatedly among all members of society to some degree. A close examination of individual artisans leads then to general as well as specific insights.

The study and presentation of folk artifacts can provide an understanding of the social frameworks that surround their production and use. Clients depend on craftsmen, but without clients to work for, craftsmen might never make a single object. The bond established by the exchange of money for goods and services is paralleled by bonds of friendship and respect. In a folk society an object may initiate a long series of reciprocal moves that ties the maker and the user of an object closer and closer together. Recognizing that folk objects are made in communities, we realize that they take on a communal aspect. If, for example, in Buncomb County, North Carolina, there is a marked preference for a particular foodstuff, say sauerkraut, then the potter will probably adjust his categories of crocks to accommodate this demand. Since the next county might not have the same food preferences, the first group's ceramics, while remaining the same salt-glazed Piedmont stoneware, will appear distinctive because of the special forms made. Thus Buncomb County's clay artifacts come to reflect specific social characteristics. Artifacts clearly reveal more than technology, since certain collective features of local culture are also presented.

From the communal level, a folklorist would next move on to the regional and cultural aspects of folk artifacts. A region consists of communities linked by a shared environment, events, and ancestry. Distinctive factors of particular times and places constitute the coordinates of a local history that may be more immediate and more comprehensible than our ultimate national and continental saga. Before Americans are Americans, they are southerners or New Englanders or midwesterners, and artifacts record these distinctions quite well. If comparative data of sufficient merit are available for several regions of the United States, or if the material from one region proves to be exceedingly rich, then broad cultural analysis can be done with folk artifacts. At this point the scholarly target is the discovery of the largest patterns in human consciousness, those universal realities common to all people. Concepts about the nature of creativity or the basis for social order can be approached at this point. Questions about the importance of symmetrical balance in furniture design or legal charters or the impact of industrial development on rural values might be raised and tested with the mute but ever-constant artifact.[18] Should any of the above objectives be met, then the folklorist's role in the museum would certainly be established and the museum's use of folklore proven worthwhile.

In a sense the rationale for including folklore in the work of museums has already been made. No one would quarrel with the advancement of knowledge and the creation of cultural awareness and sensitivity among the populace. However, since these are aims already espoused and to some degree met by museums, it would be well to clarify further the case for museological enterprise with folk artifacts. Given the close relationship between folklore and history, I will comment particularly on the advantages for the writing and exploration of history.

The current mood in historiography—to write history from the bottom up, to use oral sources, to use personal documents, to write about the unheralded—has made history an inclusive enterprise and more impossible to write than ever before. Once we acknowledge that history should be an account of all its participants, we quickly realize that we face a steep cliff to climb, with few handholds. There is so much to learn, perhaps too much. But before we are overwhelmed and despair in this gargantuan task, we can at least try to open the pages of our future books to more of history's participants.[19]

A history stemming from traditional artifacts helps us move in that direction. A history based on objects includes more people because of the social nature of folk things. Furthermore, to write extensively and comprehensively about folk technology is to write democratic history, giving time and credit where it has been long overdue. Evolutionary models of linear progress through time would have the custodians of received tradition seem like archaic dinosaurs, when in some communities traditionally sanctioned action represents the sanest and most intelligent means of earning a livelihood. To write about folk technologies as they were and are used is to restore not only a sense of balance but a sense of complexity to an oversimplified view of the past and present. A critical aspect of democracy is choice, and important choices in daily life about shelter, sustenance, and work are never as simple as they might seem to the detached outsider.

Attention to specific artifacts and their attendant technologies focuses attention on particular details and personalities, and the resulting specificity can lead to accuracy in historical reckoning. An artifact is a first-order document closely connected to people and events. It is not subject to biased viewpoint or faulty memory, as are most interpretations of documents. An object, by being itself, carries its precise history with it always. Should we be shrewd enough to understand an artifact's context both in manufacture and in use, we can improve our ability to produce a trustworthy history, as each generation must. To keep this exercise from becoming a useless overhauling of the past, we should consider the power of things to tell tales and to tell them exceedingly well. Revisionism is useless, even insidious, unless it yields a more authentic account, and artifacts can be a yardstick of authenticity.

The interpretation of history is so difficult, so complex, that all who are interested should make common cause to present it. Academic squabbles and jaw flapping over who has a right to the turf should cease. Social history requires that the unsung be sung. But questions are raised: In what key? To what tune? As we attempt to form a much needed interdisciplinary alliance, we may find ourselves worrying too much about the orchestration rather than the words of the actual song.

The folklorist's perspective would have the members of folk society come first by inverting the pyramid of hierarchical values upon which conventional history is premised. If historians go off looking for the folk, they are bound to need help at first. They will need the tools and skills in textual and artifactual analysis of the folklorist. They will have to go to the field, whether it is cityscape or farmscape, factory or barnyard, kitchen or sweatshop. And along the way they will have to reach an understanding of the concept of tradition, a philosophy as difficult to define as culture, that is vital to understanding how the consequences of events shape human nature. It is most likely to be in the museum that the beneficial alliance between historians and folklorists will occur, that the relationship of folklore and museum artifacts will be forged with trustworthy links of both theory and practice.[20]

NOTES

1. The definition of folklore as a subject and a discipline is a perplexing topic; a useful reference in this regard is Jan Harold Brunvand, *The Study of American Folklore: An Introduction*, 2d ed. (New York: W. W. Norton, 1978), see especially chaps. 1–3.

2. While there is no comprehensive history of the discipline of folklore, one can gain a general idea of its major features from Richard M. Dorson, "Concepts of Folklore and Folklife Studies," in *Folklore and Folklife: An Introduction*, ed. Richard M. Dorson (Chicago: University of Chicago Press, 1972), 1–50.

3. See Don Yoder, "The Folklife Studies Movement," *Pennsylvania Folklife* 13 (July 1963): 43–56.

4. An example of this cooperation can be found in *Material Culture Studies: A Symposium, Material Culture* 17 (1985). This special issue of the journal features commentaries by three folklorists, an architectural historian, an art historian, a social historian, and a cultural geographer.

5. On the history of open-air museums, see Jay Anderson, *Time Machines: The World of Living History* (Nashville: American Association for State and Local History, 1984), 17–23.

6. Howard Wight Marshall, "Folklife and the Rise of American Folk Museums," *Journal of American Folklore* 90 (1977): 391–413; Ormond Loomis, *Sources on Folk Museums and Living Historical Farms*, Bibliographic and Special Series 16 (Bloomington, IN: Folklore Forum, 1977), provides a list of almost nine hundred publications that describe the activities and strategies of folk museums in the United States.

7. Richard M. Dorson, "Local History and Folklore," in *American Folklore and the Historian*, ed. Richard M. Dorson (Chicago: University of Chicago Press, 1971), 145–56.

8. For an example of such an inquiry, see Michael Owen Jones, *The Hand Made Object and Its Maker* (Berkeley: University of California Press, 1975), which details the career of a Kentucky chair maker.

9. Henry Glassie, "Folkloristic Study of the American Artifact: Objects and Objectives," in *The Handbook of American Folklore*, ed. Richard M. Dorson (Bloomington: Indiana University Press, 1983), 382.

10. An instance of this sort of contribution occurred in the development of a new exhibition recently opened at the Smithsonian Institution's National Museum of American History, titled "After the Revolution: Everyday Life in the Eighteenth Century." Here folklorist John Michael Vlach was contracted to write a position paper that might illustrate themes important for the section of the exhibition dealing with Afro-American culture. See his report on file with the Department of Social and Cultural History, National Museum of American History, "Afro-American Domestic Artifacts in Eighteenth-Century Virginia," No. SF 2059410000, August 1982.

11. See Howard Wight Marshall and Richard E. Ahlborn, *Buckaroos in Paradise: Cowboy Life in Northern Nevada* (Washington, DC: Library of Congress, 1980). The

exhibition for which this book served as the catalog featured the re-creation of a cowboy line camp. This display was furnished with almost 250 items of cowboy gear collected from ranching families in Nevada.

12. Such actions were, in fact, the outcome of the exhibition "The Afro-American Tradition in Decorative Arts," staged at the Cleveland Museum of Art from February to April 1979.

13. See John A. Burrison, *Brothers in Clay: The Story of Georgia Folk Pottery* (Athens: University of Georgia Press, 1983); Charles G. Zug, *The Traditional Pottery of North Carolina* (Chapel Hill: Ackland Art Museum, University of North Carolina, 1981); Nancy Sweezy, *Raised in Clay: The Southern Pottery Tradition* (Washington, DC: Smithsonian Institution Press, 1984).

14. See Gervase Jackson-Stops, ed., *The Treasure Houses of Great Britain: Five Hundred Years of Private Patronage and Art Collecting* (Washington, DC: National Gallery of Art, 1985), for numerous examples of objects that speak principally of a small group of the superrich.

15. On the nature of the folk object, see Henry Glassie, *Pattern in the Material Folk Culture of the Eastern United States* (Philadelphia: University of Pennsylvania Press, 1968), 5–7.

16. For reviews of the scholarship in these areas, see Thomas J. Schlereth, *Material Culture: A Research Guide* (Lawrence: University Press of Kansas, 1985), especially the sections by Dell Upton (pp. 57–78) and Simon J. Bronner (pp. 127–53). See also Simon J. Bronner, ed., *American Folk Art: A Guide to Sources* (New York: Garland Publishing, 1984).

17. This sort of biographically oriented insight can be found in John Michael Vlach, *Charleston Blacksmith: The Work of Philip Simmons* (Athens: University of Georgia Press, 1981).

18. Henry Glassie, "Folk Art," in Dorson, *Folklore and Folklife*, 278–79.

19. See David E. Kyvig and Myron A. Marty, *Nearby History: Exploring the Past around You* (Nashville: American Association for State and Local History, 1982), and James B. Gardner and George Rollie Adams, eds., *Ordinary People and Everyday Life* (Nashville: American Association for State and Local History, 1983), especially Barbara G. Carson and Cary Carson, "Things Unspoken: Learning Social History from Artifacts," 181–203.

20. There now exists in the United States a network of "state folk art coordinators." Created for the most part with National Endowment for the Arts monies, this group of folklorists has been very ambitious in its museum efforts. The following selected list should provide a sample of the work folklorists are currently doing in museums: Hal Cannon, ed., *Utah Folk Art: A Catalog of Material Culture* (Provo, UT: Brigham Young University, 1980); Suzi Jones, ed., *Webfoots and Bunchgrassers: Folk Art of the Oregon Country* (Salem: Oregon Arts Commission, 1980); Patti Carr Black, ed., *Made by Hand: Mississippi Folk Art* (Jackson: Mississippi Department of Archives and History, 1980); Varick A. Chittenden and Herbert W. Hemphill Jr., *Found in New York's North Country: The Folk Art of a Region* (Utica, NY: Munson-Williams-Proctor Institute, 1982); Nicholas Curchin Vrooman and Patrice Avon Marvin, *Iron Spirits* (Fargo: North Dakota Council on the Arts, 1982); Jane C. Beck, ed., *Always in Season: Folk Art and Traditional Culture in Vermont* (Montpelier: Vermont Council on the Arts, 1982); Steven Ohrn, ed., *Passing Time and Traditions: Contemporary Iowa Folk Artists* (Ames: Iowa State University Press, 1984); George D. Terry and Lynn Robertson Myers, eds., *Carolina Folk: The Cradle of a Southern Tradition* (Columbia: McKissick Museum, University of South Carolina, 1985).

4

Paradigm Shifts in the Study and Presentation of Material Culture

The Binding Force of Artifacts

John F. Moe

A longtime colleague of John Vlach, John Moe provides an insightful perspective on the contributions of museums and of the field to cultural sustainability and material culture studies. While acknowledging the classic earlier article by John Vlach that is included in the volume, Moe calls for a more nuanced understanding of the "social nature of things." This is especially relevant today as one comes to consider the artifact as material culture—that is, "made with effort and diligence and, of course, heritage, serv[ing] to make us human." Moe argues that museum practice in the twenty-first century is informed now by deeper engagement with the visitor experience, the expectations for fund-raising with the communities they serve, and, perhaps more significantly, the need to connect with the pressing social issues that are impacting society locally and globally. He points out, "The complexity and interconnectivity of issues throughout the world have encouraged museums to think more broadly about their roles and responsibilities." In making his case for greater social inclusion by museums in all aspects of their operation, Moe examines new practices of open-air museums in Europe and Nordic countries, strategies employed by the Great Lakes Folk Festival (produced by the Michigan State University Museum in East Lansing), and the programming of the National Folk Festival (produced by the National Council for the Traditional Arts [NCTA]). In these examples, he demonstrates that innovative folklife approaches in the twenty-first century are helping realize Vlach's original call to provide a opportunities where the "unsung [is] sung."

BACKGROUND AND INTRODUCTION: "FOLKLORE AND MUSEUM ARTIFACTS" FOR THE 1980s

John Michael Vlach's essay "Folklore and Museum Artifacts" continues to remind us of our duties regarding the responsibility we carry, as academics and as citizens involved in the evaluation and public presentation of museum exhibitions. Always a passionate observer of people and their efforts, Vlach wisely urges us to understand and to practice within a democratic context and to advocate for inclusion. Vlach was proud of and knowledgeable about his own ethnic heritage, half-Czech from his father's side and his mother's family from Hawai'i. From the outset of his academic career he argued for a "history stemming from traditional artifacts." "A history based on objects," he writes, "includes more people because of the social nature of folk things. Furthermore," he declares, "to write extensively and comprehensively about folk technology is to write democratic history."[1] By looking at "the social nature of folk things," Vlach reveals an academic as well as an ethical position in favor of the efforts of human beings, everywhere, to live with dignity and to express their culture in the larger world of multiple ethnicities and nationalities. The principle of the social nature of folk things overrides all squabbles used to divide people. The validity of the primacy of the individual piece of material culture, the artifact, made by effort and diligence, and, of course, heritage, serves to make us human.

John Vlach and I have known each other and sometimes worked together for over forty years, so I write from a sympathetic and empathetic point of view. Some of my comments and all of my thoughts are framed by this shared experience. When we were graduate students, working under Richard M. Dorson, director of the Folklore Institute at Indiana University for many years, and with Henry Glassie, then the young leader of academic material culture study, Vlach and I often made modest ventures into fieldwork together. Sometimes, when we had a free afternoon, we would take my 1954 Chevy pickup out to photograph and measure an old, traditional piece of architecture. The area surrounding Bloomington, Indiana, had many old pieces of folk architecture where we could ply our skills. I-houses, double-pen houses, transverse crib barns, mountain stable barns, and even traditional hall and parlor houses could be found in the surrounding countryside.

Later, when we had finished graduate school and were both teaching folklore, we taught and studied independently the ideas of the folk artifact as part of what John Vlach terms "the social nature of folk things." We conducted fieldwork together in Hispanic and Pueblo communities in New Mexico, in the African American neighborhoods of New Orleans, and compared our fieldwork on the Scots-Irish housing archetypes and the Scots-Irish descendants in the region of Green County, Pennsylvania. We both still have small angels carved and signed in person by Gloria Lopez Cordova, one of the renowned traditional wood carvers from Cordova, New Mexico, and niece of the well-known wood carver George T. Lopez (1900–1993). Several of George Lopez's important woodcarvings are held in the collections of the Smithsonian Institution, a fact that underscores the central theme of "Folklore and Museum Artifacts."

During the annual folklore meetings in Atlanta, Los Angeles, and Milwaukee, John and I would set off to find local material folk culture. And each time I visited John Vlach in Washington, DC, we would walk a stretch of the eighteenth-century buildings and the alley architecture of the old sections of the city. We talked incessantly about the individuals we met, who made wood carvings and pottery, and what we learned while out in the field. John Vlach has always been singular in his devotion and commitment to experiencing folklore through fieldwork and the material artifacts we encountered. The item of material culture itself, experiencing the artifact firsthand, holds primacy for Vlach in his search for understanding and learning from the artifact and, therefore, appreciating the "social nature of folk things."

The original paper that formed the basis for John Vlach's essay "Folklore and Museum Artifacts" was written for presentation at an American Association for State and Local History conference in 1980. Many of the academic topics faced by folklorists, as well as the global issues that dominated world concern at the time his essay was published in 1987, were quite different from those in the first quarter of the twenty-first century.[2] In the 1980s, the United States was still in the middle of the Cold War with the Soviet Union, and academic issues in American studies, including American folklore, were largely domestic issues. American regionalism, African American (then "Afro-

American") culture, feminism, and urbanism were important scholarly issues domestically during the 1980s. Americanists, like Vlach and myself, were heavily concerned with regionalism, and in our folklore study we were guided by regionalism studies in material culture and folklore, academic studies such as Henry Glassie's seminal *Pattern in the Material Folk Culture of the Eastern United States.*[3] Scholarship in American studies during the 1980s was heavily influenced by examining the concept of regions in and regionalization of North America. Joel Garreau's *Nine Nations of North America*, published in 1981, a popular and influential study at the time, had an impact on the fields of folklore, museum studies, geography, and history.[4]

Vlach wrote his essay at a time in the late mid-century when university departments for the field of folklore and the concept of folklife study were at an early stage of development for scholars of American studies. Lamenting the dearth of understanding of folklore scholarship within the academy, he noted, "Unfortunately, the academic growth of folklore has not been accompanied by a concurrent improvement of its public perception. Most people," he remarked then, "continue to maintain a nineteenth-century view of folklore as story, as quaint survival, and worse, they see it as half-truth."[5]

John Vlach offers three areas in which folklorists can make significant contributions to museum artifact exhibition. He begins by pointing out, "No record of the past is comprehensible without some explanation of process."[6] His argument implies that the explanation of process is embedded in the strategy of the folklorist's approach to the discovery of traditional folklife patterns. Vlach specifically suggests that folklorists can contribute to the museum by participating in museum planning and policy development, implementing the folkloristic viewpoint, and programming with a sensitivity for the social arena in which the museum operates. In each of the roles, Vlach stresses the value of a fresh point of view using the perspective of the folklorist. I would argue that in the intervening thirty-five years since Vlach made these recommendations, the museum world has addressed many of his admonitions and fulfilled some of the ambitions that he set out in his initial presented paper in 1980.

TWENTY-FIRST-CENTURY ISSUES OF FOLKLORE, SUSTAINABILITY, AND MUSEUM ARTIFACTS IN A CHANGING WORLD

The evolution in museum practice has occurred not only because of Vlach's efforts and those of other folklorists all over the world but also because of a fundamental change in the ways that museums operate to attract funding and audiences, as well as museums' efforts to reflect what is happening, what is current in the world. While the folklore and museum communities may have subscribed to the predominant issues of the day in the 1980s, the issues of the first two decades of the twenty-first century are significantly different and, in some ways, more nuanced. Now, nearly thirty-five years after Vlach presented his initial paper, social, political, and economic conditions in the United States have changed, and the interconnection and interweaving of US issues and world issues have become more complex. Global change has taken many forms: global climate change, worldwide political change, demographic shifts, technological development, terrorism and wars, population displacement and migration, and, finally—in part, because of the attacks of September 11, 2001—an altered consciousness about the fragility of global stability.

The complexity and interconnectivity of issues throughout the world have encouraged museums to think more broadly about their roles and responsibilities. Indeed, significant social and political change is reflected in the exhibitions of museums at the present time, and the role of the folklorist has been a contributing factor. Early in his essay, Vlach notes the importance of the open-air museum movement in northern Europe. "One of the key arenas for cooperation between folklorists and other fields should be the museum. Folklife research in Europe has a long tradition for museum enterprise." Vlach arrives at a significant conclusion when he notes, "Hence in Europe folklorists are often seen as specialists who work in a museum."[7]

The open-air museum movement in Europe has long been an example for folklorists as a goal for the implementation of the public presentation and exhibition of traditional material folk culture. Indeed, the first American folklore PhD was Warren Roberts, who became a material culture specialist while on academic leave at the open-air museums in Scandinavia. Roberts spent his career teaching in the Folklore Institute at Indiana University and trained generations of folklore students in material culture. The open-air museum movement in Scandinavia began in Sweden with the development of Skansen, under the supervision of Artur Hazelius, and opened first in 1891. The term "open-air museum" was first in evidence in a newspaper article in 1892 and then again "in the printed annual reports of Skansen's first years in 1894."[8] The open-air museum, which was initially termed by Hazelius as the "open-air annexe," contained examples of traditional architecture from all over the Swedish countryside that were later moved to the museum site. Museum staff, including folklorists, gathered extant buildings, primarily domestic buildings, but also barns, furniture, farm work implements, and domestic items, and brought the artifacts to Skansen. The ethnologist and folklorist Gösta Berg, who specialized in rural farmland material culture, was the guiding force for material folk culture research for many years at the Skansen Museum. To illustrate the importance of folklore in the development of Skansen, Berg was the governor of the Nordic Museum (Nordiska Museet) and Skansen from 1956 to 1963.[9]

Following the lead example of the work at Skansen, national open-air museums were established in Scandinavia and the Baltic countries: the Norsk Folkemuseum (1894) in Norway, Frilandsmuseet (1897) in Denmark, Seurasaari (1910s) in Finland, and Eesti Vabaõhumuuseum at Rocca al Mare in Estonia. The Estonian open-air museum, in particular, has folkloristic roots. In 1913, folklorists who maintained themselves as a Finnish-Estonian folklore and literature club began to plan for an open-air museum—though, because of the world wars and the Soviet occupation, the Estonian museum did not open until 1957.

Though the Scandinavian open-air museums retained, for the most part, their preindustrial society focus throughout the twentieth century, during recent years, many of the museums have begun to alter their original focus by adding materials from the late twentieth century and even the early twenty-first century. For example, at the Skansen Museum, curators have been including new exhibitions that relate primarily to the years of the worldwide Great Depression. According to Charlotte Ahnlund Berg, an education director at Skansen, "The museum is now including traditional garden plots so that people can see how Swedish people lived and survived during the Depression years." The new exhibits, she stressed, "are part of the effort by the museum to educate museum visitors about how people lived in the very recent past." "We, at Skansen," Berg noted, have always been known for having an excellent historical presentation and collection, "but it is important to also show how life is changing for us in Sweden."[10]

Charlotte Berg's observations demonstrate the urge and importance of the open-air museum to retain its relevance in a changing society. Berg underscores two important factors for museums in the contemporary world. The first is to maintain their traditional focus, which is, in the case of the open-air museum, to be confident about the historical open-air museum presentation of the past. The second is to demonstrate an awareness of the importance of presenting a view of the culture that contains a conceptual understanding of traditional cultural sustainability amid the dramatic changes in the global environment. In fact, John Vlach draws upon folklorist and historian Richard Dorson to underscore this point exactly. Citing Dorson, Vlach states, "The mark of time is heavily imprinted on the products of folklore, whether they are current or ancient in origin. It follows then, that folkloristic expressions are indispensable for any historical analysis, particularly if one is concerned about the personal textures of history."[11]

Other open-air museums have adopted, or are beginning to adopt, similar changes in the outlook for the future of the museum. Museum professionals, including folklorists, are instrumental in implementing changes aimed at answering Dorson's call for an examination of the folkloristic expressions of change. The Norsk Folkemuseum in Oslo, which opened in 1894, has made some encouraging movements to an installation of an apartment building, placed on the museum grounds at some distance from the traditional log *stabbur* buildings of the 1600s and 1700s. The development of the apartment house with different decenniums of the twentieth century provides the museum with a unique way of presenting the past in an open-air museum program.

In 1998, the Oslo Cooperative Housing Cooperation offered the Norsk Folkemuseum an old three-story brick building from downtown Oslo. The building was built in 1865 and was typical of residential apartment buildings in the older parts of Oslo.[12] The apartment building was demolished in 1999 and rebuilt at the Norsk Folkemuseum during 2000 and 2001. When the project was completed in 2009, the final apartment building contained exhibition sites in individual apartments.

In all, there are eight apartments in the reconstructed building, each telling a different story of living in Oslo: a doll's house (1879), a Norwegian home in a new age (1905), Modern Living (1935), the Cleaning Lady's home (1950), Teak, TV, and Teenagers (1965), the Architect's home (1979), the student's *besitter* (1982), and, finally, a Pakistani home in Norway (2002). The museum curators argue that the apartment exhibit is, in principle, not different from other exhibitions. "The interior[s] are not simply constructed or reconstructed homes, but narratives with a defined purpose and a specific perspective. Each home in Wessels gate 15 tells a different story from different times, presenting people of contrasting social and cultural backgrounds."[13]

The open-air museum is a natural site within which to tell the story of national crisis. The Norsk Folkemuseum articulates its own response to the museum impulse toward a "democratic history." In the case of Norway, the Norsk Folkemuseum in Oslo can document the way Norwegian people lived in the sixteenth and seventeenth centuries by moving historic traditional housing and barns to the site, and the museum can also tell the story of contemporary Norway, one where Norway emerged from World War II or one that includes the Pakistani immigrant home in Oslo. Audun Kjus, one of the curators at the Norsk Folkemuseum, explains that "the next project in the outdoor museum is to move and rebuild a 50s house from Finnmark." Accordingly, this project would address the period of devastation from the time that German forces occupied Norway during World War II. During the war, the German army destroyed many towns and farms, especially on the west coast. This future project of the Norsk Folkemuseum would physically address the period following World War II by moving a house built in the 1950s as part of the "rebuilding of northern Norway" after the war.[14]

Perhaps one of the most profound adaptations of the open-air museum concept and the inclusion of folkloristic investigation is a contemporary section of the Maihaugen Museum in Lillehammer, in central Norway. Maihaugen is known as one of the finest regional open-air museums in Scandinavia and focuses its exhibition program on the region surrounding Lillehammer. Ironically, many of the eighteenth-century buildings at the Maihaugen Museum are structures that the farm owners needed to be rid of in order to modernize their farms. Magne Velure, former director of the Maihaugen Museum, explained that the museum benefitted from the fact that it was "happy to take all the buildings." Under the guidance of Velure and a staff of professional folklorists, Maihaugen has included buildings from the recent past as part of its interpretation of the passage of time.[15] Recent installations include a traditional folk architecture house from the Depression period. Gure Velure, curator at the museum, explained that by "using oral testimony as well as extant buildings, the Depression house is a structure that might have been lost to history had it not been for the folkloristic inquiry into the history of such simple structures. We are pleased to be able to present this house that is unusual for Norway today. It shows how difficult times were and how people lived at that time."[16] The Depression house is located close to a 1960s suburban house typical of the middle of Norway. Built using oral testimony as well as extant buildings, the Depression house is a structure that might have been lost to history had it not been for the folkloristic inquiry into the history of such simple structures. Had it not been in part for the folklorists' perspective, such an "inconsequential" building might have been ignored because of its lack of imposition. However, because the building was crucial to the sustenance of so many poor and unemployed Norwegians, the building remained a strong image in the oral repertoire of citizens who told stories of the Great Depression era. Many Norwegians, in folk parlance, are fond of saying, "What depression? We in Norge did not notice any change. We were in a depression before the Depression."[17]

The historical importance of creating open-air museums was current in the United States as well, and the Scandinavian/Baltic museums provided an example to emulate. For example, several museums in the midwestern United States implemented the Scandinavian open-air museum design. The Iowa Living History Farms outside Des Moines presented an open-air concept that focused on three periods of farm development in Iowa. The Conner Prairie settlement museum in Noblesville, Indiana, focused its exhibition on the 1840s in Indiana. And the Old World Wisconsin open-air museum was organized around the buildings and material culture of different ethnic groups inhabiting Wisconsin. In each of the museums, folklorists played a significant role, especially at Conner Prairie, where many folklore students, including myself, worked as docents and interns to develop the museum's "first-person" exhibition strategy.

Museums today would do well to reexamine John Vlach's suggestions regarding the role of folklore and folklorists and museum artifacts. In planning and development, in adopting a folklore viewpoint, and in a reexamination of the social arena in which the museums operate, folklorists continue to make positive inroads in the presentation of culture through the use of a folklore strategy. For example, the Norsk Folkemuseum in Oslo is famous for its outstanding collections of buildings and other material culture that date back to the sixteenth century. However, recently, in addition to developing new open-air buildings that illustrate how Norwegians lived during the 1960s, the museum folklorists have organized an oral history project on the shootings that occurred in 2011 at a summer camp on the island of Utøya, in Baskerud,

Norway. Folklorists have organized and collected artifacts for public display and oral histories and memories of the event for exhibition in a museum setting in order to preserve the oral history for future scholars to examine. Their effort is clearly in the spirit of Vlach's suggestions regarding the role of folklore and museum artifacts.

TWENTY-FIRST-CENTURY ISSUE OF SUSTAINABILITY, FOLKLORE, AND MUSEUM ARTIFACTS

In the middle of the second decade of the twenty-first century, the "civilized" world strives to make things right, à la the rights and responsibilities of "all folk." For Vlach, the artifact, the individual piece of material culture, is primary, what he calls the "first-order" piece of history. As regards museum artifacts and objects of material culture, Vlach noted, profoundly, toward the end of "Folklore and Museum Artifacts," "An artifact is a first-order document closely connected to people and events." Vlach considered the validity of traditional historical interpretation. He wrote, "The interpretation of history is so difficult, so complex, that all who are interested should make common cause to present it."[18]

At a point in time, in the new century, when we are made aware that the interpretation of history is so difficult and complex, the roles John Vlach suggests for the folklorist are broadened and emboldened. The roles he suggested in the 1980s are no less true today. Folklorists can and do provide planning and development of museum programs, with a folklore vantage point and with an awareness of the social context. Thirty years later, the only difference is the way in which the roles are conceived. In this new century, roles and issues are more nuanced; gender and violence, for example, and global sustainability, in all its forms, become common concerns. Not simply sustaining an environment, though folklore can play a role here as well, but also cultural and artistic sustainability, making sure that the folk festival creates an awareness and an affirmation of our common cultural background. Immigration is a common concern. For a long time, Americans in particular have regarded immigration in only one way, as a people coming into a culture. Increasingly it is important to understand the richness of all cultures and appreciate the reasons for sustaining the cultural heritage of all the people who live in our collective midst. John Vlach suggests that all who are interested in the interpretation of history ought to make common cause to present a broader picture of the world in which we live.

GOOD PRACTICE IN CULTURAL INCLUSION, MUSEUM ARTIFACTS, AND PUBLIC PRESENTATION

As regards the general theme of John Vlach's essay, "Folklore and Museum Artifacts," perhaps one of the finest executions of the effort to articulate the connections between the role of the academic discipline of folklore and museum artifacts is the museum at Michigan State University (MSU) in East Lansing, Michigan. At the MSU Museum, C. Kurt Dewhurst, the director for over twenty years, and Marsha MacDowell have spearheaded the development of the collection of material folk culture artifacts and organized the exhibition program for display and educational programs. Together with an outstanding staff of professionals educated in the disciplines of folklore and museum education, the MSU Museum has, over the years, managed an educational program geared to inform the visitor about the discipline of folklore and the identification and meaning of material folk culture artifacts from Michigan and the surrounding geographical area of the Great Lakes region.

During this span of over twenty years, the MSU Museum, in partnership with the city of East Lansing, has developed and maintained an important regional folk festival, the Great Lakes Folk Festival.[19] The festival exhibits folk music, traditional crafts, and educational programs about folklore from the many different ethnic populations inhabiting the Great Lakes region, the United States, and the world. The Michigan State University Museum also coordinates the Michigan Heritage Award program, which focuses on the recognition and celebration of specific individuals who have maintained and sustained ethnic traditions throughout the state. Each year individual folk performers are presented at the folk festival in a special occasion to receive their awards. As an important part of the award ceremony, the Michigan Heritage Award is presented to the individual not only by the museum director and the Michigan Traditional Arts Program coordinator but also by the individual's own state legislative representative and the governor, recognizing the official nature of the individual's achievement.

Of course, many of the individual folk festival performers and participants never thought of their pursuit as an activity that might, one day, make them regionally, and even nationally, famous. Nonetheless, from duck decoy carvers to basket makers and quilt makers, to harmonica players and traditional singers, the folk festival provides a venue for the public awareness of the vast ethnic traditional folk culture in Michigan as well as the recognition of unique individuals who happen to be outstanding representatives of their specific talents and crafts. For example, one such individual is Yvonne Walker Keshick. Her life story offers substantial credence to the efforts of folklorists and regional historians to bring more awareness of the "unsung" communities to the venue of the museum, where handmade objects and artifacts that were heretofore forgotten or ignored are now centerpieces that provide a deeper understanding of a complicated American culture.

Yvonne Keshick is an Odawa tribal member and a member of the Grand Traverse Band of Ottawa and Chippewa Indians. During the 1980s, Keshick was politically active in the effort to achieve federal recognition for her tribe. In 1992, the Michigan State University Museum honored her with a Michigan Heritage Award for her "mastery of her tradition, attention to authenticity, and commitment to sharing her cultural knowledge within her community." She has lived her entire life in northern Michigan, currently in Petoskey, in the northern part of the state's lower peninsula. She makes traditional baskets, quill working, cornhusk dolls, and other traditional handmade objects. Yvonne Keshick is primarily known for her basket making and as a quill worker, skills recognized in the Woodland Indian traditional material culture tradition. In 2015, Keshick was honored with a National Heritage Fellowship by the National Endowment for the Arts for her traditional craftwork and her continued work of sustaining the craft of Odawa traditional material culture through teaching.

Yvonne Keshick is just one of the many traditional artists the MSU Museum has completed fieldwork with and archived for future generations; however, in many ways, she is typical of the effort to bring folklore and museum artifacts into clear focus. Keshick was born in 1946 and descended from a long line of Odawa/Ojibwa quill workers, a tradition that extends to the nineteenth century. According to Keshick, her aunt Anna Odei'min was one of the finest quill workers in her region. She learned most of her stories, both humorous and serious, from the traditional oral repertoire of her aunt and other Odawa/Ojibwa tribal members.

In the folklife fieldwork with Keshick and her extended family, biographical data, photos of four-generation basket-making sessions, and illustrations of her artwork and baskets are crucial components of the future of understanding the complexity of Michigan and American societies. Indeed, an examination of Yvonne Keshick's approach to making baskets, doing quill work, and teaching her community to do this work speaks directly to John Vlach's argument in the beginning of his essay, to wit, that "All of these aspects of chair making [in Vlach's case using Michael Owen Jones's study of Kentucky chair maker Chester Cornet] taken together constitute a holistic view of the making of an artifact, moving from idea to action to object to personal and social context."[20] In traditional society, group activities are accompanied by related stories. Communal making of baskets, like quilting bees, encourages shared stories, often humorous, related to the activity. Yvonne Keshick is fond of telling traditional humorous narratives of "How the Porcupine Got His Quills," a story she heard first from her aunt. With a hint of a smile, Keshick will tell the story of the furry little animal who was defenseless, but with a little magical assistance, the furry little animal acquired the quills to defend itself against all who might attack it.[21]

There are, of course, other renditions of the traditional folk story, but combined with the baskets she made and her quill work, as well as the baskets of her children and her grandchildren, the result is an important record of the folklore and material folk culture of a specific ethnic group in Michigan, the Odawa Indians, that would surely not exist if it were not for the efforts of the Michigan State University Museum and its staff.

One result of the extensive exhibition and museum program at Michigan State University is that Yvonne Keshick's quill work is widely recognized and included in many museum collections, including the National Museum of the American Indian. In addition to her work being included in museum collections, in 2006, Keshick was a participant in the Smithsonian Folklife Festival's "Carriers of Culture Native Weaving Traditions" program. Certainly, in the intervening years since John Michael Vlach's important essay "Folklore and Museum Artifacts," many of the admonitions made by Vlach have been addressed by the folklore and museum communities.

CONCLUSIONS: "THAT THE UNSUNG BE SUNG"

In about 2011, John Vlach and I accompanied the historic preservation staff of the Smithsonian Institution and the new National Museum of African American History and Culture to a site in rural Maryland, where we would document and disassemble an 1870s log house built by a free African American family. The theme was not slavery but rather freedom. The common theme was the search for social citizenship, freedom, and a role in post–Civil War America. The exhibition of the 1870s log house will be a common cause of folklorists, historians, museum professionals, and the African American community, which sought a museum to tell another "unsung" story. The vernacular, folk piece of architecture will be one piece to articulate that story.

I am often reminded of John Vlach's insight into the nature of folklore and the public and academic construction of history. He argued, "Social history requires that the unsung be sung."[22] The primacy of the artifact is a vantage point that he and I share, our houses filled with artifacts, reminding us about the fieldwork and the individuals with whom we have done fieldwork, individuals from whom we have learned about the cultures of the world in which we live. I am reminded again, as I think about the anniversaries we celebrate during the second decade of the twenty-first century—the Civil Rights Act, the Voting Rights Act, and the March on Washington in 1963. In 2013, citizens gathered in Washington, DC, to celebrate the fiftieth anniversary of "the March," as it became known. People dug into their closets and their chests of drawers to find things from the 1963 march. They found priceless reminders of their own time in "the March" and brought out the artifacts, to share, to display, to create a social history of "the March," a social history and civil rights movement memory that the citizens shared with so many other people of their time and, to be sure, after their time was over. Citizens brought pieces of history, artifacts that reminded them of the effort of their own time.

Vlach wrote that history "requires that the unsung be sung." And, to that end, citizens brought old civil rights signs, posters from the first march, buttons that displayed the name of the March, and, of course, their old clothes, packed away in a closet or a box in the attic, waiting there for someone to rediscover the social history that had been so carefully tucked away. One of the more popular posters from 1963 contained the words of Martin Luther King Jr.: "Injustice anywhere is a threat to justice everywhere."[23] Many people still had their original buttons that displayed the official name for the March: "March on Washington for Jobs & Freedom August 28, 1963." The official button was round and pictured in the middle clasped white and black hands joined in a handshake.

Of course, the importance of folklore and material folk culture to enable the "unsung to be sung" is imbued in the construct and execution of the event itself. People, citizens, drew upon their shared social folklore and history in order to make the commemorative event memorable and meaningful. The shared experiences also enabled the original event of the March to work to perfection in 1963. Celebrated singers sang songs that the audience already knew; "We Shall Overcome" was a shared movement song everyone knew how to sing and many understood how to react to. The song was a shared part of the common folklore of the civil rights movement that helped to make the event a folkloric experience.

In many ways, the fiftieth anniversary of the March on Washington for Jobs and Freedom was a museum exhibit in itself, the people making their own exhibition of the civil rights period through the materials they gathered with which to make the march and exhibit. People intuitively understood the importance of the artifacts in a way that they did not have to be told. Citizens knew how to display the artifacts and, intuitively, understood what the display articulated. The citizens understood what to do with the pieces of historic artifacts they had kept for so many years. The event of the March drew upon the shared knowledge of how to make such an event successful because of the shared folk knowledge. As much as the Athenians of ancient Greece knew how to make a traditional folk Greek tragedy draw upon the folk preparations to make war and battle, the March drew upon citizens' understanding of the folk drama of the "protest march" and the "movement celebration." Together, the artifacts and songs of the movement were employed to add success and meaning to the event "The March on Washington," which provides a good example of Vlach's admonition that a "democratic history" relies on the "social nature of folk things."

The concept of museums and the importance of folklore and material culture artifacts could be found, in the summer of 2015, when the National Folk Festival was held in Greensboro, North Carolina. One of the main stages of the festival was situated approximately a couple of blocks from the famed Woolworths department store where, in 1960, four young students from North Carolina Agricultural and Technical State University (A&T) were denied service at the lunch counter because they were African American. North Carolina A&T, founded in 1891, is a historically African American university. The sit-in by the "Greensboro Four," as they became known, emerged as one of the primary events that catalyzed the civil rights movement during the 1960s. Standing in the location it occupied in 1960, the Greensboro Woolworths building is today the International Civil Rights Center & Museum, housing the four lunch counter seats as "unsung" symbols of social resistance to segregation and an example of the role of folklore and museum artifacts. In African American folklore, one is often reminded of the famous quote of Frederick Douglass that pertains to the four seats in the Woolworths building: "Where justice is denied, where poverty is enforced, where ignorance prevails, . . . neither persons nor property will be safe."[24] The Douglass quote reinforces Vlach's early definition of the role of folklore in "the social nature of folk things."

Vlach writes that social history requires "that the unsung be sung," and in the case of the civil rights movement, the Greensboro Woolworths store became a site to "sing," using traditional voices, the struggle for civil rights. At the National Folk Festival in September 2015, the singing for the opening of the festival was provided in a traditional African American style. The festival organizers paid homage to the importance of the Greensboro Four and their role in the civil rights movement by having the North Carolina A&T drumline begin the festival with a parade, starting at the Woolworths building and proceeding down one of the main streets of Greensboro.

The traditional African American drumline, the artifact of the drumline, was, in Vlach's terms, "a first-order document closely connected to people and events." In making the "unsung" "be sung" to a wider American audience, the folk festival drew upon a traditional folk musical experience of African American folk culture to become the heralded opening sequence of the National Folk Festival. In essence, then, the National Folk Festival, as a type of museum experience for the wider public, employed folklore and material artifact to articulate and celebrate the importance of the Greensboro sit-in experience of the civil rights movement for the audience of 2015.

The juxtaposition of the civil rights museum in the old Woolworths building and the North Carolina A&T drumline reveals the tension between real life, live performance, and the museum exhibition. The International Civil Rights Center & Museum in the Woolworths building is moving emotionally but stationary, static. The North Carolina A&T "drumline is active, a fluid display of style, and of history." One display is "cold," to use a media concept, and the other "hot"; however, American society needs both the museum and the drumline artifact to tell the story of the history of the civil rights movement and African American life in the United States. As John Vlach noted some time ago, "The interpretation of history is so difficult, so complex, that all who are interested should make common cause to present it."

When I think about John Michael Vlach's singular commitment to the field of folklore and material folk culture, especially the intensity of his powers of observation and his academic research, I remember how we felt our commitment during those early graduate school days at the Folklore Institute at Indiana University. Our collaboration and friendship continued over the years, our conversations nearly always circling back to the importance of understanding folklore. We have both done public museum exhibitions about African American folklore and history. Vlach curated a very important exhibit, "The Afro-American Tradition in the Decorative Arts," for the Cleveland Museum of Art. I helped organize an exhibit, "Elijah Pierce: Woodcarver," on Pierce's folk art, at the Columbus Museum of Art. Our teacher, Henry Glassie, wrote, providing a framework for folklore that we followed, "He [a builder] is more likely to continue building in a folk fashion because he feels that it is the best—most lasting, most moral—way to build."[25] Glassie's words provided a framework for folklore study and for the efforts made in respect for that study, efforts in scholarship and efforts in the public use of folklore.

John Vlach and I have both served on the board of the National Council for the Traditional Arts, sponsor of the National Folk Festival. There again, under the guidance of folklorist Joe Wilson, who directed the council for over twenty years, John Vlach and I learned the importance of the social contract of the folklorist to sustain the folk culture that has provided a foundation for our national culture. On the NCTA board and at the festivals, we put into action the insights we gained and shared over the course of our careers by contributing our insights on the public display of folk traditions and framing the presentation of the traditional arts. We experienced during each festival the impact of "seeing" democratic history in action, the importance of the folk voice through the traditions exhibited in an American folk festival. John Vlach remained steadfast in his devotion and commitment to making the unsung sung. It is a positive gesture and an important act to review Vlach's insight into the future of the topic "folklore and museum artifacts." Under Glassie's tutelage, John Vlach and I subscribed to the approach to folklore study and hence a devotion to the public presentation of folklore scholarship in the museum. Overall, using Vlach's words that the "unsung be sung" and Glassie's words to examine the "most lasting, most moral" leaves the contemporary folklorist and museum professional with a guidepost for the future development of exhibitions and collections.

NOTES

1. John Michael Vlach, "Folklore and Museum Artifacts" (paper presented at the American Association for State and Local History Folklore and History Conference, New Orleans, Louisiana, September 6, 1980).

2. The original paper Vlach delivered was John Michael Vlach, "Folklore and Museum Artifacts." The article discussed here was published as "Folklore and Museum Artifacts," in *Folklife and Museums: Selected Readings*, ed. Patricia Hall and Charlie Seemann (Nashville: American Association for State and Local History, 1987), 108–21.

3. Henry Glassie, *Pattern in the Material Folk Culture of the Eastern United States* (Philadelphia: University of Pennsylvania Press, 1968).

4. Joel Garreau, *Nine Nations of North America* (Boston: Houghton Mifflin, 1981).

5. Vlach, "Folklore and Museum Artifacts."

6. Ibid.

7. Ibid.

8. Sten Rentzhog, *Open Air Museums: The History and Future of a Visionary Idea*, trans. Skans Victoria Airey (Stockholm: Jamtli and Carlsson Bokförlag, 2005), 6.

9. Henry Glassie and I had a personal interview with Gösta Berg in Dalarna, Sweden, in the summer of 1991, during which he described the role of folklore in the exhibitions of the museum.

10. John Moe, personal interview with Charlotte Ahnlund Berg, June 2013, Skansen Museum, Stockholm, Sweden.

11. Richard M. Dorson, "Local History and Folklore," in *American Folklore and the Historian*, ed. Richard M. Dorson (Chicago: University of Chicago Press, 1971), 145–56.

12. http://www.norskfolkemuseum.no/en/Exhibits/The-Apartment-Building.

13. http://www.norskfolkemuseum.no/en/Exhibits/The-Apartment-Building.

14. John Moe, personal interviews with Audun Kjus, June 2013, Oslo, Norway. E-mail communication from Kjus to Moe, December 1, 2015.

15. John Moe, personal interview with Magne Velure, June 1989, Maihaugen Museum, Lillehammer, Norway.

16. John Moe, personal interview with Gure Velure, June 2008, Maihaugen Museum, Lillehammer, Norway.

17. I collected this folk saying many times while I was working at the Norsk Utvandrermuseet in Hamar, Norway, from March to June 2009.

18. Vlach, "Folklore and Museum Artifacts."

19. Over the twenty-nine-year history of the annual event, the folk festival was initially called the Festival of Michigan Folklife; then, during a three-year span, it was the National Folk Festival, sponsored in part by the National Council for the Traditional Arts, after which it became known as the Great Lakes Folk Festival.

20. Vlach, "Folklore and Museum Artifacts." For the groundbreaking material culture study of artifacts, see Michael Owen Jones, *The Hand Made Object and Its Maker* (Berkeley: University of California Press, 1975). Jones examines in depth the work of a Kentucky chair maker.

21. John Moe, personal interview with Yvonne Walker Keshick, August 7–9, 2015, East Lansing, Michigan.

22. Vlach, "Folklore and Museum Artifacts."

23. The full quote attributed to a speech in Alabama is 1963 is inscribed on one stone at the Martin Luther King Jr. Memorial in Washington, DC: "Injustice anywhere is a threat to justice everywhere. We are caught in an inescapable network of mutuality, tied in a single garment of destiny. Whatever affects one directly, affects all indirectly."

24. The famous Frederick Douglass quote is usually viewed as a precursor of a quote Martin Luther King Jr. used often: "justice denied anywhere."

25. Glassie, *Pattern in the Material Folk Culture of the Eastern United States*, 7.

SELECTED ANNOTATED READING

Over the years since John Vlach presented the original paper and later published his article, the issue of folklore and museum artifacts has become ever more complicated, involving representation, sustainability, and identity. Increasingly, folklore fieldwork and museum artefactual presence are a matter of "opening up" the system in order that more people can have a voice. This selected annotated bibliography augments the bibliographic endnotes Vlach originally made for his article and highlights some sources that discuss issues that are prevalent at the beginning of the twenty-first century.

Garreau, Joel. *Nine Nations of North America*. Boston: Houghton Mifflin, 1981. Garreau's conceptualization of North America, though published in 1981, remains a valuable and informative theoretical approach to North American cultures and is useful to studies of regional foundations and difference.

Glassie, Henry. *Material Culture*. Bloomington: Indiana University Press, 1999. This volume contains many informant stories from makers of material folk culture from which the student of material culture can learn about the trends and theories of a field largely shaped by Glassie. Through a series of vignettes of potters and rug weavers, Glassie develops his position of artifact-based humanism.

Karp, Ivan, and Steven D. Lavine, eds. *Exhibiting Cultures: The Poetics and Politics of Museum Display*. Washington, DC: Smithsonian Institution Press in association with the American Association of Museums, 1991. This early collection of articles about the exhibition of cultures remains an important source for the examination of the museum exhibition impulse.

Karp, Ivan, Corinne Kratz, Lynne Szwaja, and Tomas Ybarra-Frausto, eds. *Museum Frictions: Public Cultures/Global Transformations*. Durham, NC: Duke University Press, 2006. This volume of articles addresses the twenty-first-century tension between museum display and globalization and brings the theme of folklore and museum artifacts into the debate over ethnic identity and global tensions.

Kirshenblatt-Gimblett, Barbara. *Destination Culture: Tourism, Museums, and Heritage*. Los Angeles: University of California Press, 1998. Written by a folklorist, this volume speaks to the question of artifacts and exhibition. Kirshenblatt-Gimblett identifies the tensions between ethnological fieldwork and public museum exhibitions.

Nguib, Saphinaz Amal. "Museums, Diasporas and the Sustainability of Intangible Cultural Heritage." *Sustainability* 5 (2013): 2178–2190. This article by a Norwegian academic addresses the question of the intangible cultural heritage of migration and diasporas. The author discusses Kirshenblatt-Gimblett's theory of "metacultural production" and the notion that migratory cultures are both tangible and intangible.

Pocius, Gerald L., ed. *Living in a Material World: Canadian and American Approaches to Material Cultures.* St. John's, Newfoundland: Institute of Social and Economic Research, 1991. Edited by an early exponent of material culture study, this volume offers the student of material culture several approaches to the examination of material culture artifacts.

Prown, Jules. "Mind in Matter: An Introduction to Material Culture Theory and Method." *Winterthur Portfolio* 17, no. 1 (1982). Prown was one of the first academics in material culture, and this article is an important read for any person wanting to understand the field of material folk culture.

Rentzhog, Sten. *Open Air Museums: The History and Future of a Visionary Idea*, translated by Skans Victoria Airey. Stockholm: Jamtli and Carlsson Bokförlag, 2005. Rentzhog's work, originally in Swedish, is clearly the most comprehensive study of open-air museums. He examines both European and American open-air museums with an eye toward their historical development and orientation.

Schlereth, Thomas J. *Material Culture: A Research Guide.* Lawrence: University Press of Kansas, 1985. This early collection of essays by scholars in the field offers the student an opportunity to examine some of the classic approaches to material culture study in the 1980s and is well worth investigating.

Vlach, John Michael. "Folklore and Museum Artifacts." In *Folklife and Museums: Selected Readings*, edited by Patricia Hall and Charlie Seemann, 108–21. Nashville: AASLH, 1987. This is the collection in which John Vlach's article originally appeared.

5

Folk Art in the Fine Art Museum

Jo Farb Hernández

A vital part of an art museum's holdings may be its collection of folk or traditional art. Jo Farb Hernández shows how an art museum can attract more visitors, broaden its programming, and promote learning about a range of cultural and aesthetic spheres—all via the thoughtful presentation of folk art. She makes an excellent case for reaching beyond the precise definitions of "folk" art and "fine" art, for in so doing, a curator or director can better integrate traditional art forms into an art museum's regular programming and can begin to dispel the stereotype that folk art consists solely of quaint renderings by untrained artists. Jo Farb Hernández prepared this chapter especially for *Folklife and Museums: Selected Readings* (1987), basing it on presentations she made at annual meetings of the American Association of Museums (1983) and the American Association for State and Local History (1986). It has been revised and updated for this volume, as since that time extraordinary technological advances in a variety of innovative formats have brought the reality of interactive engagement with museum visitors—resulting in a variety of deeper learning experiences by those visitors—within reach of even the smallest museum.

Directors of art museums must be sensitive and responsive to a multiplicity of community cultural needs and desires, while at the same time remaining committed to enhancing community education by introducing members and visitors to a wider world of aesthetic interests. Not surprisingly, these two objectives sometimes conflict. Complicating matters even further, this dual focus must also correlate with the practical challenges most museums in this country routinely face—challenges that are typically linked in a variety of ways: how to attract an ever-larger and broader audience and how to secure sufficient funding to adequately maintain the museum's programs and services. The marketing of the museum and the maintenance of the institution's visibility among diverse community sectors are crucial if the museum is to compete successfully with other leisure-time activities, including movies, sports, shopping, the beach, amusement parks, and more, which are also vying for the public's entertainment dollars, hours, and interests. Although folk art and folklife exhibitions should not be expected to remedy all the troubles of an ailing institution, I have found that they may address the concerns noted above, and, if correctly coordinated and managed, they may provide an important marketing tool for an institution. At the same time, they can educate the public about new aesthetic imagery and cultural relationships and may serve as a stimulus to attract a broader audience with a wider base of backgrounds, interests, and aesthetic values. By presenting a compelling experience that ties into the museum's fundamental mission, visitors engage more deeply and begin to consider the museum as a "destination" not just for problematic out-of-town visitors but, on a regular basis, for themselves and their families.

Before discussing specifics about such programs, it is important to address commonly understood classifications and characteristics of different art genres. Infinitely minute clarifications of the definitions of folk art and fine art may be found elsewhere; it is sufficient to note here that such distinctions may blur in the face of specific artistic examples. Consequently, working to encompass all creative aesthetic expressions under the larger rubric of "art" is perhaps a more effective way to reach the short- and long-range goals noted above.

This is desirable because both fine art and folk art may be viewed and understood either exclusively or concurrently in the same two ways: (1) through an educated study of the work as a product of a particular time and space and as a predictable result of specific personal, historical, social, cultural, economic, and other influences, or (2) through the viewer's gut reaction on a purely formal level: Do I like what I see? The aesthetic experience provided by an art museum is satisfying precisely because of these two factors: first,

FIGURE 5.1
Evelio López Cruz, 2004. Attaching the handle to the vessel body. Mota del Cuervo, Spain. From the exhibition "Forms of Tradition in Contemporary Spain," Thompson Art Gallery, San José State University, 2005. (Photo: Jo Farb Hernández.)

because education about the object's form, cultural context, function, technique, or aesthetic trend will deepen the richness of the experience; second, because providing stimulation for those with no contextual knowledge about the object may inspire them to respond on a deeper level, promoting participation in a second, albeit different, kind of aesthetic experience.

Another but no less important reason to sidestep precise definitions of folk art versus fine art when mounting exhibitions in a fine art museum is their complementary nature. This may perhaps be most evident from an examination of what used to be called "primitive art." Among certain cultural groups located within broad geographic areas of Africa or Oceania, for example, both aesthetic and technique are highly sophisticated, revealing an early use of abstraction and stylization even in figurative or representational pieces. In contrast, this trend did not occur in Western art until the beginning of the twentieth century. In fact, the dawn of Euro-American abstract art coincided with the awakening interest manifested by these artists in works from African or Oceanic cultures; the European—and, later, the American—artists learned about this work when it was first introduced to the West as field expeditions began returning from abroad with artistic booty.[1] The clearly complementary nature of the two hitherto separately defined genres of art holds a potential treasure for the savvy museum curator or director. I have found that many members of the art museum-going public are willing to spend greater amounts of time learning about the unfamiliar or unusual aesthetic objects of another culture than they would spend on those emanating from their own. This increased receptivity to differing aesthetics on a worldwide basis may be extended and amplified in a spillover effect, enabling museum visitors to explore and examine (if not to understand and appreciate) differing aesthetic values within their own culture as well.

I first became pointedly aware of the potential of such an expanded reach while I was directing the Triton Museum of Art from 1978 through 1985. Located in the middle of what became known as Silicon Valley, this was an area whose earlier community base had been largely agricultural, and at that time many community members lacked reference points within their own cultural or educational backgrounds to assess new aesthetic values, whether these were presented through the art of Mexican mask makers or through the art of contemporary abstractionists. By teaching visitors to look—to *really* look—and to venture beyond an immediate gut reaction to a more educated response to "new" work, it is possible to build a more sophisticated audience that is challenged and intrigued by the different or unusual rather than being intimidated or disconcerted by it.

One of my early presentations of traditional material culture in a fine art museum was an exhibition of Mexican dance masks mounted at the Triton in the fall of 1982. This display, which to that date was the largest such exhibition presented outside Mexico, surveyed different thematic types and included masks from all regions of Mexico created over a period of two centuries. Although the masks could be (and were) enjoyed simply as intriguing, interesting, and often beautiful objects, museum staff stressed the cultural context of the works, although this aspect was handled somewhat differently than it would have been in an ethnographic, folk art, or history museum.

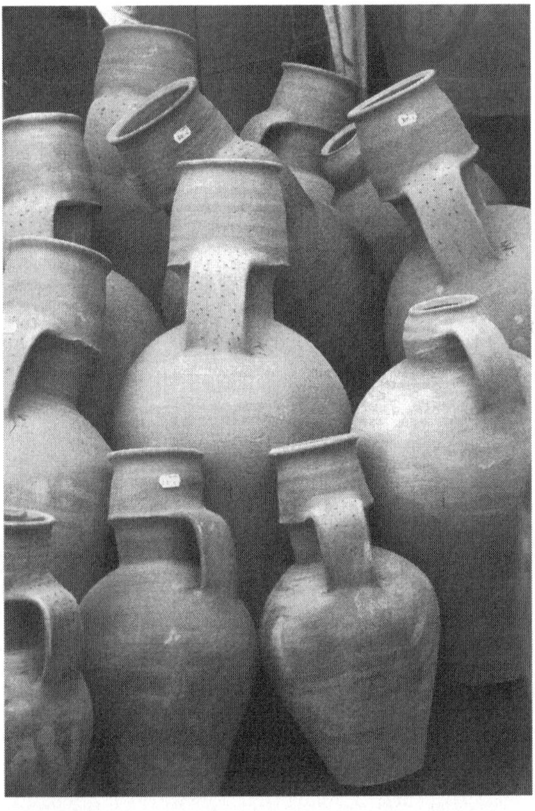

FIGURE 5.2
Evelio López Cruz. *Cántaros* (water jugs). Argentona Ceramics Fair, Spain, 2002. (Photo: Jo Farb Hernández.)

The philosophy surrounding exhibition installation at the art museums I have directed remains generally consistent over a range of subject matter, although I have often asked my designers to take a slightly different approach to display, depending on the overall level of community familiarity with a given curatorial concept or exhibition theme. Exhibitions featuring traditional material culture have therefore tended to be somewhat more educationally oriented, with staff making an extra effort to provide a contextual understanding for the objects that forms an integral part of the display. Nevertheless, all objects are still treated as art objects: they are isolated on walls or pedestals, are separately lit, and are individually labeled, not arranged in habitat-like scenes. As with the installation of "fine art," design decisions are made in conjunction with curatorial priorities regarding chronology, theme, use in social or belief systems, geography, and other considerations, all with the intent of communicating to the fullest extent possible the import and social/cultural/aesthetic value of the selected objects. An art museum installation should not try to mimic display techniques of ethnographic or history museums, but certain technical aspects of their installations can certainly be referenced.

The first decision in the case of the Mexican mask display was therefore to install the masks according to the dances or dance complexes in which they were used. Other options might have been to design the installation according to regional similarities, by chronological considerations, or on the basis of purely aesthetic concerns. But the decision to concentrate on the dance complexes served to emphasize that the masks were created with the anticipation that they would be used as part of a folkloric performance and event. Ongoing looped visual demonstrations of masks being worn and masked dances being performed further stressed that these objects, while compelling on their own as art objects, were meant to be viewed not statically but in motion. A performance at the museum on opening day featured traditional masked dances by a local group whose members had studied and apprenticed with master performers in Mexico, again emphasizing the human dimension as inseparable from the wall display. (While California audiences have been used to colorful and flashy *folklorico* dances, at our request this group performed less visually and choreographically exciting—but more authentic—works than those usually presented for the general public; their performances were thus consistent with the masking tradition, revealing the range and function of the masks' use.)

A series of illustrated lectures, presented in conjunction with the exhibition, focused on the masks' art historical context while also including information on the social functions, construction, influences upon evolution, and belief systems surrounding their varying uses. Folkloristic notions of change and continuity were explored through discussions of the constant dynamism that accompanies the masked dances, emphasizing the fact that each performance reveals changes and new interpretations, whether through the choreography, as a result of changes in the number or prowess of the performers, or in the object itself (masks were and are often repainted before each performance, and new supplementary materials, such as feathers or bells, were and are often added). Annotated wall labels, mounted photographs, educational text panels, and a small but thoroughly researched catalogue[2]—all bilingual—accompanied the display and enabled viewers to become immersed in learning about the masks' context, according to the depth of their individual interests. (Now, new technology provided by in-gallery interactive computer programs, QR codes linked to individual objects or broader curatorial questions, interpretive methodologies, and a variety of opportunities for learning through innovative formats not then available provides ever-increasing means to respond to the different ways people learn.) In whatever format, however, it is important to identify the voice of the writer, reminding audiences that art and cultural artifacts can be described and interpreted from a variety of different points of view. One curatorial strategy that has become much more widely used since the time of that early exhibition is the inclusion in labels and text panels of the voices of members of the cultural group to which the materials belong, providing first-person accounts to complement and give greater depth to the more standard "researched" third-party didactics.[3]

Had additional funds been available at the time, bringing in master artists to provide carving workshops and displays, perhaps in conjunction with a local university—as we did with a later project, "Forms of Tradition in Contemporary Spain,"[4] in which the exhibition of artisans' work at the Thompson Gallery at San José State University was complemented by a three-week workshop for sculpture students at nearby Santa Clara University (SCU), culminating in an exhibition and performance of the students' own work—would have been a desirable addition to the complementary programming. For this more recent 2005 project, components of the original exhibition traveled locally to the SCU Art Department's in-house gallery in order to enhance the academic offerings; additional educational programs, including a round-table discussion with both the visiting Spanish artists and local Mexican artists working in the same medium, and a documentary film produced to complement the larger project were also important components promoting positive learning outcomes among the students. Having the opportunity to watch, study, and learn from traditional artists from Spain helped to develop a much broader multicultural understanding among student, faculty, and community participants than would have been provided by a less experiential and hands-on approach. Couched in relation to the contemporary arts issues that university students typically study, this emphasis on traditional and folk arts broadened their bases and academic experiences, deepened their understanding of broader issues pertaining to creativity and artistic production, and greatly enriched all aspects of the university communities of both institutions.

Exhibitions such as these offer unparalleled opportunities to involve the local cultural groups whose traditions are being represented; in fact, no such project should even be attempted without their participation from the very beginning of programming discussions. The South Bay area in which the

FIGURE 5.3
David Ventura and Neus Hosta. *Capgrossos* (big-heads) and *Gegants* (giants). From the exhibition "Forms of Tradition in Contemporary Spain," Thompson Art Gallery, San José State University, 2005. (Photo: Jo Farb Hernández.)

Triton Museum is located has a large Mexican-American community, and its involvement was an essential ingredient in ensuring that the project would be community centered and meaningful. Involving community leaders at the start of exhibition planning can enable them to reach far into their community to elicit popular support, knowledge, and participation. This cannot be superficial or cursory; it will involve a series of frank discussions in which museum staff engage in dialog through "active listening" and authentic criticisms and suggestions can be heard at the point where transformative changes in programming can still be made. The museum, therefore, undertook an aggressive publicity campaign in the Spanish-language media to encourage community engagement and, indeed, empowerment: the call was not just to draw attention to the project itself but, at the beginning, to request community loans of objects and help in interpretation as well. Museum staff issued press releases and public service announcements in Spanish, presented television and radio spots on local bilingual programs, and, later, encouraged various media to cover the exhibition and opening events as "news." It was essential to have a bilingual receptionist available to answer the phone before and during the run of the exhibition, and Spanish-language docent tours were available during the display.

The participation, and even the "blessing," of the group whose material culture is being represented is particularly essential if the museum is considering presenting ceremonial or culturally sensitive material: *their* perspective must become the driving force. If the situation is thoughtfully and successfully handled, everyone can benefit: the project becomes a collaborative undertaking, blurring the lines between curator and visitor and replacing the one-way top-down teacher/student paradigm long practiced by mainstream culture institutions, in which information is handed out by an authoritative yet anonymous "expert." While some museums initially resisted (and some continue to resist) what they perceive as challenges to institutional authority, others have embraced this new paradigm of cultural pluralism. Positive outcomes include the increased pride viscerally felt by cultural groups as their voices are amplified within a perhaps heretofore unfamiliar creative space, empowering them to take part in the representation of their own cultural objects. Simultaneously, the museum itself develops and broadens its audience—an ongoing concern. Further, a somewhat peripheral but equally rewarding result is that those community members

FIGURE 5.4
Les Gàrgoles de Foc (the gargoyles of fire). Anna Sánchez, representing "Light," 2003. Festa Major, Banyoles, Spain. From the exhibition "Forms of Tradition in Contemporary Spain," Thompson Art Gallery, San José State University, 2005. (Photo: Jo Farb Hernández.)

who have become deeply involved in the exhibition process may (possibly somewhat unexpectedly) realize that they have had hands-on training in museological processes; this may spark their interest in further work in this field, something urgently needed within the still largely Euro-American staff member populations of US art museums.

One should not lose sight of the need to involve the community at large in such displays as well, in part to ensure that they don't feel excluded by an exhibition focusing on a specific cultural group. One of the major roles of the museum as an educational institution is to help people widen their views of the world and to learn to accept and appreciate unfamiliar objects and cultures, concomitantly destroying decades of received representations, images, and stereotypes. As a positive side effect, exhibitions of this nature may help to reduce the kind of intercultural friction that arises when people lack familiarity with or even misunderstand the customs and cultures of others. Educational research has defined a typical—and hierarchical—process of developing cultural sensitivity: one must pass through awareness to knowledge, then to tolerance/acceptance, and, finally, to appreciation. One moves from simply acquiring knowledge to changing previously held attitudes, something that can only take place in museums if critical thinking is fostered among visitors: audience members need to be presented with sufficient physical and conceptual materials so that they can reach their own reasoned judgments; simply passively accepting conclusions presented by institutional authority figures tends to produce only superficial and short-term learning. And again, this broadening of cultural outlook reinforces an increase in receptivity to new objects in general—even to contemporary artworks from members of the viewers' own cultural group.

Evaluation during and following such programs is essential. Locals and tourists alike should be solicited for qualitative feedback to complement quantitative reviews undertaken by staff. What was it about the exhibition/programming that visitors found compelling? Which parts were especially successful, and which may have needed more thought? When we drill down into how visitors respond to our presentations, we learn what they value, and then we learn how to better address those responses with future programming.

Exhibitions or events such as the mask display, the 2005 Spanish exhibition, and numerous others that I have curated over the years provide unequaled opportunities for complementary outreach programs to various sectors of the community. The most obvious and available partners in any area are the schools; different educational programs can be developed to accommodate all ages and levels of sophistication. Elementary and intermediate schools often focus an entire year's curriculum on a given geographic or thematic area; museum educators should connect with the appropriate class level to avail themselves of opportunities for classroom enrichment that will be welcomed by teachers and students alike. For high schools or colleges, departments or subject areas will likewise serve to widen the museum's attendance; the Spanish project exhibition enabled my staff and me to work with classes in art history, anthropology, studio art, dance, drama, and Spanish language (no folklore/folk art classes were then offered at my or other local colleges or universities). And sometimes these students will be sufficiently inspired that they will seek volunteer or internship work at the museum and may ultimately decide to pursue further study in the field.

FIGURE 5.5
Devil Group, Fira del Foc (fire festival). Banyoles, Spain, 2004. From the exhibition "Forms of Tradition in Contemporary Spain," Thompson Art Gallery, San José State University, 2005. (Photo: Jo Farb Hernández.)

Previsit educational packets for teachers—particularly for those teaching elementary or middle school levels—used to help them better prepare their classes for the upcoming visit, are often valuable; these might include an advance copy of the exhibition's catalogue or brochure or appropriate excerpts, visual representations of objects that will be viewed in the display, and contemporary as well as historical references to help establish the cultural context. Younger students in particular respond to hands-on studio classes, either at the museum[5] or subsequently back in the school classroom, as a follow-up to the museum visit. Such activity was especially positive in terms of the mask display and complemented it effectively, for the younger students were able to learn through personal experience and experiential engagement how masking can change one's actions, movements, and even persona.

A second major target area for community outreach and museum exhibitions is local businesses and corporations. Both the Triton Museum and the

Thompson Gallery at San José State University, the location of the Spanish exhibition, are located in the heart of Silicon Valley, a region where corporations are both important members of the community at large and important financial contributors to the local arts and cultural organizations. Either as thanks for past contributions or as a stimulus to potential donations, our staff was able to arrange complementary exhibitions to the mask display in the lobbies and offices of these businesses—using less valuable artifacts or providing a more educationally oriented display (for example, one focusing on mask-making techniques for a local manufacturing firm). For both these and other exhibitions, brown-bag lunchtime slide lectures, special corporate employee evenings at the museum, and articles in the in-house corporate newsletters all represented additional ways of increasing the involvement and participation of this important community sector.

Somewhat beyond the scope of this article, but worthy of consideration and analysis, is the strategy of using museum folk art collections as a base to create robust associations with folklore organizations based within a local university or as part of a governmental agency. Several well-regarded examples may serve as models, such as the Missouri Folk Arts Program, based in the Museum of Art and Archaeology at the University of Missouri; the Folk Art Society of America's collection now housed at the Longwood Center for the Visual Arts at Virginia's Longwood University; and the South Carolina Folklife and Traditional Arts Program, linked with the McKissick Museum at the University of South Carolina. Partnering with public folklore organizations that have already connected with and engaged local communities, and that have developed compelling and innovative strategies for doing so, is a desirable and dependable way for museums to expand their audience base, provide an opportunity for diverse voices to be heard, and offer a more authentic art experience that promotes the multiplicity of ways through which any individual art object may be approached. And, of course, there are other resources available to museum personnel as well, including the Folklore and Museums and Public Folklore sections of the American Folklore Society.

Practically speaking, displays of traditional material culture are very popular with the community: they attract high attendance, offer good publicity in a wider range of media organs than perhaps habitually cover museum displays, and may ultimately serve to widen the museum's membership base, thus providing a more secure and stable financial future for the institution

FIGURE 5.6
"Forms of Tradition in Contemporary Spain" exhibition installation. Thompson Art Gallery, San José State University, 2005. (Photo: Jo Farb Hernández.)

over the long term. The museum's role as an educational institution is corroborated and expanded, and it serves as well to break down older notions of museums as dusty ivory towers, conveying hackneyed platitudes about the cultural work of "others."

Distinctions between fine and folk art should be eliminated whenever possible in these instances, thereby sidestepping the need to explain what "folk art" is doing in a "fine art" museum. An exhibition of traditional material culture of the indigenous creators of the San Blas Islands might thus be titled "Art of the Cuna," not "Folk Art of the Cuna"; this change also helps museum audiences to view the display without recalling the overworked, preconceived notions of folk art as charming, cute, and quaint, something that happened long ago and always far away. In addition, people become more receptive to viewing unfamiliar objects and exploring unfamiliar aesthetic values and are more likely to try to learn from them. This is, of course, one of the museum's primary aims.

One cautionary note: I have found that because the term "folk art" may, albeit predominantly falsely, imply creators who are uneducated and untrained, it has unfortunately been the case that some museum curators in smaller to midsize institutions have felt they could transfer their art expertise to this area without specialized training. This attitude has led at least one major museum to present a most uneven—actually, embarrassing—display. In this art field as in any other, curatorial vision, combined with specialized training, is essential if the presentation is to be more than a rehash of inauthentic replicas of stereotypical conventions representing someone's less-than-knowledgeable perception of what "folk art" may be.

When researched properly and presented sensitively, however, with input from community group leaders and complemented by well-integrated contextual materials, exhibitions of traditional material culture can deepen and enrich the museum experience for various community sectors as it provides an introduction to new worlds of aesthetic interest and imagery. Furthermore, an understanding of the complementary nature of folk art and fine art genres will dispel notions of their exclusivity and the need to compartmentalize their respective productions. An exploration and presentation of traditional material culture heightens and rounds out the cultural and aesthetic experience that the art museum is able to provide.

Folklorists and anthropologists (although, typically, *not* art historians) have come to realize that "making special" is a universal human trait. Those genres typically defined and studied as "art" are not, in fact, the most primary forms of expressing aesthetic concerns, for much of everyday human behavior is aesthetic, whether it be the arrangement of fruit on a table, the way we fix our hair and dress each morning, or complex works revealing significant—if nonacademic—training. Hans Prinzhorn, the renowned psychiatrist whose early studies on the mentally ill have become a basis for the field of "outsider art," outlined six psychological traits underlying artistic creation: drives underlying self-expression, play, decoration, ordering and arranging, imitating, and reflecting symbolic meanings.[6] It is noteworthy that despite his predilection and area of study, Prinzhorn emphasized that these were universal—not psychopathological—human characteristics. Coming from a different vantage point in his book *Primitive Art*, anthropologist Franz Boas likewise asserted, "All human activities may assume forms that give them esthetic values,"[7] and decades later folklorist Michael Owen Jones riffed on this and on James West's studies of a small town in Missouri[8] when he wrote that the feeling for form and the attempt to master technique comprise a fundamental

FIGURE 5.7
Gegants (giants) in "Dancing Games." Llado, Spain, 2011. (Photo: Jo Farb Hernández.)

condition of our humanity and that the aesthetic impulse is manifested "in dozens of subtle ways in the things we make and do during the course of daily interaction, problem solving, and the accomplishing of tasks."[9] And author Ellen Dissanayake describes these impulses as so essential a "core tendency" of evolved behavior that she rechristened our species "Homo Aestheticus."[10]

By focusing on these universals—as we concomitantly study the specific differences and peculiarities of each artist's oeuvre—we can sidestep the tendency to create artificial distinctions between such genres as folk art and fine art, and we can, instead, open ourselves up to a much more expansive view of the range of influences on each creative act. And, in so doing, we can develop our institutions at the same time that we both educate our diverse publics and bring them interesting, entertaining, and worldview-broadening exhibitions to make the world more comprehensible and more enjoyable.

NOTES

1. It goes without saying that the evaluation of these objects would have been articulated in markedly different ways by members of these two cultural groups. An Ashanti fertility figure, for example, might be marveled at by Western observers for its clean lines and formalist aesthetic presence, whereas for a traditional maker or user of such a figure, its worth would have been based on its ability to promote a large family.

2. Jo Farb Hernández, *Mexican Indian Dance Masks* (Santa Clara, CA: Triton Museum of Art, 1982).

3. One early and still notable example was offered as part of one of the opening exhibitions at the National Museum of the American Indian—Heye Center in New York City in 1994. For each object, labels were separately written by an art historian, an anthropologist, and a user or maker member of the tribe from which that material came; the resulting labels were so different in focus that, taken out of context, a viewer might not realize that each voice was discussing the same object. It was a compelling way to underscore the multiplicity of ways that objects can be interpreted, analyzed, and described.

4. The original exhibition was on display at the Natalie and James Thompson Art Gallery, San José State University, in the fall of 2005. Components of this project later traveled locally to Santa Clara University, as well as further afield to China, Canada, and Barcelona. The complementary book with the same title, by the author, was published by the University Press of Mississippi in 2005.

5. Taking advantage of the timing of the exhibition and the California weather, the workshops we offered in conjunction with the Mexican mask exhibition were conducted outside, on the museum's grounds, so that more casual observers were able to attend in greater numbers.

6. Hans Prinzhorn, *Artistry of the Mentally Ill: A Contribution to the Psychology and Psychopathology of Configuration* (1922), trans. Eric von Brockdorff, from the 2nd German ed. (Vienna and New York: Springer Verlag, 1972).

7. Franz Boas, *Primitive Art* (New York: Dover Publications, 1955 [1927]), 9.

8. James West, *Plainville, U.S.A.* (New York: Columbia University Press, 1946).

9. Michael Owen Jones, *Exploring Folk Art: Twenty Years of Thought on Craft, Work, and Aesthetics* (Ann Arbor: UMI Research Press, 1987), 81.

10. Ellen Dissanayake, *Homo Aestheticus: Where Art Comes from and Why* (Seattle: University of Washington Press, 1995).

6

Folk Art and Social Change in an American Museum

The Case of the Gallery of Conscience at the Museum of International Folk Art

SUZANNE SERIFF AND MARSHA C. BOL

Over the past decade, museums and other established cultural institutions have been challenged to become places where people can gather to meet, converse, and participate in collaborative problem solving around timely issues of conscience in their lives. Folklorists have brought their particular skills as organizers, culture workers, and traditional arts advocates to such sites to facilitate new ways for such institutions to reenvision themselves as cultural centers "where multiple narratives can be told, where people can find safe spaces for cultures to mix, and where xenophobia can be overcome."[1] In this chapter, Marsha Bol and Suzanne Seriff explore one approach to incubating such an innovative space for social change within the world's largest folk art museum, the Museum of International Folk Art (MOIFA), in Santa Fe, New Mexico. The result, inaugurated as the Gallery of Conscience in 2010, has turned out to be a winning formula for success: a commitment to addressing key social justice and human rights issues of our time, backed by a sense of responsibility to address these issues through the museum's mission, and the creation of an innovative process of engagement that allows for a timely response. Marsha Bol, retired director of MOIFA, and Suzanne Seriff, director of the Gallery of Conscience, take you on a tour of both the challenges and the opportunities of such an experimental and in some ways radical endeavor in an art museum, one that museum critic Gretchen Jennings dubbed "a model of museum practice for the 21st century."[2]

INTRODUCTION

"We must come to see that the end we seek is a society at peace with itself, a society that can live with its conscience."

—Dr. Martin Luther King Jr., Alabama, 1965

Improvisation in jazz begins with a melodic phrase, invites a response, and builds on a theme. Sometimes melodic, sometimes cacophonous, the result is rooted in the magic of call and response, dialog in action. In 2012, the Museum of International Folk Art in Santa Fe, New Mexico, incubated an improvisatory approach to exhibit development in its newly created Gallery of Conscience, and the result has already created a buzz and a beat around town.

Improvisation fits both the mission and the method of the Gallery of Conscience, which draws on the words and works of living traditional artists to convey lessons from the past, share stories across generations, catalyze dialog, and promote personal reflection, communication, and action. The gallery is designed to attract new and previously underserved audiences, meet the needs of a changing, transnational population of artists, and provide a safe place in the public sphere to more directly address socially relevant issues in the twenty-first century. For these reasons, both the process and the products explored in this gallery space are fundamentally participatory and interactive.

The prototyped exhibition space—which changes continually based on visitor and community response—is specifically designed with this interactivity in mind. In addition to the folk art pieces themselves, the gallery includes multiple locales for visitors and community members to leave their thoughts, contribute to community art projects, voice their opinions, and brainstorm about avenues for personal and collective action. It is perhaps no surprise that several of the movers and shakers behind this gallery's success are PhD folklorists, trained in the public-sector sphere.

While the experimental nature of this gallery is distinctly new to MOIFA, the museum's fundamental commitment to exploring the power of folk art to transform individuals and transcend boundaries across diverse sectors of society is not. Indeed, this singularly innovative idea has fueled the museum's mission since its inception over half a century ago.

ORIGIN

Marsha C. Bol, retired director, Museum of International Folk Art

"The art of the craftsman is the bond between the peoples of the world."

—Florence Dibell Bartlett, 1953

The first museum dedicated to folk art worldwide, the Museum of International Folk Art opened its doors in 1953. Its founder, Florence Dibell Bartlett, was a witness to two world wars and a firm believer in the idea that folk art—the everyday arts of the people—was the key to promoting cultural understanding worldwide. Her words have greeted visitors to the museum for over half a century: "The art of the craftsman is the bond between the peoples of the world."

This humanistic sentiment about the universality of mankind, exhibited in the everydayness of life's cultural artworks and activities, was mirrored in a number of other arts and entertainment venues around the country at this time. In 1955 the Museum of Modern Art opened an exhibition, "The Family of Man: The Greatest Photographic Exhibition of All Time—503 Pictures from 68 Countries," organized by Edward Steichen. As Steichen says, "The exhibition . . . was conceived as a mirror of the universal elements and emotions in the everydayness of life—as a mirror of the essential oneness of mankind throughout the world."[3]

At the 1964 New York World's Fair UNICEF Pavilion, Walt Disney tested a ride slated for the Magic Kingdom of Disneyland in 1966, "It's a Small World." The water ride "featured over 300 audio-animatronic dolls in traditional costumes from cultures around the world, frolicking in a spirit of international unity and singing the attraction's title song, which has a theme of global peace."[4]

Springing from this same impulse, the Museum of International Folk Art opened a new wing in 1982 to house its latest exhibition, appropriately titled "Multiple Visions," which featured ten thousand of the over one hundred thousand objects donated to the museum by Alexander and Susan Girard. This world's largest private collection of folk art, formed by mid-twentieth-century designer Alexander Girard and his wife primarily in the 1950s and 1960s, catapulted the museum to become the world's largest museum of international folk art. Textile designer Jack Lenor Larsen, a colleague and contemporary of Girard's, described the times:

> After WWII, with the resumption of ocean crossings and the growth of global air transport, there manifested many aspects of a new global view. After years of shortages and rationing, the Allies seemed for once less keen on world markets than on sources of exotic imports unaffordable in the depression and unavailable in years of conflict. Headlines and news releases had, for years, featured far-away faces and created a keen interest in who and where they were. Other points of view, including approaches to color, sound, and dance, aroused our romantic fantasies, on the one hand, or a new world order on the other. . . . When we focused on the "One World" and spoke of the "Family of Man," we had come a far piece from the complacent isolation of prewar decades. . . . The Girards' expanding folk art collections reflected all this. . . . Repeatedly, the Girards were struck by similarities of expression in peoples far removed from each other. They had discovered the commonality of all people, especially those manifested in rural, agrarian societies.[5]

Alexander Girard was a man of his time, drawing upon the same heady moment that had produced "The Family of Man" and "It's a Small World." At the Museum of International Folk Art, he designed the ten-thousand-square-foot gallery himself, based upon several previous installations of his collections, most notably in 1963 with an exhibition of nativity scenes at the Nelson Gallery of Art (today the Nelson-Atkins Museum of Art, Kansas City, Missouri) and again at the HemisFair 1968, the World's Fair in San Antonio, Texas. He filled the gallery's cases with vignettes of folk art figures in scenes of festivals and daily life from around the world. At the entrance he chose to present an Italian proverb, *Tutto il mondo è paese*, which he translated as "The whole world is hometown." As an introduction to the gallery that bears his name, this proverb expressed Girard's approach to the world of folk art.

Through the decades since this gallery opened, hundreds of thousands of visitors have been charmed by the Girard exhibit, unlike anything that they have seen elsewhere in museums. As the only permanent gallery in the museum, "Multiple Visions" has been a major factor in the international renown garnered by the museum. Clearly it touches a chord in the minds of visitors and draws them back year after year.

Fast-forward to the twenty-first century where, in a very short period, there has been a radical change in US museums' perspectives of their mission and purpose. The trend in museums nationwide has shifted away from a singular focus on the care, study, and choreographed display of their

FIGURE 6.1
Alexander Girard in the "Multiple Visions" exhibition of the Girard Wing at the Museum of International Folk Art, 1982. (Photo: Mark Schwartz, Museum of International Folk Art Archives, Exhibitions Collection, Multiple Visions Series AR.00004.170.)

collections toward an emphasis on serving as a forum for the exchange of ideas and the value of art as a catalyst for positive social change. Indeed, the American Alliance of Museums' 2015 annual meeting theme was "The Social Value of Museums: Inspiring Change." Museums are now exploring how they can take a leading civic role in making a difference in their communities. This trend is also occurring in western Europe, as witnessed by the "Museums Change Lives" campaign launched by the United Kingdom Museum Association, for one example.[6]

Our museums are focusing more attention, staff time, and resources on engaging our communities. But our communities are also changing, even though our typical museum visitor is not. We know that traditionally American public museum visitors have been older, well-educated, affluent citizens of Euro-American descent. However, the US population demographic is shifting rapidly. In less than thirty years (sometime around 2043 or 2044), this current core audience for museums will become a minority of the population for the first time in US history.[7] If US museums continue doing business as usual, we will see a striking shrinkage of the museum-going audience.

Thus it is becoming imperative for museums to grapple with the implications of demographic changes sweeping the country if they plan to be relevant to more than a small segment of American society. Museums all over the United States are trying to update their permanent exhibits to make them more meaningful to contemporary society. At the Museum of International Folk Art, rather than tear down the "Multiple Visions" exhibition installed by Alexander Girard himself and much revered by our visitors, we looked for a way to provide balance by offering another perspective in the museum that would address topics of significance to a twenty-first-century audience, beyond the "Family of Man" and "It's a Small World" approach of a bygone era.[8]

Coupled with this need to be more responsive and relevant was a unique opportunity to more directly engage living folk artists in the museum's collections, conversations, and curations. This opportunity arose with the founding of an international folk art market right outside the front door of the museum. When 150 traditional artists from over sixty countries set up their sales booths on the museum's plaza every second weekend in July, this assembled group of firsthand experts presents an unprecedented opportunity for collaboration with the museum to connect with a truly global community. The artists presenting at the Santa Fe International Folk Art Market, founded in 2004, have made it possible for the museum staff to keep current with trends in folk arts production, such as the global rise of women's traditional arts cooperatives. Building relationships with these artists has given us the means to hear their personal and communal stories about social issues and challenges that they contend with every day back home.

As a result, in 2010 the museum launched a new initiative, its Gallery of Conscience, featuring exhibitions in collaboration with living traditional artists and focusing on the social justice and human rights issues that are expressed in their lives and their artworks. From its first exhibition on women's folk art cooperatives, the Gallery of Conscience succeeded on two basic levels: first, it provided a unique opportunity for master artists from all corners of the globe to engage with each other directly; second, it has nudged museum

FIGURE 6.2
Gathering of participants at the International Folk Art Market, Santa Fe, on Museum Hill, during the second weekend in July. Each year, the Gallery of Conscience features the words and works of market artists, along with traditional New Mexican artists and community members, in its programming and exhibitions. (Photo: Suzanne Seriff.)

visitors beyond a merely celebratory understanding of folk arts toward a more meaningful exploration of the contemporary conditions in which artists live and work and the issues that are expressed through their arts.

From the beginning, the gallery has emphasized artists' personal testimonies. Throughout International Folk Arts Week, which was launched the same year as the Gallery of Conscience, the opening of an exhibition in the gallery begins one week before the opening of the market. During the opening weekend and the ensuing weeklong series of educational activities, artists, many of whom have traveled from great distances, are present in the gallery, conversing with visitors, telling their stories, and engaging with local artists from New Mexico. In recent years, this level of engagement has extended beyond International Folk Arts Week to include an annual cycle of continuous programs, workshops, dialogues, and collaborations with local artists, visitors, students, and community arts and service agencies, all working together to explore issues of conscience that matter in their lives—including immigration, natural disaster, and health topics such as HIV/AIDS.

One of the challenges to sustaining the Gallery of Conscience was finding professionals who are trained to work directly with communities, be they local or global communities, and engage with visitors in new ways. Since this is what folklorists do best, I looked to folklorists to take the lead on the development of the gallery. Veteran folklorist and educator Suzanne Seriff, who had experience with both the museum as a guest curator and the folk art market as the long-standing head of the Artist Selection Committee, was a natural choice as gallery director. Laura Marcus Green, a local independent folklorist, brought many years of experience working with diverse communities, making her an ideal community engagement coordinator on the Gallery of Conscience team.

In the five years since its inception, the Gallery of Conscience has attracted the attention of artists, scholars, visitors, and museum educators worldwide.

FIGURE 6.3
Gallery of Conscience exhibition "Let's Talk About This: Folk Artists Respond to HIV/AIDS," July 6, 2014, to April 3, 2016. Participatory activities for visitors include a memorial wall and a prompt to make your own World AIDS Day protest march sign, 2015. (Photo by Blair Clark, courtesy of the Museum of International Folk Art.)

Its innovative approach to community engagement and collaborative exhibition development has won national recognition and support from such institutions as the National Endowment for the Arts and the American Alliance of Museums. But most significant and rewarding have been the responses from first-time visitors who are connecting to the museum experience not merely as consumers but as cocreators, whose own voice is welcomed as part of the emerging story: "I saw myself here for the first time. Thank you for that."

EXECUTION

Suzanne Seriff, director, Gallery of Conscience

"Folk art must speak to people—that is part of what puts the 'folk' in folk arts!"

—Lulama Sihlabeni, gallery artist, South Africa, 2013

What happens when a folk art museum—known worldwide for the beauty, whimsy, color, and craft of its permanent exhibition—incubates a new space to focus more on the folk in the art than the art of the folk? What happens when that same museum—internationally renowned for the quality of its collection and the beauty of its curation—reconfigures a new exhibits team to design "with" and "by," rather than "for," the folk? And what happens when that museum—celebrated for the education, erudition, and sophistication of its international visitors—dedicates this new space to engage the most underserved and at-risk audiences at home and abroad, including the illiterate, the indigenous, the impoverished, the AIDS infected, the gender queered, and the undocumented?

All hell breaks loose—that's what happens. Docents write letters of protest, curators hold closed-door meetings with the museum director, designers threaten to quit, powerful collaborators call it a "downer," guards get nervous, funders lobby complaints, and longtime museum patrons spread the word that the first prototyped exhibit in the new gallery is "the ugliest thing the Museum has ever produced in its 60-year history."

Yet responses from first-time visitors, community workshop participants, and folk artists tell a different tale:

> "I love that the Gallery is always changing, and is changed by the people who have responded."

"This is a brave thing to do."

"Look what I did!"

"This is a beautiful exhibit—accessible in ways museums haven't felt before."

"There should be a place in every museum where you have to commit your own opinions. More museums should get a hold of people emotionally, not just intellectually."

The gallery under discussion is the current incarnation of MOIFA's Gallery of Conscience, which originally launched in 2010 as a safe place within the museum to engage and connect visitors and community members around current issues of social justice through the words and works of local and international folk artists. In its first three years, the gallery featured three guest-curated and professionally designed exhibitions that each focused on a timely issue of global significance in the twenty-first century: women's empowerment (2010), natural disaster (2011), and internment in times of war (2012).[9] The first exhibit, "Empowering Women: Artisan Cooperatives That Transform Communities," opened in the summer of 2010 and subsequently traveled to museums and history sites throughout the United States and into Canada. Its positive reception, both at home and on tour, attracted widespread publicity and support for the gallery, including a generous endowment from a local family that provided a financial base for future investments and innovations.

While the gallery's first three exhibits were certainly more socially relevant and inclusive, the top-down method of curation, design, artist selection, and programmatic development was not. Both artists and community members made it clear that they wanted more. They asked, in particular, for our institutional help in creating a forum for continuing to dialog about challenging social issues, engaging underserved and at-risk communities in more meaningful ways, and extending the conversation to explore the impact of these issues in our own "backyard." There seemed to be something, ironically enough, about the polished and professional nature of the finished exhibits that prevented audiences, artists, and community members from engaging as spontaneously, deeply, or personally as they would have liked.

So in the fall of 2012, MOIFA took the next leap to transform the gallery into what we hoped would be a more effective and inviting platform for genuine community engagement and collaboration. We discovered that in order to invite and welcome that kind of community engagement, we had to do more than just alter the nature of the topics the gallery addressed. As an institutional space, it had to really *embody* the kind of honest, engaged, collaborative, and "nimble" environment we hoped to promote.

A key to this project's success—and the community's trust—began with a fundamental shift in the roles and definitions of our own personnel. Focusing on audience engagement rather than specialized knowledge, the Gallery of Conscience threw out the more traditional curator/designer/educator model of exhibit expertise in favor of a team approach that was fundamentally collaborative, improvisational, and flexible. After three years of working with MOIFA as guest curator and strategic planning consultant, I was charged with assembling such a team to lead a totally new kind of prototyping process based on visitor, artist, and community input and exchange.

The six-member team ultimately consisted of three MOIFA staff members, including an educator, curator, and preparator and two additional part-time consultants, plus myself as Gallery of Conscience director. Longtime public-sector folklorist Laura Marcus Green was hired as our community engagement coordinator, and Kathy McLean, a nationally recognized and innovative exhibition development consultant, joined the team. This "team-based" approach was chosen because it represented, for us, a more innovative structure designed to learn through doing. Rather than dividing ourselves into distinct "roles" within the team, we all worked together within the gallery to design the spaces, engage the visitors, create the interactives, write the labels, conduct visitor evaluations, and change and adjust the prototyped space for increased clarity and depth of response after each iteration. Our goal was to be as nimble and responsive with each other as we hoped to be with our visitor and community input.

While our core team of folklorists and museum professionals was experienced in community-based collaborations, we had precious little collective experience in a truly bottom-up, participatory, and dialogic model of exhibit development. This is where the experience and expertise of our resident "prototyping guru," Kathleen McLean, came in. McLean explains her idea of prototyping—drawn from the Greek word meaning "first impressions"—as "a mock up or a quick and dirty version of an idea; something flexible and changeable; a tool for learning something about the effects of an idea or object

FIGURE 6.4
Three-way community collaboration between Gallery of Conscience, Creativity for Peace, and immigrant artist Gasali Adeyemo, in conjunction with the "Between Two Worlds" exhibition project, 2015. Young New Mexican woman hangs her indigo-dyed quilt square depicting her symbol of "home" to dry at the end of a workshop led by Nigerian Yoruba adire cloth maker Gasali Adeyemo. Participants included young women from Palestine, Israel, and New Mexico. (Photo: Laura Marcus Green, courtesy of Museum of International Folk Art.)

on the end-user . . . and in the case of museums, the relevance of an exhibit or experience on the museum visitor."[10]

Like a jazz song, the exhibition development process we incubated under McLean's tutelage begins with a single social justice thread of an idea, then uses a few artworks to explore the "melody" and call for a response. In that first incubation year, the topic in the Gallery of Conscience was HIV/AIDS, and our goal was to explore the many ways in which traditional artists and local communities use their traditional storytelling and visual arts to educate, advocate, and increase awareness about HIV/AIDS both on a local and on an international scale. On World AIDS Day that year, over a dozen works of art began the conversation. They included

- A tower of six hundred beaded dolls representing the children orphaned by AIDS in one South African village
- An AIDS Memorial Quilt block commemorating eight New Mexicans who died at the height of the pandemic in the United States
- A carved wooden sculpture of an AIDS protest march in Mozambique's capital

FIGURE 6.5
Camurdino Mustafá Jethá holds his soft wood sculpture depicting refugees fleeing the violence of the civil war in Mozambique, 2013. Titled *Refugiados* (refugees), this piece depicts the displaced families and villagers carrying everything they might need on their heads, including the door to their old home, which is the first thing they set into place when they settle in a new land. This was a featured artwork in the "Between Two Worlds" exhibit in the Gallery of Conscience, 2014–2016. (Photo: Laura Marcus Green, courtesy of Museum of International Folk Art.)

Improvisation can bring out many emotions; in this case, it captured and conveyed grief, resilience, activism, and hope. People of all ages across the community responded to the call, adding miniature protest signs, memorials to loved ones, radio pieces about their own life stories, and squares later sewn into a community quilt. The yearlong project provided the community with an opportunity to discuss a subject too often hidden by silence, stigma, and misinformation. The exhibition title, "Let's Talk about This: Folk Artists Respond to HIV/AIDS," reflected the mandate felt by both artists and community members alike: "Let's Talk About This! You must not be ashamed of telling the community! When you keep quiet you sign your own death warrant."[11]

The exhibition within the gallery—which went through four separate iterations and changes—was neither finished nor polished; rather it was a kind

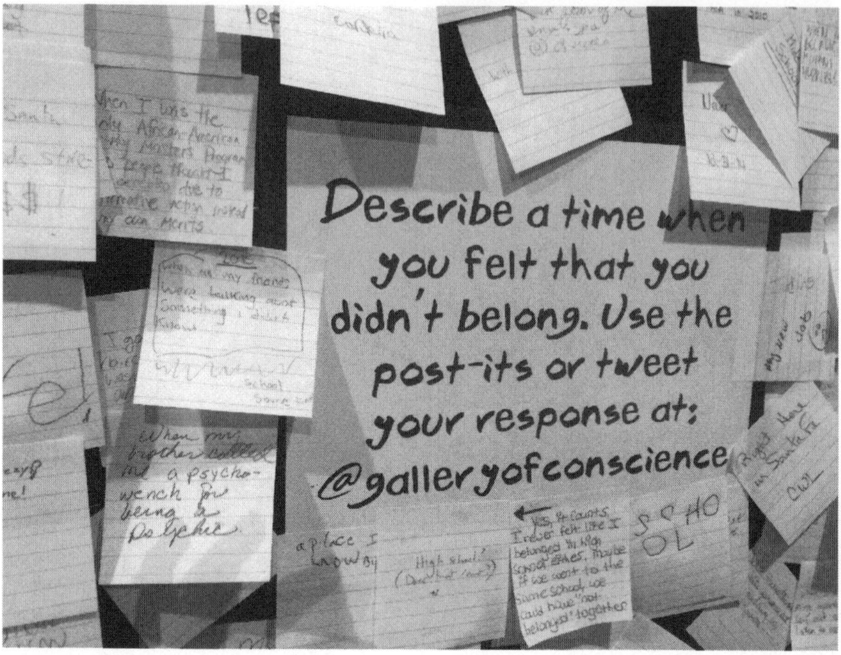

FIGURE 6.6
Talk back board participatory activity in the "Between Two Worlds" exhibit at the Gallery of Conscience, 2015. (Photo: Suzanne Seriff.)

of "call and response" lab in which visitors, artists, and targeted community members could come together to riff off of the initial artworks, dialog about issues, share their thoughts, and maybe even contribute to an ongoing, iterative art piece that was community created.

In that first prototyping year, our team experimented with a number of techniques designed to encourage visitors to feel a part of an ongoing process, able to engage easily, immediately, and meaningfully. We taped computer-generated label text directly on the wall and used existing cases, furniture, and leftover paint colors from a previous exhibit. We displayed photographs of the artwork if we didn't own the "real thing" or weren't sure if the real thing would be effective in engaging our audiences. And we hired a hip young blackboard graphic person from Trader Joe's to handwrite the exhibit title and section headings in chalk directly on the gallery walls. The opening label outside the exhibition's doors invited visitors to come in, share their thoughts, try their hand, and leave their opinion, stating, in big letters, "THIS IS AN EXPERIMENT. EVERYTHING HERE IS A WORK IN PROGRESS."

In addition to the "arts and idea exchange" exhibition lab, the prototyping process resulted in a number of programs that grew out of the grassroots community work spearheaded by our community engagement coordinator, Laura Marcus Green. In a seminal article on folk arts and social change, folklorist Betsy Peterson discusses this type of exploratory, ethnographic fieldwork as a kind of "engaged awareness"—a practice of careful listening and observation through which the multiple "narratives embedded in daily life" can offer up insights, experiences, and artworks often hidden to the more public eye.[12] Some of the gallery programs, conducted in collaboration with local arts and service organizations, included

- A series of community-based arts and dialog workshops
- A slate of public programs including films, conversation cafes, lectures, and audio listening programs
- A youth-targeted radio and digital media program collaboratively developed with community partners, which resulted in a series of short radio programs interweaving artist interviews with the personal stories of the young producers[13]

In each case, these community-based programs had been designed not as isolated instances of community outreach but as part of the prototyping process itself—a shift that fundamentally changed the level of community involvement, balance of authority, amount of staff time required, look and feel of the exhibition itself, and so forth. Although this process evolved as we went along, the ultimate goal was that each of these initially isolated programs had the potential to feed back into the exhibition itself, as the space opened up for ongoing AIDS Memorial quilt making, or listening events for radio segments were created by area youth around the topic, or the miniature protest signs made in response to an artifact interactive took over an entire wall of the gallery.

We would be wrong if we didn't admit that the results of this first incubated exhibition were both exhilarating and exasperating. Challenges arose in defining exactly what we meant by community involvement and what we meant by "art," managing work-flow expectations and responsibilities, communicating the value of "work in progress" to patrons who expect finished products, ceding the conventional authority of curator and designer, and redefining "success" in new terms—based more on reaching new audiences than on pleasing old patrons and on starting conversations rather than creating polished exhibits.

Luckily, the Gallery of Conscience team enjoyed the support of the director, the enthusiasm of our visitors, and the financial backing of both local and national funders. We were given the green light to continue the experimental "prototyping" process for another exhibition cycle.

When the Gallery of Conscience team settled on immigration as the topic for the second prototyped exhibition, we started, right off the bat, to develop a toolkit of resources to address the potential "prototype killers"[14] that we had encountered in the "Let's Talk" exhibition. We gave ourselves two years instead of one to allow the necessary time to authentically develop community collaborations, incorporate community voices and artworks over time, and more effectively prototype participatory elements within the gallery. We created a community advisory committee, consisting of immigrants, refugees, service organization leaders, and local folk artists, to more fully integrate community voices at the exhibit development table. We created a pictorial time line of the prototyping process so that visitors, docents, and patrons could see exactly where we were in the exhibition development cycle and what their role could be in its development. And we engaged local immigrant and refugee artists, poets, musicians, storytellers, performers, chefs, and advocates to accompany us on this exhibition development journey, exploring the exhibition themes through their own artistic media both within and outside the gallery walls.

Dialog was both the spark and the fuel that drove the entire process—from concept, to content, to design, to engagement, to action, and back again. Dialog was not only the primary means through which we invited diverse communities into the museum to engage with each other around relevant issues sparked by the artists' words and works; it was also the primary means through which we engaged community members to collaborate on designing the exhibit experience, select the most impactful artworks, shape the themes, develop the programs, and organize for community action.

It all began in the summer of 2013 when we held our first round of dialogues with invited immigrants, refugees, and immigrant descendants

FIGURE 6.7
The Gallery of Conscience team writes an invitation for visitor participation as part of the kickoff of a new exhibition project, tentatively titled "Under Pressure: Choices Folk Artists Make in Today's Global Marketplace," 2016. The prototyping includes an opportunity for visitors and artists to vote on their favorite exhibit title or write their own on the ballot. Team members for 2016 include, from left to right, Bryan Johnson French, Suzy Seriff, Chloe Accardi, Patricia Sigala, Carrie Hertz, and Kathy McLean. (Photo: Suzanne Seriff.)

from our local communities in New Mexico. Japanese, Nigerian, Tibetan, Mexican, Salvadoran, Korean, Cameroonian, Brazilian, and Indian community members gathered in the gallery, all bringing their own stories, perspectives, and opinions on a wide range of issues surrounding the migrant experience, from racial profiling of newcomers to what it takes to feel welcomed—or unwelcomed—in a new land.

The prototyping process we had incubated throughout the previous year assured us that we didn't need fancy bells and whistles to get the conversation started. Indeed, for that first dialog, we had nothing more than a few color photos of handmade baskets, sculptures, paintings, weavings, culinary dishes, and embroideries made by traditional immigrant artists throughout the United States. The actual pieces of art wouldn't be installed until months down the road.

The dialog process itself was one that we had developed through our membership in the Immigration and Civil Rights Network, a national network of the International Coalition of Sites of Conscience that included over forty museums and historic sites serving immigrant communities or presenting immigrant history across the United States and Europe.[15] We knew that immigration brings up strong feelings in the public sphere, both personal and political, and that we had to introduce the topic with sensitivity and care. Ask anyone what they think of when they hear the words "the American dream," for example, and they can probably tell you a personal story or spout a strong opinion, either positive or negative. This holds true whether they immigrated themselves, their families immigrated generations earlier, or they were already here when newcomers arrived. In order to create a safe space to allow for these potentially charged conversations, we knew we needed to start slow, build trust, share commonalities, and graciously explore our differences. Creating a kind of "arc" of experience through the dialog process, we began as strangers and ended up, a few hours later, as "neighbors"—having shared a profound experience that opened with introductions, moved to personal stories, escalated to issue-driven discussions, and wound down to sharing lessons learned and calls for action. It is this kind of experience that, we hoped, over time, could build capacity within our community for increased understanding, tolerance, and equity.

Based on these early dialogues, the Gallery of Conscience team crafted an initial iteration of the new exhibition, with a title reflecting the unfinished nature of the process and the invitation for audience response: "Works in Progress: Folk Artists Reflect on the Immigrant Experience." As with the HIV/AIDS prototype, we opened with a limited number of artworks (sometimes in the form of enlarged photos) displayed on the walls and in makeshift cases, computer-printed label texts and community quotes, two or three mock-ups of participatory exercises, and an invitation for visitors to explore, participate, comment, reflect, and contribute their thoughts, their stories, and their voices. Artworks included such pieces as a refugee's embroidered story cloth illustrating the Hmong people's forced exodus from Laos at the end of the Vietnam War, an ex-voto painted as a thank-you to Santo Niño de Atocha for the miracle of a mother and her baby surviving sunstroke while crossing the

US-Mexico border, a Lakota beaded cradle created to convey a contemporary social statement about immigration with the words "The Border Crossed Us" beaded across the cradle's top, and an embroidered scene depicting a young Holocaust survivor's first view of the Statue of Liberty from the ship that carried her family to freedom in the United States.

Within the first month of the exhibit's soft opening, we held another set of dialogues in the Gallery of Conscience—this time with the benefit of an actual physical exhibition as a catalyst for the conversation. We again invited refugee and immigrant community members, as well as artists, advocates, activists, and social service providers from within a hundred-mile radius. In addition to the immediate impact on the participants themselves and the concrete input we received from them about exhibit design and content, something extraordinary began to happen as relationships were formed, ideas exchanged, and creative energies ignited. Again, the trick was to be "nimble" enough to recognize what was happening and respond "on a dime."

One of these threads ultimately led to a series of new art pieces for the exhibition that had either been created, donated, or recommended by participants in one of our dialog programs. Another led to a series of collaborative performances, workshops, and classes with social service organizations throughout the community. Navigating these burgeoning relationships required its own kind of "nimbleness" and its own layer of commitment to the social justice foundation of our incubated Gallery of Conscience experience.

Responses from visitors to the gallery were immediate and enthusiastic:

> "This exhibition is very relevant to what's going on today, considering immigration law, etc. Yes, it's a very important topic. We're all immigrants in some way. It asks you to think differently about everything in the museum, not just this gallery. The show, in a very down to earth and practical way, bridges the intellectual and art appreciation with actual, real world experiences."

> "This is an excellent and timely exhibit. It brings awareness and helps people empathize by putting them in others' shoes."

> "Thank you for being here. Thanks for doing this. It makes sense for MOIFA to do this exhibit because Santa Fe is a place of convergence. It offers a nice opportunity to reflect on or participate in questions like what you would take with you (if you had to leave your home suddenly). I'd like to see the exhibit as

a resource for immigrants, so if someone is an immigrant, s/he can take from it and build on it. It's helpful to feel that you're not alone."

CONCLUSION: THE MORAL IMPERATIVE OF THE INCLUSIVE MUSEUM

As many cultural critics have noted, the demographic shifts in major cosmopolitan cities caused by widespread migration to the United States and around the world have put museums at a new crossroads.[16] While our institutions may not have been historically set up to respond quickly or nimbly to the changing needs of these new communities, some would argue that we have nothing less than a moral imperative to do just that. As folklorist and immigrant rights activist William Westerman writes, "Museums have a leading role to play in becoming cultural centers where multiple narratives can be told, where people can find safe spaces for cultures to mix, and where xenophobia can be overcome."[17] The challenge, he continues, "is how to become inclusive and relevant to the framework of civic democracy at a time when larger societies are grappling with strong exclusionist tendencies and fear."[18] He goes on to suggest four distinct yet interrelated ways in which museums might offer "inclusivity" as its own kind of capacity building and assistance.

> It can refer to programmatic decisions that integrate community input into the museum's planning . . . ; the museum can include a diverse range of people among the desired audience; the staff can be diverse and include people from varied backgrounds, origins, perspectives and approaches; and the museum can reflect a society that is itself inclusive of everyone.[19]

This range of "inclusions" is exactly what is being incubated in MOIFA's Gallery of Conscience—a range that moves beyond the "visitor as consumer" model toward a model that encompasses the full potential of community-based knowledge production, collaboration, and communication. Ever a barometer of the most contemporary issues, folk arts present a forum for response, expression, and education, as artists weave their resilience, activism, and hope into their work. Transcending silence, folk arts create an opening, an invitation to reflect upon and discuss topics that know no cultural, class, gender, or age boundaries.

Together, museums and communities have the potential to create an entirely new and replicable model for civic engagement that finds its way back to what community-based artists and storytellers have known all along. In the words of master bead worker Lulama Sihlabeni of South Africa, "Folk art must speak to people—that is part of what puts the 'folk' in folk arts!"

NOTES

1. Westerman 2008, 157

2. Gretchen Jennings, "Critique of *Between Two Worlds*," *Exhibitionist Journal* (Spring 2015).

3. Steichen 1955, 4.

4. Wikipedia 2015.

5. Larsen 1995, 30–31.

6. Lord 2015, 43.

7. Contreras 2015, A7–A8.

8. Folklorists have been involved in projects to add meaning to the "Multiple Visions" exhibition through the decades. Two projects in particular are *The Spirit of Folk Art*, a book about Alexander Girard's collection and exhibition, written by Henry Glassie in 1989, and a handheld multimedia project to add artists' voices and context to the exhibition.

9. The first three exhibits in the Gallery of Conscience included "Empowering Women: Artisan Cooperatives That Transform Communities," 2010, guest curated by Suzanne Seriff; "The Arts of Survival: Folk Expression in the Face of Natural Disaster," 2011, guest curated by Suzanne Seriff; and "The Art of Gaman: Arts and Crafts from the Japanese Internment Camps, 1942–1946," 2013, guest curated by Delphine Hirasuna.

10. McLean 2013, 2.

11. These words were embroidered on a figurative textile designed to promote AIDS education by South African folk artist Maria Rengane.

12. Peterson 2011, 28.

13. Community partners for this innovative program included Youth Media Project, teaching the craft of digital storytelling and art of listening for a socially

responsible world, and N'MPower, an LGBTQ youth-empowerment organization in Albuquerque.

14. Kathleen McLean (2013, 4) refers to "prototype killers" as those problems that "lurk in the shadows of most museums" that threaten to adversely affect the success of the prototyping process: the tyranny of the formalized label-writing and exhibit-design process; the specter of authority and control; the fantasy of perfection; and the argument that prototyping will disrupt the exhibition schedule and undermine the budget.

15. For a comprehensive look at this project, please see the forthcoming volume, edited by Sarah Pharaon, produced by the American Association of State and Local History Museums, titled *Interpreting Immigration: Connecting Past and Present at Museums*. Some parts of this chapter are excerpts from Seriff's article in this volume, "Immigration, Empathy, and Engagement: Incubating a New Approach to Immigration in the Museum of International Folk Art's Gallery of Conscience."

16. Westerman 2008, 157.

17. Ibid.

18. Ibid., 159.

19. Ibid.

SOURCES

Contreras, Russell. 2015. "Whites Could Lose Majority Sooner with Census Changes." *New Mexican*, November 19, A7–A8.

Díaz, V. Gina. 2011. "Ethics and Folk Art Production: A New Museum Initiative." *Anthropology Now* 3, no. 1: 114–22.

Farrell, Betty, and Maria Medvedeva. 2010. *Demographic Transformation and the Future of Museums*. Washington, DC: AAM Press, 1–42.

Larsen, Jack Lenor. 1995. "A Celebration of the Senses." In *Folk Art from the Global Village: The Girard Collection at the Museum of International Folk Art*. Santa Fe: Museum of New Mexico Press.

Lord, Gail. 2015. "Why Cities, Museums, and Soft Power." *Museum News* (March/April): 38–45.

McLean, Kathleen. 2013. "Museum Exhibit Prototyping as a Method of Community Conversation and Participation." American Folklore Society. http://c.ymcdn.com/

sites/www.afsnet.org/resource/resmgr/Best_Practices_Reports/McLean_and_Seriff_Museum_Exh.pdf.

Peterson, Betsy. 2011. "Folk and Traditional Arts and Social Change." A Working Guide to the Landscape of Arts for Change. Animating Democracy. http://animatingdemocracy.org/sites/default/files/BPeterson%20Trend%20Paper.pdf.

Seriff, Suzanne. 2016. "Immigration, Empathy, and Engagement: Incubating a New Approach to Immigration in the Museum of International Folk Art's Gallery of Conscience." In *Interpreting Immigration: Connecting Past and Present at Museums*, edited by Sarah Pharaon. Nashville: AASLH.

Steichen, Edward. 1955. *The Family of Man: The Greatest Photographic Exhibition of All Time—503 Pictures from 68 Countries—Created by Edward Steichen for the Museum of Modern Art.* New York: Maco Magazine Corporation.

Weil, Stephen E. 2002. "Are You Really Worth What You Cost, or Just Merely Worthwhile? And Who Gets to Say?" Getty Leadership Institute, 1–22.

Westerman, William. 2008. "Museums, Immigrants, and the Inversion of Xenophobia; or, the Inclusive Museum in the Exclusive Society." *International Journal of the Inclusive Museum* 1, no. 4: 157–62.

Wikipedia. 2015. "It's a Small World." Wikipedia.org. https://en.wikipedia.org/wiki/It%27s_a_Small_World.

7

Race and the Twenty-First-Century Museum

Aleia Brown

Aleia Brown acknowledges that while museums of all disciplines made noteworthy progress to address race in the twentieth century, the new century calls for a more systematic and meaningful assessment of the museum field's response to racial justice. She acknowledges the efforts of professional societies, and yet she challenges museums to be more accountable and to take stronger action. Brown was one of the organizers of #museumsrespondtoferguson's three-point approach to having productive conversations that lead to meaningful action. These conversations focus on the role of historically black museums and collecting institutions, the issues still not addressed by museums, and, finally, the need for museums to give greater attention to the collecting of oral histories of African Americans to enrich their collections and effectiveness. Drawing on the example of the use of Twitter chats with museum colleagues, Brown conveys the power of the oral tradition and folklore as a tool for understanding the black experience and how museums can become more active forces in response to racial issues facing society. She concludes by challenging museums to commit to a deeper understanding of race politics in the twenty-first century.

The moments, days, and months were painfully silent in museums after Darren Wilson, a white cop, shot and killed Mike Brown, an unarmed black teenager, in Ferguson, Missouri. In favor of avoiding controversy, senior leadership throughout the United States suppressed individuals interested in examining the field's role in police brutality and race relations. With the exception of notable efforts from the Missouri Historical Society, the National Museum of African American History and Culture, and a few others, museums silenced the conversation and actions related to Ferguson. Underneath a widespread blanket of ambivalence, individuals from different institutions came together online to form a cadre of museum colleagues looking to engage in meaningful dialog and action. This silence in physical spaces led to the "Joint Statement from Museum Bloggers and Colleagues on Ferguson and Related Events," a dialog in an online space. Museum consultant Adrianne Russell and I decided to continue the conversation through the monthly Twitter chat #museumsrespondtoferguson. The chat investigates Ferguson, but more important, it addresses the environment that created Ferguson. In that same vein, the chat forces participants to examine race politics in mainstream museums—the silences as well as the blatant untruths—to develop informed and sustainable solutions. As the chat became more established, we realized that examining the past had to be the foundation for our #museumsrespondtoferguson framework.[1] Conversations in the present and past did not give the history of race and museums enough attention. Taking a historical approach to analyzing race politics in museums will offer the most comprehensive solutions in dealing with race in the twenty-first century.

Public spaces in the United States were segregated longer than they were desegregated in the twentieth century.[2] On this premise, mainstream museums have a long history of cordoning off their gallery space, educational resources, and tenure in the field from African Americans. Even if individual museums operated as subversive outposts ignoring the status quo, they still existed in the broader American environment and mind-set that systemically prevented black people from interacting with them beyond service positions. While segregation is no longer legal and changing demographics push museums to interact with nonwhite audiences, the museum field never developed a formal strategic plan to transition from keeping black people out, to welcoming them in as visitors and colleagues.[3] Museums of all disciplines made both noteworthy and shaky attempts to address race in the twentieth century;

however, the twenty-first century calls for systematic and meaningful action that deconstructs the field's past dealings with race.

Already, the twenty-first-century differs from the twentieth century in that organizations have produced policies that directly or tangentially discuss race beyond what is required of public institutions. Fourteen years into the twenty-first century, the board of directors of the American Alliance of Museums (AAM) approved a diversity and inclusion policy. The brief policy communicates the organization's appreciation for diversity, claiming that it "values and celebrates the unique attributes, characteristics and perspectives that make each person who they are."[4] Producing this policy signals that the board had some inclination that the organization needed to at least acknowledge race. The actual policy is too brief to extract what inspired it, how its tenets will specifically be fulfilled, and how the organization plans to evaluate the policy's effectiveness. Its vagueness does not offer strong points of reference for accountability. In the twenty-first century, it will be imperative for museums to develop a stronger course of action in dealing with race.

To be sure, museum professionals and scholars have addressed race and museums in the current century, but the field has not moved speedily toward racial justice. Richard Sandell and Eithne Nightingale's edited volume *Museums, Equality and Social Justice* offers the most comprehensive body of work related to race and intersectional social constructs.[5] The chapters specifically addressing race, especially Janet Marstine's "Fred Wilson, Good Work and the Phenomenon of Freud's Mystic Writing Pad," tend to call for racial justice through interpretation in exhibitions in programming. This volume is not the only work focusing on interpretation to rectify the record. For example, Regina Faden's "Museums and Race: Living Up to the Public Trust" posits that museums need to offer inclusive interpretation to sustain the public's trust.[6] Faden places a premium on thoughtful interpretation, citing that museums "must honor that privilege by leading the way in presenting the stories of our lives objectively and inclusively . . . so that they may offer an objective interpretation that will foster contemplation."[7] Jennifer Scott also echoes a similar strategy while detailing work at a postemancipation site.[8] While all of these solutions certainly involve positive attributes, there has yet to be a study that solely focuses on the reasons and implications for "silencing the past."[9] These examples pose useful arguments, and new scholarship should build on them by interrogating the field's direct connection to upholding imperialism, maintaining racist tropes, and maintaining hiring practices that ensure the field's homogeneity—all actions that will prevent any real type of racial healing or rectification of the record within museums. Failure to produce criticism along this line of thinking detracts from the validity of the AAM's diversity and inclusion policy.

Understanding this scholarship has informed #museumsrespondtoferguson's three-point approach to having productive conversations that lead to meaningful action in the twenty-first century. The first point involves examining the work of historically black museums and collecting institutions. Many of these institutions started in the twentieth century and carry on their work of centering the black experience into the twenty-first century. The second point looks at issues throughout history that black people have identified as important and contrasts them with what museums actually cover about black people in exhibitions and programming. Because community engagement and shared authority have become a strong part of the twenty-first-century museum, actually engaging the traumatic histories that black people work through, rather than just covering the celebratory events that museums tend to cover, is important. The final step to this approach involves employing oral histories. This approach is long range and requires intense commitment, but it is also working against a field steeped in racial turmoil. Taking a historical approach to analyzing museums' interaction with race will offer the most comprehensive solutions in dealing with race in the twenty-first century.

Studying historically black museums and collecting institutions is beneficial because it demonstrates that institutions doing intimate work with race have existed since the nineteenth century. In 1868, the Hampton University Museum became the nation's oldest African American museum. Others like the Schomburg Center for Research in Black Culture (1905) and Howard University's Moorland-Spingarn Research Center (1914) opened early in the twentieth century. Through these institutions alone, we understand that there was a concerted effort among black bibliophiles, educators, and cultural workers to preserve and display their lives and history. The early institutions especially did so at a great risk. After all, Hampton University's museum opened not too long after slavery was abolished. The museum maintained its mission, even in the midst of what Rayford Logan termed the "nadir of race relations," the end of Reconstruction through the early twentieth century.[10]

Contemporary mainstream museums can gain inspiration from them, seeing that many avoid engaging in race work because they associate it with risk. Historically, black museums have always faced risk from white supremacy; yet they continue to pursue their work.

The second component to doing productive race work in museums involves listening and understanding what matters to black communities. In the age of community engagement and shared authority, it is absolutely critical that museum professionals listen to black communities rather than barely devoting the time. Interviews and different media will review that museums approach African American history and culture differently than African Americans approach their own history and culture. Within the last years, sustained protests have formed over issues of police brutality, Confederate symbols, education injustice, environmental justice, and more. All the while, museums have not really collected, documented, or presented these stories. Instead, they continue to opt for the safe and played approach to black history: contributionist, which highlights that black people have actually contributed to American development, or exceptionalist, highlighting a singular feat. Finding these stories will require museum professionals to possibly learn things that disrupt their own thinking or just make them uncomfortable—to do extensive work to truly learn and produce work that is meaningful rather than just scratches the surface.

Conducting informal interviews and oral histories will further reveal how black people are communicating their experience. Perusing online outlets, podcasts, and popular books on race relations, police brutality, education equity, closing the wealth gap, sexual violence, and more reveals that black communities are resisting white supremacy. Archival research, especially through the extensive papers of the National Association for the Advancement of Colored People, shows that resistance to these issues was present and documented even before the start of the classical civil rights movement. The breadth and intensity of these subjects rarely serve as the center of museum exhibitions or programs, thereby making the products more palatable and less impactful.

The work of examining racial politics in museums is a long-term commitment. It requires time, integrity, intellectual curiosity, and openness. To make substantial progress, the twenty-first-century museum will need to activate a genuine interest in museums that live up to organizations' purported commitment to diversity and inclusion. That genuine action starts with a conversation that looks at how museums have been lenses of the ingredients that made contemporary events like Ferguson possible.

NOTES

1. Gretchen Jennings, "Joint Statement from Museum Bloggers and Colleagues on Ferguson and Related Events," Museum Commons, December 11, 2014, http://www.museumcommons.com/2014/12/joint-statement-museum-bloggers-colleagues-ferguson-related-events.html.

2. To understand the #museumsrespondtoferguson framework, see the blog post "We Who Believe in Freedom Cannot Rest," Incluseum, http://incluseum.com/2015/12/17/we-who-believe-in-freedom-cannot-rest. Here, Adrianne Russell and I point to the need to center black narratives and look to the past to illuminate the implications of race politics in museums.

3. President Lyndon B. Johnson signed the Civil Rights Act of 1964, which intended to end segregation. De jure segregation, or segregation upheld by the public, remained the status quo for years afterward. In 2010 the Center for the Future of Museums produced the study "Demographic Transformation and the Future of Museums." It opens with the statistics that, from the first decade of the twentieth century to the 1970s, minorities represented 10 to 13 percent of the population. Twenty-five years ago, minorities represented 20 percent of the population. With the last census, minorities represented 34 percent of the population. Minorities make up only 9 percent of core museum visitors today.

4. American Alliance of Museums (AAM) Board of Directors, Diversity Professional Network, "Diversity and Inclusion Policy," AAM, 2014, http://www.aam-us.org/about-us/who-we-are/strategic-plan/diversity-and-inclusion-policy (accessed January 8, 2016). Prior to this policy, AAM released the report *Excellence and Equity: Education and the Public Dimensions of Museums* in 1992. This report positions museums as stewards of educational equity.

5. Richard Sandell and Eithne Nightingale, *Museums, Equality and Social Justice* (New York: Routledge, 2012).

6. Regina Faden, "Museums and Race: Living Up to the Public Trust," *Museums and Social Issues* 2, no. 1 (Spring 2007): 77–88.

7. Ibid., 79.

8. Jennifer Scott, "Reimagining Freedom in the Twenty-First Century at a Post-emancipation Site," *Public Historian* 37, no. 2 (2015): 73–88.

9. In *Silencing the Past: Power and the Production of History* (Boston: Beacon Press, 1995), Michel-Rolph Trouillot holds the West accountable for silencing the voices that narrate minorities challenging the status quo. He particularly focuses on the successful Haitian slave revolt. Not acknowledging this largely omitted event from the master Western narrative, it implies, race tensions will be left to fester.

10. Rayford Logan, *The Negro in American Life and Thought: The Nadir, 1877–1901* (New York: Dial Press, 1954).

8

Community Curation as Collaborative Pedagogy

"The Will to Adorn" Project

DIANA BAIRD N'DIAYE

Diana Baird N'Diaye presents two rich case studies of twenty-first-century museum practice that were shaped by a sincere desire to validate the perspective of community using new models of community engagement and digital tools. She describes these case studies, *Bermuda Connections* and *Will to Adorn*, where working with community teams they cocreated knowledge by documenting and interpreting the shared culture of everyday life. Both projects operated on the premise that learning about one's own culture is enhanced in the company of other learners. In addition, she stresses that there is much to learn when curators create a collaborative process of observing, recording, interpreting, and communicating knowledge. N'Diaye argues that the context of the museum is an ideal place to put these ideas into practice. She makes the case that museums are spaces that have the flexibility for convening—to draw people into meaningful conversations on society, relationships, power, and community. She concludes by citing some of the challenges presented in each project and with an assessment of what worked well and the lessons learned using participatory museology in the digital age.

"For apart from inquiry, apart from the praxis, individuals cannot be truly human. Knowledge emerges only through invention and re-invention, through the restless, impatient, continuing, hopeful inquiry human beings pursue in the world, with the world, and with each other."

—*Paolo Freire,* Pedagogy of the Oppressed

"This is what community based research is all about; learning from the experiences of our friends, our relatives and our neighbors—those in the know."

—*Charles Weber,* Bermuda Connections

When Ethan Saltus, a seventh-grade student folklife researcher in Bermuda, was asked about his plans to interview kite maker Vincent Tuzo, he responded without hesitation, "I will be interviewing, taking pictures, I will ask questions; questions that will make him think—hard questions that he might not think I would ask."[1] Ethan was a part of a community-based research project that grew out of the Smithsonian Folklife Festival program featuring the island commonwealth of Bermuda. This research began with the preparation for the program in 1999 on the National Mall of the United States in Washington, DC. By the end of the project in 2003, after the festival, the "Bermuda Connections" program had been restaged as "Bermuda Homecoming,"[2] and a commonwealth-wide research and educational project involving seasoned adult fieldworkers, intermediate and secondary school students, and community cultural practitioners had been put in place. Cultural documentation, frank discussion, and public presentation of Bermuda's culture and history had been become a nation-building project that engaged individuals and groups far beyond the narrow confines of academia and museum work. The work expanded the scope of the Ministry of Culture, Sports and Recreation, already collecting oral histories, into a space of community pedagogy—a space of reciprocal learning where the division between researcher and subject, those who teach and those who learn, blurred/dissolved if only for a while.

"The Will to Adorn," a research project that began in 2009,[3] exactly ten years later, and also inspired by Paolo Freire's work, affirmed the validating impact of community and student agency in creating knowledge by documenting and interpreting the shared culture of everyday dress. Both projects

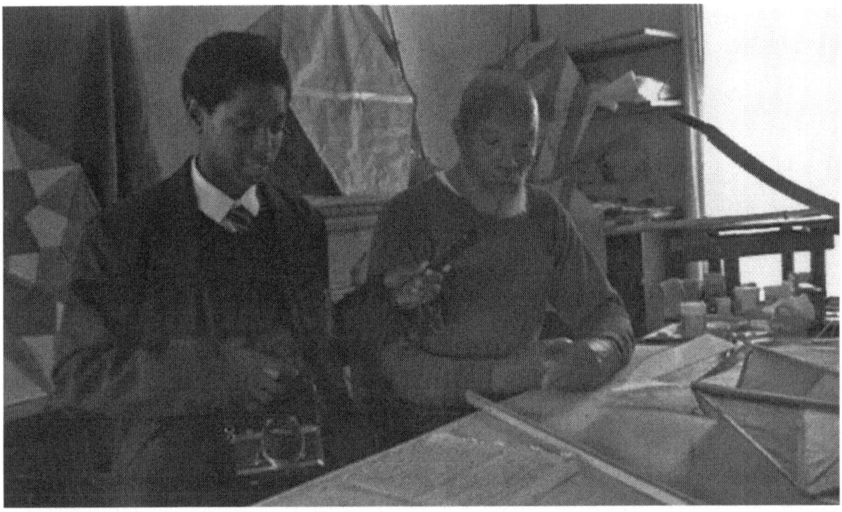

FIGURE 8.1
Ethan Saltus interviewing local master kite maker Vincent Tuzo, Bermuda. (Photo: Copyright © Smithsonian Institution.)

operated on the premise that when we learn about our own culture in the company of other learners, we learn about what is different but also what is shared as we participate together in the process of observing, recording, interpreting, and communicating knowledge. The context of the museum is an ideal place to put these ideas into practice. Museums as educational rather than scholastic spaces have the flexibility to function as convening and pedagogical spaces using both tangible and intangible cultural expression to draw people into meaningful conversations about and investigations of society and relationships, power and community.

Museums historically have been associated with collecting, conserving, curating, and interpreting objects. In addition to the collection and display of specimens of the natural world, artifacts of human creativity, invention, and works of imagination, the unfortunate legacy of museums extended to the objectification of living human beings in the nineteenth-century expositions. During the late 1960s and early 1970s, museums morphed from seeing their primary function as showcases and storehouses for collections of objects catering to exclusive audiences of collectors and scholars to being sites for object-based learning. As museums became learning environments for busloads of students during weekdays and families on weekends, the growing ranks of professional museum educators experimented and refined ways to reveal meaningful stories about nature, history, culture, and human emotion through exhibitions and interpretive programs.

In accordance with the educational role of museums, interpretive programs in museums and, notably, the Smithsonian's Folklife Festival, beginning in 1967, began publicly to recognize the authors of cultural objects as the authoritative voices of interpretation of those objects and of the cultural context in which they were created. Furthermore, the introduction of intangible culture in the museum setting—music, storytelling, the processes of making, and other intangible arts and knowledge—became established as part of the museum's offerings to the public. However, the convention remained for a curator, educator, or research staff of a museum to act as the overarching authoritative voice in determining what was worthy of researching, documenting, safeguarding, and learning about and why.

In the opening years of the twenty-first century, the focus of museums has been shifting once more in their involvement with the public[4]—with audiences that want be involved in the documentation and representation of their own communities. The expanded access of museumgoers to experiential and self-directed learning and cultural production—from independent research and documentation to Twitter posts, blogs, video, and other modes of self-publishing—has changed the imperatives and the possibilities for curating and for the kind of learning that takes place in museum settings. Museums as learning communities are partnering with the communities represented to accomplish this representation. Another change has been the call for museums to become sites of dialog and convening on issues that affect their expanding and diverse constituencies. These calls are coming from both within and outside the museum walls and spaces. The issues relating to the changing dynamics of museums and the nature of participation in and with museums are not limited to one nation. Museum constituencies and partnerships have increasingly become international and transnational. As cases in point, this chapter highlights the role of community curation in "Bermuda Connections" and "The Will to Adorn," two Smithsonian Folklife Festival projects where staff folklorists/curators, educators, students, and multigenerational researchers worked together in a reciprocal learning community.

After explaining the goals and histories of each of the two projects introduced above ("Bermuda Connections" and "The Will to Adorn"), the rest of the chapter describes how the methodologies for implementing both projects developed out of curatorial practice of festival. I pay special attention to how the recording and communication technologies that became more available to all in the decade between the two projects augmented the capacities for community-based researchers, educators, and students to work as partners with museum-based facilitators to create communities of folklore research and curation. I note some of the challenges presented in the course of each project and conclude with some comments about what worked well and some of the lessons that we are learning as folklorists and curators about participatory museology.

BUILDING CONNECTIONS IN BERMUDA: THE FESTIVAL AS AN EXERCISE IN COMMUNITY CULTURAL DEVELOPMENT

Bermuda is a sprinkling of over 170 habitable islands, linked by bridges, that are collectively the peaks of a submerged volcano, the graveyard of billions of corals whose bodies contribute the limestone that constitutes quite literally the building blocks of Bermudian homes; the nearest landmass is over six hundred miles away. Visitors first notice that the isles of Bermuda, merely 22.7 square miles, are beautifully landscaped and impeccably adorned in pastel architecture and lush gardens.[5]

Bermuda is Britain's second-oldest colony and one of its few remaining colonies, albeit self-governing, in North America; it is often described as an "island paradise." At the same time that it is a land of undeniable beauty, the island is clearly engaged in the "real world" of "multiple identities, overlapping memberships, and divided loyalties; of conflict and communion within and across boundaries; of peoples subjugated and subjugating" to which David Shuldiner eloquently referred in his call to fellow folklorists. He argued passionately for folklorists to play an active role in "confronting the challenges of cultural preservation, promoting cultural diversity, and building bridges across cultural boundaries."[6]

Ruth Thomas, cultural activist and scholar, had first approached the Smithsonian in 1987 to discuss the islands' participation in the folklife festival when she held the position of chief of Bermuda's Department of Cultural Affairs, but she was not able to secure the support of the government of the time. When Jackie Aubrey, an arts administrator within the department, approached festival director Diana Parker in 1998, things had changed quite a bit on the island. The 1994 election of the first government in the history of Bermuda to reflect the population's ethnic majority—Bermudians of African descent—and the ruling party's efforts to create a new "culturally inclusive" national identity had prompted a reexamination and negotiation of Bermudian identity and local culture. Hierarchical categories of immigration status and elaborate and contradictory notions of race, class, and ethnicity complicated the assertion of a plural national cultural identity. These were further complicated by the realities of unequal power relations within a transnational political economy. This took place against the background of controversial efforts to stem immigration and to provide jobs for native-born Bermudians in an economy facing more and more competition as a tourism destination. The "Bermuda Connections" project was conceived as a collaboration between the Smithsonian and a Bermudian government that was newly majority ruled.

Over fifty people from all parts of Bermudian society, from bank presidents and ministers of parliament to calypso singers and local educators, were invited to a meeting at a local hotel to hear from Smithsonian staff about the concept of presenting the folklife of Bermuda at a festival in the United States. We explained that the festival would be research based and that the fieldwork team would be composed of Bermudians whom we would train. The fieldwork, based on Smithsonian Folklife Festival guidelines, would first identify Bermudian cultural traditions and cultural practitioners and then present them on the National Mall of the United States. We first wanted to know what Bermudians felt was unique about their culture. From these beginnings, we worked with the Cultural Affairs Department to develop a research team that reflected a range of cultural practitioners, educators, academic scholars, artists, and journalists.

The training and fieldwork were accomplished through relatively short training sessions in Bermuda and over the course of several follow-up visits. One of the biggest challenges was climbing the technological learning curve. In 2000, cell phones were relatively new and did not include high-enough-quality video, audio, or even still photography to use in program books and signage. Local writer and actor John Zuill was hired as project photographer and shuttled between researchers' interviews to take photos. At other times researchers took their own photographs—with mixed results and much expense. Interviews were taken on audio cassette recorders and later tran-

FIGURE 8.2
"Bermuda Connections" program house builders pose on the traditional stepped roof, 2001. (Photo: Copyright © Smithsonian Institution.)

scribed. These trancriptions would prove to be invaluable and the basis for the development of Bermuda's Folklife Archive.

"Bermuda Connections" explicitly incorporated strategic planning to achieve cultural policy and educational goals to establish a national identity that recognized both the shared culture of the islands and the cultural diversity of its population. This process, which began with the initial planning sessions in 1999 for the 2001 "Bermuda Connections" Smithsonian festival program, impacted on the way that the self-governing island colony saw itself and had far reaching effects on educational, cultural, and tourism policy and even on the ways that the people of St. David's Island chose to build recognition of their Native American identity as a distinct Bermudian ethnic group.

The project was bracketed by the pursuit of cultural democratization. The dynamics of the relationship between the two institutional partners and aspects of the project and collaboration touched upon conversations about national identity, cultural policy, educational policy, and tourism on the island. It also expanded the scope of the Smithsonian Folklife Festival as an anchor for cultural-policy-related projects in pursuit of cultural democracy and in support of community cultural self-study, representation, and folklife education.

As acknowledged by participants, organizers, corporate sponsors, and the Smithsonian Institution (as the US national museum) itself, the "Bermuda Connections" folklife festival program was a resounding success. The program was attended by almost 1 million visitors, more than ten times the population of the island itself. Many visitors to the Bermuda program made repeat visits; others came from across the United States and Canada to attend. Charter trips organized in Bermuda brought many visitors to the festival—including at least one group of Bermudian seniors. One woman drove three hours from Delaware to attend a session on the Veranda (narrative) stage.

From the participants in particular, a word heard quite often was that the experience of the "Bermuda Connections" program was "transformative." Bermudian participants and visitors alike expressed pleased astonishment at the depth and diversity of their culture as showcased at the festival. Especially poignant was the sentiment expressed by some that the "Bermuda Connections" program was the first occasion in which they had significant conversations with other Bermudians across ethnic and cultural lines. Minister of Community Affairs and Sport Randolph Horton, JP, MP, wrote in his message in the "Bermuda Homecoming" program book, "Bermuda's invitation to participate in the Smithsonian Folklife Festival was an honour. But for us it also came at an important time of self-evaluation and growth. Participating in the Festival provided us with an opportunity to develop answers to questions and the restaging enables us to continue a national conversation on who we are."

Many Bermudians feel that the history and community-based culture of everyday people has been undervalued, underrepresented, and undernourished. The wealth of hospitality and sociability that helped to hold the community together in the past has apparently given way to the demands of the marketplace. Although Bermudians place a high value on ties between family members and neighbors, the exigencies of the high cost of living in Bermuda have made it necessary for families to work long hours and to forgo many of the traditional social and cultural activities. The program goals were to identify, document, and showcase the folklife and local culture of Bermudians.

If the impact of the "Bermuda Connections" program had been restricted to the ten days on the Washington, DC, mall, it could be counted a success. However, for Bermudians to truly understand and take advantage of the

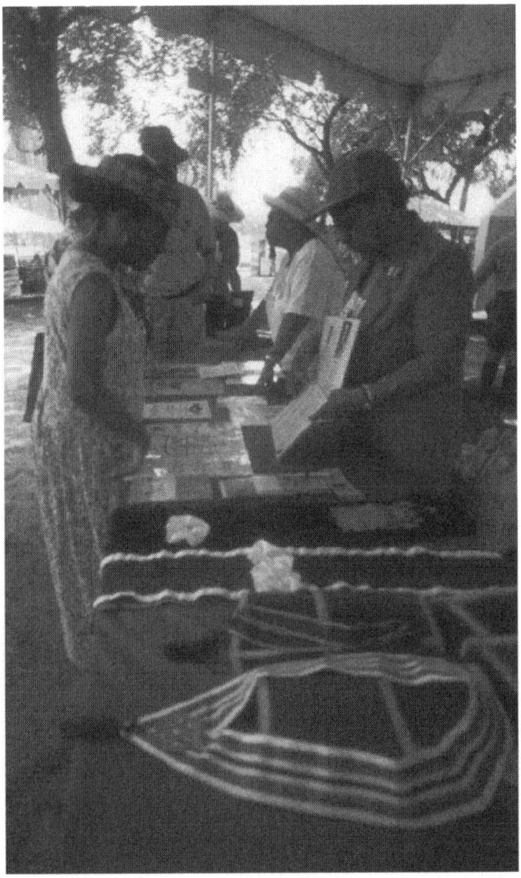

FIGURE 8.3
Participants share information and artifacts about the importance of family ties and the history of lodges organized by black Bermudians at "Bermuda Connections" program, 2001. (Photo: Copyright © Smithsonian Institution.)

potential of the program, it must be seen within the larger framework of its role in community cultural development on the island. Community cultural development involves the mobilization of culture in building community—the creation of cultural responses to social conditions. Its unifying principles, as articulated in a report commissioned by the Rockefeller Foundation titled "Creative Community: The Art of Cultural Development," are as follows:[7]

- Active participation in cultural life is an essential goal.
- All cultures are essentially equal.
- Diversity is a social asset, part of the cultural commonwealth.
- Culture is an effective crucible for social transformation.

- Cultural expression is a means of emancipation.
- Culture is a dynamic, protean whole.
- Artists (and I would add educators) have roles as agents of transformation.

Every aspect of the "Bermuda Connections" program, from the title of the program itself, to the choice of program themes, to the selection of participants, site design, and topics in the narrative sessions, was deliberately curated to address needs identified in the preliminary discussions with focus groups and in subsequent discussions with Bermuda's diverse constituencies.

The program set the building blocks for developing a new, inclusive cultural infrastructure for Bermuda. These building blocks included training of Bermuda nationals from varying walks of life in the concepts and methods of folklife fieldwork and presentation. This enabled Bermudian researchers to work as a team to survey Bermuda's local culture and living traditions; it also led to structured learning experiences for teachers at the summer seminar held during the festival and the subsequent development of classroom projects by Bermuda educators and the creation and gathering of materials for a Bermuda Folklife Archive containing fieldwork tapes and transcripts, still photography (slides), video, and audio tape of Bermudian tradition bearers at the Smithsonian Folklife Festival.

As projected in a proposal written prior to the festival,[8] Bermuda's participation in the 2001 Smithsonian Folklife Festival presented a range of opportunities for collaborative pedagogy, reciprocal learning, and support and recognition of Bermudian cultural resources and heritage, which extended beyond the time-limited framework of the ten-day festival itself. Some of these opportunities, such as the teacher institutes exploring local culture in the classroom and restaging of the festival program as the "Bermuda Homecoming," have already been implemented. The first "Bermuda Homecoming" in the spring of 2002 drew record attendance for the agricultural exhibition and led to an expansion and restructuring of the event. With the completion of *Bermuda Connections: A Cultural Resource Guide for Classrooms*, multicultural educational materials on Bermuda's cultural heritage, local history, and traditions, the Smithsonian's current commitment has now been fulfilled. Over the fifteen years since the "Bermuda Connections" festival program and the creation of the *Bermuda Connections: A Cultural Resource Guide for Classrooms* was created, Bermuda has established a folklorist within the Min-

FIGURE 8.4
Bermuda All-Star cricketers playing at the 2001 Smithsonian Folklife Festival. (Photo: Copyright © Smithsonian Institution.)

istry of Culture and Communications, an archive for Bermuda's community culture, and a cultural education website.

"THE WILL TO ADORN" PROJECT: CREATING DIGITAL COMMUNITIES OF CURATORIAL PRACTICE

"The Will to Adorn"[9] began with several ambitious goals. One goal was to bring attention to everyday dressing as a significant traditional expressive genre in African American culture—as a "folk art" with the same power and impact as music, foodways, and dance. Dress conveys powerful messages about values, beliefs, aspirations, and identities. Early in the course of the project we recognized that it was important to document not only the exemplars of style—those who had mastered the arts of dressing well—but also the master artisans, those who styled and cut hair, designed and made the articles of attire, or made them available for sale within their respective communities. The idea was to begin with the idea of sartorial autobiography, then to form study groups made up of scholars, educators, students, and cultural practitioners to document the arts of everyday dressing.

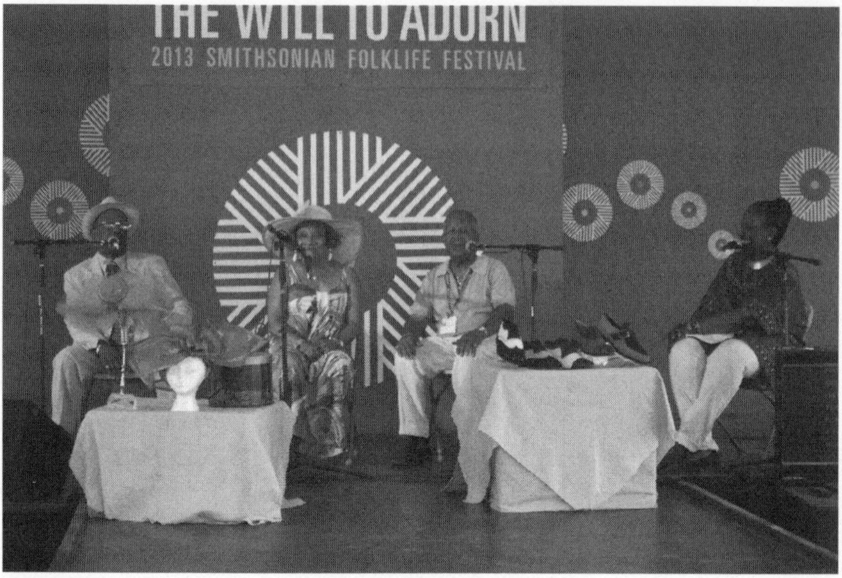

FIGURE 8.5
"The Will to Adorn" program artisans interviewed on stage, 2013. (Photo: Copyright © Smithsonian Institution.)

The Smithsonian Center for Folklife and Cultural Heritage initiated this research and community-engagement project in 2010. "The Will to Adorn: African American Dress and the Aesthetics of Identity" grew to involve the participation and support of several Smithsonian museums, including the nascent National Museum of African American History and Culture, the National Museum of African Art, and the Anacostia Community Museum. The project offered a framework for scholars, artists, students, parents, and educators in schools and community settings to explore dress as a form of expressive culture shared by communities. The pedagogical impact of the project is grounded in creating a way both to learn the tools of folklife research and also to contribute to the body of knowledge about folklife.

Nine teams of researchers in various locations—Atlanta, Detroit, Chicago, New York, Providence, Washington, DC, and the US Virgin Islands—mounted research and presentation projects to document local style. Muslim and Christian faith groups also documented body arts traditions—such as the application of henna designs and church hats. Januwa Moja, a designer/maker of African diaspora-influenced clothing, was inspired to create a collection that she presented in Cuba under the rubric of "The Will to Adorn." An arts group in Providence, AS220, worked with the youth in an after-school program to interview family members and to create videos, fashion shows, and new designs, and even worked with incarcerated youth, who created and curated photographic exhibitions of hairstyles and tattoos that preserved their privacy but showed their expressive culture. In New York's Mind-Builders, Inc., Dr. Beverly J. Robinson Community Folk Culture Program interns and youth assistants worked with the guidance of their talented instructor Jade Banks to both document and interview artisans of style at libraries and schools, and in San Francisco girls in the "Behind the Lens" summer program of the Museum of the African Diaspora documented their peers' histories of local style. The "Young Folklorists" group in Silver Spring, Maryland, a suburb of Washington, DC, presented their research in posterboard displays and readings at the Silver Spring International Festival. Several community forums at the Smithsonian drew crowds to talk about the larger social and cultural implications of style, heritage, and identity. The 2013 Folklife Festival was the largest but by no means the only convening curated around "The Will to Adorn" project.

In the ten years between the "Bermuda Connections" and "The Will to Adorn" projects, the access of ordinary people to the tools of research underwent a massive change. Virtually anyone can capture on a phone photographs and audio and video recordings that rival those produced by the most sophisticated equipment that is out of the reach of all but the most skilled researchers and documentarians. The ability to self-publish, to proactively record individual impressions of the world and opinions about self and other, has also mushroomed. The ability to represent one's culture and to comment on that of others (for better or worse) has led to the era of participatory museology. The accessibility of virtual sharing and convening through social media and online conferences—a major component of "The Will to Adorn" research methodology—has created multisited virtual museum collaborations. As artists, as well as historians, anthropologists, and folklorists, work within and with many "publics," the new community pedagogy challenges the traditional divisions between audience and participant in museums in "curating" the intangible aspects of culture. To paraphrase Pogo, we have met the curator, and it is us.

FIGURE 8.6
"The Will to Adorn" project screen shot. (Photo: Copyright © Smithsonian Institution.)

NOTES

1. Saltus 2003.

2. Horton 2002.

3. N'Diaye n.d.

4. Simon 2010; Adair, Filene, and Koloski 2011.

5. Zuill 2001.

6. Shuldiner 1993, 1–3.

7. Adams and Goldbard 2000.

8. N'Diaye 1999.

9. N'Diaye, forthcoming.

REFERENCES

Adair, Bill, Benjamin Filene, and Laura Koloski, eds. 2011. *Letting Go? Sharing Historical Authority in a User-Generated World.* Philadelphia: Pew Center for Arts & Heritage.

Freire, Paolo. 2006. *The Pedagogy of the Oppressed.* Translated by Myra Ramos. New York: Continuum.

Horton, K. H. Randolph. 2002. "Message from the Minister of Community Affairs and Sport." *Folklife Festival, 2002—Bermuda Connections: Homecoming,* edited by Jackie Aubrey. Hamilton: Bermuda Department of Community and Cultural Affairs.

N'Diaye, Diana Baird. Forthcoming. *The Will to Adorn: African American Identity and the Aesthetics of Adornment.* Jackson: Univeristy of Mississippi Press.

———. 2016. "The Will to Adorn: Style, Identity, Community." In *Curatorial Conversations,* edited by Olivia Cadaval, Sijin Kim, and Diana N'Diaye. Jackson: University of Mississippi Press.

———. 2003. "Preface: Why A Cultural Resource Guide for Bermuda?" In *Bermuda Connections: A Cultural Resource Guide for Classrooms,* edited by Diana Baird N'Diaye, 10–13. Washington, DC: Smithsonian Institution.

Saltus, Ethan. 2003. Interview by Charles Weber. *Bermuda Connections.* Pembroke, UK: Smithsonian Institution, Center for Folklife and Cultural Heritage, March.

Weber, Charles. 2003. *Bermuda Connections.* Digital video. Directed by Charles Weber. Produced by Smithsonian Center for Folklife and Cultural Heritage. Performed by Heather Whalen. Smtihsonian Institution, Folkways.

Zuill, William, Sr. 2001. "An Introduction to Bermuda." *Smithsonian Folklife Festival Program Book,* edited by Carla Borden, 16–23. Washington, DC: Smithsonian Institution.

9

Some New Thoughts on Applying Theory to Practice

Folklife and Today's History Museums

PATRICIA HALL

Patricia Hall advocates the application of several time-honored folkloristic concepts and theories to present-day historical museum programming, collecting, interpretation, and outreach. In discussing the relationship between history and folklore, she identifies ways in which folkloristic and historical approaches can complement each other and reminds us that because folklife exists in the past as well as the present, there are some natural commonalities. With an emphasis on practical applications aimed at museum and historical agency staff, some of whom may not have formal training in folklore and folklife, she explores twentieth- and twenty-first-century collecting, the "shrine" effect, text and context, interpreting sensitive topics, museum marketing, and technology-assisted community building. Drawing upon presentations made for the American Association of Museums, American Folklore Society, American Association for State and Local History (AASLH), Tennessee Association of Museums, and Kentucky Museums Association, Hall revisits concepts presented in her chapter in *Folklife and Museums: Selected Readings*[1] and suggests how folklife approaches—even at the hand of non-folklorists—can enhance museum programming, enliven and strengthen exhibits, broaden audience appeal, and better engage, educate, and entertain the diverse groups and communities—both actual and virtual—served by twenty-first-century history museums.

"So now I conclude that the role of the public historian is not as authority, but rather as a facilitator of useful storymaking based on fact, acknowledging that vastly different meanings can be assigned depending upon the perspective of individuals. All communities and societies, especially democratic ones, must have some story elements in common. Without shared stories, there is no basis for civic life and no basis for shared ambition and aspiration."

—Robert R. Archibald, 2004[2]

"In the future the authority that a museum claims will not be a function of the quality and authenticity of its collections nor its specialized content expertise. It will be secured by having a clean and distinctive mission that is well executed and relentless connectedness with its audiences in an atmosphere of mutual trust."

—Harold Skramstad, 2010[3]

"Something big shifted in our country in summer 2015. We now may be at a high-water mark for history organizations. Confronted by violent tragedy and simmering race relations, communities, politicians, and the media are engaged in vigorous debates about history's hold on the present. On a state-by-state, community-by-community basis, people are figuring out what history means in the context of today."

—John R. Dichtl, 2015[4]

Although the foregoing quotes do not specifically mention folklore or folklife, and come not from folklorists but rather from longtime leaders in the local history field, well-known for their visionary thinking and proactive follow-through, they hint at the following: folklife and history museums go together.

Throughout the twentieth century, folklorists and other cultural investigators had to argue, at times vehemently, for folklife's appropriateness as material suitable for collection, documentation, presentation, and interpretation by institutions designating themselves as *history* museums, not to mention having to staunchly defend folklore and folklife materials as deserving a place in the historical record. The same held true for the use of folkloristic methodologies.

Nevertheless, over the past half century, essential groundwork has been laid. In the academic sector, persuasive scholarship helped lay to rest arguments that a folklife emphasis isn't appropriate for a historical agency. And in the museum world, curators, researchers, exhibits specialists, and oral historians/fieldworkers have shown how effective the inclusion of folklife can be in carrying out their institutions' missions. Staffs in scores of large and small historical institutions/agencies (e.g., museums, historic sites, historical societies) have proven, in many different settings, how the inclusion of folklife (in both approach and subject matter) can enhance the programming, strengthen the mission, and broaden the visitor/member base of their institutions. Thanks to these scholars and practitioners, the idea that a history museum could present folklife no longer raises as many eyebrows as it once did.

Yet, there is still work to be done, as some of the old stumbling blocks remain. As we find ourselves at the beginning of a new millennium, staffs of museums with the word "history" or "historical" in their title may be more accepting of folklore's inclusion, yet still may not fully realize the untapped potential offered by a folklife "point of view" as they collect, document, interpret, and present their story. What follows are some suggestions on how a selection of folklife theories and approaches—some of them old, some of them new—can be put to use in a practical, hands-on fashion in the history museum.

In my chapter titled "A Case for Folklife and the Local Historical Society," in Simon Bronner's *American Material Culture and Folklife*, I pointed out ways in which a local historical society might incorporate folklife programming into its everyday activities. I stressed some ways in which folklife components might be added to existing programs such as exhibits, oral histories, and historic preservation, as well as programming for what we then referred to as "ethnic" audiences, while also taking account of the fact that more and more history museums were implementing programs that traveled out, far beyond the four walls of their facilities, to reach special audiences, often in their own environments. The time has come to reevaluate. In what ways can certain (some time-honored, some not) folkloristic approaches and methods be applied by history museum professionals, even if they are not formally trained in folklore and folklife—all with the goal of better delivering their museums' messages? Which might be most appropriate and useful, even for the small or modestly funded historical agency? Let's begin with a review of a key obstacle concerning folklife's inclusion in history museum programs.

THE HISTORICITY OF FOLKLIFE MATERIALS

Richard M. Dorson is an internationally recognized scholar and teacher in both the folklore and history fields. Throughout his career, he championed the two fields working together, underscoring the strong interdisciplinary link between folklife and history and proposing ways in which the two fields could find common ground. In his words, "How then can folklore be counted a handmaiden of history, rather than its most insidious foe? One answer lies in the conception of a fact. . . . [T]he historian reads the sources on both sides and all vantage points of the battle, or the political campaign, to reconstruct the story of what really happened. There is, however, another class of facts, in a way more solid because they are not hypostatized, and these are the traditional beliefs of a group of people as to what happened."[5]

In his many lectures, articles, and books, Dorson presented eloquent, persuasive arguments for how historians and folklorists can effectively work together to document and interpret the cultural past. To name only a few: "Oral Tradition and Written History: The Case for the United States" (1964), "Complementary Techniques and Concepts of the Folklorist and the Historian" (1967), *American Folklore and the Historian* (1971), *Folklore and Fakelore: Essays toward a Discipline of Folk Studies* (1976), and *Handbook of American Folklore* (1986). Since Dorson first wrote about folklore and history, other prominent historians and folklorists have taken up the cause, some suffering bruises and scratches along the way. In *Three Eyes on the Past* (1982), Louis C. Jones recounts the unexpected, scathing reaction he received from the president of the Schoharie, New York, historical society on a summer day in the 1930s, after addressing the annual meeting of the membership—a talk in which Jones "spoke in praise of the oral traditions of the area, the legends, ghostlore and witchcraft, beliefs and customs, songs and remedies of the farm people back in the valleys and the hunters and woodsmen in the cloves."[6]

The society's president was not amused, saying that Jones's talk had been "an insult to . . . the courageous men and women who had cleared this land, to regale them with the superstitions of the county riff-raff, the songs of drunkards, and the lies of lazy oafs who had never done an honest day's work in their lives."[7] Surprised and a bit chagrined, but also amused by this reaction, Jones took it in stride. And it was all that he needed to forge ahead, becoming an ardent, scholarly advocate for the marriage of local history and folklore.

However, despite the many who advocated folklife approaches as a way to more fully interpret history, the historicity of folklife data continued to be challenged by formal historians and other by-the-book scholars of the written word. And the challenge is not completely without merit. Many folkloric data are not the verifiable, factual information that historians seek in their quest to "set the record straight." Folklorists, in their study of culture, are concerned with folkloric truth—that is, what the individuals and groups they are studying believe to be the facts and why. Many academic historians feel that there is far too great a credibility gap between folkloric truth and historical fact for folklife to be considered reliable data.

Acknowledging the distinctions between folkloric truth and historical fact and understanding the value of each, history museum professionals can employ both to illustrate important ways in which people conceive of and interpret their own customs, beliefs, expressions, and behaviors. By presenting not only the verifiable facts about people, events, or artifacts, but also including the notions, beliefs, superstitions, and myths that shape people's lives, curators, exhibit specialists, and educators can arrive at a more well-rounded, multidimensional interpretation.

In his 1926 German-language book *Die folkloristische Arbeitsmethode* (translated into English as *Folklore Methodology* in 1971 by Roger L. Welsch), Finnish folklorist Kaarle Krohn put forth an investigative methodology he called "the folkloristic method." Although Krohn's work has been criticized by a number of modern-day scholars who came after him, several of his chapters explore the subjects of "faulty memory," "impulse toward expansion," and "laws of transformation" in an intriguing way. These could be of possible interest to a history museum curator who is mounting a program or exhibit focusing on facts and truth, memory and recollection, and how and why people tend to remember, misremember, forget, or embellish. All of this is to say that there can be some engaging folklife and history program ideas—folkloristic "prompts," if you will—tucked away in the oldest of scholarship.

Taking care to differentiate between historical fact and folkloric truth, history museum professionals can present interpretive exhibits and programs that go far beyond dates, names, and chronicled events. In his chapter "How to Interpret American Folklore Historically" (included in Dorson's *Handbook of American Folklore*), Lawrence Levine writes, "The historical use of folklore helps us to gain some sense of a people's angle of vision, to better understand the inner dynamics of a group and the attitudes of its members, and to comprehend the strategies and mechanisms a people employ to guard their values and maintain their sense of worth."[8]

It cannot be emphasized too much that folkloristic and historical approaches are not mutually exclusive and that educators or curators can benefit from using each approach at the appropriate time, taking care to make clear the different "lenses" through which they ask visitors to view the cultural information being presented. Several other excellent in-depth treatments of folklife's historicity can be found in Barbara Allen and Lynwood Montell's *From Memory to History* and in an article by William A. Wilson titled "Folklore and History: Fact amid the Legends."

TEXT AND CONTEXT

In 1966, in an article titled "Metafolklore and Oral Literary Criticism," Alan Dundes called for "fewer texts and more context." This article, a harbinger of what would become a growing movement in the folklore field, marked a theoretical and methodological shift away from the study of chiefly "products," "objects," or "texts" (i.e., tangible items of folklore) toward one focusing on "processes," "behaviors," or "contexts" (origins, surroundings, makers, production, use, and various meanings for makers, users, and participants).

In 1971, Dan Ben-Amos wrote "Toward a Definition of Folklore in Context," which succinctly described the importance of contextual studies. And in 1979, Jan Harold Brunvand's edited volume *Readings in American Folklore* (which also contained a reprint of Dundes's 1966 article) featured an entire section devoted to the topic of "folklore in context," including case study chapters by Roger Welsch, Linda Dégh, and Dorson, among others.

This emphasis on contextual approaches put folklorists on the path of documenting and interpreting culture in a more comprehensive way as they researched and ultimately placed value on "process," not just "products." Instead of studying only a ballad's words and music or a basket's shape and size, research included documenting the ongoing process of composing and singing the song or making and using the basket. The focus shifted from a study of things to a study of expressive behaviors.

More recently, Frank DeCaro addressed the subject of folklife in context from a different angle. In his 2013 book *Recycled: Old Traditions in New Contexts*, DeCaro presents case studies—some from long ago, others quite recent—in which people have reused and "repurposed" folk materials, customs, and beliefs in settings, circumstances, or arenas not thought of as being typically "folk" (for example, advertising, tourism, and promotion of regionalism or nationalism).

Pointing out that there are a number of reasons for this kind of recycling—among them, to redefine personal or ideological identity, to affirm and support unorthodox or not widely accepted beliefs about the past and present, and to feel more connected to and visibly supportive of groups and cultures other than one's own—DeCaro demonstrates how folklife can take on a broad array of meanings and values, depending on the context in which it is incorporated, used, presented, and valued. This kind of approach to materials and expressions could be full of possibility for museums mounting programs or exhibits that explore how traditional culture has, throughout history, functioned (and continues to function) in ways other than being simply "folk" survivals in a "folk" context.

This isn't to say that tangible items, objects, texts, and artifacts and architecture don't matter or are unimportant. No doubt, individual studies of an artifact yield vital and important information. But no cultural piece exists in a vacuum. The full story doesn't begin to emerge unless it can be shown how and why it got here, how it is used, and what meaning(s) it holds for its makers and users.

In his many book and articles on the subject, Simon Bronner speaks eloquently and specifically to the issue of material culture, stressing ways in which context-oriented inquiry and folklife fieldwork approaches can yield greater understanding of material things and their significance and meaning(s) for the communities from which they come or in which they are used. In his chapter "The Idea of the Folk Artifact," Bronner writes, "To understand objects and the relations they represent better, we need to keep the artifact in perspective. Know its sources and the ideas that lie encoded within the object's creation, design, and use. Know the diverse approaches to, and reasons for, unlocking the artifact's secrets. Recognize the applications to which 'object lessons' can be put. Realize the social and intellectual forces which impel analysts to hold the views they do."[9]

Today's history museums provide a tailor-made setting for the kind of contextual presentations folklorists have long advocated. And the current professional climate in museums couldn't be better. Learning about the values and beliefs of a people; becoming acquainted with the informal ways in which they interact and codify information; knowing the ways in which a given type of artifact, event, narrative, or behavior has evolved, changed, or stayed the same over several generations—all of these paths of inquiry shift history museums away from static interpretations toward seeking a much fuller, more intimate understanding.

In paying attention to interpretive context and presenting this kind of inclusive portrayal of both past and present, history museums can give much more to their audiences. Researchers and educators can present programs that quite literally surround visitors with material and sensual cues that tell the who, what, when, why, and how—stories that artifacts alone cannot impart. Even in the smallest and most modestly endowed history museums, curators and exhibit specialists can afford to accompany individual artifacts with related materials and interpretive aids that will enhance the visitor's understanding of origin, evolution, use, and meaning.

In their concern with context, both the folklorist and the history museum professional are seeking to achieve similar goals: better understanding of and enhanced ways to present and teach about human expressive behavior. With this commonly held goal, enlivened by slightly different perspectives, folklorists and history museum staffs are well equipped to collaborate on dynamic contextual presentations.

FOLKLIFE FIELDWORK AND THE HISTORY MUSEUM

Other contributors to this volume have expertly documented ways in which folklife-oriented fieldwork can enhance museum programming and interpretation. It stands to reason that an ethnographic approach that includes a folkloristic point of view will be of particular value to a museum or society that has the word "history" in its title. There are a number of good books available that address the planning and implementing of fieldwork. Some are theoretical; others are practical guidebooks; still others, a combination of both.

Some of these works about fieldwork include older references written from a folkloristic perspective. Among them are Kenneth Goldstein's *A Guide for Field Workers in Folklore*, Bruce Jackson and Sandy Ives's edited volume *The World Observed: Reflections on the Fieldwork Process*, Bruce Jackson's *Fieldwork*, Peter Bartis's *Folklife and Fieldwork: An Introduction to Field Techniques*, Barbara Allen and Lynwood Montell's *From Memory to History:*

Using Oral Sources for Historical Research, and Neil V. Rosenberg's edited volume *Folklore and Oral History*. Details about all of these are included in the "Sources" section at the end of this chapter.

Two notable books that tackle the subject of fieldwork from a history—more specifically *oral* history—perspective were written by Willa K. Baum. *Oral History for the Local Historical Society* had its genesis as a modest booklet, first published in 1969 by the American Association for State and Local History, with a foreword by then AASLH director William T. Alderson. The book (which in its revised form has become a classic) advises on how to launch a community-based oral history program and includes practical tips on interview techniques. Baum's second book, *Transcribing and Editing Oral History*, is a sequel. Initially published by AASLH in 1977, it speaks to the finer points of recorded interviewing and offers how-to advice on transcribing, processing, and indexing fieldwork data and how to negotiate the legalities of who owns what. Updated editions of both books are still available (see "Sources" section).[10]

Although technological advances have made all varieties of fieldwork, including oral historical, a whole new ballgame, these books—just a few of many—contain valuable insights for history museum staff members considering projects that will take them out in the field.

THE ESOTERIC-EXOTERIC FACTOR: A USEFUL CONCEPT FOR MUSEUMS

Because much folkloristic inquiry is aimed at the life, lore, creations, and behaviors of definable groups or communities, folklorists have concerned themselves with the differences between a group's perception of itself and its perception of other groups. In 1959, William Hugh Jansen of the University of Kentucky wrote a seminal piece about this phenomenon, titled "The Esoteric-Exoteric Factor in Folklore." This "self-and-other" contrast holds interesting possibilities for history museums as they present programs about groups and communities.

Jansen stressed that groups of people, almost universally, have specific beliefs about themselves and others, as well as what they suppose others think of them. Here is how Jansen defines his use of the terms "esoteric" and "exoteric": "The esoteric applies to what one group thinks of itself and what it supposes others think of it. The exoteric is what one group thinks of another and what it thinks that the other group thinks it thinks."[11] These beliefs may be conscious or unconscious, but to a great extent they shape interaction.

Museum research staff can benefit from understanding the esoteric-exoteric distinction as they reach conclusions about primary and secondary source material. The esoteric-exoteric distinction can also offer the museum educator or curator an excellent opportunity to teach ways in which traditions, stereotypes, and prejudices differ, depending on one's perception of oneself and of others, as well as ways in which intragroup and intergroup belief systems affect how individuals and groups relate to one another. The natural contrasts brought out through esoteric-exoteric analysis can lead to some exciting exhibits or programs exploring "points of view" in interpreting history and tackling current topics such as Internet communications (positive and negative), the effects of social media, and virtual communities.

MUSEUMS AS SHRINES AND CONTAGIOUS MAGIC

To keep current and competitive, today's history museums are spending thousands—sometimes millions—of dollars upgrading exhibits and revamping programs to be more inclusive and representative of their constituencies. Often, old exhibits, artifacts, and projects are swept out the door in favor of new, cutting-edge, and socially conscious interpretive programs and more focused collection policies. And with good reason. To remain responsive to the needs, outlooks, and values of the constituencies they serve, history museums realize their mission is not simply to amass artifacts and create programs of their own choosing, but also to adopt and implement a more democratic, inclusive mission that better meets the needs and desires of their visitors.

However, after going to such lengths to serve and educate more effectively and sensitively, many museums discover that visitors (often with children or grandchildren in tow) may sometimes come to the museum in search of the dusty case of Indian arrowheads or the taxidermy-preserved grizzly bear they remember from childhood—obsolete items that a museum may have deaccessioned or discarded years ago. Further, the same visitor who enthusiastically embraces the newest, most culturally sensitive exhibit or tech-enhanced demonstration still may want to be pointed in the direction of the cigar store Indian that made such an impression sixty or seventy years ago.

Folks love to revisit familiar artifacts that evoke memories. And they enjoy even more sharing these memories with progeny. It's human nature. By virtue of housing these special memorabilia and fondly remembered relics, a history museum can, among its other, loftier goals, function as a shrine for these visitors.

Just because people come looking for memory-provoking icons and nostalgia-laden oddities doesn't mean that museums ought to abandon efforts to improve and update programming or provide a better-informed, well-rounded interpretation. The shrine phenomenon does, however, shed light on a quest that is inherently human. We all want certain things to remain as we remember them—for ourselves and to share with our offspring. Certain museum artifacts or exhibits (interpreted or not!) can serve as memory-evoking, emotion-triggering touchstones.

Something else goes on as well. Proximity to certain artifacts (the closer the better, in some cases) can convey a special kind of magic. In this kind of intimate connection, we hope to absorb some of the artifact's significance and power—a kind of transference derived from the object's having been made or used or even slept in by someone we knew, admired, or wanted to feel closer to.

In thinking about this phenomenon, I also recalled a concept gleaned from superstition and belief studies—namely, the notion of "contagious magic." First presented years ago by Sir James G. Frazer in his twelve-volume Victorian masterpiece *The Golden Bough*, the term refers to the supernatural powers that can be transmitted through contact between magical objects and persons.

Though as enlightened members of modern society most of us profess to have moved beyond a conscious belief in the supernatural, it seems that the concept of contagious magic can help us understand present-day superstitions and feelings, particularly those concerning local and regional history. Contagious magic can help explain the undeniable appeal of certain "under-interpreted" artifacts, the popular famous-personality museums, and the "so-and-so slept here" historic sites. Objects and locations (even questionable or "tacky" ones) that were once in contact with or in use by someone special have the power to impart some of that specialness to a visitor or observer.

By acknowledging that museum visitors succumb occasionally to the shrine aspect of museumgoing and to the contagious-magic appeal of certain artifacts, history museum staff can more realistically evaluate visitor behavior that may seem to deviate from an ideal standard. Understanding this outcome can help museum staff incorporate the notion that sometimes a visitor's reasons for coming to a museum may reflect something other than a desire to be educated or enlightened.

FOLKLIFE AND THE RECENT PAST: COLLECTING AND INTERPRETING THE TWENTY-FIRST CENTURY

During the last half of the twentieth century, museum professionals began taking a special interest in collecting, documenting, and interpreting present-day life. Informed by the truism that "historical" doesn't necessarily imply "old" and motivated by the realities of rapid technological advances, artifact obsolescence, and the ephemeral, "throw-away" nature of many mass-produced items, museums began setting aside money and space to collect and house contemporary artifacts. Some of these items were acquired, quite literally, off the backs and out of the hands of their users and off the assembly lines on which they were produced.

In their urgency to responsibly collect representative contemporary cultural artifacts, many history museums focused primarily on amassing manufactured goods, mass-produced items, and industrial and technological artifacts—items that reflected a three-dimensional but by no means complete picture of so-called modern times. Not as much emphasis was placed on documenting the all-important "backstories"—the origin tales, customs, beliefs, and behaviors that surround and can lend meaning to tangible items. This somewhat myopic focus on just the products of the modern era can lead to missed opportunities to analyze and interpret such revealing subjects as high-tech factory worker shoptalk or the psychology behind "tainted fast food" urban legends.

Another pitfall is the artificial segregation of artifacts that are what is stereotypically thought of as "folk" from those that are felt to depict "modern times," acting from a belief that the two are entirely separate. Perhaps influenced by the age-old notion that folklife hails chiefly from bygone eras or rural cultures and by the premise that twentieth- and twenty-first-century life is, by nature, urban, industrial, technological, or mass-produced, many curators haven't considered folklife and the twenty-first century as at all related. But of course they are.

Folklife is ongoing and ever evolving; it exists in the present as well as the past; it can be found at neighborhood coffeehouses, in the offices of urban start-ups, and inside suburban school cafeterias; at church festivals, in mountain cabins, and on the porches of country stores. The folklorist's focus on both product and process, on tangible artifacts and expressive behaviors, can be adopted and adapted by history museum staff as they seek to broaden their contemporary collecting efforts and mount comprehensive exhibits and programs focusing on twenty-first-century life.

FOLKLIFE AND SOCIALLY CONSCIOUS SUBJECT MATTER

Folklife approaches can be particularly valuable as museums interpret today's most pressing social issues. Some of these subjects—including violence, discrimination, racial and ethnic bias, terrorism, cyberbullying, and other tragic events and traumatic legacies—are sensitive, potentially controversial subjects. The resulting programs and exhibits are provocative by nature and are likely to elicit personal and, in some cases, highly emotional reactions. A community-based, fieldwork-centered approach is one way to embrace these sensitive (and possibly "politically incorrect") subjects and can enable a museum to offer a more nuanced, engaging, and ultimately well-rounded interpretation that will encourage direct participation and enable both planners and visitors, presenters and audiences, to engage with each other in a personal, empathic way.

In her AASLH technical leaflet "Interpreting Difficult Knowledge," museum director Julia Rose suggests a strategy she calls Commemorative Museum Pedagogy, consisting of five stages of engagement—reception, resistance, repetition, reflection, and reconsideration—which, she argues, give museumgoers the time and resources to work through processing difficult subject matter. While also avoiding the pitfalls of objectifying and underscoring that all facts are questionable, all five stages of Rose's proposed framework intersect with the contextual approaches that folklorists use to focus on processes and expressive behaviors.

Heather Carver and Elaine Lawless provide a different kind of example for presenting and interpreting tough subjects. In their book *Troubling Violence: A Performance Project*, they chronicle how a performance troupe presents narrations of its members' own experiences with domestic violence and then engages audience members to join in. The book also focuses on the authors' own fieldwork and ethnographic writing as performances. This case study is an excellent example of performer/audience engagement and how performance can serve as a way to frame, present, and meaningfully document a program encompassing a highly personal topic.

The folklorist's tools and methods can also be adapted and applied by museums that are focusing on previously unacknowledged (and in some cases maligned) groups, whose histories and cultural contributions are just beginning to be recognized, documented, and interpreted in meaningful ways. Susan Ferentinos, in her book *Interpreting LGBT History at Museums and Historic Sites*, goes beyond simply calling for inclusion and acknowledgment of the LGBT community by museums, suggesting that museums underscore the long (and not just recent) multilayered histories of LGBT people and offer programming that encourages LGBT community members to tell their *own* stories as a way of engaging with a larger community legacy.

LOOKING TO THE FUTURE: MUSEUM MARKETING AND FOLKLIFE

As history museums fulfill their missions to develop and implement new, socially conscious programs, they continue to face the ongoing challenges of dwindling government and private funding sources, an ever-increasing number of real-life and virtual leisure-time competitors (including other museums), and never-ending economic belt-tightening. As a result, for the past four to five decades, history museums have had to adopt and adapt strategies long used in the business world. In short, the profession has made marketing a top priority. The design of programs to attract first-time and return visitors and the promotion and delivery of those programs to targeted and diverse audiences have become first orders of business for museums that want to *stay* in business.

According to Merriam-Webster, the first known use of the term "edutainment"—defined as "entertainment (as by games, films, or shows) that is designed to be educational"—occurred in 1973.[12] However, combining education and entertainment as a way of attracting and keeping museum visitors is not a new concept—not by a long shot. Museums have always been in the edutainment business, whether they recognized it or not.

According to Harold Skramstad, "From its beginnings, the great value of American museums has come from their diversity. It has always been a mix of collecting, inquiry and scholarship, entertainment and education."[13] Skramstad tells of late-eighteenth-century museum founder Charles Willson Peale of Philadelphia, who understood that museum objects and exhibits had to be systematically arranged, properly presented, and memorable (like his star "mammoth" mastodon). Says Skramstad, "As a businessman Peale was constantly juggling and balancing his serious collecting efforts and his entertainments in order to make his museum a financial success."[14]

P. T. Barnum (who founded his American Museum in 1841 in New York City) was another museum pioneer who knew the importance of attracting and keeping a visitor base and, according to Skramstad, "recognized in his visitors a deep curiosity, a need to know and understand things for themselves."[15]

This acknowledgment that museums can succeed by being a source of both learning and entertainment has carried through into modern times. In his 2010 master's thesis, "Entertaining the Public: To Educate the Public at Conner Prairie: Prairietown, 1975 to 2006," David B. Allison writes, "Taking a cue from a historical analysis of Conner Prairie's practices, other museums (and, to a large extent, the field of history in general) should realize that the most accurate information and authentic-seeming depictions of the past can fall on deaf ears and be ignored if not told in an engaging and entertaining way. The very survival of history's relevance in an age of declining attention spans and technological wizardry is in jeopardy. Historians have the obligation not only to tell the right stories, but to also to tell them so that people—young and old—will listen."[16]

Don Adams and John Boatright, in their 1986 article "The Selling of the Museum 1986," addressed the cultural and societal trends that museums might expect in their futures as they continued their marketing efforts. Strongly urging museums to develop specific communications strategies, Adams and Boatright also predicted certain demographic trends that could affect museums during the coming decades. And most have been borne out. Referencing predictions included in the *Yankelovich, Skelly, and White Monitor*, a widely read predictor of society's themes and patterns, Adams and Boatright forecasted, "There will be a sharp return to commitment and family. . . . There is evidence of an emerging trend toward old-fashioned ideas and nostalgia that should continue into the next decade. This is coupled with another finding showing a trend toward local identification."[17]

In his 2004 book *The New Town Square: Museums and Communities in Transition*, Robert Archibald addresses the ongoing human need for an archetypal village-style gathering place, where modern people can feel a sense of old-fashioned camaraderie and communion with one another, as well as opportunities for story sharing and community building. He suggests ways in which museums and historians can work to champion such a concept and what roles they can play in helping visitors and nonvisitors alike participate in and benefit from these shared experiences. His emphases on "the process of storymaking;" the value of "shared stories," even if they have vastly different meanings and "creates room for diverse and multiple perspectives,"[18] certainly resonate with the goals of folklife inquiry. The kind of community building and sharing Archibald advocates most certainly could be enhanced and enriched by the insights and methodologies of folklife.

It seems that every time an era has been marked by rapid industrial and/or technological change, there has been a predictable and understandable swing back to more traditional values and nostalgic touchstones, accompanied by the attendant hunger for a sense of place. Be it seeking out activities to feel closer to one's own geography, heritage, and ethnicity; giving in to the urge to "nest" in a chosen "home place"; or gathering in a real or virtual version of the type of town square that Robert Archibald describes, modern folk (quite possibly with gadgets or devices in hand) are intent on seeking out their own personal and family spaces as well as their own special gathering spots—their very own groups and communities.

The times we live in raise some important questions regarding collective identity. What are the many ways in which the Internet and social media (for example, Facebook, Twitter, LinkedIn, and Instagram) have changed the meaning of what constitutes a "group" or "community"? And what is the impact of these new "groups" on how folklorists and history professionals study and interpret human behavior? These are issues of increasing urgency and relevance in a twenty-first-century global village.

Cyberspace, the technological revolution, and the media have added a new dimension to family-centered and legacy-oriented leisure-time pursuits. Predictably, programs and services have sprung up that speak to and nurture the modern-day yearning for a "return to roots." A few of the many include StoryCorps (www.storycorps.org), a public, roving oral-history project; the Moth (www.themoth.org), a New York City–based group that offers storytelling events throughout the United States, as well as podcasts, and has even spun off an NPR program, the *Moth Radio Hour*; and *This American Life* (www.thisamericanlife.org), first a television show and now a radio show hosted by Ira Glass. Add to that the variety of web-based offerings, including

Ancestry.com (www.ancestry.com), one of many online genealogy search/research sites that also offer links to other members' family trees, and 23 & Me (www.23andme.com), featuring not only do-it-yourself, mail-order DNA genetic testing and analysis, but also online links to other genetically related family members. These kinds of programs and services yield important, "real-time" insights about what folks want and how they like it delivered. From a marketing standpoint, this kind of information can be invaluable as a history museum plans and implements cutting-edge programs designed to get more people in the door, both literally and virtually.

Since the 1980s, when Adams and Boatright first commented on what seemed to be a return to local and family identification, there has been much written, from both within and outside the museum field, regarding the importance of targeted museum marketing and how it can help attract visitors and involve them in museum programming. Museums have enlisted focus groups to provide important demographic data and evaluative material. More recently, programs like AASLH's "Visitors Count" (put in place to help history museums gather, analyze, and process information about visitor behaviors, expectations, and preferences) have come available. If staffs and board members heed the results of programs like these and sincerely subscribe to the value of a visitor- and constituency-driven mission, all the more reason to incorporate well-chosen, relevant folklife subjects and methods that can aid in the design and implementation of programs and services people will like and use.

IN CONCLUSION

There is little doubt that the kinship between folklife and history museums, if nurtured, can sustain itself and endure as a strong and valuable partnership—one that makes not only good cultural and interpretive sense, but also sound economic sense. The undeniable traditional and commercial appeal of folklife, its value as a welcoming "portal" though which to explore, learn about, and participate in one's own and others' cultural lives, and its reliability as an irresistible source of entertainment all call for folklife's inclusion as a part of a history museum's DNA. The approaches, strategies, and methods borrowed from folklife studies and folkloristic scholarship can contribute not only to better educational offerings but also to increased visitation and larger, more diverse member rolls—and ultimately to the kind of community support and participation that provides the financial stability required to keep history museum doors open well into the twenty-first century.

NOTES

1. Patricia Hall and Charlie Seemann, eds., *Folklife and Museums: Selected Readings* (Nashville: AASLH Press, 1987).

2. Robert R. Archibald, "Introduction: The Past as Context." In *The New Town Square: Museums and Communities in Transition* (American Association for State and Local History series). Walnut Creek, CA: Altamira Press, 2004, 13.

3. Harold Skramstad, "An Agenda for Museums in the 21st Century." Ann Arbor, MI: University of Michigan: Working Papers in Museum Studies, no. 1 (2010), 6.

4. John R. Dichtl, "Moving History from Nice to Essential," *AASLH History News* 70, no. 4 (Autumn 2015): 7.

5. Richard M. Dorson, *American Folklore and the Historian* (Chicago: University of Chicago Press, 1971), 147.

6. Louis C. Jones, *Three Eyes on the Past: Exploring New York Folk Life* (Syracuse, NY: Syracuse University Press, 1982), xi.

7. Ibid, xii.

8. Lawrence Levine, "How to Interpret American Folklore Historically," in *Handbook of American Folklore*, ed. Richard M. Dorson (Bloomington: Indiana University Press, 1986), 343.

9. Simon J. Bronner, ed., *American Material Culture and Folklife: A Prologue and Dialogue*, American Material Culture and Folklife Series (Logan: Utah State University Press, 1992), 36.

10. Willa Baum was a pioneer in the field of oral history, founding the University of California, Berkeley's Oral History Program, which later became the Regional Oral History Office under her directorship. Although she held undergraduate and graduate degrees in history and considered herself, first and foremost, a historian, Baum participated as a faculty member in several folklore and history AASLH seminars and was always open to discourse with folklorists regarding shared approaches and fieldwork techniques in the gathering and interpretation of oral historical material. In this way, she was a model scholar-practitioner who recognized what the fields of history and folklore could lend to each other.

11. William Hugh Jansen, "The Esoteric-Exoteric Factor in Folklore," in *The Study of Folklore*, ed. Alan Dundes (Englewood Cliffs, NJ: Prentice Hall, 1965), 46.

12. "Edutainment," Merriam-Webster.com.

13. Skramstad, "An Agenda for American Museums in the 21st Century."

14. Ibid, 1.

15. Ibid, 1.

16. David B. Allison, "Entertaining the Public: To Educate the Public at Conner Prairie: Prairietown, 1975 to 2006" (unpublished master of arts thesis, Indiana University, December 2010), 97 (https://scholarworks.iupui.edu/bitstream/handle, accessed May 19, 2016).

17. G. Donald Adams and John Boatright, "The Selling of the Museum 1986," *Museum News* 64, no. 4 (April 1986): 17–18.

18. Robert R. Archibald, *The New Town Square: Museums and Communities in Transition*, American Association for State and Local History Series (Walnut Creek, CA: AltaMira Press, 2004), 13–14.

SOURCES CITED AND RECOMMENDED READING

Adams, Donald, and John Boatright. 1986. "The Selling of the Museum 1986," *Museum News* 64, no. 4 (April).

Allen, Barbara, and Lynwood Montell. 1982. *From Memory to History: Using Oral Sources for Historical Research.* Nashville: AASLH.

Allison, David B. 2010. "Entertaining the Public: To Educate the Public at Conner Prairie: Prairietown, 1975 to 2006." Unpublished master of arts thesis, Department of History, Indiana University (https://scholarworks.iupui.edu/bitstream/handle).

Archibald, Robert R. 2004. *The New Town Square: Museums and Communities in Transition.* American Association for State and Local History Series. Walnut Creek, CA: AltaMira Press.

Bartis, Peter. [1979] 2002. *Folklife and Fieldwork: An Introduction to Field Techniques.* Washington, DC: American Folklife Center.

Baum, Willa K. 1991. *Transcribing and Editing Oral History.* American Association for State and Local History Series. Lanham, MD: Rowman & Littlefield (AltaMira Press/AASLH).

———. 1995. *Oral History for the Local Historical Society*. American Association for State and Local History Series. 3rd ed. Lanham, MD: Rowman & Littlefield (AltaMira Press/AASLH).

Ben-Amos, Dan. 1971. "Toward a Definition of Folklore in Context." *Journal of American Folklore* 84.

Bronner, Simon J., ed. 1992. *American Material Culture and Folklife: A Prologue and Dialogue*. American Material Culture and Folklife Series. Logan: Utah State University Press.

———. 2004. *Grasping Things: Folk Material Culture and Mass Society*. Lexington: University Press of Kentucky.

Brunvand, Jan Harold. 1979. *Readings in American Folklore*. New York: W. W. Norton.

———. 1986. *The Study of American Folklore: An Introduction*. 3rd ed. New York: W. W. Norton.

Carver, M. Heather, and Elaine J. Lawless. 2010. *Troubling Violence: A Performance Project*. Jackson: University Press of Mississippi.

DeCaro, Frank. 2013. *Folklore Recycled: Old Traditions in New Contexts*. Jackson: University Press of Mississippi.

Dichtl, John R. 2015. "Moving History from Nice to Essential." *AASLH History News* 70, no. 4 (Autumn).

Dorson, Richard M. 1964. "Oral Tradition and Written History: The Case for the United States." *Journal of the Folklore Institute* 1, no. 3 (December) (offprint).

———. 1967. "Complementary Techniques and Concepts of the Folklorist and the Historian." Transcript of a paper prepared for the "Folklore and Social Science" conference, Wenner-Gren Foundation for Anthropological Research, Inc., November 10–11, sponsored by the Social Science Research Council.

———. 1971. *American Folklore and the Historian*. Chicago: University of Chicago Press.

———. 1976. *Folklore and Fakelore: Essays toward a Discipline of Folk Studies*. Cambridge, MA: Harvard University Press.

———, ed. 1986. *Handbook of American Folklore*. Bloomington: Indiana University Press.

Dundes, Alan. 1965. *The Study of Folklore*. Englewood Cliffs, NJ: Prentice Hall.

Ferentinos, Susan. 2014. *Interpreting LGBT History at Museums and Historic Sites*. AASLH Interpreting History Series. Lanham, MD: Rowman & Littlefield Publishers/AASLH.

Frazer, Sir James. 1980. *The Golden Bough*. Rev. ed. New York: St. Martin's Press.

Georges, Robert A., and Michael Owen Jones. 1980. *People Studying People: The Human Element in Fieldwork*. Berkeley: University of California Press.

Goldstein, Kenneth S. 1964. *A Guide for Field Workers in Folklore*. Hatboro, PA: Folklore Associates, Inc.

Hall, Patricia. 1992. "A Case for Folklife and the Historical Society." In *American Material Culture and Folklife: A Prologue and Dialogue*, edited by Simon J. Bronner. American Material Culture and Folklife Series. Logan: Utah State University Press.

Hall, Patricia, and Charlie Seemann, eds. 1987. *Folklife and Museums: Selected Readings*. Nashville: AASLH Press.

Jackson, Bruce. 1987. *Fieldwork*. Urbana: University of Illinois Press.

Jackson, Bruce, and Edward D. Ives, eds. 1996. *The World Observed: Reflections on the Fieldwork Process*. Folklore and Society Series. Urbana: University of Illinois Press.

Jones, Louis C. 1982. *Three Eyes on the Past: Exploring New York Folk Life*. Syracuse, NY: Syracuse University Press.

Krohn, Kaarle. 1971. *Folklore Methodology: Formulated by Julius Krohn and Expanded by Nordic Researchers*, translated by Roger L. Welsch. Austin: University of Texas Press.

Rose, Julia. 2011. *Interpreting Difficult Knowledge*. AASLH Technical Leaflet #255. Nashville: AASLH.

Rosenberg, Neil V., ed. 1978. *Folklore and Oral History*. Memorial University of Newfoundland Folklore and Language Publication Series—Bibliographical and Special Series No. 3. St. John's, Newfoundland: Memorial University of Newfoundland.

Skramstad, Harold. 2010. "An Agenda for American Museums in the 21st Century." Working Papers in Museum Studies 1. Ann Arbor: University of Michigan.

Weitzman, David. 1976. *Underfoot: An Everyday Guide to Exploring the American Past*. New York: Charles Scribner's Sons.

Wilson, William A. 1979. "Folklore and History: Fact amid the Legends." In *Readings in American Folklore*, edited by Jan Brunvand. New York: W. W. Norton.

10

From Ethnology to Heritage

The Role of the Museum

Barbara Kirshenblatt-Gimblett

The very role of museums in communities continues to be redefined in the twenty-first century. One of the leading scholars of museum theory and practice, Barbara Kirshenblatt-Gimblett, offers keen insights into the movement by many contemporary museums that are embracing a focus on a new understanding of heritage to replace conventional ethnology. She effectively traces museum practice in the nineteenth and early twentieth centuries, when there was what she terms a "close fit between ethnology as a knowledge formation, collections, and museums." Today, she argues, museums are reinventing themselves as agents of heritage. She addresses the need for careful self-reflection on ideas such as the following: heritage is metacultural; tangible needs to be connected with intangible heritage; repudiation is an enabling condition; ethnology's heritage needs to be assessed; and the museum's heritage must be reimagined. She also points out the kinds of skills that are needed by museums today and how folklorists and cultural specialists can help with this transition. Kirshenblatt-Gimblett makes the case that the very notion of heritage is a mode of cultural production that creates something new and that museums should embrace this perspective in the twenty-first century. This chapter is based on a keynote lecture presented at the International Society for Ethnology and Folklore Conference in Marseille, France, in 2004.

During the nineteenth and early twentieth centuries, there was a close fit between ethnology as a knowledge formation, collections, and museums, whether museums of natural history or ethnology or *Völkerkunde* or *Volkskunde* or *les arts et traditions populaires*. The museum was the home for these fields, indeed for any field whose research produces and requires collections, including archaeology, biology, and geology, among others. During the twentieth century and especially after World War II, the situation changed, as the knowledge formations, in our case ethnology, moved into the university, leaving their collections behind. Museums became custodians of the collections of outmoded scientific disciplines. In reinventing themselves, museums have become agents of "heritage."

My remarks are organized around the following themes:

- Heritage as metacultural
- Tangible and intangible heritage
- Repudiation as an enabling condition
- Ethnology's heritage
- The museum's heritage

HERITAGE AS METACULTURAL

I define heritage as a mode of cultural production that has recourse to the past and produces something new. Heritage as a mode of cultural production adds value to the outmoded by making it into an exhibition of itself. Central to my argument is the notion that heritage is created through metacultural operations that extend museological values and methods (collection, documentation, preservation, presentation, evaluation, and interpretation) to living persons, their knowledge, practices, artifacts, social worlds, and life spaces. Heritage professionals use concepts, standards, and regulations to bring cultural phenomena and practitioners into the heritage sphere, where they become metacultural artifacts, whether "Living National Treasures" or "Masterpieces of the Oral and Intangible Heritage of Humanity." At the same time, the performers, ritual specialists, and artisans whose "cultural assets" become heritage through this process experience a new relationship to those assets, a metacultural relationship to what was once just habitus. Habitus refers here to the taken for granted, while heritage refers to the self-conscious selection of valued objects and practices. The power of heritage is precisely that it is curated, which is why heritage is more easily harmonized with human rights and democratic values than is culture. The United Nations Educational, Scientific, and Cultural Organization (UNESCO) stipulates that only those aspects of culture that are compatible with such values can be considered for world heritage designation.

Unlike things, animals, and plants, people are not only objects of cultural preservation but also subjects. They are not only cultural carriers and transmitters (the terms are unfortunate, as is "masterpiece") but also agents in the heritage enterprise itself. What the heritage protocols do not generally account for is a conscious, reflexive subject. UNESCO's declaration and conventions on intangible heritage speak of collective creation. Performers are carriers, transmitters, and bearers of traditions, terms that connote a passive medium, conduit, or vessel, without volition, intention, or subjectivity.

Living archive and living library are common metaphors. Such terms assert not a person's right to what they do but rather their role in keeping the culture going (for others). According to this model, people come and go, but culture persists, as one generation passes it along to the next. But all heritage interventions—like the globalizing pressures they are trying to counteract—change the relationship of people to what they do. They change how people understand their culture and themselves. They change the fundamental conditions for cultural production and reproduction. Needless to say, change is intrinsic to culture, and measures intended to preserve, conserve, safeguard, and sustain particular cultural practices are caught between freezing the practice and addressing the inherently processual nature of culture.

Heritage interventions attempt to slow the rate of change. *The Onion*, a humor newspaper in the United States with a national readership, published a satirical article titled "U.S. Dept. of Retro Warns: 'We May Be Running Out of Past.'"[1] The article quotes US Retro Secretary Anson Williams: "If current levels of U.S. retro consumption are allowed to continue unchecked, we may run entirely out of past by as soon as 2005," and "We are talking about a potentially devastating crisis situation in which our society will express nostalgia for events which have yet to occur." In support of these predictions, the article explains, "The National Retro Clock currently stands at 1990, an alarming 74 percent closer to the present than ten years ago, when it stood at 1969." As the retro clock speeds up, life becomes heritage almost before it has a chance to be lived, and heritage fills the life space.

The asynchrony of historical, heritage, and habitus clocks (and in particular the differential temporalities of things, persons, and events) produces a paradox, namely, *the possession of heritage as a mark of modernity*, which is the very condition of possibility for the world heritage enterprise. The contemporaneous becomes—or, rather, is at one and the same time—contemporary, to invoke the distinction made by Johannes Fabian in *Time and the Other*.[2] The dilemma for projects to safeguard intangible heritage, which requires human actors to commit themselves to embodying the knowledge, so designated, and to maintaining embodied practices, is how to reconcile the valorization of customary practices with a program of personal and social transformation. The result is a transvaluation that "preserves" custom without preserving the "custom-bound" self. Indeed, heritage becomes a resource in the project of fashioning the self.[3]

TANGIBLE AND INTANGIBLE HERITAGE

Museums, while repositories of tangible heritage in the form of artifact collections, have always had to address the intangible aspects of culture—indigenous knowledge, belief systems, techniques of the body, performance. And as those creating world heritage policy now realize, particularly within UNESCO, the division between tangible, natural, and intangible heritage is arbitrary, though not without its history and logic. Nonetheless to designate embodied knowledge and practices "intangible" is to define them by what they are not (they are *not* tangible) and to maintain the primacy of tangibility as an organizing concept in heritage theory and practice. That said, those dealing with natural heritage increasingly argue that most of the sites on the world natural heritage list are what they are by virtue of human interaction with the environment. Similarly, tangible heritage, without intangible heritage, is a mere husk or inert matter, objects that are not yet things.[4] As for intangible heritage, it is not only embodied but also inseparable from persons and their material and social worlds. "Africa loses a library when an old man dies," a quotation from Amadou Hampâté Bâ, appears on the opening page of UNESCO's Intangible Heritage page.[5] While affirming the person, the library metaphor confuses archive and repertoire, a distinction that is particularly important to an understanding of intangible heritage as embodied knowledge and practice. In contrast with the tangible heritage protected in the museum, intangible heritage consists of cultural manifestations (knowledge, skills, performance) that are inextricably linked to persons. It is not possible—or it is not as easy—to treat such manifestations as proxies for persons, even with recording technologies that can separate performances from performers and consign the repertoire to the archive.

According to Diana Taylor, the repertoire is always embodied and is always manifested in performance, in action, in doing.[6] The repertoire is passed on through performance. This is different from recording and preserving documentation of the repertoire in the archive. The repertoire is about embodied knowledge and the social relations for its creation, enactment, transmission, and reproduction. It follows, according to UNESCO, that intangible heritage is particularly vulnerable precisely because it is intangible, although the historical record does not necessarily bear this out. Though the situation today is of a different order, Australian aborigines maintained their "intangible heritage" for over thirty thousand years without the help of cultural policy, and the monumental Bamiyan Buddhas were reduced to dust in an instant.

While the categories of tangible and intangible heritage distinguish things from events (and from knowledge, skills, and values), even things are events. First, as existential philosopher Stanley Eveling has remarked, "A thing is a slow event." This is a perceptual issue. The perception of change is a function of the relationship between the actual rate of change and "the windows of our awareness."[7] Things are events, not inert or deteriorating substances, in other senses as well. A thing can be an "affecting presence," in the words of Robert Plant Armstrong.[8]

Moreover, many things are renewable or replaceable under specified conditions. Every twenty years, the wooden sanctuaries at Ise Jingū, a sacred shrine in Japan, are rebuilt. The process takes about eight years, and the shrine has been rebuilt sixty-one times since the first rebuilding in 690. Known as *shikinen sengu*, this tradition involves not only construction but also ceremony and transmission of specialized knowledge: "The carpentry work is carried out by about one hundred men, the majority of whom are local carpenters who set aside their usual work for a privileged period of two to four years. No nails are used in the entire structure. Although the plans exist for every structure, the master carpenters must remember and pass on to apprentices their expert knowledge of how to put together the complex joints, using ancient and unfamiliar tools."[9] This shrine represents "2000 Years of History, Yet Never Gets Older Than 20." Ise Jingū is a slow event.

FIGURE 10.1
Installation of the painted ceiling and reader's platform of the wooden synagogue based on the one that once stood in Gwoździec, today in Ukraine. (Photo: Magdalena Starowieyska and Darek Golik, courtesy of the POLIN Museum of the History of Polish Jews.)

As the Ise Jingū shrine demonstrates, intangibility and evanescence, which are, after all, conditions of all experience, should not be confused with disappearance or extinction.

This is a case of misplaced concreteness or literal thinking. Conversations are intangible and evanescent, but that does not make the phenomenon of conversation vulnerable to disappearance. This is true of much that is considered intangible heritage—namely, performances of all kinds. On the contrary, it could be said that because they cannot be collected, in the way that objects can be collected, because they cannot be preserved, in the way that a house can be preserved, meals and stories and songs have to be done—they have to be performed—over and over again. Indeed, the willed ephemerality of things—the destruction of the Ise Jingū shrine, for example, and commitment to rebuilding it every twenty years—intensifies the need

FIGURE 10.2
Painting workshop in the White Stork Synagogue, Wrocław, summer 2012. None of the great wooden synagogues created in the seventeenth and eighteenth centuries in the historical territory of the Polish-Lithuanian Commonwealth has survived. The last of them were destroyed during the Holocaust. The Association of the Jewish Historical Institute of Poland, the organization responsible for creating the core exhibition at the POLIN Museum of the History of Polish Jews in Warsaw, had always planned to include a wooden synagogue in the gallery dedicated to the eighteenth century. Rather than commission a theater prop company to make a copy, the association partnered with Handshouse Studio, an educational nonprofit in Massachusetts, whose mission is to recover lost objects. Laura and Rick Brown, founders of Handshouse Studio, explain that while you may never be able to recover the original object in the sense of the original material, the tangible heritage, you can recover the knowledge of how to build it, the intangible heritage, by using traditional materials, tools, and techniques. "That is precisely what we did, together with a team of over 300 volunteers and expert timber-framers, conservationists, architectural historians, and specialists in the history of Polish Jews. We chose the synagogue that once stood in Gwoździec, today in Ukraine. This synagogue was created during the 1650s, renovated in the 1720s, and destroyed during World War I, but it happens to be the best documented of the hundreds of wooden synagogues that once stood in the historic territory of the Polish-Lithuanian Commonwealth. What we created is not a copy, facsimile, reproduction, or re-creation—it is an actual object, a new kind of object, whose value lies not in the materials from which it was made but in the knowledge that was recovered from the way it was made." This approach is reminiscent of the ancient Ise Grand Shrine [Ise Jingū], which is dismantled and rebuilt every twenty years in order to keep alive and transmit the embodied knowledge of how to build it. This knowledge, this intangible heritage, is valued more highly than the original material. (Photo: Handshouse Studio.)

to maintain the embodied knowledge, the practices, that are required for making it in the first place. Ephemerality gives to things their processual and eventful character, while evanescence is the enabling condition for performing over and over again, which is itself the enabling condition for the maintenance, transmission, and reproduction of embodied knowledge. The principle: use it or lose it.

FIGURE 10.3
Timber-framing workshops on the site of the Folk Architecture Museum, Sanok, summer 2011. (Photo: Ed Levin.)

FIGURE 10.4
(Photo: Handshouse Studio.)

Finally, the possession of heritage—as opposed to the way of life that heritage safeguards—is an instrument of modernization and mark of modernity. "To have no museums in today's circumstances is to admit that one is below the minimum level of civilization required of a modern state." Indeed, museums are one instrument for the "safeguarding" of heritage, as understood by UNESCO. Safeguarding, it should be noted, requires specialized skills that are different from the practices that are to be safeguarded. There is a difference between doing the practice and doing something about it, between performing a song and recording it. Safeguarding efforts produce heritage workers, who may or may not also be heritage practitioners.

While persistence in old lifeways may not be economically viable and may well be inconsistent with economic development and with national ideologies, the valorization of those lifeways as heritage (and the integration of heritage into economies of cultural tourism) is economically viable and consistent with economic development theory and can be brought into line with national ideologies of cultural uniqueness and modernity. Fundamental to this process is the heritage economy as a modern economy. For this and other reasons, *heritage may well be preferred to the preheritage culture that it is intended to safeguard.* Such is the case at the Polynesian Cultural Center in Hawai'i, a Mormon operation where, since 1963, students at Brigham Young University, Hawaii, "keep alive and share their island heritage with visitors while working their way through school."[10]

REPUDIATION AS AN ENABLING CONDITION

Such cases point to the troubled history of museums and heritage as agents of deculturation, as the final resting place for evidence of the success of missionizing and colonizing efforts, among others, that preserve (in the museum) what was wiped out (in the community). Today's museums and heritage interventions may attempt to reverse course, but there is no way back, only a metacultural way forward.

The operations just described are the enabling conditions for the field of ethnology and for the museums dedicated to this science. This is a story of alienation, detachment, and repudiation thanks to the civilizing, colonizing, missionizing, reformation, and revolutionary projects that produce cultural outtakes in the form of dispositions and practices whose very outmodedness has made them safe for handling, studying, and display. We have here what Steven Mullaney calls the rehearsal of culture, by which he means the foreclosure of what is collected and displayed. This is the enabling condition for ethnology, its collections, and their display. *The enabling condition is willed disappearance through a process of removal, followed by the display of what has been made to disappear, as a foreclosure of it.*

This is a first step in an ongoing process of devaluation and revaluation, a process that alters the world by purging it of objects associated with pagan religions, primitive peoples, Catholicism, and subsistence lifestyles, in the name of salvation, civilization, Protestantism, and economic development, as in the case of the Congo, as described by Lotten Gustafsson in her paper at this conference on the twelve thousand Congo objects collected by the Swedish Missionary Society for the Swedish National Museum of Natural Science at the turn of the century. There, as in the Torres Strait and elsewhere, missionaries had the islanders pile their sacred objects in a heap and set them on fire, after reserving some of them for museums in Europe. Removal of objects was one step in the process of stripping subject peoples of their culture in order to convert them, modernize them, or otherwise transform them in a grand rite of separation. Ethnology, as the handmaiden of colonialism, was governed not only by intellectual concerns internal to the discipline but also by the practical concerns of better administering by studying those who were to be governed.

The success of these efforts produced a kind of crisis for ethnology to the degree that it created a disappearing subject, decimated both demographically and culturally. Imminent disappearance, an ever-advancing eleventh hour, energized salvage anthropology and a revaluation of that which was sufficiently endangered to be safe for appreciation. Salvage anthropologists, particularly those who studied Native Americans, rushed to salvage what remained, that is, to record and collect, this time in the spirit of preserving in the museum and the archive, what was disappearing in the world. *Disappearance was and continues to be an enabling condition.*

ETHNOLOGY'S HERITAGE

Heritage, it could be said, is the opposite of ethnology. Heritage is predicated on a different set of claims. But ethnology is deeply implicated in the production of heritage, first, for the historical reasons outlined above—its role in making culture disappear and then salvaging what remains—and, second, because of ethnology's own complicated relationship to its own past.

There is a double move here, two alienations. The first alienation occurs when ethnology makes culture disappear in the world and reappear, as ethnology, in the museum. The second alienation occurs when ethnology repudiates its own history, particularly as a museum field and in the museum itself.

Shame and its other face, moral indignation, are enabling conditions to the degree that they create a relationship, a strong affective and moral relationship, to that which has become a marker of ethnology's spoiled identity. In remaking itself, ethnology had to remake its relationship to its own past as well as to the present of the people it had studied.

Shifts in ethnology as a discipline—less interest in the tangible (material culture), more interest in the intangible and the theoretical—brought about a disarticulation of what was once a tight integration of knowledge formation, collection, and museum. These shifts also produced a peculiar asynchrony, as ethnology shifted from the museum to the university, forged ahead with its theories, enlarged its field of inquiry to include contemporary society, and, in a postcolonial era, faced its problematic past, while museums became the custodians of the collections and displays of an outmoded ethnology—that is, museums of ethnology became museums of ethnology's own "heritage." The devaluation of the scientific value of ethnographic collections—as ethnology moves on to other concerns—prepares the way for their revaluation as heritage, in a double sense: the heritage of those from whom those objects were taken and the heritage of ethnology itself.

Consider the so-called Bushman Diorama, the most popular exhibit at the South Africa Museum in Cape Town. This diorama has auratic power in its own right, which is precisely what makes it so dangerous. Not only are real artifacts embedded in the re-created environment, but the figures were created using life casts made from living Bushmen, as they were called, or Khoisan, as they prefer to be known. The diorama has become an artifact in its own right, which makes the museum doubly responsible for it, that is, for making it in the first place and for taking responsibility for what it says about museum practice. Every attempt to deal with this problematic display and ones like it elsewhere in the gallery—whether to cover it up, explain and apologize for it, add warning labels—foregrounds the museum itself, its operations, history, and, in retrospect, its mistakes. Such reflexive moves make the museum, its practices and its mediations, visible. They effect a shift from an informing museology (the exhibit as a neutral vehicle for the transmission of information) to a performing museology (the museum itself is on display).[11] "The diorama is now closed," the sign reads, but not gone. It is there, but it cannot be seen—except on postcards still for sale in the museum gift shop. With this performative gesture, the South African Museum publicly confronts the ideological burden of its own history. Tour guides have protested and threatened not to bring tourists to this museum until such time as the Bushman Diorama reopens.

THE MUSEUM'S HERITAGE

Post–World War II developments, really from the 1960s, arising from powerful social movements—the civil rights, free speech, antiwar, women's, and student movements; the dissolution of colonial empires and new postcolonial nations; immigration from the postcolonial periphery to the imperial center; and developments in the 1990s (fall of the Berlin Wall, collapse of the former Soviet Union, end of apartheid, emerging national consciousness of postcolonial settler societies such as Australia and New Zealand and creation of new national museums), the ever-larger European Union (and the question of European identity under such new geopolitical and demographic conditions), rise of religious fundamentalisms (Christian, Jewish, and Islamic), and now the "war on terror."

These developments have altered the nature of citizenship and given rise to policies of multiculturalism—and in New Zealand a policy of biculturalism, which recognizes the rights flowing from the treaty signed in 1840 between the Crown and the people of the land, namely, the Maori. An example of how museums responded to the policy of biculturalism is the Goldie exhibition.[12] Charles F. Goldie, New Zealand's old master (or Norman Rockwell, depending on your perspective), was a very popular painter of Maori subjects during the late nineteenth and early twentieth centuries. During the latter part of the twentieth century, *pakeha* (nonindigenous) New Zealanders became ashamed of Goldie and what they had come to see as his sentimental and stereotypical paintings of the Maori as noble savages on the brink of disappearance. He actually titled one painting *The Last of a Dying Breed.* During the 1990s, curators discovered that Maori, particularly those who identified their ancestors in the paintings, viewed them not as shameful but rather as *taonga*, as sacred treasures—indeed, as their ancestors. The decision was taken to exhibit the Goldie paintings, but in a way that reflected the value they have for Maori today. The paintings were grouped by *iwi*, or tribe. Antagonistic tribes were not hung near each other. The wall labels identified the sitter by name and tribe, not by the title that Goldie had given the painting, though the gallery guide did include Goldie's title. The audio guide provided a detailed biography of the sitter, starting with his *whakapapa*, or genealogy, followed by his travels and achievements, including in some cases a trip to England, a meeting with the queen, success in establishing a printing press, and the like. Maori related to the sitters were in the galleries to talk with visitors. Photographs of contemporary Maori life were exhibited outside the painting gallery when the exhibition traveled to the Museum of Sydney. Maori protocol was followed with respect to handling and treatment of the paintings.

A second example of how museums responded to the biculturalism policy was to take ethnology to task for the way that it had structured the old national museum, which consisted of a national art gallery featuring European-style paintings and sculpture and a natural history museum for plants, animals, Maori, and other peoples of the Pacific. This arrangement had become untenable not only on political but also on scientific grounds.

In New Zealand, as elsewhere, the early history of ethnology and of museums was defined by a close fit between the scientific project, the collection, and the museum. The scientific project was the museum's raison d'être. The museum sponsored research expeditions, developed collections, and based research on them. Permanent exhibitions of permanent collections were first and foremost exhibitions of the discipline of ethnology itself. As I have discussed elsewhere, museums exhibited "ethnographic objects" that were "objects of ethnography" in the sense that these objects were what they were by virtue of the conceptual categories and practices of ethnographers.[13] What, however, was to be done when ethnology left the museum for the university? What was to be done with old collections and modes of display and the museums that continued to house them? Should these institutions be preserved as museums of themselves? As ethnology's heritage? Or should the museum reinvent itself? In the case of New Zealand, the decision was taken to dismantle the institution, reorganize the collections, and integrate the collections in exhibitions. First and foremost, however, it was necessary to redefine the mission of the national museum. The result is the Museum of New Zealand Te Papa Tongarewa, known as Te Papa. This museum has repudiated its history as a museum. Instead, it has envisioned itself within the history of New Zealand's participation in world's fairs, from the very first one in 1851 until Seville. An expo-style building and expositionary approach to exhibition make this museum immensely popular, consistent with its promise to attract people who never go to museums and to make a good-faith effort to earn income to support at least part of the institution's operating costs.

I have tried to argue here for a notion of heritage as a mode of cultural production that creates something new. Above all, heritage as a mode of cultural production produces a new relationship—a metacultural relationship—to that which becomes heritage. Moreover, heritage is one of the ways that museums, particularly ethnology museums, reinvent themselves and redefine their relationship to their stakeholders. Rather than museums continuing to be a showcase for ethnology, they are increasingly treating their collections as heritage—of the communities from which the objects come or of the visitors to the museum. Consistent with this approach, Te Papa's motto is "Our Home," and the museum markets itself as a place for "finding ourselves."[14]

I have also argued that repudiation has historically been an enabling condition for the production of ethnology, the collections it generates, and the museums that house them. A second round of repudiation puts ethnology and museums into a problematic relationship with their respective pasts and opens up new possibilities for them to engage with their own histories and their own heritage, as well as with their responsibility to those whose heritage they have helped to produce.

NOTES

1. "U.S. Dept. of Retro Warns: 'We May Be Running Out of Past,'" *Onion* 32, no. 14 (2000), http://www.theonion.com/onion3214/usretro.html.

2. Johannes Fabian, *Time and the Other: How Anthropology Makes Its Object* (New York: Columbia University Press, 1983).

3. See Anthony Giddens, *Modernity and Self-Identity: Self and Society in the Late Modern Age* (Stanford, CA: Stanford University Press, 1991).

4. Bruno Latour, *We Have Never Been Modern*, trans. Catherine Porter (Cambridge, MA: Harvard University Press, 1993), 5; Intangible Heritage, UNESCO, http://mirror-us.unesco.org/culture/heritage/intangible/html_eng/index_en.shtml. See Diana Taylor, *The Archive and the Repertoire: Performing Cultural Memory in the Americas* (Durham, NC: Duke University Press, 2003).

5. Intangible Heritage, UNESCO, http://mirror-us.unesco.org/culture/heritage/intangible/html_eng/index_en.shtml.

6. See Diana Taylor, *The Archive and the Repertoire: Performing Cultural Memory in the Americas* (Durham, NC: Duke University Press, 2003).

7. Doron Swade, *Virtual Objects: Threat or Salvation? Museums of Modern Science*, ed. Svante Lindqvist, Marika Hedin, and Ulf Larsson (Canton, MA: Science History Publications/USA, 2000), 139–47.

8. Robert Plant Armstrong, *The Powers of Presence: Consciousness, Myth, and Affecting Presence* (Philadelphia: University of Pennsylvania Press, 1981); Robert Plant Armstrong, *The Affecting Presence: An Essay in Humanistic Anthropology* (Urbana: University of Illinois Press, 1971).

9. Japan Atlas, Architecture, Jingū Shrine in Ise, http://www.jinjapan.org/atlas/architecture/arc14.html.

10. From "History," Polynesian Cultural Center, http://www.polynesia.com/aloha/history. See also Andrew Ross, "Cultural Preservation in the Polynesia of the Latter Day Saints," in *The Chicago Gangster Theory of Life: Nature's Debt to Society* (New York: Verso, 1994), 2198.

11. Johannes Fabian, *Power and Performance: Ethnographic Explorations through Proverbial Wisdom and Theater in Shaba, Zaire* (Madison: University of Wisconsin Press, 1990).

12. Roger Blackyey, *Goldie* (Auckland, NZ: Auckland Art Gallery and David Bateman, 1997).

13. See Barbara Kirshenblatt-Gimblett, "Objects of Ethnography," in *Exhibiting Cultures: The Poetics and Politics of Museum Display*, ed. Ivan Karp and Steven Lavine (Washington, DC: Smithsonian Institution Press, 1991), 17–78.

14. Paul Williams, "Te Papa: New Zealand's Identity Complex," *New Zealand Journal of Art History* 24, no. 1 (2003): 11–24.

11

Folklife and the Rise of American Folk Museums

HOWARD WIGHT MARSHALL

The seminal article reprinted in this chapter first appeared in the October–December 1977 issue of the *Journal of American Folklore* and was published again in *Folklife and Museums: Selected Readings* (1987). Howard Wight Marshall addresses the development of a specific museum genre, the "folk" museum. In summarizing the historical and theoretical background, he defines folk museums, gives examples, and links their evolution in America to the folk museums of Europe. He discusses the living historical farms movement and examines a number of living history farms in North America. Marshall speaks of interpretation in these folk museums and of the interplay and tension between living history and folklife. He ends with suggestions as to what outdoor folklife museums should include and predicts future directions for the folk museum movement. The article is reprinted here in its entirety, in conjunction with a new chapter by Simon Bronner.

Recently in the United States there has been a movement of sorts to create outdoor folklife museums. These regional institutions are attempting serious ethnological research and the revision of local history to include folk cultural materials representative of regional life and work. A few of these museums, which portray village and farm life for the most part, are staffed by folklorists who interpret the total past in a "living history" setting complete with artifacts, sensitive communication, and a reconstructed cultural landscape. This paper examines this conscious new movement and points out the usefulness of these museums in folklife research, public education and recreation, and the selective preservation of the built environment.

DEMOCRATIC VISTAS

Folklorists believe, and sometimes overstate, that the usual history books and history museums fail to make realistic statements about ordinary past life. With justification, some folklorists, historians, cultural geographers, anthropologists, and populist scholars have set about filling in the gaps in the formal historical record to give a clearer (but often unsettling) view of the nation's many-sided cultural development. To this end, museums of all sorts could become useful centers and laboratories for research and communication of new ideas about the past. The outdoor folklife museum using first-person role-playing interpreters is a report on the past that differs from the history books and from scholarly treatments in general. The museum is an impression given substance by the assembly of artifacts and actors. Such a rigged scenario of guides interacting with old buildings and objects is not entirely accurate, and any museum's presentation will always be incomplete. But a good folklife museum will, by presenting honestly all levels of culture, be more complete than the accounts pictured by elitist history museums. The inescapable incompleteness of the presentation nags at the curator as he pieces the data together in strands of dialog and landscape; however, the incompleteness of rebuilt history is understood and acceptable when education is the goal in a "live" presentational context. These museums should give us the mood and fabric of life in the past. But they should not be entirely past-minded; they can illustrate the power of tradition and continuity of attitude—as well as of change—that characterize life then and now. A variety of needs and expediencies govern the museum's ability to portray the past accurately, and the general public usually worries little about authenticity and fact. Museum administrators know this, and some constrain curators to remember the need for "aesthetics" (pleasant, quaint scenes in good taste). Historic detail is sometimes lost to these expediencies of budget, entertainment, and administrative taste. American outdoor museums, depending as they do on public approval and financial backing, have to be aesthetically pleasing and in some way meet visitors' expectations. The curator's revisionist messages about what he perceives to be the real past operate within this framework of public needs and other pressures. Museums generally try to educate people to some degree, on the basis of research but with alertness to public relations considerations, financial alarms, the director's aesthetics, and restoration "liberties," which are much a part of working institutions.[1]

Museums that deal with local history, living history, and folklife materials call up the memory of a time when many contemporary Americans think everything was fine. American history museums and folk museums have often projected an image that visitors take to be democratic and representative but that is generally full of biases reflecting attitudes and stereotypes of noble pioneers and valiant immigrants. Many museumgoers are attracted by the imaginary or mythological past or by a vision of history coming from family saga, memorates, local legend cycles, and the folk memory. Many museums capitalize on waves of nostalgia (such as the bicentennial fervor) by building programs aimed at public sentiments about the good old days. The trends for arts and crafts and pioneer lifestyles coincide with revivalistic museum programs. These nativistic programs and public modes are usually healthy, as they invigorate and revive local awarenesses of regionality, ethnicity, genealogy, and the individual's fit in the larger historical record. On the other hand, local museums can misrepresent real history and fortify wrong notions about how the old-timers worked and lived. Misrepresentations then fortify incorrect knowledge and false stereotypes, which further skew people's feelings about what they see as an uncloudy, rustic past. Folklife museums dealing with the remote past are, like the commercial entertainment industry, a faker's paradise; curators have to deal with the images of a "golden age of homespun" and keep such images in perspective.

There is no concentrated folklife studies movement in this country comparable to the British and European movement, which generated a network of outdoor museums and research centers staffed by professionals. But there has been some meandering progress toward agreement on folklife research in America, and the arguments are visible in published examples of applied research, in Richard M. Dorson's and Don Yoder's anthologies,[2] and in the establishment of an American Folklife Center at the Library of Congress.[3] The recording, analysis, and celebration of folk culture can be accomplished in one way with folk museums as focal points for all manner of regional projects, as well as for the enrichment of studies in local classrooms and historical societies.

The mission of many outdoor museums is revisionist. Some institutions attempt to teach patrons in the fullest possible social and environmental contexts about culture change and people's history as expressed in artifacts, architecture, and the cultural landscape. This history lesson is not just about the history of furniture or the development of hay raking machinery; those ends, by means of the rows of articulately labeled and preserved objects, are successfully met by archives and collections around the country. The greatest of these are housed in such places as the Smithsonian Institution's Museum of History and Technology, Henry Ford's Greenfield Village in Michigan, the Winterthur Museum in Delaware, and the Abby Aldrich Rockefeller Folk Art Collection at Williamsburg. These collections are excellent, and their footings are firmly based on art historical theory and method. But these are not "folklife" museums of the sort described and advocated here. For the curator of the outdoor museum, the nuances of ordinary daily life and work are as important as (and often stressed more than) "the development of the broad axe."[4] The artifact is nevertheless the museum's main concern: it is the clearest representation of the old farmer's traditions, social order, and cultural milieu, privately and publicly.

E. McClung Fleming's statement of what he thought the museum's mission should be could well speak for folk museums in particular:

> To acquire and care for its objects in order to make them available for enjoyment and study; to study them in order to use them for teaching and research. I would like to see the furniture historian studying an eighteenth-century Newport high chest begin with the identification of its date and place of manufacture, its makers and owners, and then press on to wrestle with the problem of how this object, through its material, construction, design, and function, was a plastic manifestation of ideas, values, attitudes, needs, and meanings in the Newport subculture of its period. I would like to see this furniture historian reach out to grasp hands with the archaeologist, the demographer, the folk culture specialist, and the social and intellectual historian.[5]

Once having decided to take all this seriously, the museum curator must work out an apprehension of past life in his own region, and his perception should be weighted against the prevailing perception in the local community. If the curator's vision is fresh and different, that must be clearly stated in order to put the educational points across. In their attempt to educate, most museums will use entertainment and communication as the vehicle for the information presented on the tour.[6] Wilcomb Washburn discussed museum purposes and underlined the difficulty of fulfilling high goals in the face of the "bureaucratic ethos" of administrations, by which "a museum's purpose is eroded in stages" for "the perpetuation of the organization itself" and not for "the achievement of its ostensible goals."[7] It becomes critical then for museums to have a written master plan that includes a strong statement of philosophy and intended contributions. The master plan should be forthright, specific, and grounded on experience. Many museums lack a clear purpose; curators and administrators often disagree over terms and courses of action; and many museums exist without ever having to define goals or to justify existence. Often, they operate on blind faith that everyone assumes that museums do something worthwhile (if merely storing objects). Also, museums need to say clearly whether they serve as memorials commemorating a local hero or event or whether they depict a farm or town representing the period or region. Both functional intentions are viable, and some museums have both identities. For example, Conner Prairie in Indiana has among its structures an 1823 red brick "mansion" on its original site, which is something of a shrine for many Conner family descendants and local history buffs, having been built by the famous pioneer. The museum staff, however, stresses its interest as a sample of an early central and southern Indiana folk building type—a brick central-hall I house with integral ell addition and Federal style trimmings. Further, the Conner house possesses a second shrine factor, as restoration was begun in the 1930s by Eli Lilly, a contemporary Indiana philanthropist.

The ability of the folklife specialist to build an accurate picture of past life as lived by ordinary people provides the potential for attracting a wider audience than other sorts of museums if ideas of the common man are handled thoughtfully and rigorously and folklore is used to teach interesting lessons to visitors. Folklore (customs and oral traditions) is included here within folklife, and accordingly the folklife museum would study and seek to show pertinent aspects of the total folk culture. As in Europe, regional ethnology or folklife presentations refer to and touch all classes of society, following Geraint Jenkins's dictum that they "depict the life of every stratum of the community [and] . . . include material associated with the aristocracy as well as material relating to the peasant classes."[8]

FOLKLIFE AND MUSEUMS

The work done in America traces to thinkers and institutions in northwest Europe, which fostered the open-air or outdoor museum concept and the spread of ethnological research. There are ample precedents of folk museums that have been successfully operating for a hundred years, the first of these founded by Artur Hazelius in Sweden and called Skansen (literally, "open-air museum"). Hazelius sought to represent Swedish folk culture in living exhibits using artifacts and structures studied holistically and collected on his own long field trips. The contribution of the early Scandinavian outdoor museums, followed by regional British museums, has been great to folklife research in general, and European conceptual prototypes are being imitated in Canada and America. Folklife museums in Scandinavia and Britain encourage serious research and scholarship that are still rare in the fledgling American museums. Here the tendency toward simplistic educational exhibits designed for the imaginary typical visitor, with dull tours run by costumed but ill-trained interpreters, has kept museums in the shadows of respectability. Most of these museums are determined to remold history and pack it into democratic, nativistic summaries embodying "America." Recently the so-called living historical farm movement (discussed below) has taken on the presentation of rural life and work, and some of these institutions are fine and effective outdoor museums. Though they focus on tools and agricultural progress, the living historical farms carry on regional ethnological research and can be seen, at least in part, as folklife museums.

As in Europe, ours is a regional concern, and most of our museums should be powerful regional statements. And although "regionalism" is still a hazy, complex concept that begs for final definition, folklife itself is a regional pursuit.[9] "Regions" for museums generally means examples such as nations in Scandinavia and northwest Europe, divisions of the United

Kingdom (political and cultural), and major cultural geographic regions of North America. In this regard, J. W. Y. Higgs wrote a classic British treatment of folklife research and museums, urging environmental awareness and defining folklife as akin to ethnography.

> A folk museum should preserve a record of the everyday life and culture of the area it serves; it should mirror the changes in this culture whether they are of the past or currently taking place in order that they may be adequately recorded. People come to a folk museum in order to study the history and background of their own everyday life and perhaps also to see the way in which this differs from that of other people. . . . The folk museum must cater for the whole community though of necessity it will be mainly concerned with the habits of the majority. . . . The main preoccupation of a folk museum must be with the cultural and geographical area in which it is situated, but it should take into account the cultural differences that exist from region to region.[10]

Ake Hultkrantz defined folklife similarly as a part of anthropology (ethnology), saying that it is "the life and ways of the folk as subject to scientific investigation," and Sigurd Erixon, who founded *Folk-Liv* (the first real folklife journal) and is the father of the discipline, said that "the object of folklife research is to arrive at a deeper knowledge and understanding of man. It is the science of man as a cultural being."[11] And by extension Iorwerth Peate (founder of folklife research in Wales and first keeper of the Welsh Folk Museum at St. Fagans) and others included both nonverbal and verbal materials in their definitions.[12]

The coming status of American folk museums follows the acceptance of the folklife approach, and as curators and scholars try building regional museums, their guides are still the European and British institutions. Museums there issue handbooks that go beyond the simpler American ones in stating philosophies and academic intentions. These handbooks set out objectives that center around re-creation of the local environment as the stage for artifactual scenes, and all of these museums, like the newer ones in America, perform serious research, preservation, collection, and publication in addition to interpreting the cultural displays for public tourism and education. The museums there are nationalistic and proud. The object of the Danish open-air museum is "to study Danish culture in its widest sense, with particular emphasis on its material and social aspects."[13] Such museums produce valuable fieldwork, ethnological surveys, documentary films, scholarly publications, and surface archaeology in the villages and countryside. In reviewing a guide to European museums, Gösta Berg explained their mission this way: "The primary objective of the open-air museum is undeniably pedagogical, and the intention is to give the visitor a concrete and immediately understandable picture of living conditions in the past. . . . In addition to this pedagogical function, however, open-air museums have also come to play an important part for the conservation of cultural monuments."[14]

Berg's is an excellent summary of what these institutions should do; as he notes, if the work is done well, the museum can no longer be ignored by the academic community accustomed to education by bibliographies and in seminar rooms. Similar statements are found in Welsh and north Irish museum handbooks by curator-scholars Trefer Owen and G. B. Thompson:

> A folk museum represents the life and culture of a nation, illustrating the arts and crafts, and in particular the building crafts, of the complete community, and including in its illustrations the activities of the mind and spirit—speech, drama, dance and music—as well as of the hand. Such museums are in two parts: a building for the systematic display of the materials of life and culture, where the research student can study the details of folk life in exhibits emphasizing the evolution and distribution of types, their chronology and many other problems. The environment of the national life is presented in the open-air section. . . . Furniture and furnishings occupy their rightful place in the houses; carts, ploughs and other implements their place in sheds and barns. Such a museum, indeed, comes to be a cultural center of the nation which it serves.[15]

> A folk museum exists to illustrate the social history of the community which it serves. . . . While the essential aim of any folk museum is to serve its own community, it is hoped that the perceptive visitor from abroad will be able to compare the conditions of north Irish folk life with those in other countries. . . . The aim of the Museum is to represent a picture of that entity which has disappeared.[16]

A comparable statement from Scandinavia reads, "The typical Norwegian folk museum is an open-air layout consisting of groups of old buildings arranged around a . . . courtyard . . . , whose purpose it is to give an idea of life as it was lived in the past."[17]

In Europe, "experimental research" has gained attention recently, led by Peter Reynolds at England's Butser Ancient Farm Project (Hampshire) and at Lejre Research Center in Denmark. This kind of research (which studies old techniques of farming and technology and attempts to replicate methods and forms) is now being tried at Colonial Pennsylvania Plantation (Bishop's Mill Historical Institute) near Philadelphia.[18] These innovative experimental programs owe much to historical archaeological methods and theory and are valuable extensions of usual museum projects. Few museums, though, will have the ability to devote the time and staff to this experimental history until far down the road of development and financial stability.

American notions of folklife research come from European and British models but are transplanted in changed form due to different conditions of settlement, interaction with the land, and shallower historic time. To the kind of work done in Europe, Americans add what Yoder calls "the ethnographic present"[19] through fieldwork in local social settings still possessing the old ways (even if these ways are survivals gradually passing from active use). Attention to the ethnographic present is not lacking in Europe. The Ulster Folk Museum and the Museum of English Rural Life (among others) study the very recent past and the ethnographic present.

Museums in America will try to recapture the sense and vitality of the past by reconstructing logical, accurate portraits of small bits of regional history, helping communities know more of their informal histories not recorded in the standard references. The model of Hazelius's great museum in Sweden was "know yourself"—expanded later by the Swedish Tourist Association to "know your country."[20] But curators will have to beware the presumption that they are really recapturing the distant American past; theirs is an invention, hopefully artistic and honest, and not true restoration work.

Outdoor museums of folklife (or open-air museums, whichever term one prefers), then, share with the European prototypes the job of collecting, analyzing, preserving, and interpreting folklife materials and communicating their inherent messages to serve both the community and the scholar. This would indeed be Erixon's science of man as a cultural being.

The mood that compels a fascination for old things is nicely summarized by Bernard Fontana:

> There is, Thoreau reminds, something melancholy about antiquity. There is something melancholy about the village dump; about the falling adobe walls where men of the U.S. Seventh Cavalry swore and labored and loved before Taps was sounded on that final evening; about the mounds of earth which mark the remains of a late-19th century ranch house; about the slowly desiccating wooden shell where a 20-stamp mill once crushed silver and gold from its matrix of rock.[21]

The number of museums in the United States is growing at a fast clip, and the number of history museums of various sorts is growing even faster. Ideas about mass education, new museological techniques, and trends of romanticism make local history and folklife fair game for this growth industry. It becomes critical for good sense to reign in these new museums, to prevent a leveling of the past into one even, shellacked version. Ethnic identity has generally become lost in the museum reshufflings, but some institutions are reinserting ethnicity into their presentations of regional and community personality. One new museum, Old World Wisconsin (at Eagle), has the intriguing plan to depict the actual ethnic pluralism of the state by creating an assemblage of European farmsteads representing various groups at the time of initial occupancy. Such museums can become a good introduction to the diversity of earlier times and can advocate new understandings of the present. Museums ought to be able to lead visitors to alternative comprehensions about culture, beyond the familiar themes of pioneer life, sawmilling, railroads, and the like. The museum tour can show useful comparisons between the old ways and modern ones, making the visitor think a bit, but you prove nothing by analogy alone.

There are basically three categories of museums that deal with folklife materials—whatever their particular choice of title may be. First, there are *folklife museums* involving good research and articulate interpretation of the regional scene. Some of the living historical farms now gaining popularity are the closest so far to what American open-air folk museums should be. There is a good deal of tacit agreement on goals and philosophy at these educational institutions, even if the actual achievements and presentations take different profiles. Second, there are institutions which are *essentially curatorial*, maintaining and exhibiting collections which include *folk artifacts*. Third, there are many local museums without pretension that operate as romantic and nativistic community memorials and historic sites. These are very specific, very local, and appeal widely to travelers; there is little effort at interpretation or academic musing. In a sense, the small outfits nestled along highways at gas stations or in old courthouses, railroad depots, and Victorian parlors are more "folk" than the avowed folk museums—for these are not merely *about* "the folk" but are by and for them as well. As Higgs said, some of the best museums in England are the little local ones with non-professional but dedicated and knowledgeable staffs.[22] These roadside spots are telling statements about the local population's self-image and historical frame. Most museologists sniff drily at these places. In his apparent disdain, one establishment spokesman compared the "relic-filled settler's cabins in western towns" to New York's Metropolitan Museum of Art.[23] The good small museums are an important class, like the unlettered and outstanding regional ballad collections of earlier years. Fascinated amateurs often do fine work, even if they labor outside the halls of the elect of the museum world.

The three kinds of museums in some way handling folk things see different goals. The outdoor folklife museums want to revise history; the static collections want to collect and varnish; and the small organizations want to save neighborhood history and have a good time. They all "preserve," and they are all important. And, like folklife researchers, they all center attention on artifacts as the vital keys to the past.

THE NEED FOR GOOD RESEARCH

Everything hinges on research. Research programs are the backstop of authenticity, which allows for museum education and interpretation in other departments. The research department's basic function is to provide legitimate and appropriate materials, garnered from every kind of approach, from fieldwork to library, that can be incorporated into the museum's educational and "aesthetic" representations of the local historical moment. Publications, student seminars, crafts workshops, summer institutes, and other programs follow, after the initial obligation of putting on the tour is met. There are all sorts of museum researchers—wild innovators, master craftsmen, bored academics, expedient diluters, dependable journeymen, graduate students on internships—and while most researchers claim to have the data to support the programs, few really do. Researchers' titles vary greatly, from "historian" to "curator." Research staff sizes vary greatly, too, and office arrangements run from autonomous departments with libraries and photo labs to spare corners in education departments with files in shoeboxes. Fat budgets and luxurious offices have nothing to do with the quality of work that goes on.

Various academic disciplines are involved in doing museum work, and the best techniques for correctly seeing the past combine them all—folkloristics, archaeology, cultural geography, social history, anthropology, and American studies. Folklorists who are deeply trained in material culture are sometimes the best prepared for open-air museum work where proper artifacts (in both process and product) are the foundation of the whole enterprise. The museum grounds can be an emotional arena for the "folklore versus history" scraps, and every folklorist-curator will now and then feel like Darrow defending the Wobblies—searching for truths and facts with which to fight for an unpopular cause. Folklorists working in history museums face the same campaigns for recognition and acceptance as folklorists teaching in the old guard English or history departments at the university. The better historians know the worth of nonhistorical or social-scientific approaches, and folklife researchers acknowledge the importance of good history, or they ought to. In a program that centers on traditional communities, the vintage information that is defensible for tour purposes is scarce, as anyone knows who has tried to research ordinary farming in the early Midwest. The artifact once again becomes paramount. Artifacts and the cultural landscape become the vital clues to the unrecorded past, and the methods of folklife research are indispensable. The researcher learns to read artifacts for the information they contain about the "workaday conservatives" routinely ignored by history books,[24] about culture change, and about regional character. Then, lacking accurate books of history, curators ought to read literature—Twain, Faulkner, Melville, and Cooper but also Service, Eliot, and Momaday—to feel the lives they would depict with oiled tools, eager guides, and old buildings.

The importance of administrative and budgetary commitments to research cannot be overemphasized. With backing, research can become a chief goal of museums, along with public education and preservation. Solid research efforts give the institution its credibility and its authenticity; research becomes "the lifeblood of the museum enterprise."[25] Museum research teams can carve out a variety of projects leading to documentation and analysis of their region's built environment; they can produce ethnographic films, oral histories, historical archaeological investigations, and other work crossing the rickety fences between academic disciplines. American museums have much catching up to do to equal the sort of fieldwork and research carried out at the Welsh Folk Museum, at the Frilandsmuseet, at Skansen, at Kingussie, at Cultra Manor, at Reading, and at other far-off research complexes that are so relevant to America. If the essence of folk museums is to demonstrate modern man's link with past men, those links have to be hammered out on the anvil of good ethnography and rigorous criticism.

Research provides material for publications, too, which range from annotated catalogs like those issued by the Shelburne Museum in Vermont[26] to practical handbooks on restoration and other matters such as the technical leaflets from the American Association for State and Local History in Nashville. Examples of technical books that are not connected to museums but explain folklife include such tight, nonscholarly works as Eugene H. Boudreau's *Making the Adobe Brick*.[27] The better of these small publications avoid the pitfalls of the media-induced arts and crafts fad. But in publishing, as in other ways, American museums have usually been behind European counterparts. Utilizing the museum's resources, American curators have produced few scholarly works on the high level of Jenkins's *The English Farm Wagon*, Iorwerth Peate's *Tradition and Folk Life: A Welsh View*, or Alexander Fenton's *Scottish Country Life*.[28] There are notable exceptions, but most of these are not by folklorists. For example, a recent exhibition at Yale University generated the best catalog to date, a volume that includes essays going far beyond the usual exhibit catalog commentary.[29] Charles Hummel's massive work on the Dominy family of craftsmen is a classic, as are Wilbur Peat's book on Indiana housing, E. P. Richardson's treatment of American painting, Henry Mercer's book on tools, Bernard Fontana's study of an Arizona ranching complex, and Joshua C. Taylor's catalog of little-known American art.[30] The Smithsonian Institution encourages scholarly publications of the sort done by Brooke Hindle and John T. Schlebecker.[31] All these works are by writers with good museum connections, and since all deal at least partially with traditional artifacts, they are of interest to folklife students. Among other kinds of research projects the museum is suited for are experimental history and studies of neglected areas like religion, foodways, and social stratification, all helping to lead to the reorderings of local history sought by folklorists.[32]

In addition, the professional researcher will have to cope with the problem that many visitors and museum workers, having read *Antiques* and *Good*

Old Days and other popular magazines, consider themselves to be experts on history. Debates between devoted amateurs and researchers can be difficult to arbitrate, and of course many amateurs are expert in their knowledge, and their assistance should be encouraged.

THE LIVING HISTORICAL FARM

The "living historical farms" in America, at their best, amount to open-air folklife museums, though their concerns cover only part of the folklorist's total subject. The living history farms ignore some folkloristic material in their concentration on old crops, back-bred livestock, and tool collections. In addition, many of these agricultural museums focus on the development of farm equipment and methods over the years, rather than concentrating on a full reconstruction of a past moment that shows the social order and regional culture embodied in dinner table settings and architecture.

The first of the living historical farms, the Lippet Farm at Cooperstown and the Freeman Farm at Old Sturbridge Village, were both operating in the 1950s and, with Plimoth Plantation, were leaders in the early trend toward depicting old ways of work in a "live" setting. Such museums practice applied folklore and, particularly if they would use a first-person role-playing tour presentation, could accomplish what Jenkins thought open-air museums should do: "Take the visitor out of his present day environment and straight to the people that lived in some bygone age."[33] These living historical farms, some of which are folk museums, have a brilliant future. Though folk museums will eventually encompass urban populations, the emphasis has correctly been on agriculture and small village life. Up to the twentieth century, the farm and the village represent much of the substance of the American character. If properly worked out, living historical farms, in portraying "main elements of United States agricultural history,"[34] will automatically have included folk culture in their research and presentation. Like folk museums in Europe, the living farms attempt to take the visitor on "a walk into the past"[35] in order to view rebuilt historical scenes in human and geographical context. Along with Darwin Kelsey, Daryl Chase, Wayne Rasmussen, and others, John T. Schlebecker has been a driving force behind the living historical farms movement from his Smithsonian office, and he recognized that farming and small-town life were so important in national development that old-time farming holds a great fascination in contemporary America. The distant soil and the old country store cast spells on modern urban man. Kelsey, a leading theorist in the movement, noted that these reinvented farms can serve as models of the past, but only as incomplete ones that project some point of view to patrons.[36] Schlebecker and Gayle E. Peterson summarized the intentions of living historical farms: "On living historical farms men farm as they once did during some specific time in the past. The farms have tools and equipment like those once used, and they raise the same types of livestock and plants used during the specified era. The operations are carried on in the presence of visitors."[37] Kelsey defined living historical farms as "offering a patterned coherent account of the past that is intended to be true"; they do "holistic preservation: preservation of material and nonmaterial culture in context and in process."[38] There is a description of the movement by Edward L. Hawes, planner of the Clayville Rural Life Center in Illinois, which includes a list of four museum categories that indicates the current fuzziness of definition: (1) "traditional museums of agriculture or folklife," (2) "open-air museums," (3) "living historical farms," and (4) "community re-creations."[39] Museums now still in developmental stages, like Conner Prairie and Old World Wisconsin, are new enough to forge clear goals and methods and, with good staffs, can plot appropriate courses. All those categories suggested by Hawes will in some way be included in folklife museums set up in contextual natural environments. The worries over terms are expected but need not slow the growth of the museums. Some institutions choose localized titles in order to evade the word "museum"—a term with a bad reputation, connoting arid halls of musty display cases. Thus, "settlement," "village," and "plantation" occur more often than "museum," and at the moment "historic restoration" and "living history museum" (in addition to "living historical farm") are the descriptive terms in vogue. Whatever the title, most of these organizations present American folklife and will affect the discipline.

So far, among the best living historical farms where agriculture is practiced with close attention are Colonial Pennsylvania Plantation, Old Bethpage (Long Island), Living History Farms (Iowa), Westville (Georgia), Upper Canada Village (Ontario), Plimoth Plantation, and Ronald V. Jensen Living Historical Farm (Utah). None of these has "museum" in its title. They are described in a handbook that for the moment covers nearly all of the better museums based on farming in North America, the thirty-two considered by the Association for Living Historical Farms and Agricultural Museums

(ALHFAM) to be worthy of notice.[40] ALHFAM is the central organization and focus for the movement (with members from Cape Cod to Maui), and it was founded in 1970 at an agricultural symposium at Old Sturbridge Village "to encourage research, publication, and training in historical agricultural practices; facilitate the exchange of agricultural plants and animals; seek funds for a national program; and accredit living historical farms and agricultural museums."[41] Folklorists would expand that statement, and indeed few of the outfits recognized in the ALHFAM handbook measure up to the standards posed by Chase, Schlebecker, Ernst Christensen, and other leaders, all differing in details of viewpoint and practice. All, however, are probing in the right direction—toward contextual living demonstrations of rural life and work depicted in reinvented cultural landscapes.

As in Scandinavian models, attention to the natural environment is critical for outdoor museums. A visitor, for example, to an outdoor museum in the Midwest that shows pioneer modes of life can feel a little of the vastness and mood of the American frontier familiar from the writings of Flint, de Tocqueville, Peck, and Mrs. Trollope. The settlers came here to conquer nature and convert it into culture. Life was tough. In the wild and noble America—the howling wilderness—the great forest came down hard around families with their iron "falling axes" and "grubbin' hoes." That fresh landscape was the setting for the trial of the American dream. The Midwest begins here—as does its romanticization. Something of that age can be felt by modern people in a well-researched museum that boasts of the land along with displaying antiques. Although museums reconstruct these old cultural scenes with current means, good information can be presented in live demonstrations. With the right combination of artifacts, land, and interpreters, the "live" tour could convey local history very well. Folk museums are synchronic statements when they focus on one fragment of the past. For example, Plimoth Plantation shows life in 1622, Conner Prairie depicts 1836 (the 1830s), Old Sturbridge depicts 1790 to 1840, Iowa Living History Farms depict 1840, 1900, and "the farm of the future," Kipahula Living Farm (Hawaii) depicts 1848, and Westville depicts 1850. All these museums interpret a locally significant period of an earlier time, usually the period of first effective settlement by Europeans. There is still no living history farm for more recent but equally fascinating periods, such as the 1930s or the late 1940s—for which the researcher could do powerful fieldwork studying both the plentiful artifacts and the people who lived that history and could show us how they worked. Museums using a first-person role-playing guide staff, in which detail and sensitive interpretation are needed, will likely decide that a ten-year span is about the limit possible for a believable reenactment. At Conner Prairie it has been found that within the decade-long time frame, in which some stability was evident, a single year can be picked for tour purposes. The first-person interpreter has to know who is president, what events are the topic of community discussion, what the prices for corn and hogs are "this year," and so on.

The tacit agreement on goals in these museums and living historical farms is visible in the day-to-day operations. Guidebooks to institutions show this sense of purpose, although such public statements are usually laced with sentiment and are explicit in wanting to speak for the common man.

> In North Carolina: "The Pioneer Farmstead is a collection of typical pioneer structures and artifacts—but, it is much more. . . . You will see demonstrations of pioneer crafts and activities. . . . The Farmstead is more than an exhibit—it is an experience of yesterday."[42]

> In Toronto: "Black Creek Pioneer Village tells the story of rural life in central Ontario from 1793 to 1867. . . . The Village is a very specialized type of museum in which history is relived by the villagers, who portray life of more than a century ago."[43]

> In Wisconsin: "Old World Wisconsin is an open-air museum that will make history come alive. But it is an outdoor museum with a difference, because it will be the only multinational, multicultural 'living museum' in existence."[44]

> In Georgia: "Westville is a facsimile village composed of original pre-1850 buildings moved into place, restored, and furnished to house the activities for which they were originally built. . . . [The goal is] to show typical life in Georgia, complete in every aspect of the arts and crafts, of governmental and social organization, and of the everyday life of the people. . . . The dominant purpose is to provide the means of teaching successive generations of Americans the personal skills and enduring cultural values from the nation's past."[45]

In Illinois: Educational and research programs "will be devised to bring greater understanding of the past. . . . Living museums are more than collections of artifacts. At their best they are complexes of biological and cultural processes, carefully put together with patient research to recreate as much as possible of a given environment in a given time."[46]

In Louisiana: A complete plantation constitutes the museum.

For these early rural dwellers, "doin' it yourself" was a necessity, and the great variety of authentic housewares, tools, and cooking utensils displayed at the museum illustrate country ingenuity in fashioning an implement to meet every purpose. . . . For contemporary society, the LSU Rural Life Museum represents more than simply a nostalgic glimpse into our rural past: It brings to vital life the important legacy of a people whose endeavors helped to build the foundation for modern America.[47]

On the St. Lawrence River:

Upper Canada Village is a museum community recreating the life, work and development of the early settlements in the upper St. Lawrence Valley. . . . Each building . . . tells its own particular story of life in Upper Canada. . . . Upper Canada Village, however, is more than a history museum; it is a place where history comes to life. . . . It presents to those of us who live from day to day with automobiles, electricity, television, supermarkets and packaged frozen food the chance to realize that these things have not been a part of people's lives for long. The settlers of Upper Canada worked hard and long days for most of their lives, and while their age need not be romanticized, they were often rewarded with a great sense of well-being and achievement.[48]

And in Indiana:

Conner Prairie is an attempt to accurately portray, through artifacts, structures, and role-playing the social ambience of the period chosen. With education as the chief concern at Conner Prairie, all exhibits, buildings, first-person roles, and so on must be geared toward educating people about what the past might really have been like. . . . [W]e have the opportunity to create a genuine sociological assemblage. . . . Our audience is the general public, and to serve our goal of education we do what a teacher does: we fictionalize in order to teach. We select facts which convey a powerful impression of the reality of

> past living. . . . [W]e wish to portray not a change in architectural styles, but the changes in society as embodied in architecture.[49]

A sort of code is developing. But the achievement of the goals varies in styles and degree. It is fair to say that most of the institutions considered as folklife museums here (chiefly living historical farms) attain that rank by their collections and the applied folklore of their tour presentations, festivals, and special events. Whatever the merits of the newer institutions—Westville, Old World Wisconsin, Conner Prairie—the trump card is that very newness. They are starting fresh and can evade the old mistakes of false historic restoration and elitist viewpoints.

MUSEUM INTERPRETATION

In a few outdoor museums of folklife a first-person role-playing interpretive situation is being tried: at Conner Prairie and, to some extent, at Westville and Plimoth Plantation. This is an experimental educational device whereby the museum guides make an effort to live the roles of an earlier community. The method requires lengthy interpreter training periods and a mass of specific historic details. This kind of interpretation is very difficult and full of problems. (For example, will the guides use "real" artifacts or reproductions?) Reproductions should be allowed, and replicated tools, equipment, and furnishings should be used and replaced when worn out or damaged beyond repair. There are few artifacts incapable of replication by skilled museum master craftsmen. Also, the construction crew, not paid interpreters but professional carpenters and builders, ought to work on restoration and reconstruction of buildings on the tour in costume, using traditional tools and techniques proper to region and period. This is done with good effect at Plimoth Plantation but has rarely been tried elsewhere. As in other regards, seeing the process and problems of putting up a potter's beehive kiln is quite as educational to modern visitors as merely walking by the finished ("restored") "kill" on the tour. For another example, how should the museum go about truthfully and effectively showing the racial situation in these reconstructed pioneer communities? Solutions are not as simple as they might seem, and such concerns as these are naturally more critical at museums employing a thorough first-person tour.

Although it is a lively method and one that can truly involve visitors in the tour when it works well, a first-person presentation limits the amount and kind of historical information given out. At Conner Prairie, where the farm and village tour is completely in the first person, some museum patrons dislike the technique—for their questions are unanswerable if the interpreter keeps to his role (for example, "Is that a real antique flax brake?" or "Didn't they have trains in 1836?"). The visitor demanding historical information irrelevant to the museum tour or beyond the guide's knowledge and training has to hold those questions for the staff back at the visitor's center or research office. Here is where scholarly but readable visitor handbooks, clear maps, and visitor orientation are useful. The first-person scenario may not be the best approach to public education in the open-air museum context, but it is a reasonable experiment with good potential for communication of ideas. This mode of presentation actually "communicates" more than it "educates" in the usual sense of providing arrays of facts and figures. Similarly, Hazelius's exhibits at Skansen "were more intended to provide impressions than knowledge."[50] The first-person situation increases the viability of the rebuilt environment, too, and adds a human dimension to the stream of life visible in artifacts and cultural landscapes. The museums presenting the first-person tour method should have a strong formal exhibit area, removed from the outdoor section into the visitor's center or a special building. Then there would be the combination effectively used by British and Scandinavian museums: an "open-air folk park" plus a static exhibit center. There would be, as at the Farmers' Museum at Cooperstown (though it has no first-person tour), "a psychological illusion in which every visitor must take an active role. The trick is to force out of the mind all those appurtenances of contemporary living—automobiles, paved roads, television and radio, telephones—which are taken so for granted and let the mind go back freely to an earlier day."[51]

The museums' concern with the "living" and the typical past is right and complex in practice. Every institution will in its representativeness of the region want to put forth "the genius of culture,"[52] the main patterns in the old cloth. But curators know that despite a secure research base and talented guides, they cannot move backward in time into the minds and hearts of farmers, blacksmiths, teamsters, or servant girls. It is foolish to assume that the museum, with all its files and fieldwork, shows the public what the past was *really* like. Museums represent, but it is a slanted vision based on foggy diaries, spotty records, excavated shards, scholarly biases, and research dilemmas incapable of solution. Representations are mere glimpses down the tunnel at the artifacts and records that have survived. While representative museums are possible, only rarely are broadly typical ones successful when the remote past is tackled. Higgs noted that upon a closer look the "typical" village or house vanishes.[53] There is a paragraph near the end of Edward D. Ives's *Lawrence Doyle* that eloquently explains our troubles with trying to show the typical:

> Whatever Lawrence Doyle's life and works tell us about traditional songs and songmaking—and they tell us a great deal—they show us something else that is at least equally precious: the paradox of the uncommon common man. While it is of course true that in any area most lives will resemble each other, each life is also unique, and the closer we look at an average man the more we see him in all his individuality—moving through his world, making choices, and responding to life in his own way which is never quite anyone else's way.[54]

That bothersome question—what was the past really like?—is at the very center of the outdoor museum's mission. Good efforts at reconstruction can be made, but the pressures of administrative needs and compromises, the winds of national nostalgia and the Americana craze, the museum's "shrine factor,"[55] technical liberties taken, and the simple lack of information on early life will affect the true picture of local history that museum curators long for.

Nevertheless, there is room for messages about the nature of the past social order and the spirit of place. In a representative, reinvented community in a live tour there ought to be conflict and fluctuation. Scenes that depict town life can neatly show culture change and the clash of ethnic traditions as old ways meet new ones. For example, an outdoor museum with a first-person tour could show the acculturation of Germans into a dominantly British village on the Midwest frontier. Young German men and boys, whose custom it is to "shoot in the New Year," would likely find some of their English neighbors violently against such boisterous displays—which nonparticipants in the tradition may view as an excuse for the lads to fire guns at night and raise Cain.

In reinventing a "typical" village of, say, the 1830s, outdoor museums naturally tend to select bits of history for the tour that reflect the desire to perpetuate good moments and to put aside bad ones. In this light the new museum movement can be seen as revivalistic and nativistic, and the better institutions resist portraying wrong conceptions and wrong stereotypes.[56]

CONCLUSION—AND A SUGGESTION

Every folklife researcher and outdoor museum curator would quickly say that we owe much to Skansen, to Bernhard Olsen's Frilandsmuseet, to Peate's museum in the great castle, to Isabel Grant's Highlands museum, and to others. American museum curators have borrowed from European models, but refinements have been made. We share the Scandinavians' and Britons' interest in teaching people about their national (here, regional) past, teaching them to "know yourself." But in the United States the outdoor concept has been extended to include working farms and role-playing first-person interpretation, which, when it all runs right, can deeply involve visitors in an artfully contrived scene, which meets the dual goals of providing the public with recreation and with a practical source for a more truthful history. The guides here ideally use not only old-style clothes but old-style regional dialect and behavior as well, and although this is a tough educational technique to master, it may become widespread and effective—given thoughtful yet entertaining clusters of artifacts, people, and landscapes as contextual stimulation. As over there, the best museums in North America will be folklife research complexes where perceptive research excavating down through the curving layers of local history will reveal new data to fill in the hollows in the formal records of fashion, politics, and the exotic. It is becoming almost easy to argue that all this work is worthwhile.

Although an outfit like Conner Prairie runs its own show, early on the local community gathered around the museum as a focus for historical research, genealogy, and crafts festivals; currently, the college that owns and operates the museum is coming to regard it as a living laboratory for classes ranging from museum studies to Midwest history and folklife to ecology and human survival techniques.

With American museums, education has ostensibly been the immediate goal. There are institutions dealing with folklife materials whose emphasis is on scholarly experimental research and on sheer collection and preservation. Many of the living historical farms, based on good scholarship, serve this country well for outdoor folklife museums. At these places, which take account of the cultural landscape, all three basic goals of folk museums will be satisfied—*collection* (restoration, preservation, conservation, reconstruction), *education* (communication, interpretation), and *research*. These museums are regional and together will eventually form a net covering at least the more obvious chunks of American cultural history. For most of the nation, these institutions ought to have (as in Europe) two main parts: (1) an outdoor section with a genuine assemblage of artifacts and interpreters settled close into the landscape, hopefully with both a little village and working farms, and (2) a complex of buildings screened off from "the historic tour" housing static exhibits, a visitor's center (with orientation, theater, gift shop, a first-rate restaurant, and so on), an education and research complex (with library, photographic lab, meeting rooms), a collections department (collecting survivals of old plants and beasts as well as old artifacts), a master builder's shop, and administrative offices. The crowd of departments and offices differs from museum to museum. There should be a real effort to reconstruct an authentic tableau, with the farmer's yearly round of seasonal concerns and the community social configuration included. It is unimportant whether interpreters play roles and speak in the first person in dramatic serials or simply wear costumes and deliver information—so long as life, work, and the process as well as the product of tradition are shown. Technically, these are history museums, but museums that cope with that part of general history we call "folklife": revisionist history.[57] They focus down sharply on locally significant spots in time for study and interpretation. The museum is an ideogram for local history. It summarizes, symbolizes, and communicates the sense of past life. The museum's portrayal will be, for the visitor, silken or scratchy; it will attractively restate the given views of history books, or it will blast obsolete notions by laying out new and possibly irritating social history. The provocative past is seldom depicted in museum settings, but it will be shown more often as curators seek a counterbalance for the dull, usual depictions. Each worker will have to hold up the yardstick and take the measure of his region and possibilities; in old crops, while flax is cultivated, hemp and belladonna will likely be ignored. What is important is that museums recognize the impact of their work, instigating defensible missions and policies appropriate to those missions. Also, it is time for folklorists and academics in other disciplines to take these new museums seriously and to acknowledge professional folklorists who serve in them. With better work being done at these institutions, the folklore community can come to understand outdoor museums as locations for experimental research and as lively extensions of the classroom. The Scandinavian and British folk museums have long served and been served by scholars. The favorable response to a session devoted to museums at the 1976 American Folklore Society convention (the first such panel in the society's history) signals growing awareness and interest in these institutions. For folklorists, these museums and the information they can convey to an attentive public are too important to lie unnoticed. In addition, folk museums theoretically bridge the disciplines of humanities and social sciences, crossing lines of thought and welding together good ideas from all.

Folk museum curators offer a criticism of the past—"criticism" meaning showing people how to "read" cultural history. The museum tour is the edited text, arranged to explain history to a diverse audience ranging from schoolchildren to senior citizens. The briefest and clearest statement of all this is still by G. B. Thompson: "A folk museum exists to illustrate the social history of the community it serves."[58] The promise of these outdoor museums lies in the accuracy of their depictions of regional folk culture and their application of humane thought in presenting history to the general public. With the artifacts of material culture as main props in the scene, such impressionistic views of the past may help us understand ourselves as a complex nation.

NOTES

1. A section of this chapter was read at the American Folklore Society meeting in Philadelphia in November 1976; at that time I held the position of historian and expansion coordinator at Conner Prairie pioneer settlement, Noblesville, Indiana. Willard B. Moore, my colleague at Conner Prairie, read the manuscript and made helpful suggestions; see also his article, Willard B. Moore, "Folklife Museums: Resource Sites for Teaching," *Indiana English Journal* 11 (Winter 1976–1977): 3–10.

2. Richard M. Dorson, ed., *Folklore and Folklife: An Introduction* (Chicago: University of Chicago Press, 1972); Don Yoder, ed., *American Folklife* (Austin: University of Texas Press, 1976).

3. American Folklife Preservation Act, Public Law 94-201, January 2, 1976.

4. Howard Wight Marshall, "Material Culture and the Museum," *Association for Living Historical Farms and Agricultural Museums Annual* 2 (1976): 35–38.

5. E. McClung Fleming, "The Place of Research in the Museum's Mission," in *Arts of the Anglo-American Community in the Seventeenth Century*, ed. Ian M. G. Quimby (Charlottesville: University of Virginia Press, 1975), 10–11.

6. The deep problems facing the curator when education is tied to entertainment were discussed in Willard B. Moore, "Staying Honest in a Folk Museum: Education

and Entertainment" (paper presented at the annual meeting of the American Folklore Society, Philadelphia, Pennsylvania, November 11–14, 1976).

7. Wilcomb E. Washburn, *Defining the Museum's Purpose* (Cooperstown: New York State Historical Association, 1975), 7.

8. This has been the case at the Welsh Folk Museum since the start; see J. Geraint Jenkins, "The Use of Artifacts and Folk Art in the Folk Museum," in Dorson, *Folklore and Folklife*, 498.

9. Suzi Jones, "Regionalization: A Rhetorical Strategy," *Journal of the Folklore Institute* 12 (1976): 105–20.

10. J. W. Y. Higgs, *Folklife Collection and Classification* (London: Museums Association, 1963), 4–8.

11. Åke Hultkrantz, *General Ethnological Concepts* (Copenhagen: Rosenkilde and Bagger, 1960), 132; Sigurd Erixon, "An Introduction to Folklife Research or Nordic Ethnology," *Folk-Liv* 15 (1950): 5.

12. For example, see Iorwerth C. Peate's *Tradition and Folk Life: A Welsh View* (London: Faber and Faber, 1972), 18, 20.

13. Holger Rasmussen, *Dansk Folkemuseum and Frilandmuseet, History and Activities* (Copenhagen: National Museet, 1966), 5.

14. Gösta Berg, rev., Adelhart Zippelius, *Handbuch der Europaischen Freilichtmuseen* (1974), *Ethnologia Scandinavica* (1975): 165–66.

15. Trefer Owen, *Welsh Folk Museum Handbook* (St. Fagans: National Museum of Wales, 1972), 7.

16. G. B. Thompson, *The Ulster Folk Museum* (Cultra Manor, IE: Ulster Folk Museum, n.d.), 2, 5.

17. Erling Welle-Strand, *Museums in Norway* (Oslo: Royal Ministry of Foreign Affairs, 1974), 4, 7.

18. Donald W. Callendar Jr., "Reliving the Past: Experimental Archaeology in Pennsylvania," *Archaeology* 29 (1976): 173–71; Donald W. Callendar Jr., "The Colonial Pennsylvania Plantation as a Research Tool" (manuscript, Bishop's Mill Historical Institute, 1975).

19. Yoder, *American Folklife*, 6.

20. Nils-Arvid Bringeus, "Artur Hazelius and the Nordic Museum," *Ethnologia Scandinavica* (1974): 7.

21. Bernard Fontana, "Bottles, Buckets, and Horseshoes: The Unrespectable in American Archaeology," *Keystone Folklore Quarterly* 13 (1968): 171–72; reprinted in Brian M. Fagan, ed., *Corridors of Time: A Reader in Introductory Archaeology* (Boston: Little, Brown, 1974), 304ff.

22. Higgs, *Folklife Collection and Classification*, 13.

23. G. Ellis Burcaw, *Introduction to Museum Work* (Nashville: American Association for State and Local History, 1975), 26.

24. Henry Glassie, "A Folkloristic Thought on the Promise of Oral History," in *Selections from the Fifth and Sixth National Colloquia on Oral History*, ed. Peter D. Olch and Forrest C. Pogue (New York: Oral History Association, 1972), 54.

25. Fleming, "The Place of Research in the Museum's Mission," 3–5, 8.

26. For example, H. R. Bradley Smith, *Blacksmith's and Farrier's Tools at Shelburne* (Shelburne, VT: Shelburne Museum, 1966).

27. Eugene H. Boudreau, *Making the Adobe Brick* (Berkeley, CA: Fifth Street Press, 1971).

28. J. Geraint Jenkins, *The English Farm Wagon* (Newton Abbot: David and Charles, 1961, 1972); Peate, *Tradition and Folk Life*; Alexander Fenton, *Scottish Country Life* (Edinburgh: John Donald, 1976).

29. Charles F. Montgomery and Patricia E. Kane, eds., *American Art, 1750–1800: Towards Independence* (Boston: New York Graphic Society, 1976).

30. Charles F. Hummel, *With Hammer in Hand* (Charlottesville: University of Virginia Press, 1973); Wilbur David Peat, *Indiana Houses of the Nineteenth Century* (Indianapolis: Indiana Historical Society, 1962); Edgar Preston Richardson, *A Short History of Painting in America*, rev. ed. (New York: Thomas Y. Crowell, 1963); Henry C. Mercer, *Ancient Carpenters' Tools*, rev. ed. (Doylestown, PA: Bucks County Historical Society, 1975); Bernard L. Fontana and J. Cameron Greenleaf, *Johnny Ward's Ranch: A Study in Historic Archaeology* (Tucson, AZ: Kiva, 1962); Joshua C. Taylor, *America as Art* (Washington, DC: National Collection of Fine Arts, 1976).

31. Brooke Hindle, *America's Wooden Age: Aspects of Its Early Technology* (Tarrytown, NY: Sleepy Hollow Restorations, 1975); Hindle is director of the National Museum of History and Technology. John T. Schlebecker, *Whereby We Thrive: A History of American Farming, 1607–1972* (Ames: Iowa State University Press, 1975).

32. See Jay Anderson, "Foodways Programs at Living Historical Farms," *Association for Living Historical Farms and Agricultural Museums Annual* 1 (1975): 21–22; Callendar, "Reliving the Past: Experimental Archaeology in Pennsylvania."

33. Jenkins, "The Use of Artifacts and Folk Art in the Folk Museum," 510; at the time (1977), only Conner Prairie in Indiana employed first-person presentations on a full-time basis.

34. Marion Clawson, "Living Historical Farms: A Proposal for Action," *Agricultural History* 30 (1965): 110.

35. John T. Schlebecker, *Living Historical Farms: A Walk into the Past* (Washington, DC: Smithsonian Institution, 1968); see also Holly Sidford, "Stepping into History," *Rural Visitor* 15 (1975): 5–6.

36. See Darwin Kelsey, "Historical Farms as Models of the Past," *Association for Living Historical Farms and Agricultural Museums Annual* 1 (1975): 33–39.

37. John T. Schlebecker and Gayle E. Peterson, *Living Historical Farms Handbook* (Washington, DC: Smithsonian Institution, 1972), 1.

38. Darwin Kelsey, "Harvests of History," *Historic Preservation* 28 (1976): 22.

39. Edward L. Hawes, "Living Historical Farms and the Environmental Historian," *Environmental Studies Newsletter* 3 (1976): 20–21; see also Edward L. Hawes, "Living Historical Farms in North America: New Directions in Research and Interpretation," *Association for Living Historical Farms and Agricultural Museums Annual* 2 (1976): 20–21.

40. Darwin Kelsey, "Living Historical Farms as Museums?" *Rural Visitor* 15 (1975): 21.

41. Association for Living Historical Farms and Agricultural Museums, *Selected Living Historical Farms, Villages, and Agricultural Museums in the United States and Canada* (Washington, DC: Smithsonian Institution, 1976).

42. *Pioneer Farmstead* (Cherokee, NC: Great Smoky Mountains Natural History Association, 1976), 3.

43. *Black Creek Pioneer Village* (Toronto: Metropolitan Toronto and Region Conservation Authority, n.d.), 1.

44. *Old World Wisconsin: An Outdoor Ethnic Museum* (Madison: State Historical Society of Wisconsin, 1973), 3.

45. *Westville Village* (Lumpkin, GA: Old Westville, 1973), unnumbered pages.

46. Edward L. Hawes, *Prospectus for the Clayville Rural Life Center* (Springfield, IL: Sangamon State University, 1976), 2.

47. *The LSU Rural Life Museum*, rev. ed. (Baton Rouge: Louisiana State University, Office of Publications, 1974), 5.

48. *Upper Canada Village: "Ontario's Living Heritage"* (Morrisburg, Ontario: St. Lawrence Parks Commission, 1975), 1–3.

49. Reading copy of *The Conner Prairie Concept*, ed. Howard W. Marshall (Research Department) (Noblesville, IN: Conner Prairie Pioneer Settlement, 1975); from discussions with the director and the museum's main consultant, Henry Glassie, whose influence over the past five years has been substantial.

50. Bringeus, "Artur Hazelius," 11.

51. Frederick L. Rath Jr., ed., *The New York State Historical Association and Its Museums: An Informal Guide* (Cooperstown: New York State Historical Association, 1975), 38.

52. See Hultkrantz, *General Ethnological Concepts*, 156.

53. Higgs, *Folk Life Collection and Classification*, 10.

54. Edward D. Ives, *Lawrence Doyle: The Farmer-Poet of Prince Edward Island* (Orono: University of Maine Press, 1971), 252.

55. Marshall, "Material Culture and the Museum," 4–7.

56. See Ralph Linton, "Nativistic Movements," in *Reader in Comparative Religion: An Anthropological Approach*, ed. William Lessa and Evan Vogt, rev. ed. (New York: Harper & Row, 1965), 449.

57. Burcaw, in *Introduction to Museum Work*, 57, claims that "history museums are more and more being concerned with the lives of all the people, not only the rich, the powerful, and the famous." But the emphasis in most is still on the finely crafted object and not on people and process.

58. Thompson, *The Ulster Folk Museum*, 2.

12

American Folk Museums Redux

Simon J. Bronner

Simon J. Bronner considers the trends and predictions made by Howard Wight Marshall in his seminal article "Folklife and the Rise of American Folk Museums" (1977). Observing developments over a forty-year period from the perspective of someone with feet in both academic and museum areas, Bronner suggests a reconceptualization of the folk museum from its previous iteration as a rural and farm museum. In light of changes in folklife theory to break with the idea of groups rooted in the land, Bronner evaluates efforts of museums and heritage organizations to interpret traditional practices, often with a minimum of artifacts, in mobile, urban, industrial, corporate, and maritime settings. He also differentiates between organized museums of folklife and folk displays in which communities, and even individuals, provide their own versions of heritage. Viewing the modernization of folklife representation in the twenty-first century leads Bronner to address the need for enhanced integration of academic and public education in the form of folk cultural programs, centers, institutes, organizations, and heritage parks. Bronner's observations follow his previous contributions to museological and folklife theory in *American Material Culture and Folklife* (1992) and the *Encyclopedia of American Folklife* (2006).

Howard Wight Marshall's "Folklife and the Rise of American Folk Museums" was a signal document for the folklife movement that gained steam during the 1960s and 1970s in North America. His survey in 1977 can be viewed as a report from the field to complement Don Yoder's manifesto in 1963 declaring folklife "a total scholarly concentration on the folk levels of a national or regional culture" that is especially manifested through the folk or open-air museum.[1] This movement owed, Yoder and Marshall both recognized, to preservationist and nationalistic projects in nineteenth-century northwest Europe, and they viewed distinctive American contributions in the growth of living historical farms, village restorations, and folk festivals devoted to multiple aspects of a regional or local culture. If the movement was to be sustained into the twenty-first century, however, an educational component to realize the holistic goals of folklife covering what Yoder called "the analysis of a folk culture in its entirety" would be needed.[2] For Yoder, the model was to have the museum be "an adjunct institution" to an ethnological institute, typically attached to a university, but Marshall treated the museum as an independent organization capable of conducting its own research, including regional fieldwork, and within its grounds providing a historic "laboratory" of folklife.[3] Marshall thought that American museums lagged behind European predecessors in such research, particularly in field studies, and used his essay to lay out a future agenda for the American version of the folk museum as well as review its increasing popularity.

A pivotal museum-centered "teaching moment" occurring a year after Yoder's pronouncement was the launch of the Cooperstown graduate programs in American folk culture and history museum studies.[4] The programs were the brainchild of folklorist and museum director Louis C. Jones, who was influenced by the research and educational components of outdoor folk museums comparable to his Farmer's Museum in Cooperstown, New York (the museum opened to the public in 1944). Even before the program began, Jones additionally touted as "folk museums" the indoor history museums in the complex at the New York State Historical Association because they dealt with the expressive culture and daily life of ordinary people in the past. Pointing to the distinction of folk museums as immersive educational spaces, Jones in 1948 organized annual summer seminars in American culture for college credit that included hands-on craft experiences as well as folkloristic overviews.[5] Advocating museums as primary "guides to the study of our own folk life" that academic anthropologists and historians had not provided, Jones called for "a new kind of local history that considers not alone the political and institutional development of a community but which really tells us how Everyman lived, the details of his work day, how he courted, loved, married, raised his family, accepted his responsibility in the social patterns of his time, and what he thought about these experiences."[6] Forging a partnership between the State University of New York and the New York State Historical Association, Jones envisioned training combining material culture and ethnological research with museological skills to place students, as well as change public perceptions of America's past, in the burgeoning public heritage field.[7] In the central New York State locale, students fanned across the countryside to document the cultural landscape and tradition bearers for museum interpretation, exhibition, and archival use (the Archive of New York State Folklife was organized for the programs).

FIGURE 12.1
The Farmer's Museum, Cooperstown, New York, operated by the New York State Historical Association and opened to the public as a "folk museum" in 1944. View of the "Crossroads Village" representing rural life in the late eighteenth and early nineteenth centuries, 2007. Under the direction of Louis C. Jones, the museum, beginning in 1964, was a location of work by students in American folk culture and history museum studies graduate programs. (Photo: Simon J. Bronner.)

Yoder, for his part in the movement, initiated as chair of a graduate group at the University of Pennsylvania in 1966 a way for students to obtain doctoral degrees in "folklore *and* folklife." As in Cooperstown, the program had a formidable outreach and archival component. Yoder was often featured at the "seminar stage" at the Kutztown Folk Festival, although the public folk museum that he and director of the Pennsylvania Folklife Society Alfred Shoemaker envisioned to bring together archival, educational, festival, and artifactual functions of folklife work did not become a reality. Indiana University's Folklore Institute, which also granted doctoral degrees in folklore, followed suit with folklife courses led by Warren Roberts, with whom Marshall studied. Roberts also had in mind a long-term project with these courses of creating an outdoor museum of preindustrial folklife in southern Indiana that would be erected on the campus grounds. As he learned, creating an immersive environment of the folk museum was a daunting task compared to the standard house or gallery museum, although a virtual version of the project was created years later.[8] In 1967, another milestone in the folklife institute-museum collaboration was the establishment of the Festival of American Folklife sponsored by the Smithsonian Institution on the conspicuous, symbolically important outdoor location of the National Mall in the capital of the United States.

Marshall brought to the table a decade after these developments evidence that folklorists, as staff and consultants, had indeed made an impact on America's history museums as they became more socially and culturally conscious. He considered the folklife movement most effective at the local and regional levels because everyday life of communities could be integrated there into national social history. A question implied by his survey is whether folk museums would emerge as a separate category of heritage organization in North America, the way they had in Europe, or whether the folklife concept would be integrated into the more prevalent heading of history or outdoor museum. Although he saw signs of change in the great-event- and noble-figure-oriented exhibitions prevalent in history museums, particularly around the time of the roots-inclined bicentennial celebration of American independence, he hoped that folklorists and the folklife concept would have made more of a difference in visitors' perception of their past that had been forged by basic education. At the collegiate level, his criticism that American museums generally romanticized a glorious democratic past with "noble pioneers and valiant immigrants," presented an aestheticized, or cleaned-up, version of folk cultural landscapes, and did not adequately exemplify America's folk cultural diversity resounded in countless seminars and conference halls. Marshall's plaint paved the way for other critical examinations of museums and heritage organizations that questioned whether museums could, and should, take the lead in altering what Marshall called "elitist history" and other scholars have derided as "consensus history."[9] The "new history" interpreted movements and changes at the grass roots, and with its social emphasis on everyday life, it frequently employed folkloristic and sociological methodologies.

One of those seminars raising this question is the one I teach in material culture and folklife at the Pennsylvania State University, Harrisburg, which features separate certificate programs in folklore and ethnography and in heritage and museum practice, in addition to a doctoral program in American studies.[10] The seminar brings together working professionals in museums and historical agencies with academic educators. Over the thirty-five years I have led this ensemble, the discussion of Marshall's article has veered from the "rise tale" of outdoor museums as the central component of a preservationist historical enterprise to the implications of folklife in a multicultural society as a living social reform project. Building on Marshall's argument with my assessment of folklife as it has been applied in museums and other heritage organizations, in addition to the experiences of hundreds of students engaged in folklife and museums over the years, I offer perspectives for the twenty-first century on four major observations made by Marshall:

1. Outdoor museums are a primary, artifact-centered folklife space oriented particularly to local and regional history.
2. American folk museum curators have largely borrowed from European models but have distinctively extended the European precedents in working farms and role-playing first-person interpretation.
3. Application of a folklife concept in museums is challenged by aesthetic and cultural preferences of the public and museum administrators for a cheery, entertaining environment.
4. Folk museums have the potential, largely unfulfilled, of providing revisionist and critical viewpoints on the past that can affect present thinking.

Before addressing these points, a review of the folklife concept applied by Jones, Yoder, Roberts, and Marshall is in order to see if the intellectual context still holds. Following European usage (particularly the Swedish *folkliv* and the model of Skansen and Nordiska Museet in Stockholm), "life" was meant to be more inclusive than "lore." Instead of concentrating on oral texts organized by literary genres associated with folkloristic work, folklife, or folk culture, covered the full range of traditions in communities and groups. In Europe, the people represented by folklife were often peasant or homogeneous societies engaged in agriculture and preindustrial crafts. They were landed groups associated with regional locations but whose language, religion, and customs constituted the expressive, hardy soul of the nation. Since Marshall wrote his essay, the folklife concept, sometimes rendered as ethnology or ethnography, has arguably been mainstreamed into American folkloristic work. Textbooks in American folklore typically include social and material traditions, in addition to discussion of regional, religious, occupational, and ethnic "folk groups."[11] However, the concept of a group in practice has been more elastic, influenced by American folklorist Alan Dundes's definition of folk groups as "*any group of people whatsoever* who share at least one common factor."[12] This view of group identity as emergent and overlapping affected folklife studies by shifting the preservationist view of historic peasant and rural communities to ethnographic, present studies of groups as they use and invent traditions, including those in industrial, urban, suburban, and corporate settings.[13] Dundes meant the definition to reflect uses of traditions to provide social bonding and identity in modern, complex societies, and he proposed it to counter European ethnological presumptions of folk as premodern, landed groups.[14]

To be sure, American folklife scholars claimed more than historians and anthropologists the study of tradition-centered, agrarian groups such as the Amish, Appalachians, and Cajuns. They could also point to the Hasidim as an urban religious group with a totalistic folklife and studies.[15] Groups gaining attention from a folklife perspective in the United States, which often was characterized as lacking a peasant class and being massified, included students, children, older adults, factory workers, firefighters, lawyers, and cab drivers. Complicating folklife as a totalistic examination was the idea that people had cultural identities that were overlapping and malleable, depending on the situation. Folklife scholars thus pointed to novel, often temporary settings as socially constructed "frames" of tradition, such as break rooms, summer camps, hunting lodges, student dormitories, and virtual spaces. Where does that leave the function of folk museums as providing cultural landscapes of the past? Although challenging to the conventional view of folk museums representing the pioneer past, the elastic conceptualization of folklife also opens possibilities for distinctive interpretation, outreach, and research for heritage organizations to engage modern life.

One obvious shift is reconfiguration of folk museums' historic focus and Marshall's assumption that museums primarily relied on artifacts to tell their stories.[16] In many locations, history museums integrated more cultural representation into exhibitions and in some cases explained contemporary life. Cultural tourism building on the fascination of the American public with multicultural, living traditions has influenced this presentation of life as these customs are practiced in the present. A prime example of tourism oriented toward a group's folklife is the Amish and Pennsylvania Germans in Lancaster County, Pennsylvania. The county attracts over 8 million visitors annually who visit several museums, including the Landis Valley Museum, founded as a folk museum devoted to Pennsylvania German culture.[17] In the manner of folk museums, Amish Village in Ronks, Pennsylvania, and The Amish Experience at Plain and Fancy Farm, in Bird-in-Hand, Pennsylvania, provide in a village environment buildings and practices of folklife but concentrate on contemporary lifestyles rather than the past. The primary audience for the museum is non-Amish, and according to the theory of sociologist Roy Buck, such establishments serve the Amish by drawing tourists away from observing the group on their farmlands into an intensive educational-commercial zone.[18] The Amish, it should be noted, are not averse to museum going. The Rough and Tumble Museum in Kinzers, Pennsylvania, is an outdoor museum devoted to steam engines and draws plain groups to work with steam-driven tractors, equipment, and blacksmithing as part of their living tradition, although other visitors view these as historic relics. Several museums in the area invite visitors to learn about folk traditions not through artifacts but through photographic, human, and video presentations. The video of "The Story of Jacob's Choice" at The Amish Experience, for example, depicts, according to the museum's website, "the everyday lives of the Fishers, an Old Order Amish family of *today*" (emphasis added).

FIGURE 12.2
The Amish Village, Ronks, Pennsylvania, 2014. Although it contains historic buildings, it advertises its main purpose to provide visitors with "an authentic look at today's Amish lifestyle." (Photo: Simon J. Bronner.)

While the museums of the "Dutch Country" in Pennsylvania beckon visitors by emphasizing the difference of an ethnic-religious group from modern mass culture, the conventional farm museums have needed to reconsider their roles as regional and local museums within a nationalistic framework. One example is Old World Wisconsin, opened in 1976 in Eagle, Wisconsin. It claims to be the world's largest museum dedicated to rural life, with a working farm and 1880s-period village. Reflecting a concern for cultural diversity, the outdoor museum is organized into different ethnic zones, including Danes, Norwegians, Poles, Germans, and Finns, who influenced upper-Midwest culture. At the Frontier Culture Museum in Staunton, Virginia, incorporated in 1986, curators added often-overlooked African and Native American settlements to the open-air museum after German and Irish farms were erected to show colonial influences on American culture. Each of these locations became a site for folklife research connecting living practices to the past and lessons about the significant multiple ethnic influences on modern American identity. While other history museums, such as house and ethnic museums, increasingly incorporated folklife information into their interpretation by the beginning of the twenty-first century, the emphasis on living traditions and multicultural continuities in what could be called experiential settings distinguished the educational trajectory of the "folk museum" in North America.

The Frontier Culture Museum also addressed another issue faced by the conventional farm museums often associated with folk activity: twenty-first-century visitors did not relate to agrarian processes on display as they had in the mid-twentieth century, when the preserved historic farm burst onto the scene. At the time that Marshall wrote, many farm museums could be viewed as a response to the decline in the family farm. A generation of visitors flocked to the sites to recall their personal experiences probably more than to learn about America's pioneer past. The created environments lacked interpretative labels that one would find in an indoor gallery. As much as possible, curators strived to surround visitors in a landscape as it had existed in the past in living memory. Later generations were not as familiar with the agrarian past at a personal level, and surveys showed that they did not understand the significance of the environment they entered. Many farm museums built interpretative galleries to provide background to visitors before they entered the farm. The Frontier Culture Museum introduced interpretative information at its sites after visitors viewed an orientation video. As in other locations, such museums have introduced special festive events on the sites to feature performances and hands-on activities. They reimagined the museum physical plant as a festive staging area for vernacular activity, performance, and know-how rather than as a preserved site of the past.

This reorientation raises the question of whether industrial and postindustrial settings can constitute folk museums. Yoder categorized folklife as "basically . . . rural and preindustrial." Moreover, he considered it "the opposite of the mass-produced, mechanized, popular culture of the twentieth century."[19] Yet, with American deindustrialization, many communities contemplate the creation of defunct industrial sites to show the traditional lives of workers and their gritty environments as well as folk arts. Often these settings do not conform well to the pastoral ideals of the farm museums, and they challenge the tendency that Marshall mentioned of aestheticizing folk sites. More than creating memorials and galleries, community organizers of industrial museums as folk museums often have in mind a location that tells a story less about the corporate and economic history in an industry and more about the lives and traditions of workers. Considering the impact of the American labor movement and mass immigration, the number of historical labor and ethnic museums is surprisingly small in North America, and folklife provided a perspective for community-minded organizers to represent social and cultural change.[20]

One flashpoint for this discourse on industrial heritage since Marshall wrote is the former site of Bethlehem Steel in Bethlehem, Pennsylvania. Civic organizers originally envisioned it as "Bethlehem Works," an open-air site in the tradition of folk museums, to signal it as a link between the past and future revival of the rust belt region. The site stood in stark contrast in town to the preindustrial folk museum of historic Bethlehem, developed to show the original Moravian colonial-era settlement. Creating a complementary folk museum out of the industrial site proved challenging compared to farm and village museums because of the enormity of the plant buildings and the difficulty (and danger) of re-creating the steelmaking process. There was also a tussle between community members and government officials over the narrative to be presented about the site. Eventually, the project was reconceived as the National Museum of Industrial History with a more conventional progressive narrative about "building America" in a restored former Bethlehem Steel facility rather than an open-air site. Cultural critic Carolyn Kitch reported, however, that many area residents wanted a folklife-oriented story "about local more than national pride and about the town's lingering feelings of loss and betrayal."[21] As with farm museums, there was a desire to link local generations to the site, but residents desired having the social setting represented rather than the museum's plan to create a large map of the former plant "so parents and grandparents can point to it and say, 'There's where I worked.'"[22]

In York, Pennsylvania, curators linked agriculture and industry in a museum for the York County Heritage Trust that fits into the community's self-conscious, gritty, multicultural image. Under the banner of "heritage," suggesting the community's own version of history and culture, the museum takes approaches that could be viewed as an extension of Marshall's folk museum concept. Although the trust has an open-air site with log buildings for its "colonial complex," it contains the industrial exhibits in a separate factory building that showcases locally made wagons, tractors, steam engines, and farm tools. As with other appeals of folk museums to view craft and practices

FIGURE 12.3
Visitors receive a tour of the Bethlehem Steel plant site, 2004. After the plant's closing in 1995, a project to reuse the site for cultural and recreational development was organized as "Bethlehem Works." A casino was constructed on the site in 2009, and preservation groups lobbied to save the furnaces and gas-blowing engine house. (Photo: Simon J. Bronner.)

of daily life, the building contains a seventy-two-ton A-frame ammonia compressor, once used to manufacture large blocks of ice, a three-story working gristmill, a hydraulic ramp pump, and a 1930s telephone exchange. Picking up a cue from a community-wide commitment to touting the city's designation as the "city of factories," motorcycle manufacturer Harley-Davidson has a museum in its factory to show not only the history of motorcycles but also the "folk" lifestyles of workers and Harley "hog"-riding groups. Various bike rallies and meets congregate around the site to provide a haven for biker culture. Several cultural organizations at community centers also feature exhibitions on the traditional arts and practices of ethnic groups such as Jews, Germans, Latinos, and African Americans. One might view these developments as an expansion of the folk museum concept to invite participation at the grassroots level by those involved in folk life.

Marshall finds significant the American use of first-person interpretation, although it has not been mainstreamed as he thought it might. An outgrowth in educational programming, however, is to "flip" first-person interpretation by having visitors take on historic and cultural roles. Rather than viewing a schoolhouse behind a divider, visitors participate as pupils. One controversy that emerged at Conner Prairie in Indianapolis, Indiana, where Marshall worked, involved such activities to deal with difficult aspects of America's past. In an educational program called "Follow the North Star," visitors "become actors on a 200-acre stage, running from slave hunters and working together to navigate the Underground Railroad to freedom," according to the museum's website. At the end of the program, which typically shakes youths to their core, participants draw correlations between slavery in 1836 and contemporary human trafficking, bullying, and equal rights struggles. Whereas museums were often viewed as providing a sanitized, romanticized view of the past, Conner Prairie endeavored to confront hard realities of past life and relate them to the present.

There is precedent for such work in the European models that Marshall mentions. At the Netherlands Open-Air Museum, established in 1918 in Arnhem, curators relate the past of ordinary residents to contemporary issues with themes that are explored through exhibitions and events through the site. Especially with many visitors more removed from the traditional preindustrial occupations and buildings preserved in the museums, curators work to bring more educational programming into the site and reconceptualize the folk museum, from its nationalistic, preservationist roots, as a location for dialog on social and political issues.[23] The museum has refocused its mission, in keeping with the changing view within folkloristic theory of the "folk" from rural life to everyday culture nationally and in the Dutch diaspora. Themes in the museum, amid concerns for a diversifying religious and ethnic Dutch population that has witnessed increasing social conflict in the twenty-first century, have included "religion" and "migration." Behind the scenes, researchers work on documenting traditional life and mapping folk cultural traits that demonstrate the ethnic, regional, linguistic, and occupational diversity of a country as small as the Netherlands. In the midst of headlines about European countries taking war refugees from the Middle East, the museum devoted a building to show a time when it served to house refugees from World War II.

Providing an urban model for folklife and disrupting the image of the European folk museum as rural is Den Gamle By (the old town) in Aarhus, Denmark, opened to the public in 1914 to show town and urban life. It consists of seventy-five buildings collected from all parts of the country rather than showing one particular neighborhood. It also has a comparative strategy in its display by inviting visitors to consider changes, for better or worse, in environments of the 1880s, 1920s, and 1970s. The director notes that the museum defies conventional wisdom about folk museums, especially when it proposed to rethink itself, from a location to display material culture, as a "space for people and dialogue."[24] Considerable dialog among people who remembered the 1970s ensued when the museum included a gynecologist's office and apartments shared by young adults and an unmarried teacher. The museum expanded plans for the urban folk district by including a second-hand shop with pornographic magazines, a room for scouts, the environment of a homeless person, and apartments for a blind man and immigrant workers from Turkey.[25] These initiatives, the director declares, expand the mission of folk museums as "radical and highly relevant institutions. They were radical because they focused on the daily lives of ordinary people, and they were relevant because their storytelling targeted ordinary people."[26]

A transnational aspect of this thematic development is to link American folk museums with points of origin and destination. The major example is the Ulster American Folk Park in Northern Ireland. Set up to show the Irish immigrant experience, the museum includes not only folk buildings from Ulster but also a re-creation of a crammed American urban street. Embracing the critical function that Marshall discusses, the representation in one location of the immigrant experience opens questions of adjustment, prejudice, and identity. On the American side, the Tenement Museum on the Lower East Side of New York City, authorized in 1998, shows the hardscrabble surroundings that became a dense hub of immigrants during the great wave of immigration from 1880 to 1920. Costumed interpreters discuss the struggles of immigrants in the new land and their negotiation of Old World traditions in the new urban environment. They contextualize their narrative in the ongoing process of settlement and housing problems in the inner-city neighborhood that has become a destination for new Latino and Asian immigration.

Although folklorists have had a hand in developing the folk museum concept primarily on land, a few locations embrace traditions of shore and sea, summarized as maritime folklife. In the twenty-first century these locations have gained traction more than the spread of living history farms that Marshall predicted. The largest in the world is Mystic Seaport in Mystic, Connecticut, which contains re-creations of a nineteenth-century seafaring village with more than sixty historic buildings and a collection of sailing ships. In addition to developing research on material culture, the seaport museum has created a niche related to the musical folklore of sailors, with academic symposia and concerts on music of the sea.[27] Other maritime museums represent contemporary traditions so as not to give the impression that maritime folk culture is past and gone. The Chesapeake Bay Maritime Museum in St. Michaels on the eastern shore of Maryland, for example, has a floating fleet and is a center for a log canoe racing tradition.[28] Curators have designed an apprentice program to allow visitors to construct a wooden skiff under the guidance of traditional craftsworkers and thus act to facilitate cultural continuity.

FIGURE 12.4
A child participates in a program to gain a "junior sailor's certificate" aboard a historic vessel in the National Maritime Museum in Amsterdam, the Netherlands, 2005. (Photo: Simon J. Bronner.)

The maritime folk museums often make a connection to the environment, which has become an issue of cultural as well as natural sustainability. Indeed, such settings are exemplary locations for the critical examinations that Marshall thought folk museums could host. As part of their look at the cultural and political economy that supported maritime and shoreline occupations such as fishing, hunting, and shipbuilding, questions come up in interpretation of changing ecosystems, social patterns, and the roles that humans have had, and should have in the future, in these developments. On land, the use of folk museums as forums for civic engagement is evident in "heritage areas" such as those designated by the National Park Service. Beginning in 1984, the US Congress designated National Heritage Areas (NHAs) as places where natural, cultural, and historic resources combine to form a "cohesive, nationally important landscape," according to the Park Service website. Of folklife interest, the Park Service considers NHAs to be a "grassroots, community-driven approach to heritage conservation and economic development." Folklife programming at museums and temporary heritage sites has been critical to the strategies of the NHAs that integrate different cultural projects in the regions. Often the NHAs center on an industrial theme such as oil, coal, and steel in Pennsylvania. The Rivers of Steel National Heritage Area around Pittsburgh, for example, features a regional folklife directory, folklife curriculum, and ethnographic surveys that consider past as well as emergent traditions related to steelmaking. Central to the Rivers of Steel plan is the creation of a national park on thirty-eight acres of the original Homestead Steel Works mill site. As a history museum, it represents the story of the famous 1892 Homestead strike; organizers want it, as a folk museum, to feature a narrative of unions and workers, as well as their effect on the regional culture and environment, that continues into the present.

From ship to shore, folk museums have followed for the most part the formula of representing a location or central artifact to frame tradition. In the wake of more attention to traditions as processes or practices, some museums experimented with organizing activities by activity or audience. Children's museums on the rise in North America, for example, direct attention to a youth audience. For the most part, the strategy of these museums was to introduce scientific learning at a child's level rather than a folkloristic consideration of children's culture. However, the Museum of Childhood, opened in London in 1974 as a branch of the Victoria and Albert Museum, emphasizes daily cultural activities for children about their own culture in addition to exhibiting artifacts. It is also a staging area for multicultural folk traditions such as the Chinese New Year and South Asian storytelling. Indeed, one might argue that exhibits, once the mainstay of museums, are minimized and pushed to the background, and activities and events predominate in the space. In the United States, intrepid organizers working with Margaret Woodbury Strong's vast collection of toys, games, and dolls recast what was the Strong Museum into "The Strong," a national museum of play meant for families. In a museum setting typically associated with quiet, passive examination of objects, visitors are often startled to see interactive exhibits that invite participation in play. The museum includes video and digital play with learning outcomes in mind. Other potential applications of this alternative behavioral approach to the folk museum concept are in storytelling, building, and singing. Expanding the idea of vernacular media, digital folk museums covering expressions and identities of digital culture by folk groups further challenge the museum as a brick-and-mortar institution.[29] With documentary and presentational tools at the disposal of users, there is also a process emerging of the digital prosumer (users who simultaneously produce and consume content), whereby individuals create representations (or folk curations) of their own cultures or personal worlds.[30]

Many of the museums discussed do not include "folk" or "folklife" in their names. This is indicative, I observe, of an interdisciplinary movement that began with the questioning, as Marshall noted, of whether the materialization of history in museums was too narrowly defined by events and figures rather than cultural concerns. In identifying itself as a museum of play, The Strong, for instance, resists labeling as a history, children's, or folk museum. To be sure, with more concern in the twenty-first century for cultural awareness, museums often incorporate folklife as part of their resources and activities. If there is an area related to museums that prominently waves the banner of folklife, it is in "folklife centers" that frequently have a museum component and often integrate events and activities into its programming. The Western Folklife Center in Elko, Nevada, for example, features exhibitions online as well as in gallery spaces, in addition to hosting the renowned National Cowboy Poetry Gathering. Often containing archives and artifact collections, some centers such as the Vermont Folklife Center and Down Jersey Folklife Program create exhibitions of folklife at other sites. The centers often cover regional, city, and ethnic cultures and are frequently affiliated with universi-

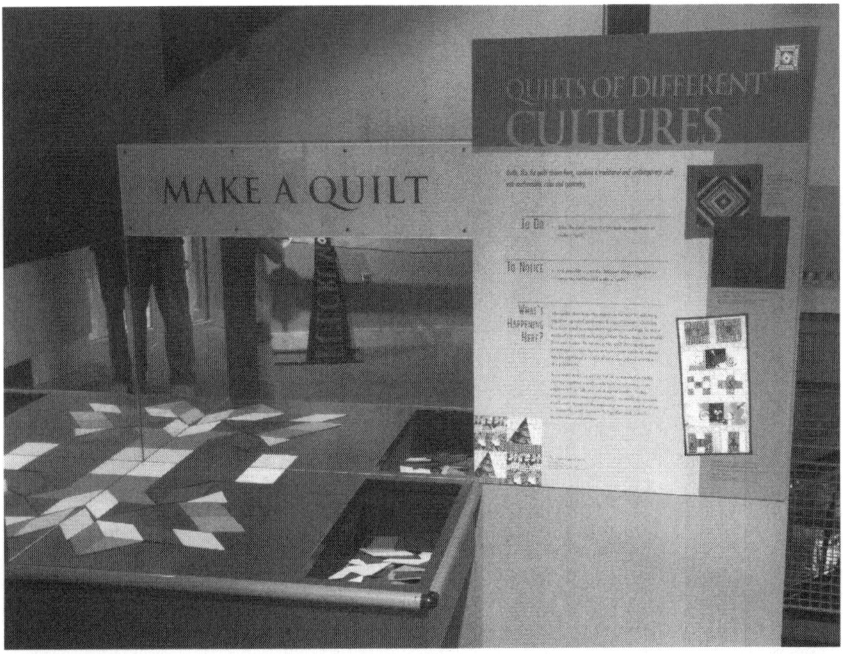

FIGURE 12.5
Folklife exhibit at the Whitaker Center for Science and the Arts, Harrisburg, Pennsylvania, 2009. The exhibit consisted of interactive hands-on activities, such as this one on making a quilt, rather than displays of historic or contemporary artifacts. (Photo: Simon J. Bronner.)

ties or cultural/governmental agencies as outreach and research organizations. At the national level, a model has been the American Folklife Center at the Library of Congress, which has sponsored exhibitions such as one on the American cowboy.[31] At the Tennessee River Folklife Interpretive Center and Museum in Pilot in Nathan Bedford Forrest State Park, there is more of a traditional notion of a permanent physical plant for a "folk museum," but it is significant that the narrative, in keeping with the folklife concept, emphasizes practices and processes of traditional life transcending the past and present: "The center features the life ways and customs of folks on the Tennessee River including musseling, crafts, commercial fishing and more."[32] The "folklife center" development is in many ways a culmination of the goals set forth by Yoder, Marshall, Jones, and Roberts to integrate research, archives, performance, and education into a single institution beyond the museum. Even if "folk museums" are not being named as such, one can witness the application of their philosophy in the rise of folklife centers.

Another evolution since Marshall wrote is in educational partnerships between museums and universities. Separate folklife training related to museums by groundbreaking university programs I mentioned earlier at Cooperstown, University of Pennsylvania, and Indiana University have given way, I daresay, to programs in heritage studies, regional studies, and American studies that take up folklife, folklore, and ethnography in a wider cultural context.[33] Museums have also created short-term programs and internships to facilitate folk museum specialization. Thus it is not only the folk material culture of concern, as the folklife centers have shown, but also the integration of various traditional practices, including music, dance, storytelling, and custom into a broader, multipronged organizational strategy. One should read the frequent labeling of "cultural heritage" (sometimes divided in scholarly discourse between tangible and intangible heritage) and "traditional knowledge" in the designation of heritage sites and concern for community perspectives as an outgrowth of the folk museum movement.[34] It still relies on folklife methodologies and theories and arguably should recognize the intellectual legacy of folklife more.[35] Indeed, it responds to the folklife concept of blurring museum boundaries as a culturally centered living display.[36]

One sign of that blurring process is Marshall's claim that the museum is at bottom an "impression" rather than a structural type. In this view, the museum as an organization of knowledge communicates by its sponsorship, audience, setting, and activity its perspective on the past and future. Folk museums since their European origins have covered a wide range of purposes but are ultimately linked together in emphasizing "folk" experience of group life. Folk museums as intellectual as well as physical constructions have evolved from preserves of local and purported national tradition in response to rapid industrialization, immigration, and urbanization into a wider folklife project to represent community and identity practices often associated with "heritage." Marshall noted that folk museums by their grassroots perspective had the potential of turning history museums on their head. Folklorists meanwhile were affected by being challenged to consider material traditions and landscapes more, in addition to being more historically aware as well as ethnographically conscious. While not quite the revolution that he predicted, the folk museum movement was nonetheless significantly evident in a growing folk, local cultural consciousness by the public and museum world, in addition to affecting various academic disciplines such as history and anthropology. I might put the transformation, if not ebb, of the folk museum movement with the development of industrial and maritime museums in the early twenty-first century, but also point to the noticeable, paradigm-changing trajectory of folklife centers as a new iteration of the folklife concept. Folklife, as a perspective people engage as well as scholars represent, constitutes a steady process of providing critical viewpoints from the ground up on past and present thinking.

NOTES

1. Yoder 1963, 43.

2. Ibid., 43.

3. See Anderson 1976–1977; Anderson 1984.

4. "American Folk Culture" 1964; Buckley 1984.

5. Clay 1960; Rath 1975, 3–4.

6. Jones 1982, 19.

7. Rath 1975, 5–6.

8. See the Warren E. Roberts Museum of Early Indiana Life (http://www.iub.edu/~wer).

9. Leon and Rosenzweig 1989; Schlereth 1978; Walker 2013; Woods 1990.

10. Bronner 2012.

11. See Brunvand 1998; Dorson 1972.

12. Dundes 1980, 6.

13. Bronner 2006.

14. Dundes 1966; see also Bronner 2007; Oring 1986.

15. Mintz 1998.

16. See Bronner 1994.

17. Johnson 2002; Trollinger 2012.

18. Buck 1978.

19. Yoder 1963, 43.
20. See Lane 1993; Stanton 2006.
21. Kitch 2012, 141.
22. Ibid.
23. De Jong 2010.
24. Bloch Ravn 2013, 49.
25. Ibid.
26. Ibid., 50.
27. Frank 1980; Grasso 1998.
28. See Glassie 1972–1973; Williams 2013, 177–79.
29. Hansen 2009; Henderson 2014.
30. See Buccitelli 2016; Papaioannou and Stergiaki 2012.
31. Taylor and Maar 1983.
32. Nathan 2015.
33. Stefano, Davis, and Corsane 2012.
34. Foster and Gilman 2015.
35. Ballard 2008; Dewhurst 2014; Feltault 2006.
36. See Dewhurst and MacDowell 1998; Kurin 2007.

REFERENCES

"American Folk Culture: A Graduate College Program." 1964. *New York Folklore Quarterly* 20: 130–33.

Anderson, Jay. 1976–1977. "Immaterial Material Culture: The Implications of Experimental Research for Folklife Museums." *Keystone Folklore* 21: 1–13.

———. 1984. *Time Machines: The World of Living History*. Nashville: AASLH.

Ballard, Linda-May. 2008. "Curating Intangible Cultural Heritage." *Anthropological Journal of European Cultures* 17: 74–95.

Bloch Ravn, Thomas. 2013. "A Museum for the Fool and the Professor." In *Museums: Social Learning Spaces and Knowledge Producing Processes*, edited by Ida Braendholt Lundgaard and Jackob Thorek Jensen, 46–61. Copenhagen: Danish Agency for Culture.

Bronner, Simon J. 1994. "From Nature to Culture and Object to Image: Challenges for the Preservation of the Past for the Future." In *Conserving Cultural Heritage in the 21st Century*, edited by Marilyn Kisly, 15–22. Ann Arbor: Historical Society of Michigan.

———. 2006. "Folklife and Folk Culture." In *Encyclopedia of American Folklife*, edited by Simon J. Bronner, 410–14. Armonk, NY: M. E. Sharpe.

———, ed. 2007. *The Meaning of Folklore: The Analytical Essays of Alan Dundes.* Logan: Utah State University Press.

———. 2012. "Folklore Studies within American Studies: The Penn State Harrisburg Model." *AFS Review*. February 13. http://www.afsnet.org/news/news.asp?id=83354#comments.

Brunvand, Jan Harold. 1998. *The Study of American Folklore: An Introduction.* 4th ed. New York: W. W. Norton.

Buccitelli, Anthony Bak. 2016. *City of Neighborhoods: Memory, Folklore, and Ethnic Place in Boston.* Madison: University of Wisconsin Press.

Buck, Roy C. 1978. "Boundary Maintenance Revisited: Tourist Experience in an Old Order Amish Community." *Rural Sociology* 43: 221–34.

Buckley, Bruce R. 1984. "New Beginnings and Old Ends: Museums, Folklife, and the Cooperstown Experiment." *Folklore Historian* 1: 24–31.

Clay, George R. 1960. "The Lightbulb Angel: Towards a Definition of the Folk Museums at Cooperstown." *Curator: The Museum Journal* 3: 43–65.

De Jong, Adriaan. 2010. "New Initiatives in the Netherlands Open Air Museum: How an Early Open Air Museum Keeps Up with the Times." *Acta Ethnographica Hungarica* 55: 333–56.

Dewhurst, C. Kurt. 2014. "Folklife and Museum Practice: An Intertwined History and Emerging Convergences" (American Folklore Society Presidential Address, October 2011). *Journal of American Folklore* 127: 247–63.

Dewhurst, C. Kurt, and Marsha MacDowell. 1999. "Gathering and Interpreting Tradition: Rethinking the Role of the Museum." *Journal of Museum Education* 24: 7–10.

Dorson, Richard M., ed. 1972. *Folklore and Folklife: An Introduction.* Chicago: University of Chicago Press.

Dundes, Alan. 1966. "The American Concept of Folklore." *Journal of the Folklore Institute* 3: 226–49.

———. 1980. *Interpreting Folklore*. Bloomington: Indiana University Press.

Feltault, Kelly. 2006. "Development Folklife: Human Security and Cultural Conservation." *Journal of American Folklore* 119: 90–110.

Foster, Michael Dylan, and Lisa Gilman, eds. 2015. *UNESCO on the Ground: Local Perspectives on Intangible Cultural Heritage*. Bloomington: Indiana University Press.

Frank, Stuart M., ed. 1980. *Songs of the Sea: Proceedings of the First Annual Symposium on Traditional Music of the Sea, Mystic Seaport Museum*. Mystic, CT: Mystic Seaport Museum.

Glassie, Henry. 1972–1973. "The Nature of the New World Artifact: The Instance of the Dugout Canoe." *Schweizerisches Archiv für Volkskunde* 68–69: 153–70.

Grasso, Glenn, ed. 1998. *Songs of the Sailor: Working Chanteys at Mystic Seaport*. Mystic, CT: Mystic Seaport.

Hansen, Gregory. 2009. "Public Folklore in Cyberspace." In *Folklore and the Internet: Vernacular Expression in a Digital World*, edited by Trevor J. Blank, 194–212. Logan: Utah State University Press.

Henderson, Amy. 2014. "Can Museums and Other Institutions Keep Up with Digital Culture?" Smithsonian.com. March 7. http://www.smithsonianmag.com/smithsonian-institution/can-museums-and-other-institutions-keep-up-digital-culture-vulture-180949926/?no-ist.

Johnson, Elizabeth. 2002. *Landis Valley Museum: Pennsylvania Trail of History Guide*. Mechanicsburg, PA: Stackpole.

Jones, Louis C. 1982. *Three Eyes on the Past: Exploring New York Folk Life*. Syracuse, NY: Syracuse University Press.

Kitch, Carolyn. 2012. *Pennsylvania in Public Memory: Reclaiming the Industrial Past*. University Park: Pennsylvania State University Press.

Kurin, Richard. 2007. "Sharing, Crossing, and Subsuming Museum Boundaries: Current Directions." *RES: Anthropology and Aesthetics* 52: 59–64.

Lane, James B. 1993. "Oral History and Industrial Heritage Museums." *Journal of American History* 80: 607–18.

Leon, Warren, and Roy Rosenzweig, eds. 1989. *History Museums in the United States: A Critical Assessment.* Urbana: University of Illinois Press.

Mintz, Jerome R. 1998. *Hasidic People: A Place in the New World.* Cambridge, MA: Harvard University Press.

Nathan Bedford Forrest State Park. 2015. "About." http://tnstateparks.com/parks/about/nathan-bedford-forrest.

Oring, Elliott, ed. 1986. *Folk Groups and Folklore Genres.* Logan: Utah State University Press.

Papaioannou, Georgios, and Athanasia Stergiaki. 2012. "Students as Co-curators in the Virtual Museum of Folk Musical Instruments for Children: Roles, Rules and Realities." *International Journal of Heritage in the Digital Era* 1: 632–45.

Rath, Fred. 1975. "The Great Adventure: Louis C. Jones and the New York State Historical Association." *New York Folklore* 1: 1–6.

Schlereth, Thomas J. 1978. "It Wasn't That Simple." *Museum News* 56 (January/February): 36–41.

Stanton, Cathy. 2006. *The Lowell Experiment: Public History in a Postindustrial City.* Amherst: University of Massachusetts Press.

Stefano, Michelle L., Peter Davis, and Gerard Corsane, eds. 2012. *Safeguarding Intangible Cultural Heritage.* Woodbridge, UK: Boydell Press.

Taylor, Lonn, and Ingrid Maar. 1983. *The American Cowboy.* Washington, DC: American Folklife Center, Library of Congress.

Trollinger, Susan L. 2012. *Selling the Amish: The Tourism of Nostalgia.* Baltimore: Johns Hopkins University Press.

Walker, William. 2013. *A Living Exhibition: The Smithsonian and the Transformation of the Universal Museum.* Amherst: University of Massachusetts Press.

Wallace, Michael. 1996. *Mickey Mouse History, and Other Essays on American Memory.* Philadelphia: Temple University Press.

Williams, James C. 2013. "Sailing as Play." *Icon* 19: 132–92.

Woods, Thomas A. 1990. "Getting beyond the Criticism of History Museums: A Model for Interpretation." *Public Historian* 12: 76–90.

Yoder, Don. 1963. "The Folklife Studies Movement." *Pennsylvania Folklife* 13: 43–56.

13

The National Cowboy Poetry Gathering

A Case Study in Folklorist and Tradition Bearer Collaboration

Meg Glaser and Charlie Seemann

Meg Glaser and Charlie Seemann provide a case study of the National Cowboy Poetry Gathering (NCPG) of the Western Folklife Center (WFC), its genesis in fieldwork by professional folklorists, and its close collaboration with tradition bearers in all stages of development of the event. They discuss how the WFC's museum programs grew out of the gathering and how fieldwork, collaborative planning, and involvement have continued to shape WFC programming beyond the National Cowboy Poetry Gathering. Involving tradition bearers in key roles beyond just being advisors, such as recruiting them as guest curators, has given community members a feeling of being real stakeholders and having ownership in the representation and presentation of their own cultures. It has enabled the building of deep, long-lasting relationships that have benefited both communities and the presenting organization.

The Western Folklife Center, a 501(c)3 nonprofit, was founded in Salt Lake City, Utah, in 1980, dedicated to exploring, presenting, and preserving the diverse and dynamic cultural heritage of the American West.[1] Over the years, the WFC developed into a major cultural institution in the western United

States, with a broad range of activities and programs working with indigenous, occupational, ethnic, and other communities throughout the West and internationally. Performances, exhibitions, educational programs, media productions (radio and television), research, documentation, and preservation projects celebrate the wisdom, artistry, and ingenuity of western folkways. The WFC's flagship event is the National Cowboy Poetry Gathering, started in 1985 by a collaboration of folklorists and working cowboys, ranching people, and tradition bearers, a model of partnership that would become the base methodology for all of the organization's work going forward.

GENESIS AND DEVELOPMENT OF THE NCPG

The first gathering located and brought together cowboy poets, bearers of a tradition of occupational poetry dating back to the cattle trail-driving days of the late 1800s, for a public presentation in Elko, Nevada. Elko, with a lively cowtown heritage, central location, local leadership, poets, partners, and facilities (Northern Nevada Community College [Great Basin College], Northeastern Nevada Museum, and Elko Convention Center), provided an ideal setting. Center founding director Hal Cannon, working with state folklorists in western states and other contract fieldworkers, conducted extensive fieldwork and eventually selected about forty poets and reciters from across the West and invited them to come to Elko. Seeded with funds from the National Endowment for the Arts, the event was to be a onetime affair, but it was so enthusiastically received by the ranching community and the general public that it became an annual event and sparked a renaissance in cowboy poetry and song, spawning more than a hundred similar spin-off events throughout the ranching West. In 2000, the US Senate proclaimed the event the National Cowboy Poetry Gathering.

ACQUISITION OF HEADQUARTERS FACILITY AND IMPACTS

Growth in size and importance of the gathering shaped the trajectory of the organization, leading it increasingly in the direction of becoming a full-fledged cultural center with a strong museum component. While the early emphasis was on the intangible cultural expressions of poetry and music, the event was, from the beginning, complemented by exhibits of related material culture and art. These exhibitions, presented in partnership with Northern Nevada Community College (Great Basin College) and the Northeastern

FIGURE 13.1
National Heritage fellows third-generation Montana rancher and poet Wallace McRae and cowboy singer Glenn Ohrlin perform onstage at the 2011 National Cowboy Poetry Gathering. (Photo: Copyright ©Jessica Brandi Lifland.)

Nevada Museum, featured occupational crafts such as saddle making, bit and spur making, and rawhide braiding. They attracted larger and larger audiences, especially working cowboys, craftsmen, and collectors. Eventually, a renaissance of handcrafted horse and riding gear developed parallel to that of poetry and music.

From 1984 to 1991, the Elko office of the Western Folklife Center operated out of donated space at the Northeastern Nevada Museum, Northern Nevada Community College (Great Basin College), and Elko Convention and Visitors Authority. Commitment to continuing the gathering in Elko led the organization to seek a facility for year-round offices and visitors, as well as the building of collections and exhibition space for longer-term installations. In 1991, board member George Gund III purchased the historic Pioneer Hotel building in downtown Elko as a permanent home for the Western Folklife Center. Renovation began immediately, with support from the state of Nevada, foundation grants, and private support, and over the next two decades a performance theater, exhibition gallery, archives space, and museum store were created. The building also housed the historic Pioneer Saloon, which was restored to its original splendor.

The acquisition of a permanent facility allowed for an expansion of programs beyond the annual National Cowboy Poetry Gathering: the Wiegand Gallery became a venue for year-round exhibitions, including traveling shows; designed for multiple-uses, the theater made year-round concerts and other presentations possible; the Western Folklife Center's Pioneer Saloon and GIII Theater are popular venues for community events, allowing the earned income from rentals to increase the organization's revenue base.

COLLABORATIVE PROCESS

A key WFC practice is a collaborative approach to the design, curation, and production of the National Cowboy Poetry Gathering, its exhibitions, and other programs. As a natural extension of research and fieldwork, the engagement of advisors and knowledgeable individuals—often folk artists—has provided valued solutions at every step of the process. Input is sought out of necessity, out of respect, and to expand knowledge, networks, and resources. This approach has nurtured long-term relationships and deeper investments in and understanding of our work. In early years, input about the future of the gathering was sought at meetings convened during the event. More recently, meetings organized during the NCPG have focused on seeking involvement from the next generation. Periodically, ad hoc steering committees serve as sounding boards for programmatic directions for the gathering. In the months leading up to the event, the WFC convenes an artist selection committee, usually comprising a cowboy poet, musician, and folklorist to jury and recommend performing artists. Stakeholders, artists, and colleagues are regularly surveyed to collect input. Over the three decades of gatherings, the relationships forged between artists, colleagues, patrons, and volunteers have enhanced a collective sense of ownership of the event.

For exhibitions, the collaborative model takes many forms. The selection of artists and show themes is arrived at in various ways. Staff members often work with folk artists, colleagues, and guest curators to arrive at a focus and an artist invitation list. The involvement of artists as curators, installers, advisors, and more has been critical to the successful production of these exhibitions.

EXHIBITION DEVELOPMENT IN THE CONTEXT OF THE NATIONAL COWBOY POETRY GATHERING

The production of exhibitions within the context of the National Cowboy Poetry Gathering has afforded numerous opportunities for learning and experimentation that have carried over into the year-round exhibition program at the Western Folklife Center. What began as an organic planning approach to the gathering and related exhibitions became more formalized and refined as the organization made a commitment to produce the festival on an annual basis and eventually invest in the Pioneer Hotel facility in Elko.

With over one hundred invited artists and participants coming together for a week of activities, there are abundant opportunities for exhibition-related programming. These have included demonstrations of leather carving and cinch making; hands-on workshops in silver engraving, photography, and rawhide braiding; discussion panels on how to value artwork; gallery talks and performances; artwork appraisals and films. Gallery docents, reception hosts, and exhibition-related volunteers are recruited and trained along with other festival staff. Artists, exhibitors, and sponsors benefit from a large and enthusiastic audience—peak conditions to open an exhibition, acknowledge exhibition sponsors and donors, and bring attention and sales to featured artists.

The expansive approach to programming generates endless ideas for exhibition subjects. Exhibitions curated and hosted as part of the National Cowboy Poetry Gathering often draw inspiration from the event's programmatic themes. These have included surveys of Native American cowboys and regional ranching traditions of Hawaii, the Great Basin, Florida, the Northern Plains, and the Southwest. Over the years, programs have also included international exchanges with the herding cultures of Australia, Mexico, Hungary, Mongolia, Scotland, Wales, Ireland, Northumberland, Canada, France, Colombia, Brazil, Italy, and Argentina. All of these programs build from folklife fieldwork and research—whether conducted by WFC staff or colleagues—and ideally have at least three years for planning. Sufficient time is especially required for paperwork and international shipping of exhibition artifacts, with regulations and procedures varying from country to country and year to year. Occasionally, elements of an exhibition have arrived in a suitcase with a guest artist.

The gear of the working cowboy makes up a significant part of over thirty years of presenting exhibitions. Artisans in this multigenerational community have experienced a transition from viewing their work simply as a utilitarian occupational craft to seeing it as an art, which has led to exhibitions that push the boundaries of tradition. For several years, master artisans Jeremiah and Colleen Watt worked with WFC staff to create "Gathering of Gear" exhibitions for the gathering. Many of these were organized by genre, such as "Cowboy Chrome," a silver and metalworking exhibition, "Saddle Up," a saddle-making exhibition, and "Braided, Twisted, and Tied," a leather, rawhide, and horsehair exhibition. The Watts juried and communicated with artists, installed displays, and facilitated sales. Their role was eventually given the title of guest curator, with a job description that varied depending on the holder's skills and availability. A guest curator is contracted for exhibitions requiring special expertise and assistance and has become increasingly important as WFC staff resources are focused on other areas of program development.

EXHIBITION PROGRAM

The Western Folklife Center typically presents two to four exhibitions a year in its Wiegand Gallery and occasional off-site installations of its traveling exhibitions. This rotation schedule works well within a larger program schedule. In-house exhibition staff has numerous responsibilities beyond exhibition development and production. The number of return visitors does not demand a more intensive exhibit rotation schedule. Exhibitions are a combination of in-house productions and affordable traveling exhibitions. The special exhibitions that open during the gathering usually remain on display for seven to eight months for maximum exposure.

The WFC is a folklife organization with a long history of fieldwork, professional media production, and event documentation, and its archival collection is a rich resource for exhibitions. Increasingly, the organization incorporates media installations into all public exhibition space, including its Wiegand Gallery, Pioneer Saloon, and website (www.westernfolklife.org), such as a popular production *Why the Cowboy Sings* in the gallery's black box theater, an interactive Cowboy Music Jukebox, a series of short videos on the art of gear making, and highlights from the "Deep West Videos" program. Most media installations require push-button, computer-driven technology, requiring another layer of expertise to install and maintain, especially in an area with numerous power bumps.

Because of the Western Folklife Center's reputation as headquarters for the National Cowboy Poetry Gathering, visitors expect to see exhibitions of ranch culture year-round. This is certainly the strength of the WFC's collections. In 1992, with acclaimed western artist William Matthews's support and leadership, the Western Folklife Center established a Contemporary Gear Fund as a means of building a collection of contemporary handcrafted gear representative of the region and its respected makers. Over the years the collection has grown incrementally through the generous donation of gear and funds and is the foundation of an online exhibition, "Back at the Ranch—an Artful Life," a series of short videos on the art of gear making, and semipermanent installations in the Wiegand Gallery.

The WFC fulfills its broader mission through a variety of exhibitions showcasing contemporary folk arts of other western cultural communities. These have included exhibitions of Shoshone and Paiute basketry, Navajo weaving, Basque sheep ranching and music, and more. Some of the most popular exhibitions mix folk art with other visual art (e.g., pairing William Matthews's watercolors with buckaroo gear or Craig Sheppard's artwork with the WFC's contemporary gear collection).

CHALLENGES OF EXHIBITION PROGRAMMING IN A RURAL SETTING WITH LIMITED STAFF AND BUDGET

Unlike larger museums in urban settings, the WFC has no staff solely dedicated to exhibition oversight and development. The organization's artistic director is also involved in the curation and production of the National Cowboy Poetry Gathering, year-round programs, planning, fund-raising, and outreach. Titles are blurred, and roles of typical museum staff are often fulfilled by fewer people, including volunteers. Because of budgetary limitations, the center is always seeking volunteers with special skills—curation, record keeping, writing/editing, construction, fabrication, installation, lighting, electrical, and technical. When possible, contract staff is brought on to assist, most often from out of town. These have included professional photographers, fabricators, designers, cowboy craftsmen, blacksmiths, welders, woodworkers, lighting designers, and audiovideo technicians. Operating a museum and cultural center in a rural setting has inherent challenges. There is a limited skill base, availability of resources, and specialized materials. You can't go to a local store to purchase many things. It is necessary to plan well ahead when ordering supplies or make do with what you can find locally. Typically, exhibitions must be produced within a short period.

With international programs, where language and communication are a challenge, much of the work of writing exhibit text has to wait until international folk artists and partners are in town and installation is well under way. When possible these special guests are brought in early to make final adjustments to installations, lead tours for school groups, and train docents. When translators are limited, communication is overcome in other ways (drawings, working side by side in the workshop to construct things, and going to local hardware stores to shop the aisles together). When the center conducted an international exchange with Baja California *vaqueros* and ranchers, a local Spanish-speaking Basque craftsman worked side by side with a Baja California–based professor and artist to build a typical Baja ranch house in the exhibit gallery. Skills were shared through the intensive production phase, and strong, lasting international friendships were formed.

FIGURE 13.2
Baja California *vaquero* exhibit in the E. L. Wiegand Gallery at the Western Folklife Center, 2015. (Photo: Steve Green.)

WHAT FOLKLORISTS HAVE CONTRIBUTED TO MUSEUM EXHIBITIONS, WHAT MUSEUMS HAVE CONTRIBUTED TO US, AND HOW FOLK ARTISTS HAVE BEEN WOVEN INTO THE PROCESS

Staff folklorists bring their skills to the exhibition production process in various ways. Fieldwork underlies all of the Western Folklife Center's programming. The collaboration of folklorist staff and tradition bearers has contributed valued professional development to hundreds of folk artists. Staff interview traditional artists to write and edit biographical sketches, artist's statements, and artwork descriptions; arrange for professional photographs of artists and their work; assist with assessing sales values of their work; offer educational forums for discussing the valuing of work and other issues/topics; and bring their work to the public through workshops, demonstrations, and onsite and online exhibitions.

In return, folklorists have learned how to properly display horse gear from the cowboys. Cowboys are often enlisted to help install work and as a result are increasingly skilled in the art of display in a museum context.

Working with this community over time has allowed staff to see artists grow and evolve. The long time frame has also brought on the next generation of artists working within artistic families and from a long legacy of master-apprentices. For example, silver artist Nevada Watt, daughter of guest curators Jeremiah and Colleen Watt, was instrumental in the design and maintenance of the Facebook page for the exhibition "Expressing the Rural West—into the Future." Facebook artisan groups organized around interests of leatherwork, silverwork, and more share educational videos and tips, advertise workshops and trade shows, trade and sell, and offer ever-new resources for curatorial staff.

EDUCATIONAL COMPONENT OF NCPG

Education programs for both youth and adults are an integral part of the National Cowboy Poetry Gathering. For youth, participatory and cultural opportunities span two weeks during the gathering and annually engage more than seventy-two hundred youth from almost twenty schools and home-school programs in Elko County. Through these programs, young people learn about the value of traditional arts in the rural West, visit exhibits, create original artwork, meet and learn from internationally acclaimed musicians, writers, and artists, and perform for NCPG audiences. Extracurricular and enhanced classroom learning opportunities are scarce for young people in Elko County, an underserved rural area. Special guests from international cultural exchanges spend a week in Elko to present educational programs in the schools, workshops, performances, discussions, and exhibit-related programming.

These include a Western Folklife Center Youth Festival inviting third- and fourth-grade students to visit the Western Folklife Center to learn about cowboy life, be the first visitors to the latest exhibition, participate in a hands-on leather-stamping activity, and finish up with a glass of sarsaparilla in the Pioneer Saloon. Art teachers and instructors from K–12 schools are encouraged to work with students to create work especially for a student art show that opens during the National Cowboy Poetry Gathering. Teacher-juried artwork from students around Elko County is displayed at the Western Folklife Center for four months, culminating in a popular student reception. Early in the week of the National Cowboy Poetry Gathering, cowboy artists travel to schools throughout Elko County and students travel to the Elko Convention Center Auditorium to present entertaining and educational programs about cowboy poetry and traditional music. The "Young Buckaroo Open Mic and Talent Showcase" provides an opportunity for students eighteen and under to perform original poetry, classic recitations, western music, and dance in a supportive, welcoming atmosphere.

Educational programs for high school students include "Poetry Writing for Teens," bringing together local teens to receive heart-to-pen guidance on finding inspiration and expressing passion on the page from word wrangler and poet Paul Zarzyski. "From Page to Stage," a poetry recitation class with some of the finest cowboy poets and reciters, presents a hands-on coaching session for interested teens. Students involved in the national "Poetry Out Loud" program are often among the participants. A "Teen Poetry and Music Slam" invites teens to share original work or classics onstage at the Western Folklife Center. Participants in the poetry writing and reciting workshops are especially encouraged to sign up.

Educational programming for adults takes several forms. Hands-on workshops, led by master craftsmen, offer opportunities for participants to learn traditional arts such as leather working, rawhide braiding, hat making, and silver engraving. Musical workshops, such as in fiddle, guitar, and mandolin, are taught by virtuoso traditional musicians. Writing workshops, including

FIGURE 13.3
Rancher and singer Trinity Seely talks with grade school students during a school program. (Photo: Charlie Ekburg.)

in poetry, songwriting, and narrative, are presented by leading wordsmiths, many of whom are performers at the gathering. Cooking workshops focus on cuisines ranging from Dutch oven cooking and Basque food to the cuisines of Mongolia, Hungary, and other countries.

In addition to workshops the artistic and performance aspects of the gathering are complemented by keynote addresses, panel discussions, and humanities lectures on topics having to do with ranching culture and various related issues in the West. The discussion panels and lectures provide information and foster participation in conversations about rural life and western residents' relationships to animals and the land. Over the years, these programs have had a significant impact on ranching, sustainable agriculture, and conservation issues in the West. In 1992 a Zimbabwean ecologist and the originator of holistic range management (HRM) gave the keynote address at the gathering and introduced many western ranchers to methods of restoring grasslands through the practice of holistic management. Many of those ranchers adopted aspects of HRM and have helped transform western animal husbandry. Panel discussions on topics like land stewardship, watershed

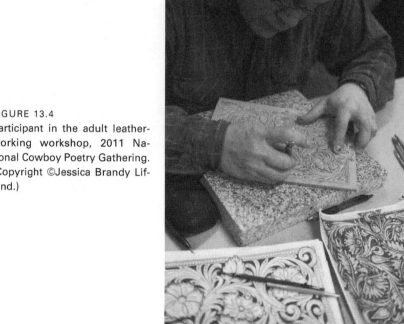

FIGURE 13.4
Participant in the adult leatherworking workshop, 2011 National Cowboy Poetry Gathering. (Copyright ©Jessica Brandy Lifland.)

preservation, water rights issues, niche marketing of grass-fed and organic beef, and horse training have provided practical knowledge that attendees could take with them and apply to their own operations. Humanities lectures have been given by people like former secretary of the interior Stewart Udall, ethnobotanist Gary Nabhan, and western historian Patricia Limerick.

EDUCATIONAL PROGRAMS BEYOND THE NATIONAL COWBOY POETRY GATHERING

As the Western Folklife Center has expanded programming beyond the National Cowboy Poetry Gathering, a number of collaborative educational projects with exhibit components have been developed. One such program was "Voices of Youth," a multiyear, multistate program that brought together small groups of teenagers to learn ethnographic documentation skills of photography, interviewing, audio recording, and editing for radio. The center enlisted nationally recognized photographer Bruce Hucko and aural historian and radio producer Jack Loeffler. These two, along with WFC staff, led participants through a multimonth series of workshops to practice the arts of interviewing, identifying informants, scheduling interviews, photo documentation, darkroom magic, matting and framing, audio recording, transcribing, editing, story scripting, and creating radio pieces. Their work led to the production of an exhibition (writing of text, creation of labels, installation, lighting, promotion, hosting a reception, public speaking). The program resulted in various exhibitions, including one for the Nevada Arts Council's traveling exhibition program, presentations at state arts conferences, and radio programs distributed throughout the West. Several of the "Voices of Youth" participants have returned to the WFC as adults to assist with exhibit production, volunteering, marketing efforts, and fund-raising.

"Be a Tourist in Your Own Town," partially funded by a National Endowment for the Arts–US Forest Service joint grant, was designed to encourage community building by working with visible and not-so-visible cultural and occupational communities to host a series of convivial events and exhibitions in the Elko area. Over a two-year period, center staff worked with Jewish, Asian Indian, Basque, Shoshone-Paiute, Hispanic, and mining communities. The process involved identifying and convening leaders and organizations representing these communities to discuss project goals. The group became the curators of a public program, sometimes centered on a holiday and often involving foodways, music, dance, and a small exhibit. The program was hugely successful in bringing communities together. For many of them, it was the first time they had done anything for the public, outside their own community, and it opened the door to further opportunities and invitations.

One of the most successful ongoing programs is both educational and involves community outreach. "Deep West" was initially funded in 2000 by a multiyear grant from the Wallace Foundation. Since then, the Western Folklife Center has been working with people from throughout the rural West to produce short videos about their lives on the land. Created using the tools of digital communication, these homemade productions are simple yet elegant; they are not glossy and commercial but from the heart.[2] Videos have been made by ranching families, by students from one-room schoolhouses, and by the Owyhee Public School on the Duck Valley Indian Reservation, about sheepherders with cell phones, a Basque country journal, the Oregon Range War, and many other topics. The videos are presented annually at the gathering by the filmmakers and are available on the WFC website.

The WFC has also reached a large national audience with a strong media presence, through television documentaries such as *Why the Cowboy Sings* and *Healing the Warrior's Heart* (which examines the emotional trauma of war through the lens of Native American tradition and ceremony), both of which aired on PBS television. The center has also produced numerous radio programs for National Public Radio, including series like *The Open Road*, which visited places throughout the West, and *What's in a Song*, which featured important western songwriters.

CONCLUSION

As a result of the longevity of the National Cowboy Poetry Gathering, the WFC has had the benefit of developing a long and ever-deepening (and -widening) connection with the culturally rich ranching occupational community and, subsequently, with related ethnic, tribal, and immigrant communities. These relationships have been built through fieldwork by staff folklorists and extensive collaboration with community members, inviting them to participate as full partners in planning programs and exhibitions, as guest curators, exhibition installers, and volunteers, with ownership in their projects. The primary role of the WFC has been as a facilitator, helping communities tell their own stories in their own voices. This approach has proved successful enough that the WFC was the recipient of the Institute of Museum and Library Services (IMLS) award in 2004 for its work. The IMLS said that year that the four recipient organizations "share a view of collaboration as the strategy for success and have expanded their outreach with strong, sustainable community partnerships. The recipients are not content to serve just their regular patrons, but reach out in exemplary ways to provide service to even the most marginalized in their communities."[3]

NOTES

1. "About," Western Folklife Center, https://westernfolklifecenter.wordpress.com/about (accessed May 8, 2016).

2. "Deep West Video," Western Folklife Center, http://www.westernfolklife.org/Audio-Video/Deep-West-Video (accessed May 9, 2016).

3. "2004 National Awards for Museum and Library Service," Institute of Museum and Library Services, https://www.imls.gov/sites/default/files/publications/documents/2004awards.pdf?p (accessed May 8, 2016).

14

Folklife and Historic Preservation

Traditional Cultural Places and the Casita Rincón Criollo

MICHAEL ANN WILLIAMS AND VIRGINIA SIEGEL

A historic site's eligibility for inclusion on the National Register of Historic Places serves as a gold standard by which significance is ascribed in historic preservation practice and policy. Michael Ann Williams and Virginia Siegel survey historic preservation's intersections with the discipline of folklore over the past half century and detail an initiative of the Working Group in Folklore and Historic Preservation Policy of the American Folklore Society (AFS). Aiming to better represent the variety of sites tied to cultural practice, the pilot project focuses on nominating the Casita Rincón Criollo, a Puerto Rican community site in the South Bronx of New York, to the National Register as a "traditional cultural place." The authors make the case that folklorists offer more inclusive definitions of traditional groups and are uniquely poised to assess traditional cultural places (TCPs) through ethnographic fieldwork and folklore methodology. Earlier versions of this work have been presented at the American Folklore Society annual conferences (2014, 2015) and the "Learning from the Reservation" Traditional Cultural Places conference (2015) at Delaware State University.

American folklorists entered the realm of historic preservation policy for much the same reasons they became engaged in museum work.[1] Although their counterparts in a number of European countries had long been engaged in the study of material culture and in working with museums, during the first half of the twentieth century folklorists in America tended to focus exclusively on oral tradition. The development of applied or "public" folklore parallels the development of historic preservation policy in many ways, from early grassroots efforts, to active engagement of the federal government during the New Deal, to the creation and maturation of contemporary systems in the 1960s and 1970s. In 1966, the National Historic Preservation Act (NHPA) created the federal preservation system as we know it today. Four years later, the National Environmental Policy Act (NEPA) mandated that both cultural and natural resources be included in environmental impact statements accompanying federal construction projects. Similarly, the federal government established the National Endowment for the Arts, which included folk arts in its enabling legislation, in 1965 and the American Folklife Center at the Library of Congress in 1976. For the most part, however, the twin developments of federal preservation law and public folklore did not intersect until the late 1970s.

Coincidentally, just as the NHPA and NEPA legislation reshaped the contours of historic preservation in the United States, the folklife movement began to introduce American scholars to the holistic approach of Scandinavian research, which incorporated material culture and belief studies into the study of folk tradition.[2] During the 1960s and 1970s, as the newly refashioned National Register of Historic Places program took shape, the study of American folklore expanded to include material culture and the study of vernacular architecture. By the late 1970s and early 1980s, individual folklorists increasingly worked within historic preservation contexts on comprehensive surveys, National Register nominations, and other forms of documentation. Folklorists' expertise in vernacular architecture, a subject at the time largely ignored by architectural historians, gave them a special role to play as comprehensive surveys and impact studies became crucial to preservation work in the United States.

The expanding world of public folklore also engaged in the development of preservation policy. During the 1970s, a growing awareness emerged among heritage specialists that "cultural resources" could and should include more than buildings and archaeological remains.[3] Section 502 of the 1980 amendments to the National Historic Preservation Act directed the American Folklife Center at the Library of Congress to devise a program to preserve intangible cultural heritage. The report, published in 1983, declined to arbitrarily separate the tangible and intangible aspects of culture, instead proposing the concept of "cultural conservation," a cohesive and integrated approach to the protection of cultural heritage.[4] The Library of Congress followed the publication of this report with several pilot projects that examined the intersection of folklore with preservation and land use planning.[5]

While the 1980 amendment to the NHPA potentially opened the door to the integration of historic preservation and public folklore policy, two key decisions during that era had a lasting negative impact on further interconnections. The American Folklife Center (AFC) had contracted to conduct an impact study for the proposed construction of the Tennessee-Tombigbee Waterway in 1978. However, political opposition from within the membership of the American Folklore Society ultimately led to the withdrawal of the AFC from the project. While the caution and skepticism of the AFS membership toward federally funded impact studies is understandable, it overlooked the potential positive impact that folklorists could have on such a project, and it led to further neglect of the protection of intangible cultural resources as part of federally mandated impact studies. More than a decade later, AFS president Peggy Bulger, the second director of the American Folklife Center, concluded that in this decision, "despite well-meant impulses, folklorists missed an opportunity to be central to the work of cultural conservation and the environmental survey work that is still going on today."[6]

In addition to the withdrawal of the American Folklife Center from a federally mandated impact study, the relatively timid approach of the *Cultural Conservation* report (perhaps responding both to the disciplinary uproar over the proposed Tennessee-Tombigbee project and the changing political climate in Washington during the early 1980s) resulted in a failure to break new ground in proposing a federal system for protecting intangible culture. The report cautioned against the use of register systems for living cultural forms or engagement in "reactive Federal involvement in the preservation process" (i.e., mandated impact studies).[7] While the reluctance to arbitrarily distinguish between tangible and intangible cultural resources is justifiable from an intellectual point of view, the report's rejection of this division ultimately led to the failure of the report to fulfill the mandate of the NHPA amendment, and it guaranteed that intangible cultural heritage would continue to be ignored within the context of American preservation law. More recently, as international concern for the safeguarding of intangible cultural heritage has grown under the auspices of the United Nations Educational, Scientific, and Cultural Organization (UNESCO), folklorists in the United States have had little to add to the dialog, except intellectual critique of the process, as America has no comparable recognition of intangible resources.[8]

Despite these fateful decisions of the late 1970s and early 1980s, the next decade continued to show promise for the involvement of folklorists in historic preservation. The Grouse Creek survey and the Pine Barrens study initiated by the American Folklife Center demonstrated useful models for integrating the work of folklorists with preservationists and land use planners, although, unfortunately, the specific recommendations of the reports seemed to have little impact and the models were not taken up in any systematic way.[9] In 1990, under the leadership of the American Folklife Center, a conference was held at the Library of Congress, which brought folklorists into dialog with individuals involved with planning and preservation policy. Papers from this conference were published several years later in an edited volume, *Conserving Culture: A New Discourse on Heritage.*[10]

THE CONCEPT OF TRADITIONAL CULTURAL PLACES

The same year that the national conference at the Library of Congress brought folklorists, preservationists, and planners together to engage in a dialog on cultural heritage, the National Park Service (NPS) took a major step forward in recognizing the significance of the cultural practices of living communities. Periodically the NPS publishes new bulletins, providing guidelines for the preparation of nominations to the National Register of Historic Places. The publication of the 1990 TCP bulletin *Guidelines for Evaluating and Documenting Traditional Cultural Properties*, written by Patricia L. Parker and Thomas F. King, held great promise for folklorists working within historic preservation. Although it does not specifically recognize intangible cultural resources as eligible for the National Register, intangible culture constitutes the significance of the property or place. As the bulletin states,

> A traditional cultural property, then, can be defined generally as one that is eligible for inclusion in the National Register because of its association with cultural practices or beliefs of a living community that (a) are rooted in that

> community's history, and (b) are important in maintaining the continuing cultural identity of the community.[11]

By emphasizing properties that derive significance from cultural practices or beliefs of living communities, the bulletin took an important step forward in integrating the protection of tangible and intangible cultural resources. Just as important, it recognized the significance of living communities and their values, the neglect of which was often a source of frustration for folklorists working within the preservation world. Indeed, coauthor Tom King later wrote that part of his inspiration for writing the bulletin had been the efforts of folklorists working in the public domain.[12]

Unfortunately, the promise of traditional cultural properties (or "places," as they are now generally known) soon faded for folklorists. Although the bulletin was written, in part, in response to the American Indian Religious Freedom Act, it also specifically cited the 1980 amendments to the NHPA and the *Cultural Conservation* report. From the outset, the bulletin clearly states,

> The fact that this Bulletin gives special emphasis to Native American properties should not be taken to imply that only Native Americans ascribe traditional cultural value to historic properties, or that such ascription is common only to ethnic minority groups in general. Americans of every ethnic origin have properties to which they ascribe traditional cultural value, and if such properties meet the National Register criteria, they can and should be nominated for inclusion in the Register.[13]

Despite the fact that the bulletin says otherwise, National Register coordinators at the state level frequently took the line that TCPs were to be used exclusively for Native American properties, and in actual practice few non–Native American nominations were produced. However, because the TCP designation is considered an "overlay" and not a property type, the National Park Service has kept no official records of the number of properties nominated as TCPs, making it difficult to assess when and how often the designation was used. While the bulletin did have an impact in not eliminating sacred Native American sites from National Register consideration (for reasons of separation of church and state), its potential for protecting a broader range of properties went untapped.

Public folklorists interested in the preservation of traditional places instead turned to the model of grassroots registers, such as Place Matters in New York City. Emerging in part from City Lore's "Endangered Spaces" program and a Municipal Arts Society taskforce on encouraging protection for significant places, Place Matters was formally established in 1998 to foster the conservation of New York's historically and culturally significant places.[14] Inspired by Place Matters, as well as the TCP bulletin, Varick Chittenden, founder of Traditional Arts in Upstate New York (TAUNY), in turn created the Register of Very Special Places (RVSP) in 2005.[15] While these efforts have the advantage of providing local communities with the tools for nominating places that they find significant, they rely largely on publicity and public opinion for their impact, since they cannot offer the protection of federal law.

With the change of leadership at the American Folklife Center, national engagement of folklorists with preservation policy declined. At the leadership level, engagement in heritage policy focused more on the international stage, especially the programs of the World Intellectual Properties Organization addressing "traditional cultural expressions" and UNESCO's intangible cultural heritage convention (although the United States had not ratified the latter).[16] However, individual folklorists have continued to work with preservation agencies at the local, state, and national levels, but until recently no central point of communication existed for those who engaged in this work. This changed in 2010, when the American Folklore Society issued a request for proposals for the creation of its second working group on folklore and public policy. A group of folklorists engaged in historic preservation put together a successful proposal, led by cochairs Laurie Kay Sommers, an independent folklorist, and Michael Ann Williams, head of the Department of Folk Studies and Anthropology at Western Kentucky University (WKU), which has the only graduate program in folklore with a designated historic preservation track.[17] The group subsequently issued a white paper, titled "Integrating Folklore and Historic Preservation Policy: Toward a Richer Sense of Place."[18]

THE FOLKLORE AND HISTORIC PRESERVATION WORKING GROUP

The Folklore and Historic Preservation Working Group first met in July 2011 at the Library of Congress. By this time, word was about that the National Park Service was potentially reworking the TCP bulletin. Among the individuals who met with the working group during the two-day meeting was Paul Lusignan of the National Register. The working group itself included representation from both City Lore/Place Matters (Steve Zeitlin and Molly Garfinkel) and TAUNY (Jill Breit and later Varick Chittenden). In brainstorming various actions for the working group, Williams suggested that the group pursue model TCP nominations based on properties already nominated through the grassroots process offered by Place Matters and RVSP. A few months later, Williams secured funding from Western Kentucky University to support graduate students to do this initial research.[19]

The broader purpose of the project was to investigate ways in which folklorists could add to the dialog on TCPs, much of which has focused on defining what constitutes traditions. Folklorists recognize that traditional culture is not an exclusive possession of native peoples and, further, that *all* people (assuming they have social contact with other human beings) possess traditions. Equally problematic are notions of what constitutes a traditional community or group. The Park Service seems inclined to accept ethnicity as a primary criterion in defining a traditional community, despite the fact that for almost a half century social scientists have questioned the notion of bounded ethnic groups. Even folklorists' much-cherished notion of "group" has come under scrutiny in recent years.[20] Issues of self-ascription and situational identity challenge any easy definitions of traditional group. While the notion that nonindigenous ethnic groups have TCPs may take us one step beyond the limitation of restricting the concept only to Native Americans, the notion of traditional community still seems firmly rooted in a concept of otherness.

Folklorists have also long studied the traditions of occupational groups, although the Park Service has seemed initially reluctant to acknowledge that occupation or avocational associations could be the basis of traditional practice. Traditional occupations often are jeopardized in development and land use planning and are critically in need of attention within heritage protection. When the working group began its project, no examples of TCPs based on occupation could be found. The 2013 listing of the Green River Drift Trail in Wyoming brought traditional occupation, in this case ranching, into the scope of TCP nominations.[21] Additionally, the Tarpon Springs Greektown Historic District nomination, prepared by folklorist Tina Bucuvalas and listed in 2014, included consideration of occupational culture, although in this case within the context of ethnicity.[22]

A folklorist has also been involved in a groundbreaking use of the TCP designation in an environmental impact statement. In environmental review, determination of eligibility for, rather than actual listing on, the National Register is the relevant criteria in the process. In 2005, folklorist Alan Jabbour (former director of the American Folklife Center) and anthropologist Philip E. Coyle successfully argued for the eligibility of the decoration day practice and its associated cemeteries in the North Shore area of the Great Smoky Mountains National Park. In doing so, they argued for eligibility despite "criteria considerations" that can rule properties ineligible except under specific exceptions. These include cemeteries, religious properties, and properties achieving significance in the last fifty years. Although the revival of the current decoration day practice is less than thirty years old (access to the cemeteries had become limited due to the construction of the Fontana Dam in the 1940s), Jabbour and Coyle documented that the practice itself was much older, preceding the construction of the dam and resulting lake.[23]

The fifty-year rule of thumb that guides National Register practice continues to pose issues for the nomination of traditional cultural places. Not only do properties ideally have to have achieved significance more than fifty years ago (unless they are of exceptional importance), but also it is common practice in writing nominations to end the listed period of significance no later than fifty years ago.[24] In some cases this practice has led to the writing of nominations that exclude important aspects of significance for the existing community. For example, in the nomination of a historic African American district in Kentucky (not listed as a TCP), the community requested that the period of significance be brought up to the present in order to include the impact of redevelopment and current revitalization efforts. The National Park Service returned the nomination, and the period of significance was altered by the state preservation office. Only then was the district listed. If TCP nominations place the practice and beliefs of living communities at the heart of the nomination, then obviously the period of significance needs to be extended to the present. This important change could potentially yield far richer and better-detailed nominations and allow more consideration of what living communities themselves deem significant.

While the designation of traditional cultural places does potentially expand the period of significance to the present, the TCP bulletin still states that "significance ascribed to a property only in the past 50 years cannot be considered traditional."[25] This places our understanding of tradition as something that endures over a great length of time—again, a notion that folklorists have soundly rejected in the past fifty years. Traditionality is ascribed by a community, and tradition continually reinvents itself anew. Virtually no contemporary folklorist believes that cultural practices have to be of a certain age to be defined as "traditional."

Little did the working group suspect when it embarked on this project that one of the main challenges would be identifying the individual properties to be nominated. Project members wanted to push the envelope, yet not engage in challenges that had little chance of being considered. For instance, while folklorists could see how a Coney Island Ferris wheel might have traditional significance (a project considered by Place Matters and the TCP team), they decided that they probably could not sell the idea to the National Park Service. Therefore, the team started with a relatively conservative (for folklorists) notion of traditional community. Another unanticipated roadblock occurred when some individuals and communities who were happy to be publicized as part of a grassroots register decided that they did not want to be listed by a federal agency. The team considered the nomination of a matzo factory, long a center of the Jewish community in New York City. One of the owners was keen, but another family member was not (the business has recently closed, and the building is being sold to property developers). Of the four places ultimately chosen, one community withdrew after the documentation was complete, deciding that it wished to avoid potential federal scrutiny (mostly fearing violation of health laws in its social events).

As the project proceeded, it became clear that the properties listed by TAUNY's Register of Very Special Places were possibly just not "other" enough. Rural communities in upstate New York, although definitely communities with traditions, lacked the ethnic identity or other qualifiers that helped state and federal officials perceive them as traditional communities. In the review of one of the places documented by the team, a town square, Varick Chittenden was told by a state preservation official that the property was clearly eligible for the National Register but not as a TCP. Overall within preservation circles, an attitude seemed to exist that TCP designation should only be used if other, easier approaches to the nomination were not viable. While this pragmatic approach may have its merits, the unfortunate by-product is that nominations are often written without mention of the continuing significance of a place to a living community.

The two properties chosen from the Place Matters roster were both clearly identified with ethnicity. One was Nom Wah, the earliest known dim sum restaurant in New York.[26] As we discovered, however, the building was already included in the massive Chinatown nomination, although virtually no information on Nom Wah was included in the nomination. The research raised an interesting point, however. By whose standards is something deemed "traditional practice"? A member of the state preservation staff questioned the traditionality of Nom Wah because dim sum is no longer served on rolling carts. While this may be of concern to non-Chinese seeking the "authentic" dim sum restaurant experience, it didn't seem to lessen the importance of the place to the Chinese American community, which saw the restaurant as a place to gather even in the years when the restaurant did not serve food at all. While ultimately the research on Nom Wah might be added to the Chinatown nomination, the team decided, in the end, to focus on another New York City property as the most promising as a model nomination.

THE CASITA RINCÓN CRIOLLO

Casita Rincón Criollo is a Puerto Rican casita and community garden in the South Bronx, known most significantly for its role as an important incubator of the musical genres of *bomba* and *plena* in the region and nation. Though Casita Rincón Criollo is one of the city's oldest and best-known casitas, the site is just one of many that dot the landscape of greater New York City. The word "casita" means "little house," and in New York the earliest recorded examples of Puerto Rican casita creation appear to date from the early 1970s.[27] In the 1960s and 1970s, a combination of different factors (including industry relocation and urban renewal) brought much devastation to many parts of the city, with the South Bronx among the more seriously affected areas. With vacant and abandoned properties rising in number, concerned individuals and grassroots organizations began to take action. It was against this backdrop that the urban community garden movement began in New York City.[28] Emerging at the same time and with the same concerns, the New York Puerto Rican tradition of creating casitas and gardens on vacant city lots also began. Casitas tended to be built as impermanent structures because community members often erected them illegally on abandoned lots by clearing litter and constructing community spaces in their stead. Further, casitas were designed to physically evoke the environment of Puerto Rico, and over time gardens and other recreational amenities were added. This was the case with Casita Rincón Criollo, founded by José "Chema" Soto around 1970 and built with care by many family and friends. Rincón Criollo is an excellent example of a traditional cultural place with significant practices tied to the structures and site—namely, the musical traditions of *bomba* and *plena*, but also other practices such as Puerto Rican festival celebrations, gardening, and games.

When choosing a site for the model nomination, the American Folklore Society Working Group in Folklore and Historic Preservation Policy felt that Casita Rincón Criollo served as an ideal candidate for several reasons: first, it had already been listed on City Lore's Place Matters, and second, as a result of City Lore's work, the Puerto Rican community that had built the site was experienced and open to working with outside researchers.[29] Also pertinent to the AFS working group were several factors that might have made other preservationists shy away from the nomination process. Casita Rincón Criollo was built less than fifty years ago, and, equally problematic, its structure and gardens had been moved to a new location in 2006. The AFS working

FIGURE 14.1
(Photo: Virginia Siegle.)

group set out to push the boundaries of what could be considered eligible for the National Register of Historic Places, and the Casita Rincón Criollo would certainly push boundaries. Perhaps most importantly to the working group, though, the community would also greatly benefit from inclusion on the National Register of Historic Places as a traditional cultural place.

In 2011, graduate students at Western Kentucky University began researching Casita Rincón Criollo under the guidance of Michael Ann Williams. As per the AFS working group's vision, WKU students sought from the beginning to incorporate folklore methodology into the research process for the site. Oral history interviews and face-to-face conversations are fundamental to folklore methodology. Written sources would not be enough, especially when the casita was so important to a community that is still actively using the site. Graduate student Rachel Hopkin pioneered the first stages of the nomination process from 2011 to 2012. Fluent in Spanish, Hopkin not only compiled existing scholarship on Rincón Criollo and casitas in general but also visited New York City in person to conduct oral history interviews with many casita members and scholars. Her interviewees included casita founder José "Chema" Soto and his son Carlos Soto. Hopkin also interviewed casita members who attribute Rincón Criollo with the fostering of the musical genres of *bomba* and *plena*, both of which are performed at the casita. *Bomba* and *plena* are both musical traditions of Puerto Rico, reflecting the African roots of present-day Puerto Rico. *Bomba*, described simply, is a highly rhythmic genre that relies on participation from both musicians and dancers, with dance and call-and-response lyrics as key components of the performance. *Plena* was developed from *bomba* and also features a call-and-response format but differs from *bomba* in instrumentation, dance steps, rhythm, and structure.[30] Regarding the casita's musical traditions, Hopkin spoke with Juan Gutiérrez, National Heritage Award fellow and founder of the highly successful musical group Los Pleneros de la 21. Gutiérrez recalled,

> Well, to tell you a little bit more about it, you know, the group that we put together, now it's an organization Los Pleneros de la 21. It was formed there in la casita. And we—I met most of the original founders of the group, you know, there, in la casita. They used to hang out there. There was a time when I was there every single day.[31]

In addition to casita members, Hopkin interviewed many scholars who had completed earlier research on the site as well, including photographer Martha Cooper and folklorist Joseph Sciorra. The WKU research team was by no means the first to use ethnographic research to document Rincón Criollo; Joseph Sciorra, in particular, generously shared his own extensive research gathered in the late 1980s and 1990s.[32] Hopkin's interviews, both of casita members and with scholars such as Sciorra, proved especially important, and many quotes from the interviews were woven throughout the body of the nomination. Most important, though, the interviews were primary source material for the types of daily activities that take place at the Casita Rincón Criollo and their evaluation by those who partake in these activities.

In 2012, Rachel Hopkin finished the first full rough draft of the nomination with the research she had, focusing on the role the casita played in the dissemination of Puerto Rican folk culture, with a small section on the musical practices of *bomba* and *plena*. She laid the foundation for the nomination's fundamental message: the age of Casita Rincón Criollo and its 2006 relocation do not threaten the integrity of the site or disqualify it for eligibility on the register; in fact they define what a casita is and form the backbone of why Casita Rincón Criollo stands out among other casitas. Casitas are by their nature impermanent. Further, when many casitas were being demolished or forced out by landowners for redevelopment, Rincón Criollo's members rallied behind their site.[33] When development forced their move in 2006, casita members successfully found a new site, just one block from the original site, and the casita community flourishes to this day. As Hopkin's interviews would be used to show, casita members painstakingly saved what they could, including a treasured apple tree and much of the architectural fabric of the original casita house, and re-created their environment on their new lot.[34]

While Hopkin's draft was effective in demonstrating, in their own words, the importance of Casita Rincón Criollo to the community members who use it, it became apparent that in the eyes of the New York State Historic Preservation Office, a successful nomination would need a stronger argument for why this particular casita stood out among other existing casitas. However, City Lore and the WKU research team did not know which casitas were still in existence. Martha Cooper and Joseph Sciorra had completed the last full survey of casitas in 1988. AFS working group member Nancy Solomon had completed some measured drawings at the time as well, including one of Rincón Criollo prior to its move. However, researchers did not know which casitas had quietly survived, been demolished, or were no longer actively used.[35] In order to contextualize the casitas' fight for survival and to help reveal Casita Rincón Criollo as an exemplary casita, there would need to be a survey of the other remaining casitas, no easy task by any means. In 2013, Caitlin Coad took over Hopkin's research and became the second Western Kentucky University graduate student to assist the AFS working group in the model nomination project. While the research team did not have the means to complete a full ethnographic survey of all casitas in New York City, it decided to do what it could. In the summer of 2013, Coad traveled to New York City to complete a windshield survey of the sites surveyed in 1988, while also noting any new sites that had arisen after that time. Coad, to the best of her abilities, recorded what was lost and what survived and found that casita sites appeared to have had the highest survival rate in the Bronx. Further, she found that most casitas in existence in 2013 appeared to be much newer than the Casita Rincón Criollo. To supplement the oral histories and published sources that Hopkin had gathered, Coad compiled her survey data into a chart that could be included in the additional historic context of the National Register nomination.[36]

FIGURE 14.2
(Photo: Virginia Siegel.)

At the same time that Coad gathered information on the survival rate of the casitas of New York City, the WKU researchers came to the conclusion that they had undersold one of the most significant aspects of Casita Rincón Criollo in Hopkin's first draft of the National Register nomination form. In 2013, graduate student Virginia Siegel was tasked with finalizing Rachel Hopkin's draft of the nomination form in light of Coad's comparative data, as well as some new scholarship that had recently been completed on Rincón Criollo's tradition of musical performance. César Colón-Montijo, a Rincón Criollo member, had shared with the nomination research team his thesis work and ethnographic research on the musical performance of *plena* at Rincón Criollo.[37] Through his scholarship, as well as a revisiting of the casita members' oral histories, it became clear that the previous draft of the nomination had understated the importance of Casita Rincón Criollo's musical traditions of *bomba* and *plena*. The performance of *bomba* and *plena* is one of the most distinctive aspects of the community, and the influence the casita has had on these traditional music forms sets this particular casita apart from other contemporary casitas.[38] Rincón's musical tradition was perhaps the most important reason for the nomination of Casita Rincón Criollo as a traditional cultural place. Siegel restructured the nomination, taking this new information into account, including Colón-Montijo's own personal communication with Juan Gutiérrez in which he quotes Gutiérrez as saying that traditional *plena* is "a song-driven musical genre that takes its dynamics responding to the circumstances where and when it is performed."[39] This new insight would become a key component of the second draft's statement of significance because, as Siegel would go on to write in the nomination, if "plena responds to its environment, the physical experience of the casita has therefore played a critical role in the manifestation of the genre today."[40]

While this new information would address the exemplary quality of the casita, there still remained the issue of Rincón Criollo's relocation. The first draft of the nomination stated that the continual rebuilding of the casita was not an impediment but, in fact, part of the nature of casitas. Drawing parallels to *arrabal* homes, urban vernacular structures found in Puerto Rico, Sciorra notes that like the *arrabal*, "Rincón Criollo is constantly being transformed and renewed, and must be seen as unfinished, that is, continually becoming."[41] In June 2014, Virginia Siegel traveled to New York City and, accompanied by Molly Garfinkel of City Lore and Place Matters, measured and created detailed drawings of the casita house and gardens. Today, the site for Casita Rincón Criollo features the casita house, a small performance stage, and a small storage shed. Siegel created a drawing of the site plan and floor plans for both the casita and the stage and then reworked large portions of the architectural description based on these sketches and photographs from the site visit. Using known historic photographs of the casita before its move to the new site, as well as descriptions of the site provided in Hopkin's oral history interviews, Siegel expanded the narrative description of the site to discuss and contrast the original casita structure with its reconstruction after the 2006 relocation and to note known continuities and differences in the structures of the site over the years. In May 2015, Siegel returned for Rincón Criollo's Mother's Day celebrations and noticed that in just one year's time, the casita had been repainted yet again. In short, the casita remains "continually becoming."

Several years into the project, ethnographic methodology remains at the heart of the nomination of Casita Rincón Criollo. Considering the words and actions of the casita's community members, Siegel writes in the most recent draft of the nomination, "The community at Casita Rincón Criollo continues their traditional cultural practices at this location. As demonstrated in the statement of significance and by the site's continued use, the community believes the structure and site maintain their integrity, a key component when considering integrity for traditional cultural properties."[42] It was because of the combined tactics of interviews, physical recording of the structure, comparative data, and written documentation and scholarship that these conclusions could be drawn. Oral histories, though, were central.

CONCLUSION

Though several years have passed, the nomination process for the Casita Rincón Criollo is still ongoing. The second draft currently stands at forty-five pages total, with a diverse range of source materials and data to support the nomination. Kathleen LaFrank of the New York State Historic Preservation Office has been generous in providing several rounds of feedback. In both 2014 and 2015, Virginia Siegel presented papers at the American Folklore Society on the project. The year 2015, in particular, was bittersweet for Casita Rincón Criollo and the project. In July, beloved founder José "Chema" Soto passed away. On the positive side, in November, with the aid of Kathleen LaFrank,

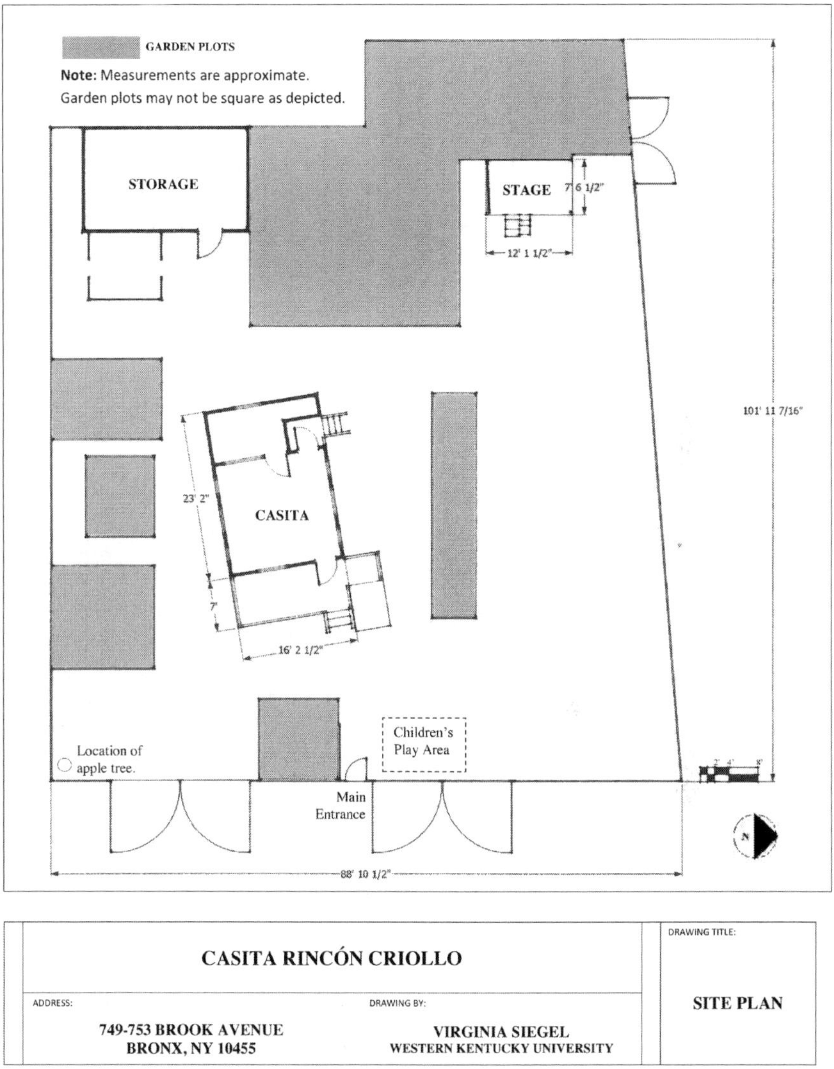

FIGURE 14.3
(Photo: Virginia Siegel.)

Molly Garfinkel of Place Matters received a grant from the National Park Service aimed at documenting historic resources associated with underrepresented communities in the National Register of Historic Places.[43] The grant will support the so-needed intensive survey of New York City's casitas, as well as the continuing work of the traditional cultural place nomination, which will no doubt be supported and enriched by the survey to come. In short, those involved in the working group and project feel a measure of success in the project and with the National Park Service and New York State Historic Preservation Office's response and support. The American Folklore Society Working Group in Folklore and Historic Preservation Policy and Western Kentucky University have passed the draft on to Place Matters and the New York National Preservation Office with the hope that the nomination will lead ultimately to the listing of the Casita Rincón Criollo as a traditional cultural place.

For over half a century now, the American discipline of folklore has embraced the study of material culture. During this time, folklorists have lent their expertise to and taken leadership roles in folk art and ethnographic museums and the study and preservation of vernacular architecture. Folklorists are now uniquely poised to assess and document traditional cultural practices associated with specific places and to weigh in on the use of the TCP designation within the National Register of Historic Places.[44] Through ethnographic fieldwork and oral histories, folklorists (and other ethnographers) offer documentation strategies to supplement those most commonly employed in National Register nominations. Furthermore, traditional cultural practices and places have been at the heart of folklorists' enterprise. While appreciating the reluctance of the National Register to fling open the doors that restrict eligibility to the National Register and adopt some of folklorists' more expansive definitions, folklorists invaluably add to the dialog. It makes sense that, having already embraced the notion that traditional cultural places should be eligible for the National Register, the National Park Service and state historic preservation offices would engage the expertise of those who study traditional cultural practice.

NOTES

1. See C. Kurt Dewhurst, "Folklife and Museum Practice: An Intertwined History and Emerging Convergences" (American Folklore Society Presidential Address, October 2011), *Journal of American Folklore* 127 (2014): 247–63.

2. For a history of the introduction of folklife studies in the United States, see Don Yoder, "Folklife Studies in American Scholarship," in *Discovering American Folklife: Studies in Ethnic, Religious, and Regional Culture*, ed. Don Yoder (Ann Arbor: University of Michigan Research Press, 1990), 43–61.

3. Alan Jabbour, "Some Reflections on Intangible Resources," in *Rescue Archeology: Papers from the First New World Conference on Rescue Archeology*, ed. Rex L. Wilson and Gloria Loyola (Washington, DC: Preservation Press, 1982), 251–56.

4. Ormond Loomis, *Cultural Conservation: The Protection of Cultural Heritage in the United States* (Washington, DC: Library of Congress, 1983).

5. Mary Hufford, *One Space, Many Places: Folklife and Land Use in New Jersey's Pinelands National Reserve* (Washington, DC: American Folklife Center, Library of Congress, 1986); Thomas Carter and Carl Fleischhauer, *The Grouse Creek Cultural Survey: Integrating Folklife and Historic Preservation Field Research* (Washington, DC: American Folklife Center, Library of Congress, 1988).

6. Peggy Bulger, "Looking Back, Moving Forward: The Development of Folklore as a Public Profession" (AFS Presidential Plenary Address 2002), *Journal of American Folklore* 116 (2003): 387.

7. Loomis, *Cultural Conservation*, 16, 83.

8. Barbara Kirshenblatt-Gimblett, "Intangible Heritage as Metacultural Production," *Museum International* 56 (2004): 52–65; Dorothy Noyes, "The Judgment of Solomon: Global Protections for Tradition and the Problem of Community Ownership," *Cultural Analysis* 5 (2006): 27–56.

9. Thomas Carter, "'That Was Fun, Let's Not Do It Again': The Curious Legacy of the Grouse Creek Cultural Survey," American Folklore Society, 2012, http://www.afsnet.org/?pages=FHPGrouseCreekStudy.

10. Mary Hufford, ed., *Conserving Culture: A New Discourse on Heritage* (Urbana: University of Illinois Press, 1994).

11. Patricia L. Parker and Thomas F. King, *Guidelines for Evaluating and Documenting Traditional Cultural Properties*, National Register Bulletin 38 (Washington, DC: National Park Service, Department of the Interior, 1990).

12. Thomas F. King, *Places That Count: Traditional Cultural Properties in Cultural Resource Management* (Walnut Creek, CA: AltaMira Press, 2003), 75–77.

13. Parker and King, *Guidelines for Evaluating and Documenting Traditional Cultural Properties.*

14. Steven J. Zeitlin, "Conserving Our Cities' Endangered Spaces," in *Conserving Culture: A New Discourse on Heritage*, ed. Mary Hufford (Urbana: University of Illinois Press, 1994), 215–28.

15. Varick A. Chittenden, "'Put Your Very Special Place on the North Country Map!': Community Participation in Cultural Landmarking," *Journal of American Folklore* 119 (2006): 47–65.

16. Richard Kurin, "Safeguarding Intangible Cultural Heritage in the 2003 UNESCO Convention: A Critical Appraisal," *Museum International* 56 (2004): 66–77.

17. The initial members of the working group included Laurie Kay Sommers (Laurie Sommers Consulting, LLC, Okemos, Michigan), Michael Ann Williams (Western Kentucky University Department of Folk Studies and Anthropology), Jill Breit (Traditional Arts in Upstate New York), Tom Carter (emeritus, University of Utah), Nancy Solomon (Long Island Traditions), John Vlach (George Washington University), Molly Garfinkel (City Lore's Place Matters in New York), Steve Zeitlin (City Lore), and Jay Edwards (Louisiana State University). Breit was replaced by Chittenden, retired director of TAUNY, after the initial meeting.

18. Laurie Kay Sommers, "Integrating Folklore and Historic Preservation Policy: Toward a Richer Sense of Place," AFS Working Group in Folklore and Historic Preservation Policy White Paper, American Folklore Society, 2013, http://www.afsnet.org/default.asp?page=FHPPolicyPaper.

19. The original graduate student team consisted of Sarah McCartt-Jackson, Katie Wynn, Caitlin Coad, and Rachel Hopkin.

20. Dorothy Noyes, "Group," in *Eight Words for the Study of Expressive Culture*, ed. Burt Feintuch (Urbana: University of Illinois Press, 2003), 7–41.

21. Laura Nowlin, *Green River Drift Trail*, National Register of Historic Places Nomination, 2013.

22. Tina Bucuvalas, *Tarpon Springs Greektown Historic District*, National Register of Historic Places Nomination, 2014.

23. Alan Jabbour and Philip E. Coyle, *North Shore Cemetery Decoration Project, North Shore Road Draft Environmental Impact Statement* (National Park Service, 2005), 84–89.

24. Although the nomination process requires a "period of significance" to be defined, the practice of ending this period more than fifty years ago is not articulated in the National Register Bulletin 16A, "How to Complete the National Register Form."

25. Parker and King, *Guidelines for Evaluating and Documenting Traditional Cultural Properties.*

26. The research on Nom Wah was conducted by Caitlin Coad.

27. Exact dates are unknown, especially with regard to Casita Rincón Criollo. Casita members and scholars have cited varying dates for the founding of Casita Rincón Criollo.

28. For a more complete history of the community garden movement in New York City, see "History of the Community Garden Movement," NYC Parks, http://www.nycgovparks.org/about/history/community-gardens/movement.

29. To read Place Matters' profile of Casita Rincón Criollo, visit "Casita Rincón Criollo," Place Matters, http://placematters.net/node/1445.

30. The National Register of Historic Places nomination form for Casita Rincón Criollo features a much more detailed explanation and history of the musical genres of *bomba* and *plena*, which are key to the identity of the casita. For more information on the genres, readers are encouraged to visit the Smithsonian Folkways website (http://www.folkways.si.edu), which features articles on *bomba* and *plena*. Smithsonian Folkways also offers several recordings and video performances of Los Pleneros de la 21.

31. Juan Gutiérrez, interview with Rachel Hopkin, New York City, May 22, 2012.

32. See Joseph Sciorra, "'We're Not Here Just to Plant. We Have Culture': An Ethnography of the South Bronx Casita Rincón Criollo," *New York Folklore* 20 (1994): 19–41.

33. Casita Rincón Criollo's history of threat of demolition or relocation spanned several years prior to its 2006 move. In addition to Rachel Hopkin's research, Joseph Sciorra's work with the casita during the late 1980s and 1990s reveals the community's persistent spirit. Oral accounts by community members to Sciorra revealed that the casita was continually regenerated and rebuilt, even before the 2006 move, in response to events such as a fire in the mid-1980s. See Sciorra, "'We're Not Here Just to Plant.'"

34. Rachel Hopkin and Virginia Siegel, *Casita Rincón Criollo*, National Register of Historic Places Nomination Form, draft, 2014, 5.

35. Some surviving casitas, unlike Rincón Criollo, have been gentrified through their incorporation into the New York City GreenThumb park system. Casita Rincón Criollo, on the other hand, though a GreenThumb garden, remains under the control and guidance of its original founders and founders' children.

36. By neighborhood and borough, Coad found nine casitas in the Bronx, whereas there had been thirty-five in 1988. Five of these casitas were not included in the 1988 survey. Coad surveyed five sites in Harlem where there had been twenty originally. One of these casitas was not included in the 1988 survey. In Brooklyn, Coad found one casita where there had been six in 1988. This casita was not in the original 1988 survey. Last, Coad found one casita in the Lower East Side where there had been two in the 1988 survey. The surveyed casita was not in the original 1988 survey. With regard to this data, "casita" is used to mean site, not individual structure. More detailed survey results may be seen in Hopkin and Siegel, *Casita Rincón Criollo*, National Register of Historic Places Nomination Form, 32.

37. César Colón-Montijo, "The Practices of Plena at Las Casita de Chema: Affect, Music and Everyday Life" (thesis, Columbia University, 2013).

38. Casita Rincón Criollo's influence has included the formation of several musical ensembles that grew out of musical relationships formed at the Casita Rincón Criollo, including Los Pleneros de la 21, Conjunto Cimarrón, Cumbalaya, and Los Instantaneos de la Plena. Juan Gutierrez, founder of Los Pleneros de la 21, is also a founder of BomPlenazo, a biennial celebration of *bomba* and *plena* hosted by the Hostos Center for Arts and Culture in the Bronx. This large celebration draws participants from across the nation and features events held at Casita Rincón Criollo during the celebration as well.

39. Colón-Montijo, "The Practices of Plena at Las Casita de Chema," 17.

40. Hopkin and Siegel, *Casita Rincón Criollo*, National Register of Historic Places Nomination Form, 17.

41. Sciorra, "'We're Not Here Just to Plant,'" 25.

42. Hopkin and Siegel, *Casita Rincón Criollo*, National Register of Historic Places Nomination Form, 20.

43. "Interior Department Announces Grants for Underrepresented Communities through Historic Preservation Fund," US Department of Interior, https://www

.doi.gov/pressreleases/interior-department-announces-grants-underrepresented-communities-through-historic.

44. In April 2015, a national meeting focusing exclusively on traditional cultural properties, called "Learning from the Reservation: Using the Traditional Cultural Place Perspective for Better Decision Making in a Diverse Cultural Landscape," was held at Delaware State University. Folklorists presenting at the meeting included Tina Bucuvalas, Alan Jabbour, Beth King, Virginia Siegel, and Michael Ann Williams.

BIBLIOGRAPHY

Bucuvalas, Tina. 2014. *Tarpon Springs Greektown Historic District*. National Register of Historic Places Nomination.

Bulger, Peggy A. 2003. "Looking Back, Moving Forward: The Development of Folklore as a Public Profession" (AFS Presidential Plenary Address, 2002). *Journal of American Folklore* 116, no. 462 (Autumn): 377–90.

Carter, Thomas. 2012. "'That Was Fun, Let's Not Do It Again': The Curious Legacy of the Grouse Creek Cultural Survey." AFS. http://www.afsnet.org/?pages=FHPGrouseCreekStudy.

Carter, Thomas, and Carl Fleischhauer. 1988. *The Grouse Creek Cultural Survey: Integrating Folklife and Historic Preservation Field Research*. Washington, DC: American Folklife Center, Library of Congress.

Chittenden, Varick A. 2006. "'Put Your Very Special Place on the North Country Map!': Community Participation in Cultural Landmarking." *Journal of American Folklore* 119: 47–65.

Colón-Montijo, César. 2013. "The Practices of Plena at Las Casita de Chema: Affect, Music and Everyday Life." Thesis, Columbia University.

Dewhurst, C. Kurt. 2014. "Folklife and Museum Practice: An Intertwined History and Emerging Convergences" (American Folklore Society Presidential Address, October 2011). *Journal of American Folklore* 127: 247–63.

Gutiérrez, Juan. 2012. Interview with Rachel Hopkin. New York City. May 22.

Hopkin, Rachel, and Virginia Siegel. 2014. *Casita Rincón Criollo*. National Register of Historic Places Nomination Form, draft.

Hufford, Mary. 1986. *One Space, Many Places: Folklife and Land Use in New Jersey's Pinelands National Reserve*. Washington, DC: American Folklife Center, Library of Congress.

———, ed. 1994. *Conserving Culture: A New Discourse on Heritage.* Urbana: University of Illinois Press.

Jabbour, Alan. 1982. "Some Reflections on Intangible Resources." In *Rescue Archeology: Papers from the First New World Conference on Rescue Archeology,* edited by Rex L. Wilson and Gloria Loyola, 251–56. Washington, DC: Preservation Press.

Jabbour, Alan, and Philip E. Coyle. 2005. *North Shore Cemetery Decoration Project, North Shore Road Draft Environmental Impact Statement.* Washington, DC: National Park Service.

King, Thomas F. 2003. *Places That Count: Traditional Cultural Properties in Cultural Resource Management.* Walnut Creek, CA: AltaMira Press.

Kirshenblatt-Gimblett, Barbara. 2004. "Intangible Heritage as Metacultural Production." *Museum International* 56: 52–65.

Kurin, Richard. 2004. "Safeguarding Intangible Cultural Heritage in the 2003 UNESCO Convention: A Critical Appraisal." *Museum International* 56: 66–77.

Loomis, Ormond. 1983. *Cultural Conservation: The Protection of Cultural Heritage in the United States.* Washington, DC: Library of Congress.

New York City Department of Parks and Recreation. N.d. "History of the Community Garden Movement." NYC Parks, http://www.nycgovparks.org/about/history/community-gardens/movement (accessed November 16, 2015).

Nowlin, Laura. 2013. *Green River Drift Trail.* National Register of Historic Places Nomination.

Noyes, Dorothy. 2003. "Group." In *Eight Words for the Study of Expressive Culture,* edited by Burt Feintuch, 7–41. Urbana: University of Illinois Press.

———. 2006. "The Judgment of Solomon: Global Protections for Tradition and the Problem of Community Ownership." *Cultural Analysis* 5: 27–56.

Parker, Patricia L., and Thomas F. King. 1990. *Guidelines for Evaluating and Documenting Traditional Cultural Properties.* National Register Bulletin 38. Washington, DC: National Park Service, Department of Interior.

Sciorra, Joseph. 1994. "'We're Not Here Just to Plant. We Have Culture': An Ethnography of the South Bronx Casita Rincón Criollo." *New York Folklore* 20: 19–41.

Sommers, Laurie Kay. 2013. "Integrating Folklore and Historic Preservation Policy: Toward a Richer Sense of Place." AFS Working Group in Folklore and Historic Preservation Policy White Paper. AFS. http://www.afsnet.org/default.asp?page=FHPPolicyPaper.

US Department of Interior (DOI). 2015. "Interior Department Announces Grants for Underrepresented Communities through Historic Preservation Fund." DOI. November 6. https://www.doi.gov/pressreleases/interior-department-announces-grants-underrepresented-communities-through-historic (accessed November 16, 2015).

Yoder, Don. 1990. "Folklife Studies in American Scholarship." In *Discovering American Folklife: Studies in Ethnic, Religious, and Regional Culture*, edited by Don Yoder, 43–61. Ann Arbor: University of Michigan Research Press.

Zeitlin, Steven J. 1994. "Conserving Our Cities' Endangered Spaces." In *Conserving Culture: A New Discourse on Heritage*, edited by Mary Hufford, 215–28. Urbana: University of Illinois Press.

15

Smithsonian Folkways Recordings

The Role of Music in Blurring the Barriers of the Box

Daniel Sheehy

Smithsonian Folkways Recordings is the nonprofit, educational record label of the US national museum. Guided by the Smithsonian's mission—"the increase and diffusion of knowledge"—and playing to its own strengths as a museum collection built and disseminated through active revenue generation as a record label, Folkways addresses in its own way the question "Increase and diffuse what, how, and to what end?" Driven by its mission of "supporting cultural diversity and increased understanding among peoples through the documentation, preservation, and dissemination of sound," Folkways seeks to strengthen people's engagement with their own cultural heritage and to enhance their awareness and appreciation of the cultural heritage of others. This imperative requires it to reach far beyond the walls of the museum and to align itself with community-based local and global agendas worldwide. The curatorial philosophy of "great music and a great story" grounds Folkways' work in both musical connoisseurship and telling a cultural and/or social "story" in collaboration with local actors.

Smithsonian Folkways Recordings is the nonprofit record label of the Smithsonian Institution, the United States' national museum. Folkways pairs with the Smithsonian's annual Folklife Festival in honoring and bringing to public attention the keepers of intangible cultural heritage traditions from many parts of the world. At the Folklife Festival, which takes place on the National Mall in Washington, DC, each summer, the culture bearers speak for themselves in a presentational environment designed to promote interaction among the participants and audience members. In 2011, Folkways recordings of regional music from Colombia sparked an entire Folklife Festival program.

In previous years, four major Folkways recordings programs, featuring artists from Latin America and Latino USA, attracted millions of visitors in 2004, 2005, 2007, and 2009. The Smithsonian is a complex of nineteen museums and galleries and twelve research and cultural centers guided by its institutional mission: "the increase and diffusion of knowledge." Each part of the Smithsonian addresses in its own way the questions—increase and diffuse how and to what end?—that arise in pursuit of this mission. Smithsonian Folkways Recordings has found its own answer in "supporting cultural diversity and increased understanding among peoples through the documentation, preservation, and dissemination of sound." Folkways seeks to do two things: strengthen people's engagement with their own cultural heritage and enhance their awareness and appreciation of the cultural heritage of others. The range of possibilities offered by this dual intention is vast. The "Staff Picks" section of the online Folkways website-and-catalogue, for instance, leads with *Ballads, Banjo Tunes and Sacred Songs of Western North Carolina, Performed by Bascom Lamar Lunsford* (1996); *Abayudaya: Music from the Jewish People of Uganda* (2003); *More Multicultural Children's Songs from Ella Jenkins* (2014); and *The Mississippi River of Song: A Musical Journey down the Mississippi* (1998).

For Smithsonian Folkways Recordings, the museum setting is more a means than an end. While the audio recordings held in its archival collections are used inside museums for a wide range of things—audio components of exhibitions, science education curriculum materials, "music on hold" when people are placed on hold during telephone calls, and much more—our main presence is outside the walls of the museum. Folkways was born "out of the museum box"—that is, with the intent to engage people and cultural issues in settings located anywhere. One of the most pressing contemporary challenges for museums is how to be relevant to society—as well as the associated challenge of reaching people beyond a museum's physical location. Maria Rosario Jackson, an American researcher specializing in studies of community cultural assets, has envisioned the importance of museums in playing a more meaningful role in communities. "Too often, they are on the sidelines of civic life," she writes. "The museum field [faces] a noble challenge—to stretch its boundaries, step away from the sidelines, come to the center of civic life, and become a more active participant and even a leader in social-capital and community-building processes."[1]

What does music have to do with social capital and community building? Music can be a powerful communicator of social and cultural values and an attractive invitation to public engagement. Music bonds, and music bridges. Music has the potential to strengthen ties within cultures and to build understanding, mutuality, and empathy across cultural differences. The product of these bonds and bridges is a kind of "social capital"—shared values and ties that enable and encourage mutually advantageous social cooperation. In the case of Smithsonian Folkways, this often means directly and deliberately working with people who are themselves using music to express their identity and aspirations in the public sphere. In 1948, Moses Asch, founder of the private record label Folkways Records in New York City, set out to create an encyclopedia of humanity through recorded sound. By the time he died in 1986, he had published 2,168 albums of music and sounds from around the world—averaging about one album per week. This was the collection that came to the Smithsonian in 1987. Asch had a special interest in publishing recordings of music that were relevant to current issues. For example, in the 1950s, the American public knew very little of cultures from around the world, so he partnered with scholars such as anthropologist Harold Courlander to make music of many cultures available. In doing so, he set a standard for what would be called "world music" recordings. One of these was the 1951 recording *Folk and Classical Music of Korea*, produced in collaboration with Kyung Ho Park. Note that this was published during the time of the Korean War (1951–1953), bringing greater awareness of Korean culture to an American public more familiar with Korea through images of violence. The American civil rights movement prompted many Folkways recordings of music that inspired it. During the war in Vietnam, Folkways published *Music of Vietnam* in 1965 and *Folk Songs of Vietnam* in 1968. Today, Smithsonian Folkways Recordings both keeps this legacy alive and builds on it. At the website (www.folkways.si.edu) you can hear samples of that 1951 recording from Korea as well as the others mentioned; you can download them or order them on CD.

"Great music" is music performed at a high level of standards, as determined by its home culture. "Great story" is music that has a compelling extramusical role—for example, bringing to public attention a culture with a future threatened by globalization, countering cultural inequities by reinforcing a minority culture's identity, adding momentum and meaning to a cultural movement, bringing people together across cultural barriers, or amplifying a little-known cultural story that needs to be told. The recording *¡Soy Salvadoreño! Chanchona Music from Eastern El Salvador* is a good example. The music is a mountain tradition, with its loose-jointed and joyous sound rooted in rural country life. It is performed by members of an accomplished, respected family of musicians steeped in the tradition for four generations. They play in the style of their community and their ancestors, and they do it well. The spirit behind the music is the same rural-life spirit behind its name—*chanchona* means "big sow pig" and was playfully applied to the music around 1960 in reference to the homemade string bass that anchors the group. The "story" is that of a community from the eastern department of Morazán, severely battered by El Salvador's civil war of the late 1980s and early 1990s. Forced by poverty and violence to leave their homes, many emigrated to Washington, DC, and the surrounding area in the states of Virginia and Maryland. In their new homes, their neighbors knew little about them, their plight, and their music. This recording is the first recording of *chanchona* music with educational notes that tell their story. A central theme of their story is the cultural and social power of music to bond them together. In their own words, when they hear their music, they feel "at home," no matter where they may be. The story here, then, is about the culture and values of a recent immigrant group to the United States and the power of music as a means of building a strong sense of community. It also introduces the broader public and schoolteachers to a little-understood immigrant community in an enticing way.

In eastern Uganda, a group of people call themselves the Abayudaya—"People of Judah," in the Luganda language. In 1919, under the guidance of their leader, the entire community converted to Judaism. This conversion brought many challenges—especially under the repressive regime of dictator Idi Amin in the 1970s—as well as spiritual rewards. The Abayudaya have long sought to live their cultural and spiritual lives in peace and to connect with, and be recognized by, the larger world of Judaism. About ten years ago, an ethnomusicologist and rabbi, Jeffrey Summit of Tufts University, came to

FIGURE 15.1
Videographer Charlie Weber and audio recordist Pete Reiniger of Smithsonian Folkways Recordings document the Chanchona Los Hermanos Lovo in Pajigua Arriba, Guatajiagua, Morazán Province, El Salvador, 2009. (Photo: Daniel Sheehy; copyright © Smithsonian Institution.)

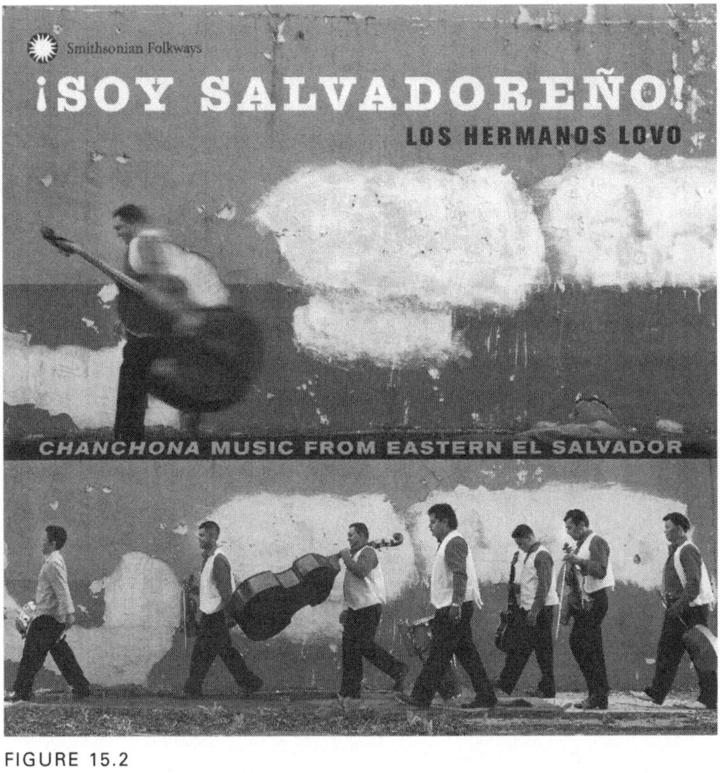

FIGURE 15.2
Album cover for *¡Soy Salvadoreño! Chanchona Music from Eastern El Salvador* (2011). (Photo: Courtesy of Smithsonian Folkways Recordings; copyright © Smithsonian Institution.)

us with a project to publish a CD offering a glimpse of the musical life of the Abayudaya to tell the story of their cultural aspirations. Two years later, the CD was released. The recording was nominated for a Grammy Award—the American music industry's highest honor—for best traditional world music album. This public visibility aligned with the community's desire to be recognized more broadly as a unique Jewish people. Several years later, the royalties generated by the sale of the CD paid for scholarships that enabled several of their young people to go to college. The recording project clearly helped the community tell its story to a broader public and to build pride in its heritage.

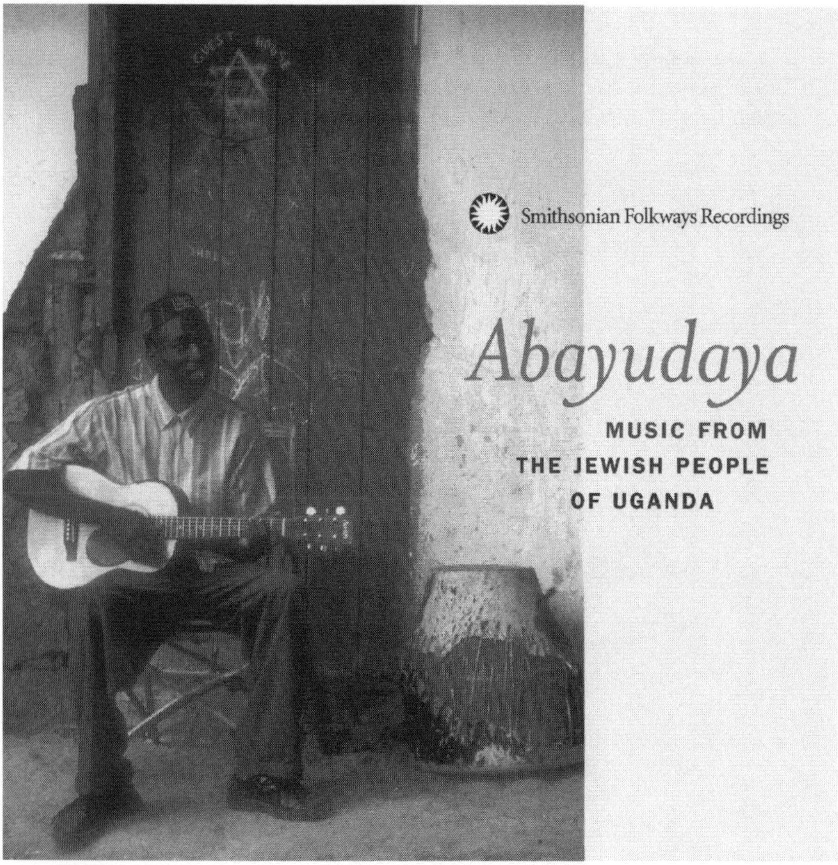

FIGURE 15.3
Album cover for *Abayudaya: Music from the Jewish People of Uganda* (2003). (Photo: Courtesy of Smithsonian Folkways Recordings; copyright © Smithsonian Institution.)

In the South American country of Colombia, the eastern tropical plains region bordering the Orinoco River and Venezuela historically was distanced from mainstream national cultural life and the cultural capital of Bogotá in the Andean highlands. A local musician, educator, and plains cultural consultant, Carlos Rojas Hernández, was eager to raise the national and international profile of his music and regional culture, which he felt had been neglected and unrecognized in the cultural life and identity of his country. The regional music had emerged as a national musical icon of neighboring Venezuela in the 1950s, further overshadowing its presence in Colombia. Collaborating with the Smithsonian Folkways team, Rojas produced an album of plains music demonstrating three generations of traditional musical style. The album, *¡Sí, Soy Llanero! Joropo Music from the Orinoco Plains of Colombia*, earned a Grammy nomination, generating much attention in the Colombian news media. This recording was the first Colombian music recording, recorded in Colombia, to receive Grammy recognition. The recording made cultural headline news nationwide and forwarded the cultural agenda of gaining broader recognition. Rojas later reflected on this achievement: "Our relationship with Smithsonian Folkways Recordings launched us onto the world music stage, bringing visibility to our plains *joropo* tradition both internationally and at home in Colombia. The albums they produced and the inclusion of our recordings in the Smithsonian's collection confirm the artistic and cultural value of our musical traditions; a recognition that we hope will inspire new generations of participants and contribute to the conservation and revitalization of *joropo* as part of Colombia's cultural heritage." The group that emerged from that recording, named Cimarrón, parlayed that broader recognition into many international tours and a spotlight appearance at the World Music Expo in Europe.

In bringing the voice of the people to the forefront, Smithsonian Folkways uses several important methods. First, it employs the already-mentioned "good music, good story" philosophy. Second, the "first-voice" of the artists and cultural stakeholders is privileged in telling the story. One way of doing this is to include the first-voice words of the artists in the liner notes that accompany each recording. Third, in presenting the first-voice story, video is used whenever possible, offering a much richer sense of the musicians, their techniques, their thoughts, the cultural context, and the physical setting. These videos are short—about five minutes in length—and are posted on

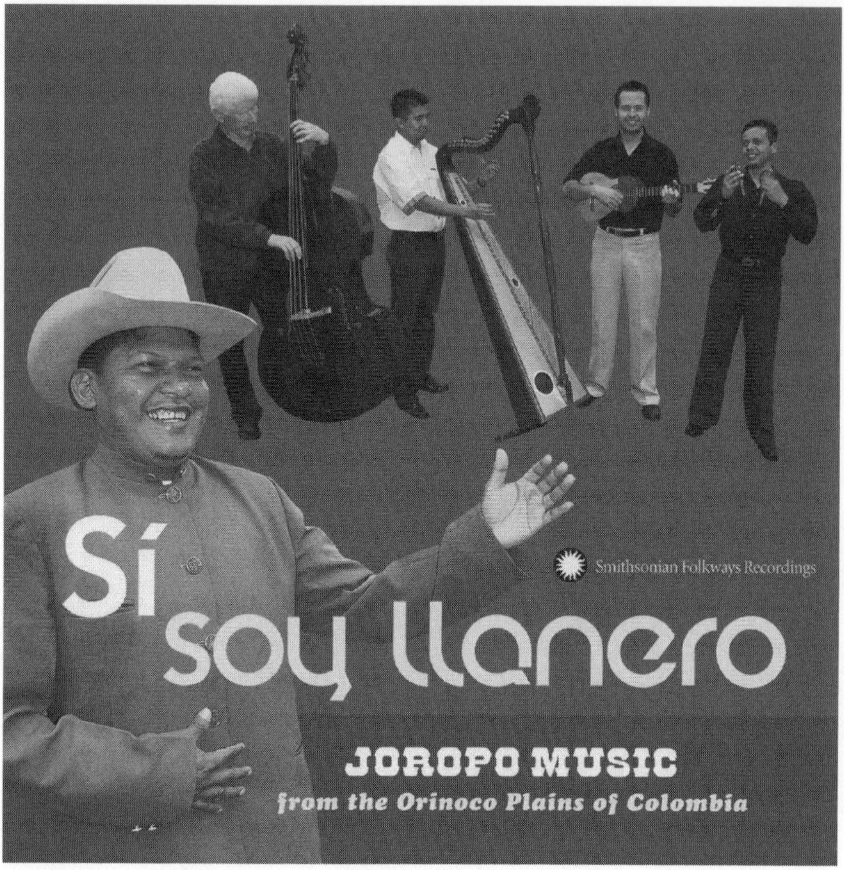

FIGURE 15.4
Album cover for *¡Sí, Soy Llanero! Joropo Music from the Orinoco Plains of Colombia* (2004). (Photo: Courtesy of Smithsonian Folkways Recordings; copyright © Smithsonian Institution.)

the website when a companion CD is launched. A sampler of seven of these videos accompanies the Tradiciones/Traditions series of music from Latin America and Latino communities in the United States.

Fourth, seeking maximum public impact is central. It occurs through sales of CDs, downloads, streams, and social media. Folkways distributes forty-seven thousand tracks of music and sound originating in more than 160 countries to people throughout the United States and around the world. More than 10 million audio tracks were delivered to our audiences by forty-plus distributors of physical product (CDs), digital music retailers such as iTunes in more than one hundred territories internationally, streaming services such as Spotify, and subscriptions to libraries. The collection comprises twelve historical record labels, including the recently added United Nations Educational, Scientific, and Cultural Organization (UNESCO) collection, with its 127 volumes of traditional music of the world. Fifth, Folkways collaborates with other parts of the Smithsonian and with outside organizations and individuals to extend both impact and reflexive research. Folkways has worked with the Aga Khan Trust for Culture to produce a ten-volume series of CD-DVDs on the music of Central Asia, for instance. Strategic targeting of educational resources reaches hundreds of thousands more people each year. More than one hundred lesson plans for teachers were downloaded nearly 127,000 times in 2015, touching the lives of countless students.

These examples offer a deeper understanding of our engagement with traditions and keepers of intangible cultural heritage, in our own nation and around the world. To the museum, our presence brings deep and active engagement with communities in safeguarding their traditions of intangible cultural heritage and in adding new meaning and value to those traditions. To the public, our position in the museum underscores and reinforces our role as something more than a mere record label. Smithsonian Folkways Recordings is a mission-driven force intent on bringing the work of the museum more into civic life and doing what it can, in collaboration with community members themselves, to safeguard intangible cultural heritage.

NOTE

1. Jackson 2002, 29.

DISCOGRAPHY

Jenkins, Ella. 2014. *More Multicultural Children's Songs from Ella Jenkins.* Smithsonian Folkways 45078.

Lunsford, Bascom Lamar. 1996. *Ballads, Banjo Tunes and Sacred Songs of Western North Carolina, Performed by Bascom Lamar Lunsford.* Smithsonian Folkways 40082.

Los Hermanos Lovo. 2011. *¡Soy Salvadoreño! Chanchona Music from Eastern El Salvador.* Smithsonian Folkways 40535.

Various artists. 1951. *Folk and Classical Music of Korea.* Folkways FE 4424.

———. 1965. *Music of Vietnam*. Folkways FE 4352.

———. 1968. *Folk Songs of Vietnam*. Folkways FTS 31303.

———. 1970. *Cancion Protesta: Protest Songs of Latin America*. Paredon 1001.

———. 1998. *The Mississippi River of Song: A Musical Journey Down the Mississippi*. Smithsonian Folkways 40086.

———. 2003. *Abayudaya: Music from the Jewish People of Uganda*. Smithsonian Folkways 40504.

———. 2004. *¡Sí, Soy Llanero! Joropo Music from the Orinoco Plains of Colombia*. Smithsonian Folkways 40515.

WEB RESOURCES

http://www.folkways.si.edu/search/civil-rights

http://www.folkways.si.edu/music-of-vietnam/world/album/smithsonian

http://www.folkways.si.edu/los-hermanos-lovo/soy-salvadoreno-chanchonamusic-from-eastern-el-salvador/latin/album/smithsonian

http://www.folkways.si.edu/video/traditions_series_field_trip.aspx

http://www.folkways.si.edu/search/central-asia

REFERENCES

Jackson, Maria Rosario. 2002. "Coming to the Center of Community Life." In *Mastering Civic Engagement: A Challenge to Museums*, Washington, DC: American Alliance of Museums, 2002.

16

The Smithsonian Folklife Festival in Museological Perspective

RICHARD KURIN

The Smithsonian Folklife Festival has been described as a living museum. Over its history it has challenged negative perceptions of museums and influenced museum practice, and it continues to do so in the twenty-first century. Richard Kurin has played a leadership role in the festival for decades, and now, as acting provost and undersecretary for museums and research of the Smithsonian, he provides keen insights into how the festival has evolved and its continuing contributions to museology. He captures the way that the festival provided a context where visitors became participants in the exhibitions, demonstrations, and performances as they sang, danced, ate, and interacted with people of other cultures. The festival challenged conventional museological practices of curators and directors as musicians, artists, and tradition bearers were given a setting where they could speak for themselves. Kurin also reminds readers that thousands of academic and community scholars have contributed fieldwork on forms of cultural traditions that have resulted in published scholarly work as well as films, recordings, and educational curricula. The festival has also come to be viewed as a model for other major public cultural presentations, including programs on the Mall, as well as the cultural programs for the Olympics and other international festivals.

Ornithologist S. Dillon Ripley well understood the importance of museums and their collections through his own use of specimens in researching the bird species of India and Asia, as well as in running Yales Peabody Museum of Natural History—but when he came to the Smithsonian as its secretary in 1964, his agenda was more public and expansive. Visiting museums was "essentially very dull. You did it on Sunday afternoon after a big lunch," he wrote.[1]

This less-than-tepid endorsement of the stodgy displays in what was called "the Nation's Attic" gave Ripley his cause. He wanted to liven up the place and make museums accessible, fun to visit, and exciting—an interest he shared with his younger contemporary, J. Carter Brown, across the way at the National Gallery of Art. Ripley liked the "attic" moniker, not because of its association with the old and packed away but for the idea of serendipity and discovery: Who knows what a child might find in an old trunk and what playful flights of imagination might be inspired by it? Ripley's impetus in the 1960s toward heightened levels of civic participation ran counter to the first secretary, Joseph Henry, who sought—from the institution's founding in 1846 through his three-decade-long tenure—to stem the almost irresistible drive to turn the Smithsonian from the research institution he envisioned into the national museum.

The institution's purpose, penned in the will of its eponymous founder, James Smithson, was the "increase and diffusion of knowledge among men," and Henry was squarely on the increase side. Ripley, a scientifically oriented naturalist, favored diffusion. To leave no doubt about whose vision would rule the day, Ripley, ever a consummate symbol-manipulating showman, ordered the statue of Henry—which for decades had faced the Smithsonian Castle—turned around to face the National Mall. It signaled a more conceptual turn, from an inward to an outward focus, from juggling the competing demands of self-driven expertise to assuming responsibility for encouraging public knowledge and resultant civic virtue.

Though the west end of the Mall with the Lincoln Memorial had been the site of the March on Washington in 1963, the east end of the Mall, closer to the Capitol and the front yard of the Smithsonian, was little used. "Forest Lawn on the Potomac," Ripley called it—a cemetery-like dead space in the center of the nation's capital.[2] Ripley, recalling his youthful visits to Paris and its people- and entertainment-filled Tuileries Garden, thought his end of the Mall should be overflowing with lively wonders. Ripley hired impresario James Morris to produce concerts, sound and light shows, performances, and even a temporary annual theater on the Mall.

Ripley had envisioned something like a New England town gazebo and concerts on the lawn as part of the Smithsonian's summer programming. Morris, familiar with the Newport Folk Festival, and having produced his own festival in Asheville, North Carolina, with the participation of folklorist Alan Lomax and singer Pete Seeger, channeled Ripley's impulse toward a folk festival for the Smithsonian. Morris hired Ralph Rinzler to run it. Rinzler was the field research director for Newport and a documentarian who—with folk musician and folklorist Mike Seeger and others—sought out authentic, grassroots artists. Rinzler recorded and learned from such musicians as Doc Watson, Bill Monroe, and Dewey Balfa; befriended Woody Guthrie; worked for Moses Asch and produced Folkways Records; and brought his ethnomusicological pickings to his own music, playing the mandolin and banjo for the old-time folk revival group the Greenbriar Boys. Bob Dylan had been their opening act at Greenwich Village's Gerde's Folk City when he was "discovered."

As an urban "folkie," Rinzler was knowledgeable and sophisticated, the son of a physician and teacher, educated at Swarthmore and the Sorbonne, and a good fit to help Ripley expand his museological vision. Ripley famously said, "Take the instruments out of their glass cases and let them sing."[3] He was noting that the objects in the museum meant something to the people who made, used, and listened to them—and that museums really had to convey that if they were truly to come alive. Rinzler, influenced by scholars like Don Yoder, Roger Abrahams, and Henry Glassie, chose the more academic term "folklife" rather than "folk" for the festival—trying to position the activity as having a serious ethnographic approach aligned with the Smithsonian, rather placing it in the domain of entertainment and youthful, somewhat scruffy counterculture.

The initial Festival of American Folklife, as it was titled, was a four-day event held over the Fourth of July holiday in 1967, outdoors on the Mall and in front of the Museum of History and Technology. As with the Smithsonian's museums, there was no admission charge. The festival featured more than a hundred musicians and artisans from around the United States, demonstrating a variety of Appalachian, Puerto Rican, African American, Native American, and ethnic traditions. Its success seemed immediately apparent, drawing hundreds of thousands of visitors and praise from a few members of Congress, who lauded the fact that their folks from "back home" were featured. The press was effusive: "Fresh air for the Nation's Attic," gushed the *New York Times*; "A ball on the Mall," toasted the *Washington Post*.

The festival did have its doubters both in and out of the Smithsonian. Some worried about having a "carnival" on the Mall and producing an exposition that lacked the seriousness and standing of the museums. Rinzler and Morris developed a language for talking about the festival, its purpose and organization, over the ensuing years. Programs like the "African Diaspora," or "Ohio," or "Working Americans" were named components of the festival—much in the way that museum exhibitions or galleries focused on a particular culture group, form, or region. Performers, artisans, craftspeople, cooks, and others who demonstrated their traditions were called "cultural practitioners," "bearers," or "exemplars." People introducing performances or providing background information on demonstrations were called "presenters."

The overall purpose was for the festival to illustrate the diversity and beauty of long-lived traditions still practiced in many communities across the United States but often ignored in a modern, urban context. It would feature authentic practitioners of those traditions—not reenactors as one might find at the so-called living history museums of the time. The festival was conceived as giving voice to the less known and underrepresented. Finding many American traditions closely connected to and derived from those in Europe, Asia, Africa, and other parts of the world, the festival quickly added participants from other nations—something that years later led to a name change as the Smithsonian Folklife Festival.

Ripley had been right—the public embraced the spirit of the festival as the Smithsonian come alive. Visitors too became participants in the displays, demonstrations, and performances as they sang, danced, ate, and ritualized with people of other cultures. The festival grew in popularity and audience, featuring hundreds of artists, becoming longer in duration and more expansive on the Mall.

In the first few years, the festival's organizers and presenters came from among Rinzler's Newport contacts. But that group quickly expanded. Planners, presenters, interpreters, and translators increasingly came from the communities of the represented. Musicians and artisans spoke for themselves and offered their interpretations and their points of view. Rinzler took criticism from some Smithsonian museum directors and curators for demeaning museological practice; the festival was seen as the curatorial equivalent of turning hospital patients loose to make the diagnoses and offer the treatments rather than leaving it all in the hands of the well-trained, experienced, and rational physicians.

But the festival had its advocates, supporters, and champions, like Margaret Mead and others in the museum, academic, and public intellectual worlds. Festival literature promoted ideas of America's diverse and authentic grassroots culture; the value of the artistry, skill, knowledge, and wisdom of its cultural exemplars; and the importance of hearing their voices.

Rinzler saw the festival as a corrective to the rather narrow representation of American history and culture in the Smithsonian museums. He pointed out that American Indians were represented not in the history museum but rather in the natural history museum, along with the dinosaurs, flora, and fauna—as objects of nature rather than agents of culture. Rinzler recruited a strong group of American Indian cultural scholars and educators—Clydia Nahwooksy, Lucille Dawson, Helen Schierbeck, Rayna Green, Alfonso Ortiz—and with their help, the festival became an important platform for native cultural leaders, scholars, artists, and ritual experts to publicly represent their traditions and concerns.

Similarly, within the museums there was little representation of African American culture; Rinzler recruited Bernice Johnson Reagon, Gerald Davis, James Early, John Franklin, Bill Ferris, and others to devise programs and interpretations for the festival. Rinzler brought in Mick Maloney to help explore Irish and Irish American culture; Ethel Raim and Martin Koenig to present the traditions of eastern European immigrants; Américo Paredes to examine ways of presenting Hispanic culture; Archie Green to develop a framework for occupational cultures; and so on. The festival became a way for the Smithsonian to expand its representation of the American people. Morris called the festival an exercise of "cultural democracy" and suggested that its message would be a corrective to America's longtime insecurity vis-à-vis European high culture—a point well made as the United States approached its bicentennial celebrations.

To bring that point home, the festival became one of the official centerpieces of the bicentennial of the United States and was provided a budget of about $9 million—a whopping amount at the time—to produce a three-month extravaganza in the summer of 1976. The Smithsonian collaborated with cultural scholars and activists from across the United States and around the world to bring more than five thousand musicians, artisans, cooks, workers, healers, and other cultural exemplars to Washington to demonstrate their traditions to more than 3 million visitors.

Programs featured a sweeping view of diverse cultural histories: Native American traditions through the involvement of scores of tribes; the "African Diaspora," looking at connections between American, Caribbean, and African traditions through performances and demonstrations of artists from more than a dozen nations; "Regional America," examining everything from New England's seafaring history to the cowboy traditions of the West; "Old Ways in the New World," pairing up Americans of numerous ethnic groups with exemplary artists from more than twenty countries of Europe and Asia; and, with the cooperation of labor unions, "Working Americans," with a host of occupational folklore demonstrations by construction workers and seamstresses, miners, and farmworkers. There was even a "Family Folklore" program to feature children's games and traditions and to collect stories from the public. All of this, spread over fifty acres for three months, represented a diversity and intensity of participation never before seen at the Smithsonian.

It took some getting used to for the Smithsonian to produce the festival. There were parallels, to be sure, between museum and festival production schedules, regimens, and logistics. But the festival demanded a new level of complexity. To put people on display, they needed to be transported; exhibition and display contexts needed to be built. Those from other countries needed visas and documents.

Organizers had to accommodate the dietary preferences, religious needs, and hygienic practices of its diverse participants—bringing in special cooks, providing prayer spaces, even constructing specialized toilets and holding culturally appropriate exorcisms when needed. Scores of translators and cultural liaisons and hundreds of volunteers were required for each festival to assure participants were taken care of, communicated with, and treated with respect. The festival had to grow real crops like corn and cotton and install a working rice paddy on the Mall to accommodate presentations. It would have to build a New Mexican adobe village; bring in a dozen mud masons from Mali to construct a Djenne-like gate down the hill from the US Capitol; and transport everything from an iceberg from Alaska to a temple from Bhutan so as to provide a realistic context to its presentations.

Over the years, the rest of the Smithsonian got used to the festival as a kind of people-messy, once a year, topsy-turvy ritual that happened outside—not within—the carefully curated and scripted halls of the museums. Sometimes the contrast was startling. Anthropologist James Boon captured the spirit in an article, "Why Museums Make Me Sad," contrasting the loud, vibrant, youthful, messy disorder of the festival with the hushed halls of the galleries.[4] Smithsonian undersecretary Dean Anderson said it succinctly at one of the festival's opening ceremonies: "Museum is a noun; the Festival is a verb."[5]

The *Washington Post* and other media loved the festival because it was in many ways so counter to the self-absorbed seriousness and power suffusing the nation's capital. The juxtapositions were just too seductive to ignore: A calf escaping the festival, followed by a cowboy on horseback chasing it down Constitution Avenue, only to finally lasso it in the parking lot of the Kennedy Center. Lumberjacks demonstrating their skills on timbers raised hundreds of feet high next to the Washington Monument. Indians staging their Ram Lila spectacle, firing burning arrows into massive, fireworks-loaded, exploding effigies of the evil king Ravenna under the watchful eye of twenty fire trucks lining the Mall to guard against the festival burning down the museums and other public buildings.

While supping on the drama of these antimuseum, antiofficial juxtapositions—Are they really sheering sheep, making moonshine, and spray-painting graffiti on a New York subway car on the National Mall?—the festival also partook of the Smithsonian-museum idiom. The festival had explanatory signage and photo-text panels; it had a catalogue or program book; its programs were "curated" and its "exhibitions" reviewed. Though its "collection" was essentially ephemeral, festival staff and volunteers took great pains to document performances and demonstrations, so that over the years there has been an impressive record made—through video and film, sound recordings and images—of the traditions represented.

Overall, the festival has hosted tens of thousands of artists in programs featuring scores of countries; just about all US states and territories, from New Hampshire to Texas, Mississippi to Iowa, New Mexico to Hawaii; a few cities like New York and Washington; hundreds of tribes, communities, and ethnic groups; and dozens of occupational groups. It's even represented the cultural traditions running through federal agencies—the White House, NASA, the Forest Service, and the Peace Corps. Some programs have been more thematic, examining a cultural form or issue in different societies—such as the "Musics of Struggle," "Culture and Development," and "Cultural Conservation." Some programs have looked at particular types of cultural connections, such as "Borderlands"; a massive program about the Silk Road was organized with Yo-Yo Ma and involved more than five hundred artists from twenty-three countries. Many programs have focused on cultural "hot spots" when an appearance at the festival could help play a role in resolving difficult issues; programs on Northern Ireland, American Indian access to resources, and the Tibetan diaspora, with participation by the Dalai Lama, were of this type.

In all of its manifestations, the festival's museology has as its core the foregrounding of the cultural exemplars and the primacy of their voices in the presentations. The festival makes the key philosophical and ethical statement that the people of a culture should play the lead role in shaping the character of their own representation—with scholars, curators, and others engaging in dialog, facilitating, and providing context for that presentation.

Even though this method has now, decades later, become standard practice for the public programming of artists, musicians, storytellers, and others in most of the Smithsonian's museums and in hundreds of those around the country and the planet, not everyone agrees with this approach. Some have argued that festival programs, with names of nations and groups heralded on massive signs and banners on the Mall and trumpeted in promotional material, can overessentialize the nature of a community's identity—so that individual participants are falsely placed in a role of representing nations and groups of people that are themselves historically and often problematically construed. Some think this leads to more celebratory and sanitized presentations and less critical representations of self, community, and historical reality than a more dispassionate curatorial or scholarly approach would yield. Other critics have argued that rather than giving voice to participants, the festival thrusts people on stage, out of context, putting them on zoo-like display where they are somehow forced to act out their ethnicity in a manner recalling the sad and even sordid ethnographic voyeurism of the late nineteenth and early twentieth centuries.

I think this criticism is way off base—because participants are briefed, aware, and much more sophisticated about what they are doing than these critics imagine. Indeed, one of the contributions of the festival has been that thousands of cultural exemplars have gained added experience in representing themselves and their cultural communities to new audiences. Many have learned from this, developing new tactics and strategies for advancing their own cultural agendas, forming new networks of support and advocacy, and discovering new connections with other practitioners and their traditions. Some have benefited both materially and spiritually from their participation.

The festival has made other contributions as well, some of which Ripley would probably never have anticipated. Because of the festival, thousands of academic and community scholars have engaged in fieldwork to document and analyze numerous forms of cultural expressions; this has resulted in scores of books, recordings, articles, book chapters, and other publications—as well as the acquisition of historic Folkways Records and its ongoing, successful documentation and dissemination work at the Smithsonian. The festival has provided a model for other large-scale public cultural presentations, including programs for the Olympics, the Black Family Reunion, the opening of the National World War II Memorial, the National Museum of the American Indian, presidential inaugural activities, and other national celebration events. Festival programs have also been restaged "back home" in places like Texas and Kentucky, Bermuda and India, and have contributed to a larger, more sustained effort to research, exhibit, and utilize local cultural heritage for positive purposes.

Festival programs have played a key role in generating economic activity—through music and crafts sales, by opening up markets to communities previously excluded from them, by encouraging new cultural products, and by stimulating tourism to the nations or regions featured. The festival has inspired and contributed to changes in policies and laws, which have enabled nations and communities to better recognize, preserve, sustain, extend, and benefit from their heritage.

The festival has also played a pivotal role in helping expand what governments now regard as heritage—adding, to the built sites and environments on the world heritage list, the more ephemeral forms of intangible cultural heritage that people enact as part of who they are and what they do. In short, the festival has energized new possibilities for what can be done in the Smithsonian and on the National Mall, but also in the lives of people, communities, and institutions well beyond.

NOTES

This chapter is a republication of Richard Kurin, "The Smithsonian Folklife Festival in Museological Perspective," *Curator: The Museum Journal* 57, no. 4 © 2014, Wiley-Blackwell on behalf of the California Academy of Sciences, with permission.

1. Parker 2001, 14.
2. Kurin 1998, 24.
3. Kurin 1997, 110.
4. Boon 1991.
5. Kurin 1998, 30.

REFERENCES

Boon, James A. 1991. "Why Museums Make Me Sad." In *Exhibiting Cultures: The Poetics and Politics of Museum Display*, edited by Ivan Karp and Steven D. Lavine, 255–78. Washington, DC: Smithsonian Institution Press.

Kurin, Richard. 1997. *Reflections of a Culture Broker: A View from the Smithsonian.* Washington, DC: Smithsonian Institution Press.

———. 1998. *Smithsonian Folklife Festival: Culture of, by, and for the People.* Washington, DC: Smithsonian Institution.

Parker, Diana. 2001. "A Tribute to S. Dillon Ripley." In *Smithsonian Folklife Festival 2001*, 14–15. Washington, DC: Smithsonian Institution.

17

Museums and Ethnography in the Digital Age

MARSHA MACDOWELL
AND JASON BAIRD JACKSON

Ethnographic museums were among the earliest adopters of digital computing technologies to advance the public service and professional goals of the field. In the history of one key area of current digital activity—databases—American Folklore Society fellow William Fenton, writing in the pages of *Curator* in 1960, called for the creation of a unified index of ethnographic museum collections information.[1] By the middle of the 1960s, and in response to this call, experimental projects were under way using mainframe computer database systems as a means of aggregating and extending knowledge of ethnographic object collections.[2] Present-day multi-institutional collections database projects, such as the Quilt Index and the Reciprocal Research Network (RRN), thus represent the flowering of long-standing professional commitments by ethnographically oriented museum professionals.[3] In an era in which the digital has become a ubiquitous obsession, folklorists and other museum ethnographers can be proud that their current work has deep roots and responds to needs long recognized.

As our world has become increasingly one in which digital tools are fundamental to all aspects of human life, museums have also become more digitally dependent. As institutions dedicated to the preservation and use of material cultural heritage, museums were early adopters of digital tools and have steadfastly worked to use new digital tools to strengthen their abilities to meet their missions.[4] While earlier museum engagements with computer technologies centered on the specialized challenges of museum collections and cataloging, today digital tools, networks, and data are central to nearly every aspect of ethnographic museum practice, from marketing to disaster planning. Digital practices have also been transforming fundamental assumptions about what the museum is and where its boundaries might lie.[5] This chapter's brief review cannot survey all of the areas in which folklorists, museums, and digital tools and techniques presently intersect. Such a survey, along with a more theoretical and overarching meditation on the current state of change generally, are needs that can only be highlighted here. In keeping with other chapters in this overview of the current folklore museum scene, a few key areas are described with accompanying case study introductions. Examined here are several prominent and increasingly interdigitated realms of activity: digital exhibitions, collections-focused databases, and collaboratory tools, along with digital aspects of museum research and education. Social media, video production, open access scholarly communication, and the everyday use of general and specialized software, including open source software, are all topics deserving of attention in future surveys of digital practice in folklore and other ethnographic museums.

DIGITAL EXHIBITIONS

Digital exhibitions are no longer a new genre of scholarly communication. We can see this in their proliferation as well as in our growing ability to chronicle the history of change within the genre.[6] Earlier Internet-based digital exhibitions were built—as were other websites, following the birth of Internet browser software—out of computer code and digital assets (such as object photographs) assembled on what amounted, metaphorically, to blank sheets of (digital) paper. To take one typical example, in 2001–2002 then museum graduate assistant Rhonda S. Fair was charged with creating a simple digital exhibition presentation of the Sam Noble Museum's collection of Mayan clothing. In response, she built "The Fabric of Mayan Life: An Exhibit of Textiles," a website combining text and digital photographs that was built using the HTML editor Dreamweaver.[7] While digital exhibitions—some very simple, some very complex—are still built "by hand" in this way, the current norm (ca. 2015) is to construct digital exhibitions using a general-purpose content management system such as WordPress or Drupal or a special purpose tool, such as Omeka, that has been designed to (among other tasks) facilitate the production of digital exhibitions. Illustrating this later case is an exhibition developed with Omeka by folklore graduate students at the Mathers Museum of World Cultures in 2014: "Ojibwe Public Art, Ostrom Private Lives."[8] Content management platforms such as those increasingly in use provide digital exhibition builders the means by which projects are more easily accessed on mobile devices (through "responsive design"), are more easily updated, are better able to connect with users (via social media), and can be linked to or incorporated into other digital projects (through technical "interoperability"). While the exhibitions just cited as examples are relatively modest undertakings, folklorists have been central to many major digital exhibition projects. A relatively early example is "Dane Wajich | Dane-zaa Stories and Songs: Dreamers and the Land," an award-winning Virtual Museum of Canada exhibition cocurated by a team that included folklorist Amber Ridington.[9]

Digital resources and tools are also impacting the design of physical museum exhibitions in a range of ways. Behind the scenes, digital tools—from computer-aided design systems and photographic editing software to 3-D printers—play a key role in the making of gallery exhibitions, including ethnographic ones. In public view, documentary fieldwork video not only serves as a means of documenting new ethnographic collections but also, when present in exhibition galleries, enables the presentation of first-person narratives about objects as well as the processes, uses, and meanings that provide their contexts. Increasingly, it is not just video that accompanies objects in ethnographic exhibitions; an ever-growing range of digital games and active-learning activities is used in such projects. As an illustration, the collaborative exhibition "c̓əsnaʔəm, the city before the city" was organized by the Musqueam Indian Band, the Museum of Vancouver, and the Museum of Anthropology at the University of British Columbia. As part of the exhibition, a team led by museum anthropologist Kate Kennessey of Simon Frazier University developed an exhibition element called "ʔeləw̓k̓ʷ—Belongings: A Tangible Table." This tangible table gave visitors a chance to hold and manipulate 3-D models of exhibited objects and to deploy them interactively on a digital surface that responded in complex ways, engaging visitors and providing

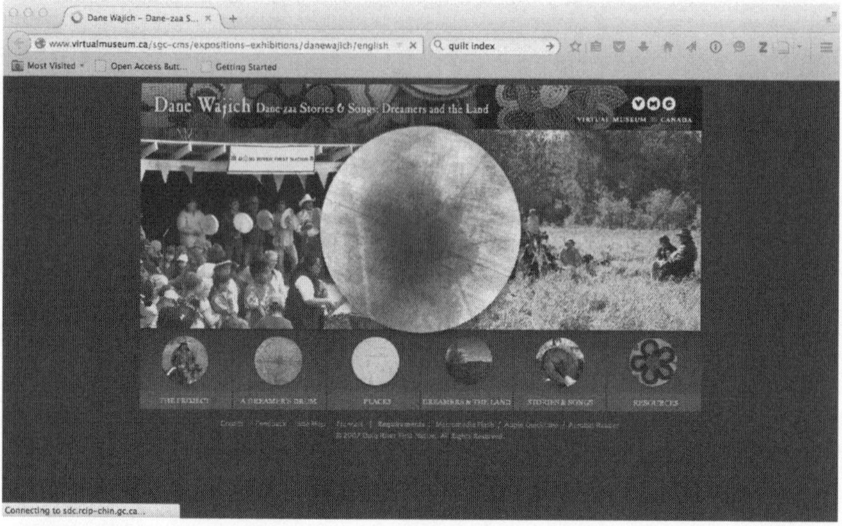

FIGURE 17.1
"Dane Wajich | Dane-z̲aa Stories and Songs: Dreamers and the Land" is a widely discussed and critically acclaimed digital exhibition and archive produced under the auspices of the Virtual Museum of Canada. The work of a large team of native and nonnative participants, the project centered on work done over a month in summer 2005, when Doig River First Nations elders, youth, and leaders collaborated with ethnographers, linguists, and technologists to produce a documentary digital exhibition focused on place-based stories and traditions of the Dane-z̲aa people. See http://www.virtualmuseum.ca/sgc-cms/expositions-exhibitions/danewajich/english/index.html. (Photo: Dane Wajich | Dane-z̲aa Stories and Songs: Dreamers and the Land.)

rich cultural content bridging past and present and helping visitors engage uniquely with the stories of Musqueam Indian Band elders, places, historical artifacts, and contemporary objects.[10] Such hybridization of tangible and digital environments—in the service of providing visitors with self-guided inquiry—is a key theme in current digital exhibition work.

Parallel to the changes in associated technology are new curatorial choices. Many digital exhibitions relating to ethnographic collections were online spin-offs of physical exhibition projects, but more and more digital space is a coequal realm, and digital projects increasingly unfold unmoored to associated gallery exhibitions or programs. This dynamic has many contextual features but includes a desire to explore the unique affordances of digital media for ethnographic representation, collaboration, education, research, and outreach. Digital exhibitions pursued independently of physical ones in turn point to new questions about the institutional underpinnings of exhibition activity overall. Museum-relevant projects based on a museum's content may be produced by agencies outside the collecting museum. For instance, the multifaceted "Inuvialuit Living History" project is deeply focused on Smithsonian Institution collections, but Smithsonian staff are modest participants in an effort led by a consortium of First Nations cultural workers and nonnative, non-Smithsonian scholars.[11]

The "Osage Weddings Project," another exhibition project at the Sam Noble Museum, exemplifies the way in which digital tools are changing the very nature of how museums engage with communities in ethnographic research. Knowledge is contributed in digital space, and museum activities—collection preservation, exhibition, publications, and educational programs—are intentionally and openly derived from this public interface.[12] The traditional notion of curatorial authority is challenged, and the multiplicity of voices and knowledge becomes integral to the ways in which collections are formed and understood. New digital technologies are increasingly central to the fruitful decentering and democratization of museum authority structures, opening up new possibilities for cultural collaboration and innovation.

DIGITAL COLLECTION RESOURCES

Increasingly, digital exhibition projects (and other cultural heritage–related, website-based projects) sit atop and integrate richly with, rather than simply draw content out of, associated collections databases. The "Inuvialuit Living History" project just mentioned, for instance, is dependent first on the collections databases of the Department of Anthropology at the National Museum of Natural History, Smithsonian Institution, but more importantly and directly on collections data that has been placed within an exemplary resource aggregating ethnographic and archaeological collections data from a large number of partner institutions—both museums and indigenous governments. The Reciprocal Research Network is one of a number of such multi-institutional collections databases. The RRN was developed jointly by the Musqueam Indian Band, the Stó:lō Nation/Tribal Council, the U'mista Cultural Society, and the Museum of Anthropology at the University of British Columbia. The RRN lets users research cultural items held at twenty-two institutions. It is also structured technically to allow for a range of additional uses above and beyond accessing core collections data. Some of these will be highlighted below, but among them are the ability for related and unrelated projects to draw data out of the RRN system for use in endeavors such as "Inuvialuit Living History."[13] Other new digital resources born of an effort of linking and making accessible ethnographic collections in geographically dispersed archives, libraries, and museums are the American Folklore Society's National Folklore Archives Initiative, the American Memory Project at the Library of Congress, and Open Folklore, a partnership of the American Folklore Society and the Indiana University Bloomington Libraries.[14] Similarly, the Quilt Index is continuing to move from being a dynamic, multi-institutional database of stories and images to being a wider resource that can also feed content into digital exhibitions, host scholarly essays, and provide lesson plans and other resources. Importantly, it is becoming a laboratory for developing and testing digital tools, such as for automated pattern recognition, that advance the ability of scholars and educators to use collections in new and unexpected ways.[15]

FIGURE 17.2
The Quilt Index is a project of the Michigan State University Museum Matrix and MSU's Center for Digital Humanities and Social Sciences to preserve images and stories about quilt artists, quilts, and quilting activities and then to make this information searchable and freely accessible for research and education. The index houses tens of thousands of images and stories of artists and quilts from private and public collections (including over 250 museums) around the world. See www.quiltindex.org.

FROM COLLECTIONS TO COLLABORATORIES

Multipurpose collections platforms such as the RRN and the Quilt Index point to another newer development among digital practices within the museum ethnography realm. Such sites not only integrate or further collections documentation and collections interpretation goals but also constitute examples of the phenomena known as collaboratories. Collaboratories are more than collections of information and communication technologies; they are new modes of social organization that foster new social practices, collaboration techniques, norms, values, and rules.[16] While general users encounter core collections information when consulting the public face of the RRN, registered users have access to additional collaboration tools that can, for instance, facilitate object selection for a gallery exhibition or provide discursive space for weighing competing interpretive claims regarding a collection. These tools are an especially powerful means toward the widely shared goal of including source communities more fully in the curatorial and interpretive work of ethnographic museums. They also further the long-standing scholarly and outreach mission of collecting institutions, facilitating otherwise impossible collaborations on distributed collections by distributed partners.[17]

TOOLS AND PLATFORMS FOR DIGITAL MUSEUM ETHNOGRAPHY

The rise of the field of digital humanities in higher education and the proliferation of digital humanities centers are fostering new strategies for documenting, preserving, and using ethnographic and heritage collections. Digital tools with possibilities for use in humanities and social sciences are being developed at an amazing speed and being employed in creative ways with collections. For instance, digital tools such as StoryMap JS, Timeline JS, and Tableau Public, for georeferencing, visualization, mapping, and creating time lines with museum collections, are seeing collections used by new audiences in diverse ways.[18] Massive collections of systematic data—now referred to as big data—are affording new opportunities for inquiry and portend new uses of museum collections in ethnographic studies and other disciplinary arenas. One example of the use of digital tools in research can be seen in the "Runaway Quilt Project," a recent study of quilting during the period of slavery in the United States.[19] These new digital tools provide scholars with unprecedented means of seeing data in new ways and opening up lines of humanistic inquiry that would not have been possible previously.

It also might well be noted that digital tools allow for individuals to curate their own collections of images, text, music, and videos they own or make as well as to connect to data made and or owned by others, including museums. Tools like Pinterest and Spotify increase the ways in which individuals create or curate digital collections. A growing number of museums are providing tools for users to create personal digital albums of objects owned by the museums. The lines between collections built and held by museums and those built and held by individuals blur as the digital environment allows for connecting and sharing these personally and institutionally held materials. This realm of connectedness comes with new issues of curatorship, authenticity, intellectual property, and copyright, but by tapping into expanded pools of expertise and information, this sharing provides a means by which our understanding and knowledge about objects and their place in human experience can exponentially increase.

NEW LEGAL AND ETHICAL PRACTICES

Technology centrism in mainstream North American culture can cause participants and observers of digital initiatives such as those discussed here to emphasize software tools, platforms, and networks and to be less self-aware of everyday practices, legal regimes, economic contexts, and associated cultural shifts. While the larger theme is beyond the scope of this chapter, it is worth noting that some of the most crucial technologies shaping digital museum ethnography—by both opening up new opportunities and precluding them—are not in a narrow sense digital technologies. While they respond to the rise of digital technologies and are recursively connected to them, the kinds of practices and frameworks that we have in mind are more centrally legal, ethical, and, most broadly, cultural in nature. Two examples of relevance for museum-based ethnography can be flagged here.

The Creative Commons is a "nonprofit organization that enables the sharing and use of creativity and knowledge through free legal tools." Creative Commons licenses build upon national and international copyright law, providing an easy-to-use means by which creators can license their work for reuse and adaptation. The widespread use of Creative Commons licenses has been transformative in many sectors, including in the scholarly publishing and museums sector.[20] Museums can, for instance, use Creative Commons licenses or a Creative Commons–designed public domain designation to facilitate sharing and reuse of collections documentation, museum publications, curricular materials, and other resources created for public benefit.

The way that Creative Commons licenses add a useful layer on top of copyright, one that provides content creators with a means of sharing their work in more granular ways than are otherwise provided through all-or-nothing copyright alone, provides one inspiration for a project of special relevance to museum ethnographers working in digital environments. Developed through collaboration with a range of indigenous communities worldwide, "Traditional Knowledge [TK] licenses and labels recognize that Indigenous, traditional and local communities have different access and use expectations in regards to their knowledge and cultural expressions. These different expectations of access and use depend heavily on the material itself and the local context from which it derives. These TK licenses and labels help identify this material and establish culturally appropriate means of managing control and access."[21] Thus, like Creative Commons licenses, Traditional Knowledge licenses and labels, when attached to cultural objects, images, and documents, help communities convey cultural expectations to users—including museum users—who otherwise would not be aware of them. The potential uses of such licenses and labels in museum catalogs, digital exhibitions, curricular materials, and other museum ethnography domains are great. Developing legal/ethical "technologies" such as these is a crucial need running alongside the development of new digital platforms and projects.

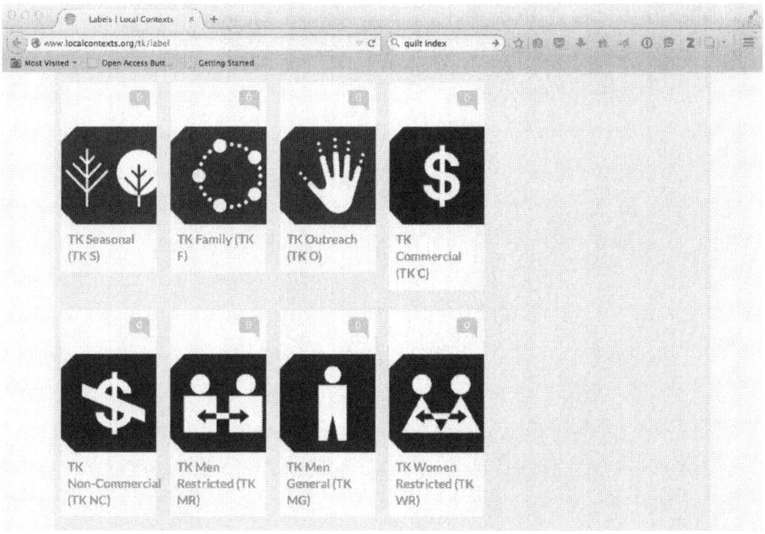

FIGURE 17.3
Traditional knowledge. (Photo: licenses and labels TK.)

MUSEUM EDUCATION

Another realm of museum-based activity impacted by growth of digital technologies is education. Educators are using digital tools to engage K-gray audiences in using collections in multiple physical and online learning environments and activities. Local Learning, an informal "network of people interested in engaging young people with their own traditional culture and with the local culture and folklore of their families, regions, and the larger world," recently published three online classroom modules designed to facilitate use of ethnographic collections.[22] The Quilt Index has its own Quilt Index wiki, with a section devoted to suggestions and resources—including lesson plans and a serious game—that promotes the use of the digital repository in learning.[23]

USER EXPERIENCE DESIGN AND VISITOR STUDIES

Investigation into how and why visitors make sense of their museum experiences and how museums can make more effective, impactful learning environments and experiences for their visitors has become a specialized field of museum study and practice referred to as visitor studies.[24] A parallel arena of investigation in the realm of digital studies is user experience design (UXD or UED or XD), or "the process of enhancing user satisfaction by improving the usability, accessibility, and pleasure provided in the interaction between the user and the product."[25] The emphasis here for museum professionals is to construct experiences that resonate with, have meaning for, and respond to the needs of audiences, be they visitors to the museum's physical resources (exhibitions, programs, and collections) or to the museum's online resources. Here, too, folklorists in museums are exploring the intersections of how to enrich the visitor and user experiences contributing to and using museum-based ethnographic collections and exhibitions, both physical and digital, to engage participants in active learning, and to do so in ways that respect and honor traditional knowledge systems and protocols. As an example, at the Michigan State University Museum, visitor studies have been conducted with those who attend the museum's annual folklife festival to ascertain whether or not the festival fostered a deeper appreciation by visitors of their own cultural traditions or the traditions of others, prompted an interest in learning more about these traditions, or inspired visitors to be more active in their traditions.[26] In recent years, festival visitors have recorded their responses on iPads (digital tablets) at evaluation stations at the festival or during or after the festival on SurveyMonkey (a web-based survey platform).

DIGITAL RESOURCES AND MUSEUM CAREERS TODAY

Separate from more elaborate collaboratories, everyday digital technologies and platforms increasingly shape the ways that museum practitioners and museum communities more broadly interact with one another. Social media platforms like Facebook and Twitter are the means by which museum people exchange news and announce publications, exhibitions, and other resources. More specialized professional forums such as Museums and the Web and Webwise offer increased opportunities for sharing new applications of digital tools in museum activities.[27]As in other fields, museum professionals learn about new career opportunities in digital environments, apply for such jobs in digital environments, and—if hired—do much of their work in them as well.

CONCLUSION

Museums and communities are being mutually transformed through their co-engagements with digital practices. Technology is blurring the lines between curator and visitor, between documenter and documented, and between collection managers and users. While museum ethnography began its digital journey in the age of mainframes and punch cards, the field's digital work reached an important level of maturity in the era of Web 2.0 when the Internet shifted from being a means of consuming information into a space with increased opportunity for users to contribute to, and not simply consume, museum-centered and collections-centered activities. In his webography of websites and web resources of folklore museums, Gregory Hansen has shown the growing use of digital technology by museums engaged in ethnographic activities to simply make their activities and resources known to others.[28] In the present era, new technologies are presenting new opportunities and challenges in a voyage that is clearly a long-term endeavor. In the realm of ethnographic work that is based in or linked to museums, it is also clear that the use of digital tools and technologies has become an integral and important factor in deepening the capacity for excellence in museum and ethnographic practice.

NOTES

1. William N. Fenton, "The Museum and Anthropological Research," *Curator: The Museum Journal* 3, no. 4 (1960): 327–55. doi:10.1111/j.2151-6952.1960.tb01697.x.

2. Alex F. Ricciardelli, "A Model for Inventorying Ethnological Collections," *Curator: The Museum Journal* 10, no. 4 (1967): 330–36. doi:10.1111/j.2151-6952.1967.tb01490.x.

3. Quilt Index (http://www.quiltindex.org, accessed November 14, 2015); Reciprocal Research Network (http://www.rrncommunity.org, accessed November 14, 2015).

4. Two good summaries of the intersection of museum practice and new digital technologies are Ross Parry, *Recoding the Museum: Digital Heritage and the Technologies of Change* (New York: Routledge Press, 2007), and Katherine Jones-Garmil, ed., *The Wired Museum* (Washington, DC: American Association of Museums, 1997).

5. Susana Smith Bautista, *Museums in the Digital Age: Changing Meanings of Place, Community, and Culture* (Lanham, MD: AltaMira Press, 2013).

6. Jason Baird Jackson, "On the Review of Digital Exhibitions," *Museum Anthropology* 29, no. 1 (2006): 1–4. doi:10.1525/mua.2006.29.1.1.

7. "The Fabric of Mayan Life: An Exhibit of Textiles" (https://web.archive.org/web/20150223223953/http:/www.snomnh.ou.edu/collections-research/cr-sub/ethnology/mayan/Home.html, accessed November 14, 2015).

8. Ojibwe Public Art, Ostrom Private Lives (http://dlib.indiana.edu/omeka/mathers/exhibits/show/ojibwe-public-art--ostrom-priv/introductio, accessed November 14, 2015).

9. "Dane Wajich | Dane-zaa Stories and Songs: Dreamers and the Land" (http://www.museevirtuel-virtualmuseum.ca/sgc-cms/expositions-exhibitions/danewajich/english/index.html, accessed November 14, 2015).

10. "ʔeləw̓k̓ʷ–Belongings: A Tangible Table" (http://hennessy.iat.sfu.ca/mcl/%CA%94el%C9%99w%CC%93k%CC%93%CA%B7-belongings, accessed November 23, 2015).

11. Inuvialuit Living History (http://www.inuvialuitlivinghistory.ca, accessed November 14, 2015).

12. Osage Weddings Project (http://osageweddings.com, accessed November 14, 2015).

13. Susan Rowley, "The Reciprocal Research Network: The Development Process," *Museum Anthropology Review* 7, no. 1–2 (2013): 22–43, http://scholarworks.iu.edu/journals/index.php/mar/article/view/2172.

14. National Folklore Archives Initiative (http://www.folklorecollections.org, accessed November 14, 2015); American Memory Project (http://memory.loc.gov/ammem/index.html, accessed November 14, 2015); Open Folklore (http://www.openfolklore.org, accessed November 14, 2015).

15. Marsha MacDowell et al., "Quilted Together: Material Culture Pedagogy and the Quilt Index, a Digital Repository of Thematic Collections," *Winterthur Portfolio* 47, no. 2–3 (2013): 139–60. doi:10.1086/671567. See also Amanda G. Sikarskie, *Textile Collections: Preservation, Access, Curation and Interpretation in a Digital Age* (Lanham, MD: Rowman & Littlefield, 2016).

16. "Collaboratory," Wikipedia, last modified September 10, 2015, https://en.wikipedia.org/wiki/Collaboratory.

17. Consideration of digital collections and digital collaboration strategies points to a neighboring topic: digital repatriation or return. These practices involve providing ("returning") digitized cultural heritage resources to the communities of origin (aka source communities) out of which they came prior to being curated by museums and other repositories. Digital repatriation practices relate not only to digital museum practices generally but also to actual processes of repatriation, wherein physical collections, as well as human remains, are restored to their communities of origin. For a collection providing an overview of digital repatriation, including both positive and critical assessments, see *After the Return: Digital Repatriation and the Circulation of Indigenous Knowledge*, a special issue of *Museum Anthropology Review*, edited in 2013 by Joshua A. Bell, Kimberly Christen, and Mark Turin (http://scholarworks.iu.edu/journals/index.php/mar/issue/view/233).

18. Story Map JS (http://storymap.knightlab.com, accessed November 14, 2014); Timeline JS (https://timeline.knightlab.com, accessed November 14, 2014); Tableau Public (https://public.tableau.com/s, accessed November 14, 2014).

19. The Runaway Quilt (http://runawayquiltproject.org, accessed November 2014); Deimosa Webber-Bey, "The Runaway Quilt Project: Digital Humanities Exploration of Quilting during the Era of Slavery," *Journal of Interactive Technology and Pedagogy*, http://jitp.commons.gc.cuny.edu/runaway-quilt-project-digital-humanities-exploration-of-quilting-during-the-era-of-slavery (accessed January 24, 2015).

20. "What We Do," Creative Commons, http://creativecommons.org/about (accessed November 14, 2015).

21. "Welcome to Local Contexts," Local Contexts, http://localcontexts.org/about (accessed November 14, 2015).

22. Local Learning (http://locallearningnetwork.org, accessed November 14, 2015); "Dress to Express Classroom Modules: Museum Collections as Literacy and Discovery Tools," Local Learning, http://locallearningnetwork.org/index.php/guest-artist/dress-to-express-museum-modules (accessed January 24, 2015).

23. Quilt Index Wiki (http://www.quiltindex.org/wiki/index.php/Main_Page, accessed November 14, 2015).

24. One of the most oft-used publications that provides a theoretical approach to visitor studies is John H. Falk and Lynn D. Dierking, *Learning from Museums: Visitor Experiences and the Making of Meaning* (Walnut Creek, CA: AltaMira Press, 2000).

25. "User Experience Design," Wikipedia, last modified November 15, 2015, https:en.wikipedia.org/wiki/User_experience_design.

26. Copies of these studies are housed at the Michigan Traditional Arts Research Collections, Michigan State University Museum.

27. Museums and the Web (http://www.museumsandtheweb.com, accessed November 14, 2015); Webwise (http://www.imls.gov/about/webwise.aspx, accessed November 14, 2015).

28. Gregory Hansen, "Webography of Public Folklore Resources," in *Folklore and the Internet: Vernacular Expression in a Digital World*, ed. Trevor J. Blank (Logan: Utah State University Press, 2009), 213–30.

18

Public Folklore Curatorship

Collaborating with Emerging Refugee Communities

CARRIE HERTZ

Using her fieldwork with the Bhutanese-Nepali population of Buffalo, New York, as a case study, Carrie Hertz explores how museums in the twenty-first century can adopt community-oriented approaches in their programming, making them more responsive to the diverse communities they serve. Citing several different museum-based exhibits and programs, Hertz underscores the importance of reciprocity and multidirectional communication, demonstrates how fieldwork can form a vital bridge, and proposes that the concept of "inclusion" is not simply a technique but also a philosophy that can have profound influence on how groups conceptualize their own and others' history, society, and culture and their respective places in each. She also questions what collaborative role museums might play in exploring how community members respond to new living situations; what cultural practices and traditions are preserved, changed, or abandoned; and how these choices might contribute to cohesion or tension within the larger community. Conceiving of their missions in this way is an invaluable opportunity for twenty-first-century museums to move beyond simply being repositories of cultural artifacts to becoming more responsive, inclusive, and proactive—in effect, becoming "good neighbors" with their multicultural constituencies.

FROM THE FIELD: INTRODUCTIONS

Bishnu Adhikari leads me down a long driveway to a side door. The house is bustling with guests in colorful clothes. They spill out into the yard where a mandap *stands, draped in garlands and Christmas lights. Leaving our shoes in a pile by the door, we slide through the kitchen, past heaping plates of* sel roti *and pots of steaming* kheer. *Bishnu ushers me up a narrow flight of stairs and leaves me with a group of young women. Singing snippets of folk songs and brandishing makeup brushes, the women surround Meena Siwakoti, insuring she looks resplendent on her wedding day. Graciously, they include me in their conversation, eager to practice English and to have their picture taken. They splay out their palms to show off the henna designs they applied the night before.*

When the groom's family arrives, everyone gathers in the driveway to watch the procession of foods they carry—glossy bunches of fruit, a pair of silver fish, a plate of syrupy jalebi. *These will be elegantly displayed while the bride rushes off to change out of her own sari into a new, bright-red one provided by the groom's family. When she reemerges, the couple meets at the edge of a temporary altar created with designs drawn in tinted rice flour. Later, each guest will offer his or her blessings, applying a smudge of* tika *(a paste made from cooked rice, yogurt, and vermilion powder) to the bride's and groom's foreheads. Before we leave, Bishnu gently scolds me for not sitting down to eat. In my excitement to see everything I have not performed my social obligation as a guest. I immediately sit down in a room off the kitchen where a woman brings me a huge plate ofdelicious food. I ate it all.*[1]

As a wedding guest, a museum representative, and a pro bono photographer, I experienced my first introduction to the rapidly growing Bhutanese-Nepali population of Buffalo. I was also new to the area, having recently accepted a position as the curator of folk arts at the Castellani Art Museum (CAM) of Niagara University. Fresh from graduate school in Indiana, I was excited to explore western New York, documenting and presenting local artistic traditions within the potentially provocative context of a contemporary art museum. The fields of museums and public folklore do not always intersect,

FIGURE 18.1
With the help of friends and relatives, Meena Siwakoti dresses for her wedding day. Buffalo, New York, 2012. (Photo: Carrie Hertz.)

despite the parallel currents running through them. Managing a museum-based folk arts program dedicated to local culture gave me the opportunity to synthesize my understanding of both worlds, working toward more accountable curatorship using folkloristic methods. I have been heartened by the growing demands for inclusivity, dialog, and social justice within museology and believe folklorists have much to contribute to these discussions. I offer my own experiences trying to enact these ideals by developing new curatorial processes in collaboration with an emerging community in Buffalo.

COMMUNITY ENGAGEMENT IN CURATORSHIP

Museums face serious challenges in the twenty-first century: demographic changes resulting in shrinking core audiences and growing demands for inclusiveness; increasing competition for leisure time, disposable income, and charitable giving; and technological innovations that nurture individual contributions and participation over other forms of involvement.[2] These dynamics call into question conventional collecting and didactic display models that position curators as arbiters of elite tastes and official narratives.

Not long ago, prominent debates in museum studies (as well as folklore and anthropology) centered on the "politics of representation" and how best to incorporate diverse source communities as participants in the process of collecting, interpreting, and displaying their cultural lives.[3] Folklorist and curator Frank Korom predicted that questions about who controls representation in the public sphere would drive twenty-first-century curatorship, but he also cautioned folklorists to consider what such collaborations could actually achieve for our partners.[4] His calculation and his counsel still ring true.

With current discussions focused on "community engagement," the catalog of participants and the potential roles they may play have broadened.[5] A wealth of museum literature encourages reaching "new communities," usually framed as underserved groups defined by economic status, class, gender or sexual orientation, ethnicity, education level, religion, ability, or age.[6] The prevalence of the term "communities" as a synonym for cultural groups inappropriately excluded from structures of power, authority, and equal participation signals a general desire within the museum profession to promote more democratic institutions.[7] By constantly reframing and multiplying who acts as protagonist in the museum—curators, educators, artists, community members, audiences—perhaps museums can expose the (co)constructed and dynamic nature of meaning making and communication. We are not "sharing authority," that is, giving away something that inherently belongs to museums; we are acknowledging our "shared authority" to define the world through the dialogic process of knowledge production.[8]

Even as we continue to expand the list of stakeholders we are in dialog with, we are still asking how we can better impact their lives in real and substantive ways. As museums embrace more community-minded, multiperspective, people-centered approaches, curators are in a better position to advocate for the needs and desires of diverse constituencies. In 2015, the American Alliance of Museums highlighted issues of social justice and activism with the annual conference theme "The Social Value of Museums: Inspiring Change." The development of ambitious initiatives like the International Coalition of Sites of Conscience, a network of museums and historic sites dedicated to using dialogic techniques to collectively "envision and shape a more just and humane future," similarly attests to a general belief in the power of museums to be active agents of positive change in civic life.[9]

Aware of these intellectual currents, I arrived in Buffalo looking for ways to frame my work as a curator in terms of local needs. Such an orientation required a better understanding of place and the unique opportunities it may hold for deeper engagement.

BUFFALO, "THE CITY OF GOOD NEIGHBORS"

Buffalo, sometimes known as "the city of good neighbors," is experiencing tremendous changes, demographically and economically. Home to the largest population of recent refugees in New York State, Erie County resettles fifteen hundred to two thousand people every year, totaling nearly ten thousand since 2003. Like other places in the rust belt, Buffalo has become a "welcoming city," in part because of the large swaths of vacant housing left after decades of population decline.[10] While some longtime residents and government officials tout resettlement programs as contributing to the first population increase since the 1960s, others articulate fears about the shifting cultural landscape and the increased strain on public resources in an already economically disadvantaged and racially divided county.[11] The topic of immigration and refugee resettlement, as it does throughout the United States, raises heated debates and complicated emotions for Buffalonians. Witnessing the burgeoning activity resulting from resettlement, both positive and negative, I knew this was an issue of special significance for the area, one that will have a profound and evolving influence on how Buffalonians understand themselves, their home, and what it takes to be "good neighbors."

Through one of four resettlement agencies, I met Bishnu Adhikari in the summer of 2012, less than three years after he and his wife, Chitra, arrived in Buffalo.[12] Previously, they had spent nearly two decades living in a Nepali camp after fleeing persecution in Bhutan. In the camps, Bishnu taught English, social studies, and computer skills as a volunteer teacher, served in various leadership positions, and formed a support group for survivors of sexual violence. Today, he works as a vocational trainer and employment specialist for Journey's End Refugee Services, the same agency that assisted with his own resettlement. "Journey's End provided me with the strength that I am someone in the world," he told me. "Now I'm working full-time for Journey's End and helping my community." In his spare time, Bishnu organized the Bhutanese-Nepali Hindu Community of Buffalo, a group dedicated to helping individuals adjust to American life while maintaining a sense of cultural continuity. Bishnu is well respected for his education and his commitment to others. I spent more than one Sunday afternoon drinking sugary cups of tea in the Adhikari home as community members, one after another, dropped by to socialize, seek advice, and share their concerns with him.

In 2012 and 2013, coinciding with my residency, Bhutan was the second most common nation of origin for refugee resettlement in Buffalo, contributing more than three thousand residents. By the 1990s, more than one hundred thousand ethnic Nepalis had fled or been driven out of southern Bhutan after the Buddhist Ngalong government initiated ethnonationalist "One Nation, One People" policies outlawing Nepali language and cultural practices.[13] Many sought refuge in Nepal, where they were registered into one of seven camps. Third-country resettlement became an option in 2007. Choosing this route could be difficult, as it would result in fractured families and social networks as people were scattered across North America, Australia, New Zealand, and a few European nations.[14]

As a scholar concerned with the dynamic processes of tradition, I wondered how individuals and families were creatively responding to their new situations. What cultural practices were being transformed, preserved, or jettisoned, and how were these choices contributing to cohesion or tension within both the Bhutanese-Nepali community and the larger population of Buffalo? As a curator, I wondered what role CAM could play in helping to answer these questions.

Bishnu expressed similar concerns to me. "We lost our citizenship for twenty years. We were nowhere in the refugee camp," he confided. "Our goal is how to make you our own siblings. We are here to exist here, to make friends here, to make this land as our motherland." For Bishnu, the task of forging new, thriving lives in the United States can be viewed through the lens of kinship and necessitates intercultural communion, not only for new Bhutanese-Nepali Americans, who must reconsider their sense of identity and social belonging, but also for others living in Buffalo, who may choose to welcome or reject what is unfamiliar. The stakes are high. Comparing refugee status to other diasporas, Bishnu stresses, "We can't go back. We are here permanently." Bishnu and I, quickly realizing our shared interests, looked for ways to collaborate.

I began working closely with members of the Bhutanese-Nepali community, in part, because I met leaders early, like Bishnu, who welcomed the potential for collaboration, who desired increased visibility for their group's struggles and cultural worth, and who were already organizing cultural preservation efforts at a grassroots level. Not all recent refugees wish to bring heightened public scrutiny to their everyday lives. Feeling vulnerable, socially isolated, or stigmatized, they understandably would rather pass under the radar.

Most curatorial work, being publicly funded, should increase public knowledge in some capacity, whether through programming, exhibitions, collections/archives, or publications. However innovative or meandrous the path, I knew I could not commit to curatorial collaborations that would not eventually benefit heterogeneous, pluralist audiences. Successful cocreation necessitates a "spirit of mutuality," meaning that all partners can contribute special skills or knowledge *and* gain from their investment of time and resources.[15] Museum professionals, especially when working cross-culturally, must be thoughtful and transparent about their institutional responsibilities as well as what they can offer. Partners, similarly, should feel empowered to articulate their conditions for participating. Simply receiving an institution's momentary attention is not enough. Collaborations can, and should more often, originate from and serve community needs rather than beginning with what museums want.[16]

The barriers to orchestrating such nuanced communication with emerging refugee communities are fairly sizable, language being a major one. According to the Centers for Disease Control and Prevention, only about 35 percent of Bhutanese refugees, for example, arrive in the United States with even a functional grasp of English, instead speaking Nepali, a regional dialect, or Dzongkha (the official language of Bhutan).[17] How to speak to each other is only one consideration. First you must locate enough interlocutors. Refugee groups can be difficult to reach.

"Community" is a term bandied around easily, but by 2014 Bhutanese-Nepali Americans in Buffalo had forged strong, active social networks that impacted experiences and interpretations of daily life. Many had lived together previously within refugee camps, carrying collective frames of reference with them to Buffalo. As a self-identified community, however, they had not made many gains establishing public spaces—either physical (e.g., temples or community centers) or discursive (e.g., social media sites or the ethnic newspapers connecting Polish or African American groups in Buffalo). As an institution, how do museums, then, make contact and forge relationships with community members?

Publications analyzing collaborations between American museums and the recent refugee groups in their localities are still fairly uncommon. Public folklorists, in contrast, have been more prolific. Fine work has focused on identifying and supporting—whether through granting opportunities, apprenticeship programs, archival documentation, or educational and celebratory public presentation—the traditional art forms, skills, and intangible cultural knowledge that "new neighbors" bring with them to the United States. Public folklorists have worked with or within all manner of refugee social service organizations to foster awareness and appreciation for traditional arts, storytelling, and the role these may play not only in economic and professional development but also in memory and healing. These efforts operate at every scale, sometimes serving individuals (such as by helping artists access resources, including raw materials, performance venues, audiences, and markets), while others focus on influencing policy.[18] By examining this record, we ascertain the importance of ethnographic fieldwork for initiating and sustaining active ties between agencies and emerging communities.

FIELDWORK AND FORMING ALLIANCES

Fieldwork can form an important, necessary bridge between a museum and specific local communities. Like most folklorists, I expect to learn about a place and its people through fieldwork (including methods of participant observation, interview, oral history, and audiovisual recording). Knowing little about Buffalo and needing to articulate comprehensible, goal-oriented projects to my new institution, I started with what I understood well and would help me survey cultural activity broadly: weddings. When I met Bishnu, weddings became an effective way to introduce me to individual community members, as well as to Bhutanese-Nepali Hindu culture as it was developing in Buffalo.

To Bishnu, wedding celebrations were a sign of cultural resiliency. "Two years ago," he told me, "there were no marriage ceremonies. But now there are marriage ceremonies. There are pujas. They are exercising their rights now." One of the first communal celebrations to be reintroduced, traditional weddings were soon followed by others. "Journey's End and other American people, they encouraged me to celebrate our Nepali culture, which was denied for many, many, many years in Bhutan. In the refugee camp," he said, "we were unable to celebrate our cultural programs. This land is free for culture. Our lives are blooming like marigolds." Marigold blooms, being closely associated with Hindu ritual practice, serve as an apt metaphor for growing religious visibility following a period of suppression.

During weddings, individuals from multiple generations enact conscious choices against a backdrop of shared expectations, collectively negotiating the perpetuation of cultural values, aesthetics, and norms. What better window into how people come together and creatively shape meaningful lives using traditional forms—from ritual, to music, to foodways and dress? Weddings can also be times when outsiders are welcomed into otherwise private spaces, especially if they deliver high-quality photos free of charge. Tila Bastola, a woman I met at a wedding, assured me, "Nepalis love guests and they love getting their picture taken." Participating in "reciprocal community service projects," like making photographs and films of ceremonial events readily available to participants, should be understood as a critical aspect of maintaining museum community relationships.[19]

FIGURE 18.2
Bishnu and Chitra Adhikari (standing) pose in their home with their nephew Narayan Dhungana and his new bride, Bishnu. Buffalo, New York, 2013. (Photo: Carrie Hertz.)

Bishnu ushered my entrance into the community by inviting me to weddings as his guest. Soon, however, I was attending other celebrations and meeting individuals who could teach me about the complex viewpoints and social positions under the surface of similarity.

Twenty-first-century curatorial practice is now regularly conceptualized as a continual process of relationship building that requires reciprocity and multidirectional communication. Since the development of museum anthropology, museums have long been recognized as potential field sites for ethnographic investigation and cultural critique. Increasingly, museum professionals of all orientations require the skills of an ethnographer to recognize and navigate the plurality of both internal and external agendas, perspectives, motivations, and positions at play. Corrine A. Kratz, describing this turn in museums, defines ethnography as "a mode of knowledge production" that utilizes "extended research, diverse social relationships, and fundamental grounding in communication exchanges."[20] Ethnography in this model is inherently collaborative, intersubjective work—an ideal methodology for nurturing a "shared authority."

Folklorists are well suited for an ethnographic museology, especially as curators. Contemporary material culture studies resist the decontextualization of collection objects by emphasizing the role of individuals in animating and personalizing conventional artistic forms through performative acts of creation and use. Through fieldwork, we can untangle complicated systems of meaning, balancing the tensions between personal and collective expressions. Cultivating this level of understanding through "cultural conversations" requires a great investment of time.[21] Trust and reciprocity, the building blocks of productive relationships, arise through participation in social life—sitting in living rooms, offering *tika*, or accepting traditional hospitality by eating foods spicier than you once thought you could handle.

Can conventional museums provide the kind of flexibility and funding required for sustained community fieldwork? Interactions "in the field" necessitate time outside an office, often outside office hours, and only produce results in relation to long-term investment. Museums can learn a great deal from the struggles of public folklorists working in government or nonprofit arts agencies. Many write passionately about the need for open-ended neighborhood explorations and face-to-face conversations, even when market-driven productivity models and skeptical coworkers discount them.[22] The best way to ensure democratic inclusiveness starts with first identifying and then befriending those living far from centers of power, those with limited historical interaction in museums, those unlikely to reach out uninvited. Newcomers are preoccupied with daily survival, with achieving cultural literacy and self-sufficiency. Individuals who have experienced political and social upheavals may express deep mistrust of bureaucracy and cultural institutions. An imposing museum narrowly dedicated to elite tastes and histories offers little apparent value.

Patient fieldwork does more than identify "underserved" people and initiate new relationships with them. By asking questions, learning biographies and genealogies, and observing social exchanges, we can discover more, over time, about the hidden complexities of community composition, thereby avoiding further social ruptures or tokenism in representation.[23]

One afternoon, I was visiting Bishnu and Chitra. I had just finished recording part of an oral history when a few relatives dropped by and joined us. Seeing an opportunity, they refocused attention, questioning me about American culture—about women's married names, gender relations, and burial customs. Out of a sense of reciprocity, I did my best, but I felt foolish, an inadequate spokesperson, and wondered how my fumbling questions about cultural practices within the Bhutanese-Nepali community must sound to them, especially those implicating delicate subjects like the residual impact of caste systems.

Individuals' interpretations are limited by their personal experiences, positionalities, and agendas. When language skills restrain nuanced conversation, the impulse is to rely on a small number of people for understanding. Engaging with many, even nonverbally, can help reveal social divisions, internal disputes, generational divides, historical legacies, and sensitivities that may not be openly discussed.[24]

Incorporating new communities promotes equality within museums only when we take the time to comprehend and account for internal diversity and viewpoints, values, and protocols. Equipped with this awareness, we can better develop effective strategies for equitable collaboration and partnership. Long-standing strategies, such as forming advisory committees or formalizing cooperative endeavors with indigenous communities, have become more sophisticated and integrated over the past decades but may not translate easily for newcomers.[25] Dialogic models originating from Western ideals of democracy, similarly, may not be compatible with cultural norms or hierarchies relating to gender, age, class, or education level. More than once, I was cautioned by well-meaning community members not to take seriously the perspectives of those "from the jungle," illiterate farmers who clung to old ways. Older women, lagging behind in language acquisition, were also more difficult to engage directly. Attempts to organize more formal conversations with groups of people often went nowhere—unreliable transportation, demanding schedules, and the foreignness of "meetings" being contributing factors.[26] In these early stages, when objectives remain open-ended, it can be challenging to articulate convincing rationales for why individuals *should* engage, especially against the urgency of other obligations. Even if we cannot literally bring "everyone to the table," perhaps we can still develop creative ways to do so representationally.

Part of the struggle with finding the most effective, sustainable approaches to engagement is directly related to the tyranny of project-based work. Arts funding, granting cycles, and exhibition schedules compress time lines, expect premature clarity about outcomes, demand immediate "products," and put an end date on activities to the detriment of long-term interactions that could otherwise accrue meaningfully over time. At CAM, I was responsible for producing a fieldwork-generated exhibition every six months, a grueling turnaround without juggling multiple endeavors of varied levels of depth simultaneously. I found it better to consider emerging community collaborations as part of a longitudinal, iterative process—one that balances short-term, low-commitment projects with longer-term, exploratory ventures that begin without clear outcomes or hasty deadlines. Working in this way advances opportunities for the museum's expanding toolkit and the community's local rootedness to mature together, learning from each other and developing new patterns for decision making along the way. More open-ended, responsive approaches that build organically upon fieldwork may also open new avenues for advocacy by revealing needs and breaking down assumptions among participants. Fieldworkers do tend to become "closet social workers," a natural by-product of listening and growing emotionally invested in the lives of others.[27]

There are, of course, dangers that accompany fieldwork-based relationship building. Museum community engagement is always about unique individuals coming together as representatives.[28] If a museum lacks wider institutional commitment, relying on the activities of a single "community engagement" specialist, the museum-community link may collapse with inevitable staff turnover. Person-to-person connections are an effective starting point. Museum fieldwork, however, should also include forming networks of diverse partners with mutual interests—inside institutions, across institutions, and among varied community members.

Alliances in which diverse colleagues share responsibility for problem solving, together imagining more consequential undertakings for everyone involved, can unlock new pathways for potential transformation—individual, institutional, societal.[29] When collaborating with newcomers, museums can promote holistic approaches to engagement, project development, and community well-being by enlisting a consortium of partners (e.g., community translators, sister museums, health-care professionals, social workers, academics, and resettlement agencies).

The experience of resettlement is also transformative. Increasingly, we understand that lasting success for refugees entails a more thorough awareness of their long-term needs, especially those stemming from histories of violence, trauma, and insufficient health care. Incorporating collaborators with special expertise in these areas could help curators avoid artificially separating physical from spiritual well-being or art from daily existence.[30] While we may consider ourselves cultural-sector workers, our partners' cultural lives are deeply affected by political, economic, and social justice concerns. Refugee lives are inundated with bureaucratic interventions. Writing about the emerging Bhutanese-Nepali community in nearby Erie, Pennsylvania, anthropologist Joseph Stadler stresses that the construction of social collective memory takes place within the context of a past of religious and linguistic persecution and a present of resettlement and, therefore, "begins with a politicization of cultural heritage."[31] To talk about culture is to talk about changes wrought by displacement and resettlement. Bhutanese-Nepali newcomers, when asked about rites of passage, want to discuss how employee attendance policies and government recognition of clergy affect their ability to continue traditional mourning and wedding practices. Public policies of all kinds are ultimately "cultural policies" influencing how traditions are practiced and interpreted.[31] In the midst of so many logistical and conceptual barriers, developing useful collaborative work will require more responsive curatorial processes.

FROM THE FIELD: COLLABORATIVE CONVERSATIONS

Program manager Tara Lyons leads me, Bryana DiFonzo, Bishnu Adhikari of Journey's End Refugee Services, and a couple of members of the Bhutanese-Nepali community (Nars and Ram) on a tour of the Buffalo History Museum's galleries. In an exhibit of new acquisitions, she points out a handwoven shirt made by a local Burmese Karen woman. In another room dedicated to early European settlement of the Niagara frontier, Tara encourages everyone to touch a floor loom on display. Like many have done across the country, she hopes to establish a monthly sewing and weaving circle with immigrant and refugee women. At the end of a permanent exhibit called "Neighbors: The People of Erie County," Tara describes the museum's plans to update its representation, incorporating materials from newcomers who are contributing to the development of local history. The list of new and planned programs to reach emerging communities is heartening, but Tara stresses how much thoughtful effort is still needed to accomplish the museum's ambitions.

For weeks, our little group has had conversations—some formal, others informal—about possibilities for collaboration. We each have personal goals and collective obligations; we don't feel particularly comfortable speaking for ourselves alone. Although we hoped to have more people actively involved in these early group discussions, participation from the Bhutanese-Nepali community has been inconsistent, comprising primarily those people Bishnu brings with him. We've looked at alternative meeting times and locations but realize that we might structure our work instead around the very concept of informal dialog, one managed by participants.

Together we have identified key community concerns: strained communication between generations, vanishing or nonexistent records of life in and exile from Bhutan, and troubling suicide rates. Youth who have no memory of Bhutan, who were born and raised in refugee camps, have told me they consider themselves Nepali, not Bhutanese. Such identity claims can be painful for elders who keenly miss the land and lives they lost when stripped of citizenship. Through Bishnu, one man explained why separation from Bhutan—whether physical or cultural—was intolerable: "I never want to change my mother's name." For similar reasons, Bishnu had asked me to make digital copies of his badly battered documents proving he was once a Bhutanese citizen. He wanted these to be a matter of public record in CAM's archive, available for future generations who will undoubtedly forget in the process of assimilation.

We conceive of a series of storytelling (truth telling?) sessions in private homes, bringing multiple generations together to listen, ask questions, and share experiences of living in Bhutan, in Nepali camps, and in Buffalo. Community members will organize sessions. Institutional partners will record them and pay interpreters from the community to generate bilingual transcripts. The records will then be given to families and archived in both museums.

Tara ends our tour in the Buffalo History Museum's library, where archival collections are stored, where, if our partnership moves forward, testimonies of community memory and personal experience will be kept. Bishnu has had limited familiarity with museums in the past. Now having spent time in both the Buffalo History Museum and CAM, he describes his growing realization of their purpose to me. "You come, you hear the voice of your father, and you cry," he says. "That is called museum." The legitimizing authority and permanence of museum collections promise stable recognition for subjective histories and impermanent expressions. They may also serve functions of personal and collective catharsis and healing. Bishnu, looking far into the future, wants Bhutanese Americans to still be able to learn from their ancestors. Museums have an important role to play for them.[33]

DIALOG AND REFUGEE STORYTELLING

Proponents of dialogic processes—those who acknowledge issues of authority and subjectivity in the production of knowledge—argue that museums, as public institutions, are responsible for uncovering marginalized perspectives and making them widely available. Inclusion is not simply a technique but a philosophy that has profound influence over how we conceptualize history, society, culture, and our place therein. Such a philosophy insists we incorporate "communities of people who did not have the power to document and archive their perspectives, to develop historians and institutions that would then represent their point of view."[34] How do museums ethically, respectfully, and realistically integrate the voices of refugee communities emerging in their localities?

From the moment they seek resettlement or asylum, refugees must frame personal "stories" for outsiders, adequately translating their experiences and sense of self into purposeful "public policy narratives" that will meet bureaucratic expectations.[35] The rigorous review and approval process can feel cruel, requiring an applicant to repeatedly recount traumatic experiences in detail for authentication. In *The Politics of Storytelling*, anthropologist Michael

Jackson writes, "Not only do refugees struggle with a sense that language cannot do justice to their experience, the suspicions and indifference of administrators in both camps and countries of asylum reinforce this tragic sense of not only having lost one's autonomy and homeland, but having one's life history doubted or dismissed as a form of deceit."[36]

Even after resettlement, refugee stories of trauma, survival, and perseverance are continually solicited and transformed by well-meaning advocates into products to serve multiple agendas, from political debate to policy discussions, educational outreach, or organizational fund-raising.[37] Because of their precarious positions, these stories rely on an uncomplicated "mythico-history" that presents refugees as innocent victims of immoral state violence.[38] Yet, as Jackson argues, constructing narratives out of personal experience and sharing them with others is fundamental to the "reclamation of a person's humanity."[39] "Without stories, *without listening to one another's stories*, there can be no recovery of the social, no overcoming of our separateness, no discovery of common ground or common cause."[40] For some, however, the ways in which they are asked to frame their identity in order to be acceptable to others is simply "incompatible with recovering a sense of dignity or personal integrity following a trauma."[41]

When I first met Bishnu, he expressed a sense of responsibility to "tell his story" to anyone who would listen if it might help his community. But he was also frustrated by the one-dimensional way this painted his identity. "I *was* a refugee, not *am*. I'm American now," he insisted.[42] By constantly asking newcomer communities to frame their identities as political victims, survivors, and martyrs, dependent on their past for definition, we are missing potential opportunities to support futures pursuing creative, culturally rooted lives of self-determination.

When we came together in Buffalo as a group of partnering individuals and organizations, we recognized a need to foster spaces for community conversations where stories could be told within close networks mutually invested in making sense of personal and collective experiences, not directed at outsiders. These could be the stories individuals wished to share with families, including imagined future generations. Such a process would encourage community partners to identify themselves as active agents in the negotiation of local expressive culture and history, not only within their personal networks but also more broadly.

Before leaving Buffalo, I had the opportunity to record only one storytelling session, a sort of test case, in the home of Surjiman Khadka, an elder selected, in part, for his leadership in Bhutan as an elected official.[43] Perhaps more than anyone in Buffalo, he could speak to issues of power and political conflict leading up to expulsion.

I sat quietly, with my audio recorder and my tea, among a group of ten or so individuals spread across two adjoining rooms. Surjiman sat in a single chair between the living room and dining room. Most of the women and young people stayed in the adjoining dining room. (The informal separation of men and women was typical for most social interactions and will raise interesting questions about the compatibility of museum and community protocols when women or youth are given the main stage in storytelling sessions.)

I understood little of the conversation, spoken in Nepali, but occasionally someone would consider a point too important not to summarize it for me in English. My presence, in this manner, was acknowledged but not underlined. Surjiman talked about his youth, about his time as a volunteer service worker, parliamentary member, and district head. He talked about being a wealthy and influential man in Bhutan and his feelings of uselessness without work in the refugee camp. He shared his opinions about the problems facing the community in Buffalo. Women, experiencing more isolation in the home, committed suicide more often than men. He said people cannot live "like cattle, contained." They must be able to express themselves and dance. "We don't know how to dance over here. It's slippery."

The tone of the conversation vacillated between lighthearted laughter and nostalgic reminiscences to furrowed seriousness. Throughout, like on any other Sunday afternoon that I've experienced in a Bhutanese-Nepali home, friends and extended family dropped by, sat for a while, asked questions, and then left. Despite the artificialness of arranging and recording the session, it felt seamlessly interwoven with everyday life. When it was over, people posed for photos.

Constructing space for these conversations and recording them may lead to a better understanding of how individuals are negotiating belonging, cultural continuity, and traditional expressive practices within Buffalo. How are people interpreting their new lives and activities in relation to the past and present? What do they see as their most important challenges and opportunities for the future? How do traditional forms of creativity, like dance—both actual and metaphorical—enhance quality of life and community health? For a museum, starting here means that community questions, desires, and needs can inform continued collaborations and museum products (like future exhibits, programming, and collecting), eventually making it possible for more intelligible and balanced civic dialog to take place within the museum around experiences of immigration within the city. Eventually, these collaborations can also build capacity within the community, assisting individuals with technical training so they may pursue more self-directed heritage initiatives.

Developing this project was slow and sometimes stilted. What it might become and ultimately achieve still unfolds, now in the hands of my successor, Ed Millar, and the remaining partners. Before leaving Buffalo, however, I wanted those I worked with to know that CAM was committed to more than conversation and had interest in them beyond their status as refugees.

FROM THE FIELD: ON DISPLAY

Everyone lines up for a photo: two Hindu priests, Khem and Bishnu Khanal; and two assistants, Bishnu Adhikari and Shyam Ghana Khanal. They pose in the Folk Arts Gallery of the Castellani Art Museum behind a beautiful rice-flour drawing, painstakingly created for the exhibition "(Almost) Too Good to Eat: Marking Life Transitions with Food." Known as rekkhi, *drawings like this serve as a base for temporary altars. The flour designs, tinted with vermillion and turmeric, sanctify the space and "create a map," the priests tell me, for numerous rites that will take place around it. Designs and colors vary with occasion. This style belongs to wedding ceremonies. When I'd seen* rekkhi *created on the floors of several brides' family homes, I'd noted how carefully and precisely the priests worked, taking most of the day to complete what would typically be done in little time. In the art museum, in a gallery already filled with photographs and cultural objects related to diverse ritual food traditions, the four understood that their work would represent their culture, their religion, and their local community against the backdrop of a multicultural landscape. In response, they heightened aesthetic excellence.*

First, using measuring tape and an iPhone calculator, they sketched the pattern with pencil and chalk, ensuring perfect symmetry. When Khem finally began pouring flour from his fist, Shyam followed closely behind, sharpening the lines with a damp paper towel. A vigorous discussion in Nepali broke out

FIGURE 18.3
The wedding of Lokesh and Karma Rai takes place in the bride's home around a temporary altar created for the occasion, 2012. A sacred drawing of rice flour, poured onto butcher paper, serves as the foundation. (Photo: Carrie Hertz.)

after Khem completed two of four planned swastikas. Bishnu turned to me and asked, "There are problems with this?" In the United States, I explained, many people associate the symbol with Nazis and genocide, but I assured them this would be an excellent opportunity to educate the public about other meanings. After further discussion, Shyam announced a plan to replace swastikas with "Om," since it also communicates peace without risk of offending. "We want to make peace in America," he explained. "We don't want anyone to question." I worried that their self-censorship would weaken authenticity, but Khem stressed that both symbols are appropriate to the design and left to the discretion of an acting priest. They all agreed that everything should be "true," Bishnu reiterated. A practicing Hindu from their community should recognize it as a proper place for prayer (if they added the additional ritual elements, of course, namely, a sacred fire). Later, Bishnu explained their readiness to make contextual adjustments to cultural practices. "We want to adopt American system and carry our system too."[44]

FIGURE 18.4
Bishnu Adhikari, Khem Khanal, Shyam Ghana Khanal, and Bishnu Khanal pose behind the *rekkhi* (sacred rice flour drawing) they have just completed for an exhibition of ritual foods held at the Castellani Art Museum of Niagara University, 2013. (Photo: Carrie Hertz.)

MAKING ROOM FOR CELEBRATION

Many refugees arrive in the United States wishing to create lives that simultaneously look forward and backward, balancing new belonging with identities built on tradition. For Bishnu, for Surjiman, for the priest Khem, the adaptation of traditional celebrations not only represents cultural survival but also signals lives worth living—lives of joy, social and spiritual connectedness, and hope. Folk art, always changing, always central to fashioning identity, is generally understood as a resource for carving out and justifying a place in a transnational world.

I wanted to curate an exhibition of ritual foods, both edible and purely ceremonial, to introduce audiences to some of the individuals and groups I had begun working with over the previous two years and to demonstrate to those collaborators that CAM was committed to showcasing the beauty and value of their traditions. The thematic conceit served other important curatorial goals.

In a museum otherwise filled with fine art paintings and sculptures, an exhibit honoring the artistry of ceremonial foodways emphasizes main achievements of public folk arts programs: expanding the definitions of art and artist to reflect more pluralistic understandings and recognizing art as a transformational, performative, aesthetic process, not simply a material product with lasting, formal properties.[45] The show also explicitly connected newcomers with established immigrant groups readily celebrated within local social history. Representations of Bhutanese-Nepali *rekkhi* and Ethiopian coffee ceremonies were juxtaposed with more familiar arts, like Polish Easter butter carving and lamb cakes. In Buffalo, people say, "Everyone's Polish at Easter," acknowledging the widespread celebration and adoption of these ethnic customs within the city. This conceptual link was positively acknowledged in local media when a reviewer, discussing the inclusion of "new Americans" in the show, wrote, "We know them. They are us."[46]

When I spoke with Bhutanese-Nepali community members about what ceremonial foods might be appropriate in the exhibition, rice flour altar drawings emerged as especially poignant. In Buffalo, the practice has intensified in meaning, being a means for temporarily creating sacred space anywhere, whenever needed. *Rekkhi*, destroyed in the act of prayer and created anew, operates as an active metaphor, a reminder of the transient and cyclical nature of existence, a symbol of resilience in change, a cultural resource ready to be adapted. As a nonverbal expression of skill, beauty, and shared religious knowledge, it also stands in contrast to personal narratives of hardship.

Amplifying stories of displacement and endurance is vital to promoting social justice through meaningful and informed civic dialog. Equally important are the celebratory methods, long fundamental to public folk arts practice, that illustrate the multifaceted, creative identities of individuals and the value of cultural traditions in the lives of all people.

As museum professionals, it feels right that we should push the boundaries of what we can achieve, ambitiously exploring new techniques and critiquing our own practices and assumptions. We should continue to justify and extend our value to society. Yet, we should not forget the long-held belief that celebratory representation in the museum, especially when undertaken in a spirit of mutuality and shared authority, is a civically engaged, political act. As a "factory of identity" in which the interpretation of self, society, heritage, and belonging is constructed, a museum is never neutral.[47] We know our depictions have consequences, not only conceptually, presenting as reasonable certain ways of seeing each other, the world, and what changes could be possible, but also substantially, impacting daily interactions, policy and human rights decision making, and social service development.

I was recently reminded how relevant discussions around the "politics of representation" still are to museums. At my new institution, the Museum of International Folk Art, we hosted a panel discussion on transgender issues using folk art as a focus for dialog.[48] During a dynamic and surprisingly intimate conversation among audience members, one of the panelists, Adrien Lawyer, codirector and founder of the Transgender Resource Center of New Mexico, argued, "We can't actually *represent* each other. We can only *advocate for* each other." We can learn how to do this, he says, from the civil rights struggles that have come before: advocacy requires education and personalization, so that when others start talking about "those people," we actually think of our friend or our neighbor. In short, we still need to create public spaces in which diverse people can come together, learn about each other, and know each other as interesting, valuable individuals. Public folklorists have long known this as we focus positive attention onto communities through their art and artists. Bishnu Adhikari knows this, wishing to remake Americans into siblings.

Just as folklorists emphasize the cultural process of art making—how social, ethical, and aesthetic values become enacted and materialized through individual choices—so can curators reframe museum practice by interrogating how professional values are enacted and materialized in the making of museum products. Process matters. Collaborating with local, emerging communities may present unique, challenging opportunities for exploring new approaches, guiding the museum to become more responsive and accountable, while also supporting newcomers to feel more emotionally connected to a museum and to the society to which they now belong. In Buffalo, this is one way to co-construct what it means to be "good neighbors."

NOTES

1. Drawn from field notes, September 22, 2012.

2. For relevant studies, see Betty Farrell, Maria Medvedeva, Center for the Future of Museums, and American Association of Museums, *Demographic Transformation and the Future of Museums* (Washington, DC: AAM Press, 2010), http://www.aam-us.org/docs/center-for-the-future-of-museums/demotransaam2010.pdf; Steven

Shewfelt and the National Endowment for the Arts, *How a Nation Engages with Art: Highlights from the 2013 Survey of Public Participation in the Arts*, Research Report 57 (Washington, DC: National Endowment for the Arts, 2013), http://arts.gov/sites/default/files/highlights-from-2012-SPPA-rev.pdf.

3. See Karp and Lavine 1991; Karp, Kraemer, and Lavine 1992.

4. Korom 1999.

5. See Adair, Filene, and Koloski 2011.

6. For some representative texts, see Golding and Modest 2013; Peers and Brown 2003.

7. Gable 2013.

8. Frisch 2013.

9. "About Us," International Coalition of Sites of Conscience, http://www.sitesofconscience.org/about-us.

10. Cities like Buffalo are also known as "preferred communities" by the US Department of State and the Office of Refugee Resettlement.

11. For relevant statistics, see Chung and Riordan 2014; Johnson and McManus 2015. For examples of media discourse, see Zremski 2015.

12. I met with Bishnu many times over the course of nearly three years and keep up a long-distance friendship now. During my time in Buffalo, I recorded an oral history with him on November 11, 2012, now archived at the Castellani Art Museum of Niagara University. Some quotations are transcribed from this recording; others come from field notes.

13. For a more thorough and nuanced discussion of the conflict leading to expulsion, see Hutt 2003. Bhutanese-Nepali refugees are Hindu, Kirat, Buddhist, and Christian, but I primarily worked with Hindus, who constitute the vast majority in Buffalo. During a phone conversation in December 2015, after I shared a draft of this chapter, Bishnu told me of increased efforts within the community to bring all members closer together through heritage and advocacy activities, explaining that "all religions are children of the same mother." In Bhutan, those of Nepali ancestry who lived in the south are sometimes referred to as Lhotshampas (Dzongkha for "southerners"). I do not use this term, as I found no individuals who identified themselves this way. Most people referred to themselves as Bhutanese, Nepali, or Bhutanese-Nepali. For the sake of inclusiveness, I will primarily use Bhutanese-Nepali.

14. Ilse Griek (2013) documents an interesting response to these conditions of diffusion: the reversal of declining rates of minor marriages within Nepali camps as young sweethearts eloped, hoping to avoid separation during resettlement.

15. Dewhurst and MacDowell 2015.

16. McMullen 2008.

17. Find relevant statistics at "Bhutanese Refugee Health Profile," CDC, http://www.cdc.gov/immigrantrefugeehealth/profiles/bhutanese/background/index.html.

18. For examples of analyses of American museum-emerging refugee collaborations, see Kendig-Lawrence 2010; Westerman 2008. American museums have lagged behind the work of Europe, Australia, and New Zealand; see, for examples, Day 2009; Goodnow 2008. There are too many examples examining folklore-refugee collaborations to cite, but in addition to others cited elsewhere in this chapter, some excellent highlights that have informed my thinking include Proschan 1992; McMahon 2009. Marcus and Westerman 2006 discuss salient issues in working with and for social service agencies. See Modic et al. 2007 for an example of an instructional publication merging folkloristic and social service concerns. For an excellent example of a folkloristically driven examination and critique of asylum policy, see Bohmer and Shuman 2008.

19. Swan and Jordan 2015. Similarly, as part of collaborative relationships with organizations like Journey's End Refugee Services, I donated time and resources by helping to fill tables at fund-raisers or providing photography at events for use in promotional materials. These community service endeavors do more than cement relationships. As Frank Proschan (1992) argues, they can also lead to deeper interpersonal and cultural understanding.

20. Kratz 2013, 64–65.

21. Spitzer 1992.

22. For particularly persuasive examples, see Nusbaum 2004; Wells 2006; Westerman 2006.

23. Nusbaum 2004, 203. This scenario—of inadvertently exacerbating community strife and difference—is explored by Heather Hindman (2013) in her comparison of experiences between Bhutanese-Nepali refugees and Nepali asylees in Austin, Texas.

24. My experiences echo those of Béatrice Halsouet (2013, 43), who found that most people verbalized equality, but, on observation, some continued to adhere to caste taboos related to things like food or home visitation.

25. For a recent discussion of museum–Native American community collaborations, including a useful bibliography, see Swan and Jordan 2015.

26. Bau Graves, Juan Lado, and Patricia Romney (2005) have written in detail about their attempts—successful and less successful—to bring fractious communities together in conversation by organizing community events that also serve as dialogue planning sessions.

27. Wells 2006, 10.

28. Onciul 2013.

29. Westerman 2006.

30. There have been recent efforts to create an international network of researchers working on Bhutanese refugee resettlement. In 2013, a workshop titled "The Bhutanese Refugee Resettlement Experience" was held at the School of Oriental and African Studies, University of London. Organizers cited the need to bring people who have been otherwise working in isolation together with new communities emerging in dispersed locations across the globe. For a brief report on the workshop, see Chase 2014. A resulting publication also gathered papers in a special issue of the *European Bulletin of Himalayan Research* 43 (Autumn-Winter 2013).

31. Stadler 2013, 88.

32. Feltault 2006.

33. Drawn from field notes, February 28, 2014, Buffalo, New York.

34. Tchen and Ševčenko 2011, 89.

35. Shuman and Bohmer 2004.

36. Jackson 2013, 106.

37. These documents have deep significance for Bishnu and other Bhutanese-Nepalis. Heather Hindman (2013, 110) explains, "Amassing papers that might give one's presence in Bhutan legitimacy by documenting their landholdings and history was one that many refugees had chased as the rules changed or were applied unevenly in the late 20th Century in Bhutan." Like many refugees, Bishnu lost rights to his family lands when his father was pressured by the government to sign them away.

38. Stadler 2013, 90.

39. Ibid., 115.

40. Ibid., 114.

41. Shuman and Bohmer 2004, 406.

42. For examples of this specifically within Bhutanese-Nepali resettlement contexts, see Stadler 2013; Evans 2009.

43. Bishnu became a US citizen in 2015.

44. Drawn from field notes, July 20, 2013, Niagara Falls, New York; "(Almost) Too Good to Eat: Marking Life Transitions with Food" was on exhibit at the Castellani Art Museum of Niagara University from July 14 to December 8, 2013.

45. See Westerman 2006 for a discussion of how folklorists have been instrumental in the development of these philosophical refinements in understanding "aesthetics in the twentieth century" (118).

46. Adams 2013, 37.

47. Kaplan 1994.

48. "Between Two Worlds: A Transgender Perspective" was a public program held on November 15, 2015, in conjunction with the Gallery of Conscience exhibition "Between Two Worlds: Folk Artists Reflect on the Immigrant Experience."

REFERENCES

Adair, Bill, Benjamin Filene, and Laura Koloski. 2011. *Letting Go? Sharing Historical Authority in a User-Generated World.* Philadelphia: Pew Center for Arts and Heritage.

Adams, Bruce. 2013. "On View: The Art of Food." *Buffalo Spree* (November): 36–37.

Bohmer, Carol, and Amy Shuman. 2008. *Rejecting Refugees: Political Asylum in the 21st Century.* New York: Routledge.

Chase, Liana E. 2014. "The Bhutanese Refugee Resettlement Experience: A Workshop Report." *Himalaya: The Journal of the Association for Nepal and Himalayan Studies* 34, no. 1: 130–31.

Chung, Subin, and Emily Riordan. 2014. "Immigrants, Refugees, and Languages Spoken in Buffalo" (Buffalo Brief). Partnership for the Public Good. http://www.ppgbuffalo.org/wp-content/uploads/2011/01/Immigrants-Refugees-and-Languages-Spoken-in-Buffalo.pdf.

Day, Annette. 2009. "'They Listened to My Voice': The Refugee Communities History Project and Belonging: Voices of London's Refugees." *Oral History* 37, no. 1: 95–106.

Dewhurst, C. Kurt, and Marsha MacDowell. 2015. "Strategies for Creating and Sustaining Museum-Based International Collaborative Partnerships." *Practicing Anthropology* 37, no. 3: 54–55.

Evans, Rosalind. 2009. *Inheriting the Past and Envisioning the Future: Young Bhutanese Refugees' Political Learning and Action.* PhD diss., Oxford University.

Feltault, Kelly. 2006. "Development Folklife: Human Security and Cultural Conservation." *Journal of American Folklore* 119, no. 471: 90–110.

Frisch, Michael. 2013. "From *A Shared Authority* to the Digital Kitchen, and Back." In *Letting Go? Sharing Historical Authority in a User-Generated World*, edited by Bill Adair, Benjamin Filene, and Laura Koloski, 126–37. Philadelphia: Pew Center for Arts and Heritage.

Gable, Eric. 2013. "The City, Race, and the Creation of a Common History at the Virginia Historical Society." In *Museums and Communities: Curators, Collections and Collaboration*, edited by Viv Golding and Wayne Modest, 32–47. London: Bloomsbury.

Golding, Viv, and Wayne Modest. 2013. *Museums and Communities: Curators, Collections and Collaboration.* London: Bloomsbury.

Goodnow, Katherine. 2008. *Museums, the Media, and Refugees: Stories of Crisis, Control and Compassion.* London: Berghahn Books and Museum of London.

Graves, Bau, Juan Lado, and Patricia Romney. 2005. "African in Maine Case Study: Center for Cultural Exchange." Animating Democracy. http://animatingdemocracy.org/sites/default/files/documents/labs/african_in_maine_case_study.pdf.

Griek, Ilse. 2013. "A Daughter Married, a Daughter Lost? The Impact of Resettlement on Bhutanese Refugee Marriages." *European Bulletin of Himalayan Research* 43: 11–25.

Halsouet, Béatrice. 2013. "Nepali-Speaking Bhutanese Refugees in Canada: How to Be Hindu in a Regional Quebecois City?" *European Bulletin of Himalayan Research* 43: 36–51.

Hindman, Heather. 2013. "Social Service Provider Perceptions of 'Nepali-ness' among Asylum Seekers and Refugees in Austin, Texas." *European Bulletin of Himalayan Research* 43: 103–19.

Hutt, Michael. 2003. *Unbecoming Citizens: Culture, Nationhood, and the Flight of Refugees from Bhutan*. Oxford: Oxford University Press.

Jackson, Michael. 2013. *The Politics of Storytelling: Variations on a Theme by Hannah Arendt*. Copenhagen: Museum Musculanum Press, University of Copenhagen.

Johnson, Robert, and Clint McManus. 2015. "Racial Disparities in Buffalo-Niagara: Housing, Income, and Employment" (Buffalo Brief). Partnership for the Public Good. http://www.ppgbuffalo.org/wp-content/uploads/2011/01/Racial-Disparities-2015.pdf.

Kaplan, Flora E. 1994. *Museums and the Making of "Ourselves": The Role of Objects in National Identity*. London: Leicester University Press.

Karp, Ivan, and Steven D. Lavine. 1991. *Exhibiting Cultures: The Poetics and Politics of Museum Display*. Washington, DC: Smithsonian Institution Press.

Karp, Ivan, Christine Mullen Kreamer, and Steven D. Lavine. 1992. *Museums and Communities: The Politics of Public Culture*. Washington, DC: Smithsonian Institution Press.

Kendig-Lawrence, Julie. 2010. "In Our Own Image: Stories of Refugee Youth." In *Narratives of Community: Museums and Ethnicity*, edited by Olivia Guntarik, 128–47. Edinburgh: MuseumsEtc.

Korom, Frank J. 1999. "Empowerment through Representation and Collaboration in Museum Exhibits." *Journal of Folklore Research* 36, no. 2/3: 259–65.

Kratz, Corinne A. 2013. "The 'Ethnographic' in the Museum: Knowledge Productions, Fragments, and Relationships." In *Beyond Modernity: Do Ethnography Museums Need Ethnography?*, edited by Sandra Ferracuti, Elisabetta Frasca, and Vito Lattanzi, 61–78. Rome: Espera Libreria Archeologica.

Marcus, Laura R., and William Westerman. 2006. "Report from the Field: A Dialogue on Immigrant and Refugee Issues." *Voices: The Journal of New York Folklore* 32 (Fall–Winter), http://www.nyfolklore.org/pubs/voic32-3-4/refugee.html.

McMahon, Felicia R. 2009. *Not Just Child's Play: Emerging Tradition and the Lost Boys of Sudan*. Jackson: University Press of Mississippi.

McMullen, Ann. 2008. "The Currency of Consultation and Collaboration." *Museum Anthropology Review* 2, no. 2: 54–87, https://scholarworks.iu.edu/journals/index.php/mar/article/view/88.

Modic, Kate, Ron Kirby, Laura R. Marcus, and Amy E. Skillman. 2007. *Newcomer Arts: A Strategy for Successful Integration (A Manual for Refugee and Immigrant Service Workers and Newcomer Artists)*. Harrisburg, PA: Institute for Cultural Partnerships.

Nusbaum, Philip. 2004. "Folklorists at State Arts Agencies: Cultural Disconnects and 'Fairness.'" *Journal of Folklore Research* 41, no. 2/3: 199–225.

Onciul, Bryony. 2013. "Community Engagement, Curatorial Practice, and Museum Ethos in Alberta, Canada." In *Museums and Communities: Curators, Collections and Collaboration*, edited by Viv Golding and Wayne Modest, 79–97. London: Bloomsbury.

Peers, Laura, and Alison K. Brown. 2003. *Museums and Source Communities: A Routledge Reader*. London: Routledge.

Proschan, Frank. 1992. "Field Work and Social Work: Folklore as Helping Profession." In *Public Folklore*, edited by Robert Baron and Nicholas R. Spitzer, 145–58. Washington, DC: Smithsonian Institution Press.

Shuman, Amy, and Carol Bohmer. 2004. "Representing Trauma: Political Asylum Narrative." *Journal of American Folklore* 117, no. 466: 394–414.

Spitzer, Nicholas R. 1992. "Cultural Conversations: Metaphors and Methods in Public Folklore." In *Public Folklore*, edited by Robert Baron and Nicholas R. Spitzer, 77–104. Washington, DC: Smithsonian Institution Press.

Stadler, Joseph. 2013. "Refugees and Advocates: Bhutanese Refugees, Resettlement NGOs and the Co-construction of a Social Memory of Victimhood." *European Bulletin of Himalayan Research* 43: 86–102.

Swan, Daniel C., and Michael Paul Jordan. 2015. "Contingent Collaborations: Patterns of Reciprocity in Museum-Community Partnerships." *Journal of Folklore Research* 52, no. 1: 39–84.

Tchen, John Kuo Wei, and Liz Ševčenko. 2011. "The 'Dialogic Museum' Revisited: A Collaborative Reflection." In *Letting Go? Sharing Historical Authority in a User-Generated World*, edited by Bill Adair, Benjamin Filene, and Laura Koloski, 80–97. Philadelphia: Pew Center for Arts and Heritage.

Wells, Patricia Atkinson. 2006. "Public Folklore in the Twenty-First Century: New Challenges for the Discipline." *Journal of American Folklore* 119, no. 471: 5–18.

Westerman, William. 2006. "Wild Grasses and New Arks: Transformative Potential in Applied and Public Folklore." *Journal of American Folklore* 119, no. 471: 111–28.

———. 2008. "Museums, Immigrants, and the Inversion of Xenophobia; or, the Inclusion Museum in the Exclusive Society." *International Journal of the Inclusive Museum* 1, no. 4: 157–62.

Zremski, Jerry. 2015. "Immigrants End the Decline in Erie County Population." *Buffalo News*. March 26. http://www.buffalonews.com/city-region/erie-county/immigrants-end-the-decline-in-erie-county-population-20150326.

19

Folklife Museums, Sustainability, and Social Entrepreneurship

CANDACE TANGORRA MATELIC

In this chapter, Candace Tangorra Matelic explores how and why folklife museums, open-air museums, and historic sites can and should challenge old assumptions and evolve to engage more fully with the communities they serve. Citing examples of several museums she has worked with, located in different parts of the world, she argues that folklife museums in particular have a unique opportunity to use input and insights from audiences they serve as a way of engaging community members, strengthening relationships with them, and moving toward a proposed model for what she calls social entrepreneurship. The ultimate outcome is a museum for the twenty-first century that is a strong and relevant model of public service.

CONNECTING THE DOTS

When Lou Jones and I wrote the introduction to the 1987 version of this book, we focused on where folklife museums had come since the 1940s and 1950s and where they were heading. I want to once again look at some important trends of the last three decades and then posit that folklife museums are poised to be leaders of a sustainable and bright future if they accept the challenge of moving toward community engagement and social entrepreneurship.

In the earlier piece we chronicled how the early pioneers challenged folklorists, museologists, and historians to collaborate much more closely as they developed the dozens (hundreds? thousands?) of representative museums that celebrated ordinary people rather than the elite and showed the history of average families, typical businesses, and common community activities. The result was a burgeoning network of living historical farms, villages, forts, mining camps, industrial sites, and individual estates, which drew millions of visitors each year, employed an army of volunteers to help operate them, and raised museological questions about collections, interpretation, and administration at each step along the way. Along with the growth came a maturation of understanding about education and interpretation as a fundamental purpose and function of museums, equal to research, collection, and preservation.

Folklife museums, open-air museums, and historic sites experimented with a multitude of program approaches, ranging from living history and craft demonstrations to hands-on activities for visitors of all ages. These museums utilized stories, music, dance, and theater to depict the joys and tribulations of everyday life, and they developed adult education classes, summer day camps, workshops and seminars, activity centers, thematic special events, computer games, and multisensory, experiential presentations to bring their sites alive and personalize visitors' connections between past and present. The interpretive content for many of these approaches was drawn from folklife research, social history, and material culture studies. Simply put, the more visitors got involved in their museum experience, the more they wanted to know about everyday life and about average people like themselves, supporting the need for better integration of folklife studies into ongoing museum research and collecting interpretation and programs.

My expertise in the arena of community engagement comes from almost two decades of working with museums of all kinds to begin their engagement journeys. Since much of my work in museums was in education, interpretation, and public programming, I was already an advocate for meaningful visitor experiences. But community engagement is much more than offering wonderful programs. It is more than audience development. It goes much deeper and addresses why museums can matter. As I worked with museums, I quickly realized that the best ideas often come from community members.

They do not have hidden agendas about power and control or "emotional baggage." When the American Association of Museums launched its "Museums and Community" initiative twenty-plus years ago, I was excited and hopeful. The association sent teams of museum colleagues to communities across the United States to have dialogs with community leaders about their issues and how museums could become more involved in civic affairs. The reports were exciting and inspiring. There was a lot of talk, but very few museums understood how to shift their paradigms and assumptions and transform their operations. The action was slow in coming. For me, this was very frustrating, so I just started doing it as I worked (as a consultant) with many organizations. Whether it was an interpretive planning project or a strategic planning process, I started with community engagement. I was amazed at how things started to change, and the overall quality of the results was dramatically increased. I witnessed the museums shifting their own thinking and starting to move toward partnerships and collaborations rather than trying to control (and do) everything themselves.

My passion for helping museums serve a deeper purpose in their communities was ignited after the events of 9/11, and I started learning about the worldwide movement in social entrepreneurship. During my dissertation research on organizational change in museums, I was steeped in the experiences of seven museums that had undertaken major change over the course of two decades[1] and read the organizational literature on change, transformation, development, and learning. I discovered that museums around the world were courageously addressing the tough issues in their communities, often beginning with offering a safe and neutral place for dialog and then using their resources—collections, exhibits, and programs—to raise awareness, provide a historical or cultural context, and advocate for social change. Wow! This was what I thought museums should be doing—making a real difference in people's lives. And long story short, I realized that if an organization embraced community engagement to its fullest, it naturally moved toward social entrepreneurship.

RECENT BEST PRACTICES AND FORCES FOR CHANGE IN MUSEUMS

In the last three decades, bolstered by an explosion of research about how visitors learn in museums, the museum policies and teaching approaches that were experimental or innovative have become best practices. Museums are no longer measured and judged solely by their internal resources—collections, endowments, facilities, and staff—but rather by the external benefits and value they create for individuals and communities. Growing numbers of museums are learning to make their organizations more meaningful and relevant by involving their communities in ongoing planning and decision making. They are reframing museum activities to focus on what matters to their communities. By getting involved in community challenges and developing new partnerships, they are identifying underserved audiences and creating memorable visitor experiences. As museums begin this journey toward community engagement, they are initiating and facilitating social change and moving toward social entrepreneurship.

Current best practices for facilitating meaningful visitor experiences include:

- Designing interpretation as a transformative communication process to evoke a response at many levels—cognitive, affective, behavioral, and spiritual
- Employing the philosophy of visitor meaning making—recognizing that visitors are actively engaged in constructing personal meaning as they experience programs and exhibits at museums and historic sites
- Utilizing experience design as a strategy to engage visitors in a personal and memorable way—borrowing techniques from theater, retail spaces, food operations, and themed attractions
- Recognizing that visitors are sophisticated learners who choose to participate in museum educational offerings—drawing on new scholarship on adult education, lifelong learning, experiential learning, informal or voluntary learning, communities of practice, and organizational learning
- Teaching through interpretive processes and hands-on activities—that can bring objects, settings, processes, and interpretive concepts to life for visitors
- Offering multiple perspectives in interpretation—a strategy that draws visitors into dialog and cuts across many normal barriers, such as race, class, economic status, and cultural or ethnic traditions
- Respecting that visitors to museums and historic sites have a series of rights—as articulated by Judy Rand to include comfort, orientation, welcome and belonging, enjoyment, socializing, respect, communication, learning, choice and control, challenge and confidence, and revitalization[2]

- Incorporating visitor perspective and focus into program and exhibit planning and implementation from the beginning—through a program of ongoing visitor studies[3]

For those readers who are new to the field or have not followed the events and trends of the last few decades, it may be helpful to summarize the transformational shifts in our thinking and some of the forces for change that are shaping why and how museums are moving toward more inclusive and engaged practice. There are numerous forces for change, including the challenging global economy and our continuing efforts to embrace diversity and serve a multicultural society. With a deeper understanding of visitors' needs, interests, and learning, we are now moving toward a point where visitor participation, buy-in, and ownership are the norm—visitors want to have a voice, a role, and some control over their time and activities when engaging with our exhibits, programs, spaces, and content. The traditional roles of museum staff have changed so dramatically that we might as well throw out the old job descriptions—directors faced with a myriad of complex responsibilities to keep their organizations running smoothly, curators sharing their sole authority for content and collections decisions, and educators assuming a larger role in the development of exhibitions and other delivery venues. Museums are fundamentally complex organizations, and we need to operate them as such, drawing on the rich body of research and practice about improving organizational behavior and effectiveness (this is "the second agenda," or the necessary foundation to accomplish a museum's primary mission and goals). Technology continues to transform the way we interact with the world in our daily lives and certainly the way we work in museums.

Framing these forces for change, three significant paradigm shifts, or transformative shifts, in our thinking in the museum field are now guiding our work:

- *Mandating public service:* The central purpose of museums is to serve our many publics at the level of making a meaningful difference in the lives of individuals and making a significant contribution to the communities we serve. This mandate means that our organizations must demonstrate their public value and positive social outcome and state these goals in mission and vision statements, as well as in program descriptions for all activities.[4] For many museums, this mandate is about reframing our organizational models to focus on long-term effectiveness rather than short-term efficiency, a task that is easier said than done.[5] It is a new way of thinking, a new perspective for planning, budgeting, and organizational assessment. Strategically, it is about doing the right things rather than doing everything right. Often the most difficult transition is the understanding that the inherent worth of collections and facilities is necessary but not sufficient to demonstrate public value. These things matter only if the organization matters.

- *Making interpretation, programs, and community engagement everyone's business:* A second paradigm shift is the understanding that everyone in the organization, from the board to curatorial staff to the front-line staff and volunteers, is responsible for community engagement as well as the public dimension of the museum. These components of a museum's operation must be organizational priorities rather than delegated to whoever is responsible for programs. A useful interpretive framework—that puts stories into the context of universal concepts and ideas—provides guidance for research, collections, marketing, and fund-raising, as well as public programs, exhibits, publications, events, and other methods of communicating to audiences. Museums of all sizes and focuses can utilize interpretation as a powerful way to engage people and facilitate timely dialog and deep reflection about important issues because people come to museums to learn about people—their lives, values, trials and tribulations, joys, and contributions. They come to reflect on their own lives and the lives of their families, friends, neighbors, and business associates. They come to get a new perspective, a new understanding of other people, places, and times, and to get renewed, reinvigorated, and even inspired. By making interpretation, programs, and community engagement everyone's responsibility, museums can become "dialogic places" as described by Stan Carbone, director of the Jewish Heritage Centre of Western Canada.[6] To embrace this shift, many museums must transform their internal values and organizational cultures to embrace leadership at all levels, redefine roles of professional staff, empower all staff, volunteers, and the community to participate in planning and decision making, utilize teamwork with community involvement, and integrate ongoing visitor studies into their operations.

- *Becoming learning organizations:* This third shift is about "walking our talk," or valuing learning for stakeholders, those people who have an existing relationship with the museum, such as staff, board members, and volunteers, as well as for visitors. It is about understanding the inherent difficulty and complexity of organizational change and touching hearts and minds before expecting any transformation to occur. Learning organizations use their knowledge and experience to become more effective by going beyond the status quo to grow and evolve. If an organization has embraced this concept, then the criteria for making organizational decisions and setting priorities include learning outcomes as well as short-term performance and the bottom line. The organization values innovation, experimentation, flexibility, and initiative. Knowledge is openly shared, and everyone is encouraged to apply it for problem solving. Leaders at all levels use systems thinking to improve the organization as an integrated ensemble, establish relationships with external groups and organizations, and build long-term sustainability. For museums and historic sites to move toward becoming learning organizations, they must learn to value people as their most critical resource and help people develop their knowledge and skills. They must also understand that "organizational development" means much more than building new facilities and getting more money. It is learning about effective teamwork and designing new operational structures that focus on long-term effectiveness as well as short-term efficiency. Organizational development includes deepening relationships and collaboration with other community organizations through meaningful work and visioning the museum's future as a highly valued community player.[7]

Hence, to be innovative, museum programs must go beyond best practices to break new ground, change old assumptions and behavior patterns, and transform participants and possibly the organizations involved. Criteria for current innovative programs include:

- Engaging a wide range of community groups and organizations in program conception, planning, evaluation, and ongoing refinement
- Developing and nurturing long-term collaborations, partnerships, and relationships with community organizations, sharing risks, rewards/losses, and resources

- Targeting new and/or underserved audiences, going beyond existing stakeholders
- Developing transformative interpretive content, addressing the things that people care about and the issues that matter in their daily lives
- Integrating mission-related sustainable enterprise as a part of program planning and implementation, including products and services to generate ongoing income to supplement traditional sources of support
- Moving toward social entrepreneurship, working with other community partners to make a real difference by addressing social needs, drawing on the "spirit" of the people who are connected to our organizations (What did they deeply care about? What really mattered in their lives? What would they be pushing us to do to shape the future of our organizations?)
- Adapting to forces of change and important trends in our external environments, using our creativity to continually respond, reflect, learn, and innovate[8]

These new directions represent enormous shifts in thinking about museums, sites, and cultural organizations, with different underlying values, and for some colleagues and stakeholders, they are downright scary, in part because they challenge traditional professional standards, roles, and practices. Also, it is difficult to predict exactly where an organization will end up once this transformation process is under way. For some people and risk-aversive organizations, this uncertainty is very disconcerting. It requires a leap of faith. However, once embraced, and the journey begun with openness and sincerity, these new directions and roles can be exciting, rewarding, and even liberating, because they move our organizations closer to a path of broad community support.[9]

THE HEART OF THE MATTER: BUILDING A RELEVANT AND SUSTAINABLE FUTURE

Let's get to the bottom line: in order for folklife studies to thrive as an integral component of folklife museums, open-air museums, historic sites, and history museums, our organizations need to be perceived by the communities they serve as relevant and sustainable contributors. In other words, they need to demonstrate their ongoing value as civic players, contributing to addressing the compelling issues and enduring needs of the community.

Community engagement and moving toward social entrepreneurship is not a casual endeavor. Rather it is often a dramatic metanoia, or shift in the way we think about the business of running museums. Our focus must move away from internal survival, asking what the community can do for us, to an external focus, asking what we can do to build a better community. In terms of long-term organizational relevance and sustainability, our organizations must move toward addressing what matters in our communities. In this day and age, with so many pressing global concerns around the world and near home, we cannot hide behind mission, using it as an excuse for nonengagement—this is an arrogant and elitist posture that will not serve museums well in the future. Museums often think they know what matters to communities, what they care about. This is usually very far from the truth! We need to listen and pay attention to what we hear. We need to ask our communities for help. We need to learn about the issues that people grapple with in their everyday lives. We need to work with many other individuals and organizations in our communities to address what matters to them and respond when people need help, regardless of our missions. We need to get involved in the lives of our communities, however we define community. When challenges come to our communities and people organize to respond and help, many of our organizations are never even considered as part of the solution—we're not at the table or even on the radar screens of the problem solvers. We need to change that perception.

For many colleagues and institutions, this shift is scary and difficult. This topic was never discussed as many of us were trained for our museum careers (thankfully, many more museum studies programs are now offering courses about museums and communities and integrating principles of community engagement into the entire curriculum).[10] If you perused the programs of recent professional conferences, you would see increasing numbers of sessions about community engagement. However, in many cases, it is audience development rather than community engagement that is discussed. Both processes are important, but they are not the same thing. The transformation of a museum toward community engagement and social entrepreneurship also challenges traditional professional standards, roles, and practices. Since it is difficult to predict exactly where an organization will end up once this transformation process is under way, for some colleagues and risk-averse organizations this uncertainty is very disconcerting. It requires a leap of faith.

However, once embraced, and the journey begun with openness and sincerity (no hidden agendas), these new directions and roles can be exciting, rewarding, and even liberating, because they move our organizations closer to a path of broad community support.

To begin the journey toward community engagement and social entrepreneurship, focus first on building better communities—this is the conversation starter, the reason why people will agree to gather with us, and many others. If we take this approach, I promise that the conversation will come around to your organizational needs. But we cannot start with our own museum needs—this just closes doors. I've seen this situation directly many times. The process has to first be about community; we need to pay it forward. The bottom line is that communities take care of the things that matter to them, in good times and bad. If our organizations don't matter, then what is our future?

MOVING FROM AUDIENCE DEVELOPMENT TO COMMUNITY ENGAGEMENT TO SOCIAL ENTREPRENEURSHIP

To understand where your organization is on this journey toward social entrepreneurship, it is useful to clarify some terms and then articulate some steps to guide the organizational development process. First we must understand what community engagement is and is not. Then it is critical to comprehend the difference between audience development and community engagement—there is a lot of confusion about and misuse of these terms in the museum field. Both are valid processes, but when community engagement is used to describe audience development, a museum's efforts can seem token and patronizing.[11]

There are many ways to define "community," including shared interests and experience, common affiliations, demographics, and the geographic location of your organization. While it is fine to build networks of stakeholders, including members, volunteers, reenactors, and past participants in your organization's programs, I am defining community as the people who live in the geographic location of your museum. Depending on the scope of your organization's mission, this geographic community could be local, regional, state, provincial, or national. For our purposes, it is more useful to think in terms of geography than in terms of stakeholders and affiliations. This geographic definition of community is important because the place where your organization does business is your foundation—your organization is a member of this community, regardless of how active it has been in civic affairs, and the people who live in your community are your organization's constituents. Your geographic community provides resources for your organization, such as supplies, equipment, marketing, knowledge, and expertise. As your organization becomes a more active contributor to community life, these resources grow. Also, every geographic community has a distinguishing character and spirit that emerges over time from its people and history. This means that community engagement and service are different in every community, and each organization must forge its own way. Yet another way to think about community engagement is pushing beyond your organization's existing stakeholders and friends.

Community engagement *is* identifying and addressing what people care about and doing things that really matter, for example, activities focused on building better communities (see Table 19.1). It is identifying and establishing long-term relationships and partnerships with other community groups and going beyond the traditional alliances with other cultural or educational organizations. The focus of the engagement must first be on the whole community. This is part of the process of building trust, learning about enduring needs and issues, and seeking new connections through discovering shared visions, often with the most unlikely groups and community organizations. The focus can and will come back to your organization, and it will be much more productive if you begin with the larger focus of building a better community. Let me offer a definition of *engagement*:

> *Engagement* means more than consulting (as by traditional audience research methods). It means ongoing involvement in planning, governance, making decisions, resource acquisition/allocation, and program delivery. It is a long-term strategy, not a short-term fix.

Community engagement, if done correctly, will fundamentally transform the business we are in as well as the way that our organizations do business. It changes everything. For many museums, this is now a lifeline to survival. It is also the right thing to do.

It is also important to understand what community engagement is *not*. It is not occasional stakeholder-input meetings, an annual visitor survey, or token

Table 19.1

Community Engagement Is	*Community Engagement Is Not*
Identifying and addressing what the community cares about	Identifying what the community can do for your organization
Doing things that really matter (e.g., activities focused on building better communities)	Token exhibits and programs about or with community groups
Establishing long-term relationships and partnerships with other community groups	Occasional stakeholder input meetings or an annual visitor survey
Working with community groups to plan and offer your programs and activities and sharing the control, acknowledgment, and proceeds	Continuing to control and run your programs and activities, yet expecting other community organization to participate and donate
Getting involved in community activities outside your organization	Expecting reciprocity for contributions to the community outside your organization

exhibits and programs about or with community groups. In fact, sometimes this approach is worse than doing nothing as it raises expectations of meaningful involvement without the follow-through. Community engagement is also not about identifying what the community can do for your organization. This second point may sound counterintuitive, but if the community perceives that the engagement process is solely about your organization, there will be people who decline to participate because they do not feel that they have any connection with or expertise about your organization. Also, they may tell you what they think you want to hear instead of offering creative ideas and solutions that address shared, broader challenges.[12]

Remember that your organization can define the scope of the community that you serve, but once you've done that, then you have a responsibility to serve that community—all of it, not just select parts. We do this in different ways, and it may be a building or layering process, but it must be inclusive rather than exclusive. After working in and with museums for a number of decades, I often bemoan that arrogance runs rampant in our field, and it has not helped us connect to and serve our communities at the level of making a meaningful difference. It is why so many museums are struggling to become relevant and demonstrate the value they provide to their communities. Community engagement, as I define it in this chapter, can change that situation and help museums and communities to heal and move forward.

How does community engagement differ from audience development? It is critical to understand the differences between these processes. It is true that audience development is a legitimate and useful process in itself and may lead to community engagement. But please understand that they are different processes in terms of scale and scope. Please don't confuse the terms. In Table 19.2 I offer a comparison of audience development and community engagement.[13]

Table 19.2

Audience Development	*Community Engagement*
Short-term marketing strategy to increase the number of people who visit your organization: builds and broadens your audience, which can turn into support for your organization.	Long-term organizational development strategy to build community ownership, participation, relationships, and support for your organization: builds a better community, which in turn builds your audience and position of importance in the community.
Looks at who is and who is not coming and why or why not; identifies potential audiences for marketing existing museum services.	Looks at what matters to the community and how your organization is or is not responding; identifies how existing museum services are relevant or could become more relevant.
Focus on increasing visitation numbers from existing and new groups and building membership numbers; the relationship with community remains the same as it is currently.	Focus on developing relationships and increasing partnerships and collaborations with a variety of community groups, benefiting all participating partners.
Internally focused approach: how can the community serve us and our needs (this approach potentially closes doors as it does not address what other organizations need—it is all about your organization).	Externally focused approach: how can we serve the community's needs, working with others (this approach opens doors as it is a shared goal with other community organizations—it is about what we all need).
Involves education, marketing, and development staff members.	Involves all stakeholders, including staff, trustees, and volunteers.
A consultant can complete the bulk of the work, working on your behalf, conducting interviews in the community and facilitating focus groups and then summarizing salient points (a consultant goes to the community and reports back to you).	A consultant can facilitate and guide the initial conversations and summarize the collective input from community participants, but your staff needs to be actively involved to make it work (a consultant helps to bring the community to you for collective dialogue).
Organizational identity, goals, and priorities remain essentially the same, as does the organization's current reputation, public service, value, and standing in the community.	Organizational identity, goals, and priorities could be fundamentally transformed in response to community input and ideas, substantially increasing reputation, public service, value, and standing in the community.
A more conservative approach, with more predictable and focused outcomes and, if completed thoughtfully, impacting a limited portion of the organization.	A riskier approach, but if completed with sincerity and honesty, outcomes can far exceed initial expectations, impact all aspects of the operation, and last longer.

Social entrepreneurship, or social innovation, is a growing worldwide movement in which individuals, foundations, organizations from all sectors (business, public, and nonprofit), and the academy act as change agents. With bold social missions, social entrepreneurs are creating systemic sustainable improvements in society. Duke University professor J. Gregory Dees, in a 2001 article, "The Meaning of Social Entrepreneurship," articulates that social entrepreneurs act as change agents by

- Adopting a mission to create and sustain social value (not just private value)
- Recognizing and relentlessly pursuing new opportunities to serve that mission
- Engaging in a process of continuous innovation, adaptation, and learning
- Acting boldly without being limited by resources currently in hand
- Exhibiting heightened accountability to the constituencies served and for the outcomes created

When most museum colleagues consider these actions of social entrepreneurs, they do not envision museums as examples. But why not? When folklife museums, open-air museums, and historic sites engage their communities, discover what people care about (now and always), and transform their visions, programs, and services to address what matters, they are moving toward becoming social entrepreneurs. As new roles in the community emerge, ranging from facilitating dialog about important civic issues[14] to collaborating with other organizations to provide needed services, our organizations become change agents for building better communities.

These actions echo the broad paradigm shifts that I described at the beginning of this chapter about our mandate for meaningful public service, embracing interpretation, programs, and community engagement as everyone's business, and becoming learning organizations. So, while many museums initially consider it a big leap to move toward social entrepreneurship, it is happening, with rewarding results, as enlightened leaders realize that they must be more proactive in response to increasing societal needs. In engaging communities and moving toward social activist roles, most folklife museums, open-air museums, and historic sites will undergo major organizational change and transformation.[15]

A FEW INSPIRING EXAMPLES OF MUSEUMS BEGINNING THIS JOURNEY

Let me mention a few organizations that have begun their engagement journeys. I hope that you will find a story that is similar to an organization that you know and, more importantly, find inspiration to begin or deepen your own organization's work as an agent for social change.

The Ulster Folk and Transport Museum, in Belfast, Northern Ireland, began to bring Catholic and Protestant children together in the late 1970s to learn about their common Irish heritage. By that point, there was already an entire generation that had been raised in different neighborhoods and schools due to the ongoing social conflict.[16] In this very divided society, educators from the Ulster Folk and Transport Museum joined with their peers at the Ulster-American Folk Park and the Ulster Museum to develop cross-community programs that promoted better community relations. By the mid-1990s there were dozens of integrated schools and an emerging political stability after the Belfast Agreement of 1998; yet the challenge remained as to how to tell the multiperspective history of conflict while helping people to heal and move forward. The Ulster Folk and Transport Museum created an Educational Residence Centre in the center of the open-air museum that opened in the early 1990s to accommodate cross-community groups for weekend living history immersion visits. The Ulster-American Folk Park also created residential experiences, and the Ulster Museum mounted a series of exhibits offering multiple perspectives, collected oral histories, and created a Science Discovery Bus to engage thousands of children in both Catholic and Protestant areas of the inner city that were affected by "the Troubles." These activities are inspiring examples of museums working as agents of social change, regeneration, and reconciliation.[17]

The Australian Museum helped to foster reconciliation between Aboriginal people and descendants of European settlers as they reached out to Indigenous people and created communities of practice throughout the country. Museum staff worked with Indigenous communities to tell their stories, interpret collections, and develop exhibits at the national museum, as well as at numerous community museums, known as Keeping Places and Cultural Centres. The community museums were developed by Indigenous people and exhibited repatriated artifacts, creating pride and self-esteem along with programs and employment. Museum policies were revamped to include Indigenous staff members (including Dawn Casey, who was director from 1999 to 2003), incorporate Indigenous history, voices, and material culture into education and exhibits, and develop a robust repatriation program. This has been a many-decades-long journey, and all of these actions worked toward healing the injustices of the past and building a more positive attitude toward and recognition of the Indigenous population as a part of the community.[18]

The District Six Museum in Cape Town, South Africa, was created in response to the forced relocation of neighborhoods of people under the policies of apartheid. The museum, housed in a Methodist church building, features, on the floor, a large map of District Six before it was leveled. As former "District Sixers" identify their former homes, businesses, and other places of interest on the map, the museum is helping them reconstruct their past, tell their stories, and understand their new identities. As this former heterogeneous community contributes to the museum's exhibits and programs, the museum uses the mapping of memories to engage and heal, reclaim their history, and build community for the future.[19]

The Museum of Malawi worked with local community leaders to offer mobile museum programs that address malaria prevention, HIV/AIDS prevention, and support for cultural expression in schools through songs, dance, and theater presented in the appropriate indigenous language and honoring community traditions.[20]

The Lower East Side Tenement Museum in Lower Manhattan, New York City, is well known for its efforts to go beyond the traditional operations of a historic site. Visionary founder Ruth Abram has written about the museum's engagement journey in a number of articles, documenting its efforts to directly respond to the events of 9/11, as the World Trade Center towers fell down near it, and then develop programs that taught about diversity and tolerance. The museum reached out to its neighbors and got involved in addressing their needs through offering English as a second language classes at the museum and developing an immigrant resource guide. It is using its history to create dialog, address contemporary issues, and affect social change. By founding the International Coalition of Sites of Conscience, Abram created a worldwide "network of museums, historic sites, and memory initiatives connecting past struggles to today's movements for human rights and social justice." Now with more than two hundred members, the coalition is advocating, creating programs, training in facilitated dialog, and connecting sites within and across regions to collectively address new threats to democracy and human rights as they arise.[21]

The Santa Cruz Museum of Art and History in California, led by Nina Simon, has embarked on a journey that began with a focus on visitor participation in exhibits and programs. As many museums do, it has learned about the transition from audience development to community engagement by doing it, listening to and learning from the community along the way, creating a multigenerational advisory community group, and partnering with community organizations. The museum's journey is well documented in Simon's blog, *Museum 2.0*, and a thesis by staff member Stacie Marie Garcia in 2012.

At a larger level, in the United Kingdom, the Museums Association (MA) embraced an inspiring vision for the increased social impact of museums, titled *Museums Change Lives*, with the goal to "enthuse people in museums to increase their impact, encourage funders to support museums becoming more relevant to their audiences and communities, and show organisations the potential partnerships they could have with museums, to change people's lives."[22] The MA articulated a series of key principles for this bold initiative:

- Every museum is different, but all can find ways of maximizing their social impact.
- Everyone has the right to meaningful participation in the life and work of museums.
- Audiences are creators as well as consumers of knowledge; their insights and expertise enrich and transform the museum experience for others.
- Active public participation changes museums for the better.
- Museums foster questioning, debate, and critical thinking.
- Good museums offer excellent experiences that meet public needs.
- Effective museums engage with contemporary issues.
- Social justice is at the heart of the impact of museums.
- Museums are not neutral spaces.
- Museums are rooted in places and contribute to local distinctiveness.

The Museums Association believes that every museum, regardless of size or focus, should commit to increasing its social impact through "improving health and wellbeing, helping to create better places, and championing a fairer and more just society." The Liverpool Museum has been a leader in this engagement and social justice movement, modeling the principles in its exhibits, programs, staffing, and policies. Museums throughout the United Kingdom are beginning this journey, working with health and social service agencies and reaching out to and offering exhibits and programs that share the voices of underserved audiences.[23]

Once a museum decides to embark on an engagement journey, it can start wherever it is as an organization. Although community can mean many things, it is powerful to look to your immediate neighbors, start a conversation, and find ways to work together. A wonderful example of this process can be found at Dallas Heritage Village (DHV), which engaged a neighbor school that served homeless children. As Melissa Prycer, DHV president and executive director, reported,

> In March 2014, Vogel Alcove moved into the new renovated City Park Elementary located directly across the street from Dallas Heritage Village. Vogel Alcove is a fellow non-profit who provides childcare for homeless children 6 weeks to 5 years old. As soon as DHV heard their plans, they immediately reached out to the staff of Vogel Alcove. At that first meeting, DHV said, "Please consider our museum an extension of your classrooms." Since that time, DHV and Vogel Alcove have partnered in countless ways: we share parking. They've used some of our excess mulch. We're in each other's disaster plans. The kids decorate one of the trees for Candlelight, DHV's major event. DHV staff volunteer regularly at Vogel. Most importantly, the kids have become some of the Village's most active users. Twice a month, there are curriculum-focused field trip experiences at the Village. But some classes walk across the street almost daily to enjoy a walk through the shady grounds or a visit with the resident donkeys, Nip and Tuck. Some of these partnerships are a result of our shared mission of serving children, but some of this is simply a part of being a good neighbor. In October 2015, Vogel Alcove created a new award for their annual fundraiser, Ambassadors of Hope. They presented the Community Partner Award to Dallas Heritage Village.

In a chapter titled "New Roles for Small Museums," I've written about five other museum engagement journeys.[24] There are other important compilations of case studies of which readers should be aware, including Richard Sandell's *Museums, Society, Inequality* (2002), Bob Janes and Gerald Conaty's *Looking Reality in the Eye: Museums and Social Responsibility* (2005), and

FIGURE 19.1
The children of Vogel Alcove enjoy the Miller Playhouse at Dallas Heritage Village. (Photo: Courtesy Dallas Heritage Village.)

Sheila Watson's *Museums and Their Communities* (2007). And there are many other important engagement journeys that I didn't describe, due to space, but that should be explored. Places like the Brooklyn Museum, Oakland Museum of California, Wing Luke Museum, Liberty Science Center, Missouri Historical Society, Museums of Kenya, and The Strong come immediately to mind.[25] Thankfully, the literature is rapidly expanding as museums and historic sites around the globe share their engagement stories and lessons.

Let me reflect briefly on these inspiring case studies. By focusing on what matters to people, these organizations have developed synergy and shared visions with other community organizations, resulting in innovative, collaborative programs and initiatives. There were some similarities in the challenges faced by these organizations. They all required courage to begin their journeys and perseverance to keep going, even when faced with obstacles. They took risks and usually challenged their (sometimes long-held) assumptions about museums. They were all better off for beginning an engagement process, sometimes dramatically so, and sometimes in very unexpected ways. In every case, the community responded without reservation and often in a manner that far exceeded their wildest hopes. When some of the organizations encountered resistance from internal stakeholders (I've never seen resistance come from the community), the community created momentum (sometimes pressure) for change. These journeys required courage to begin and faith to keep going. They are all inspirational in their own way, and I hope they will take us to a deeper level of understanding of and appreciation for the power of community engagement and moving toward social entrepreneurship.

CLOSING THOUGHTS

In this chapter I have argued why and how folklife museums, open-air museums, and historic sites can and should transform to address what matters in their communities and become more relevant and sustainable organizations. Within the context of some broad paradigm shifts that are occurring in the field, the challenge remains for museums to address what communities deeply care about. One could argue that folklife museums have a unique opportunity to undergo this type of transformation because they can draw on their existing community connections to deepen their relationships, find new friends, and use the input from the community to articulate an inspiring vision and shape a more meaningful future of public service. However, this will only occur if museum leadership is willing to let go of old-school museum models, honestly listen to community ideas, discover what really matters to people, and realign their programs and services in response. Most likely, the progression will be from audience development to community engagement and then to facilitating social change. It will require courage, faith, and integrity to initiate and nurture the journey. To move toward relevance and sustainability, the most enterprising folklife museums, open-air museums, and historic sites will transform their organizational identities, priorities, and community roles toward becoming social entrepreneurs.

NOTES

1. The seven history museums in the dissertation study were

- Henry Ford Museum & Greenfield Village (now The Henry Ford), Dearborn, Michigan
- Detroit Historical Museum, Detroit, Michigan
- Minnesota Historical Society, St. Paul, Minnesota
- Missouri Historical Society, St. Louis, Missouri
- The Strong Museum (now the Strong National Museum of Play), Rochester, New York

- Historical Society of Washington, DC (now the City Museum of Washington, DC)
- National Museum of American History, Smithsonian Institution, Washington, DC.

2. Rand 2001.

3. I have included longer descriptions of these best practices for interpretation and public programs in teaching notebooks, presentations, and strategic interpretation and program plans developed for numerous clients over the last two decades, sometimes under the title "Guiding Principles."

4. Skramstad 1999.

5. Weil 2002.

6. Carbone 2003.

7. Colleagues across the United States and Canada who have attended the many keynote presentations, workshops, and courses that I have given over the last two decades will recognize these paradigm shifts and forces for change. They continue to hold saliency for me as key organizing concepts, as they have withstood the test of time, and I've received a lot of confirming feedback from participants.

8. As with the best practices, I have included longer descriptions of the criteria for innovative programs in teaching notebooks, presentations, and strategic interpretation and program plans developed for numerous clients over the last two decades.

9. For more information on whom in the community to engage and guidelines for beginning this journey, see Matelic 2011, 141–62.

10. In 2012, I developed and taught a graduate course, "Social Engagement," for the University of Victoria, and a graduate course, "Museums and Community Engagement," for the Johns Hopkins Museums Studies Program. I teach these courses annually. Also, I teach the "Museums and Communities" component of the Association of Nova Scotia Museums museum certificate (offered every third year) and taught the overview component of the Alberta Museums Association 2013 community initiative.

11. Hirzy 2002.

12. There is widespread misunderstanding in the museum field about what constitutes community engagement. Most of what I learned about this process came from the many communities that I've worked with, and community members usually don't mince words when expressing their frustration about the arrogant stance that many museums still take about engagement. It is a humbling experience,

but a critical step, to listen to communities articulate their own issues and needs, rather than to assume that we know what they need. On the other hand, we should feel comfortable asking the community for help—I've never seen a community refuse, if there is no ulterior motive or hidden agenda.

13. Matelic 2009. As with the concerns articulated in note 7, there is widespread confusion about these processes. When this material is covered in teaching and presentations, it is often an "aha" moment for participants. So, I hope that this comparison will help colleagues to clarify the differences and use the appropriate terms when describing the processes. I'm happy that this chart already has some use in the field—please credit accordingly!

14. I call readers' attention to a number of very useful resources listed at the end of this chapter, in particular Sam Carbone's inspiring article on becoming a dialogic place, Elaine Gurian's brilliant writings on museums as congregant spaces and safe places for unsafe ideas, and Margaret Kadoyama's thoughtful piece on the hard work of listening.

15. For colleagues who are ready to learn more about organizational change and transformation in museums, see Matelic 2008, which I wrote about some key understandings. This piece will appear in an expanded version in an upcoming (2016) AASLH book, *Making History in the* 21st *Century*, edited by Bob Beatty. I do teach regularly about this subject and about transformational leadership at museum conferences and gatherings—please contact me for more information.

16. Visiting there in 1977 and learning from then director George Thompson about the primacy of their educational mission was a defining experience early in my career.

17. Crooke 2007; Speers, Montgomery, and Browne 1994.

18. Kelly and Gordon 2002; Casey 2007.

19. McEachern 2007.

20. Baker 2011.

21. Abram 2002. To learn more about the coalition's inspiring work, visit its website (www.sitesofconscience.org).

22. Museums Association 2013.

23. It is important to recognize that the Liverpool Museum was a centerpiece of a six-week MOOC on the twenty-first-century museum offered in spring 2015 by the

University of Leicester. The course covered aspects of the Museum Association's "Museums Change Lives" initiative. David Fleming, Liverpool Museum's director, also spoke about their journey at the 2014 annual meeting of the American Alliance of Museums, in a talk titled "Museums and Social Justice."

24. Matelic 2011.

25. Please forgive me if I did not mention an important example of a museum embarking on a transformative engagement journey. My oversight in no way diminishes the important work that so many museums are now doing to move toward social entrepreneurship. After decades of pushing for this direction for museums, all of a sudden, it feels like we are experiencing a tipping point (hurrah!). I was focusing on folklife museums, open-air museums, and historic sites, but I know that I've only scratched the surface in those arenas, let alone captured the important transformations that are happening in art and science museums. Please feel free to contact me to tell me about what your organization is doing and/or refer me to articles written about your journey so that I do not overlook your important contribution in future writing. I am particularly interested in organizations that are openly and actively pursuing a path toward social entrepreneurship.

REFERENCES AND RESOURCES FOR FURTHER REFLECTION AND ACTION

Abram, Ruth J. 2002. "Harnessing the Power of History." In *Museums, Society, Inequality*, edited by Richard Sandell, 125–41. London: Routledge.

Abungu, George H. O. 2001. "Museums: Arenas for Dialogue or Confrontation." *ICOM News* 54, no. 3: 15–18, http://archives.icom.museum/pdf/E_news2001/p15_2001-3.pdf.

Baker, K. 2011. "Embracing Community Development: A Case Study of the Museums of Malawi." *International Journal of the Inclusive Museum* 3, no. 4.

Black, Graham. 2012. "From Engaging Communities to Civil Engagement." In *Transforming Museums in the Twenty-First Century*, 202–39. London: Routledge.

Bergeron, Anne, and Beth Tuttle. 2013. "Magnetism and the Art of Engagement." In *Magnetic: The Art and Science of Engagement*, 21–33. Washington DC: AAM Press.

Born, Paul. 2006. "Community Collaboration: A New Conversation." *Journal of Museum Education* 31, no. 1 (Spring): 7–14.

Carbone, Sam. 2003. "The Dialogic Museum." *Muse* 31, no. 1 (Winter): 36–39.

Casey, Dawn. 2007. "Museums as Agents for Social and Political Change." In *Museums and Their Communities*, edited by Sheila E. R. Watson, 292–99. London: Routledge.

Center for Advances in Public Engagement. 2008. "Public Engagement: A Primer from Public Agenda." Center for Advances in Public Engagement. http://www.publicagenda.org/files/public_engagement_primer.pdf.

Crooke, Elizabeth. 2007. "Museums, Communities, and the Politics of Heritage in Northern Ireland." In *Museums and Their Communities*, edited by Sheila E. R. Watson, 300–312. London: Routledge.

Dees, J. Gregory. 2001. "The Meaning of Social Entrepreneurship." Stanford Center for Social Innovation. http://csi.gsb.stanford.edu/sites/csi.gsb.stanford.edu/files/TheMeaningofsocialEntrepreneurship.pdf.

Garcia, S. M. 2012. "Community and Civic Engagement in Museum Programs: A Community-Driven Program Design for the Santa Cruz Museum of Art & History." Thesis, Gothenburg University, http://www.academia.edu/1776769/MastersThesisStaceyMarieGarcia.

Gurian, Elaine Heumann. 2006. *Civilizing the Museum: The Collected Writings of Elaine Heumann Gurian*. New York: Routledge.

Hirzy, Ellen. 2002. "Mastering Civic Engagement: A Report from the American Association of Museums." In *Mastering Civic Engagement: A Challenge to Museums*, edited by M & C, 9–20. Washington DC: American Association of Museums.

Janes, Robert R., and Gerald T. Conaty, eds. 2005. *Looking Reality in the Eye: Museums and Social Responsibility*. Calgary, AB: University of Calgary Press.

Kadoyama, Margaret. 2007. "The Hard Work of True Listening." In *Civic Discourse: Let's Talk, Museums and Social Issues*, edited by Judy Koke and Marjorie Schwarzer, 201–6. Walnut Creek, CA: Left Coast Press.

Kelly, Lynda, and Phil Gordon. 2002. "Developing a Community of Practice: Museums and Reconciliation in Australia." In *Museums, Society, Inequality*, edited by Richard Sandell, 153–74. London: Routledge.

Koster, Emlyn H., and Stephen H. Baumann. 2005. "Liberty Science Center in the United States: A Mission Focused on External Relevance." In *Looking Reality in the Eye: Museums and Social Responsibility*, edited by Robert R. Janes and Gerald T. Conaty, 85–111. Calgary, AB: University of Calgary Press.

Kretzmann, John P., John L. McKnight, Sarah Dobrowolski, and Deborah Puntenney. 2005. "Discovering Community Power: A Guide to Mobilizing Local Assets and Your Organization's Capacity." Asset-Based Community Development Institute, School of Education and Social Policy, Northwestern University. http://www.northwestern.edu/ipr/abcd.html.

Matelic, Candace Tangorra. 2008. "Understanding Change and Transformation in History Organizations." *History News* 63, no. 2: 7–13.

———. 2011. "New Roles for Small Museums." In *Reaching and Responding to the Audience*, ed. Cinnamon Catlin-Legutko and Stacy Klingler, 141–62. Small Museum Toolkit 4. Nashville: AASLH.

McEachern, Charmaine. 2007. "Mapping the Memories: Politics, Place and Identity in the District Six Museum, Cape Town." In *Museums and Their Communities*, edited by Sheila E. R. Watson, 457–78. London: Routledge.

Museums Association. 2013. *Museums Change Lives*. Museums Association. http://www.museumsassociation.org/download?id=1001738.

O'Neill, Brian. 2014. "21 Partnership Success Factors." *History News* (Autumn): 17–21.

Prycer, Melissa. 2015. E-mail exchange about the partnership between Dallas Heritage Village and Vogel Alcove, November.

Rand, Judy. 2001. "The 227-Mile Museum." *Curator* 44, no. 1.

Scott, Carol. 2002. "Measuring Social Value." In *Museums, Society, Inequality*, edited by Richard Sandell, 41–55. London: Routledge.

Silverman, Lois H. 2010. *The Social Work of Museums*. London: Routledge.

Skramstad, Harold K. 1999. "An Agenda for American Museums in the Twenty-First Century." *Daedalus* (Summer): 109–28.

Speers, Sheela, Sally Montgomery, and Diedre Brown. 1994. "Toward Reconciliation: A Role for Museums in a Divided Society." *Journal of Museum Education* 19, no. 1 (Winter): 10–13.

Tamarack: An Institute for Community Engagement. http://tamarackcommunity.ca.

The Learning Coalition. 2009. *Building Responsive Museums: A Discussion Framework*. Ontario Museums Association. https://members.museumsontario.ca/sites/default/files/members/buildingresponsivemuseumspolicyandplanning.pdf.

Watson, Sheila. 2007. "Museums and Their Communities." In *Museums and Their Communities*, edited by Sheila E. R. Watson, 1–23. London: Routledge.

Weil, Stephen E. 2002. "New Words, Familiar Music: The Museum as Social Enterprise." In *Making Museums Matter*, 75–80. Washington, DC: Smithsonian Institution Press.

———. 2002. "Transformed from a Cemetery of Bric-a-Brac." In *Making Museums Matter*, 81–90. Washington, DC: Smithsonian Institution Press.

Wing Luke Museum. N.d. "Community Process Model." Wing Luke Museum of the Asian Pacific American Experience. http://www.wingluke.org/process.htm.

Worts, Douglas. 2006. "Measuring Museum Meaning." *Journal of Museum Education* 31, no. 1 (Spring): 41–48, http://worldviewsconsulting.org/uploads/3/1/1/2/3112423/measuring_museum_meaning.pdf.

Zamora, Herlinda. 2007. "Identity and Community: A Look at Four Latino Museums." In *Museums and Their Communities*, edited by Sheila E. R. Watson, 324–29. London: Routledge.

20

Serious Fun

A "Strong" Model for Play and Folklore in Children's Museums

SUSAN ASBURY

Susan Asbury focuses on play as a folklore concept and explores both its historical and its contemporary uses within museums, specifically children's museums. Asbury devotes particular attention to the utilization of play as a teaching methodology, and she turns her attention to The Strong in Rochester, New York, as a case study of methods that children's museums and other cultural institutions could employ to incorporate play as both a learning tool and a lens onto cultural manifestations. The Strong, while not a children's museum, offers an excellent example of the opportunities and challenges of integrating the theme and practice of play into museums' collections, exhibitions, publications, and programming. Children's museums, Asbury contends, are uniquely positioned to utilize play as a historical and folkloristic tool to interpret childhood. Asbury draws on her research as an American studies scholar who focuses on the material culture of play, as well as on her previous work at institutions within the museum field, including a tenure at The Strong.

In the summer of 2014, my family and I visited Plimoth Plantation in Massachusetts. This living history center is famous for its first-person interpretation in which costumed staff interact with guests as though everyone is living in the seventeenth century. The interpreters never break character, and guests can navigate from house to house, street to street, witnessing Plimoth's "citizens" perform a variety of daily tasks. My sons, ages four and nine at the time, struggled with how to communicate with staff members portraying the year 1627. Neither of my children had the cognitive ability to envision what life was like nearly four centuries ago. About one-quarter of the way into the tour, during a walk down one of the streets, a costumed interpreter approached my sons and asked if they knew how to play marbles. Both nodded in agreement. The interpreter then proceeded to remove several marbles from a sack he was carrying and engage them in a game. While playing, he talked with them about some rules with which they were unfamiliar and answered their questions about the types of marbles he was using. All the while, the boys reflected on how those rules compared with their own. My sons enjoyed the marbles game, and they seemed surprised to encounter a museum interpreter who would participate in play with them while they were on a tour of a historical site. Clearly they did not expect to meet someone who would talk with them about childhood at the museum, not to mention play a game with them. This encounter and their reaction forced me to think about how children approach history museums. Generally speaking, they envision them as places to be serious and learn, not play.

Fast-forward three months, to October 2014, when my sons and I were on another museum tour. This time, we visited The Strong in Rochester, New York, a museum dedicated to the study of play as a window onto the past and as a tool that promotes creativity, learning, and discovery. While in a shopping exhibit sponsored by the Rochester-based Wegmans grocery store chain, my sons assumed several role-playing opportunities as shoppers, checkout clerks, and restockers. They spent the majority of their time, however, in the café area of the grocery store—preparing meals, serving tasty dishes, and busing tables. This activity involved not only them but also my husband and me. They assigned us to the role of customers, and we were expected to order, eat our dishes, and provide rave reviews about the food and service. In this scenario, play occurred spontaneously and organically, including both parents. While the interaction with interpreters regarding play and childhood at Plimoth Plantation seemed surprising, play in a children's exhibit did not. But why? Both at Plimoth and at The Strong, play was similar and steeped

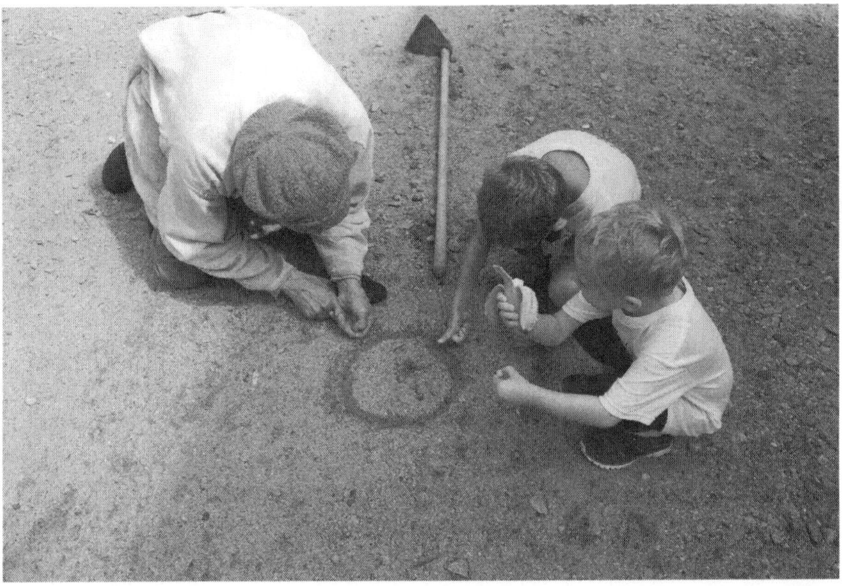

FIGURE 20.1
While learning about seventeenth-century colonial life, the author's sons enjoyed the experience of playing a game of marbles with a costumed interpreter at Plimoth Plantation. (Photo: Susan Asbury.)

in folklore. The marbles game was a play-based interactive with concepts and physical objects that for centuries have stayed essentially the same. My sons' playful experience in the "Wegmans Super Kids Market" exhibit at The Strong exemplified play as a frame of performative behavior encompassing cultural values related to consumerism, foodways, and family rituals. Was the difference between how play occurred at each of these places because one encounter occurred in a museum deemed more serious in topic and scope and the second in an exhibit designed for children?

In typical history and living history museums, the visitor is expected to approach the topic or theme in a more solemn manner than the ways in which one navigates an experience at a children's museum. Over the past few decades, while some "traditional" museums have incorporated hands-on projects for children, the contemporary children's museum primarily frames the visitor's experience around activities that allow for engagement with artifacts and other interpretive concepts through experiential lessons and play. Since the inception of the children's museums movement, these institutions have been utilizing play in innovative ways—from teaching science in a more tactile fashion to underscoring past traditions of previous generations or exploring current traditions related to childhood culture. The Strong, in particular, recently arose as an institution that provides meaningful discussions of its interpretive topics through play. While this institution does not position itself as a children's museum, its focus on play as an overarching theme for analysis of childhood traditions, lifelong hobbies, and the intersections of history and popular culture has applicability to the field. The Strong's method of incorporating play—as a way not only to understand the past of adults and children but also to explore folkloric patterns, traditions, and cultural nuances—underscores the importance of play in human life and development. Beyond providing an instructive case study, The Strong's work also reveals that analysis of play has both limits in a museum setting as well as potential to influence how museums can use a thematic interpretive concept that combines both interactivity and object-focused learning for a broad audience. Although The Strong has created an interpretive niche around the topic of play, museum administrators, curators, and educators could nevertheless expand the use of play in exhibits, programming, and artifact acquisitions in ways that lend credence to their own missions. Because play is viewed as a folk practice and portal for culture, folklorists and other play studies scholars can assist with the interpretation of play in children's museums and other types of cultural institutions.

PLAY AS A FOLKLORE CONCEPT AND A SCHOLARLY INQUIRY

Defining play is a difficult task. One knows it when one sees it, but its meaning is difficult to articulate. As historian Jean-Paul Dyson notes, "Play escapes tight definition and eludes attempts to nail it down."[1] Play is complex and multifaceted, incorporating both individual and group activities, but many observers will agree it is about doing something engaging that delights us. Play is also defined by what it is not: work. Oftentimes play has been viewed as a phenomenon relegated to childhood, emphasizing the belief that once that developmental stage ends, play then ceases and work begins. Initial scholarly inquiries into play reflected this point of view. In 1693, John Locke highlighted the importance of play, arguing that children learn more readily when subjects are introduced in an engaging way and not "imposed on them as a task."[2] Since Locke advocated the training of both mind and character, he posited that children's lessons should "take the form of play," emphasizing the association of study with pleasure.[3] Locke connected play with education, but he did so with a utilitarian purpose in mind. His theories influenced parenting for generations and shaped the development of the American educational system. Both parents and teachers coupled interactivity with practical knowledge and skills to mold children into productive adults, fostering a temporal use for play deemed acceptable only in the youngest stages of life.

Nineteenth-century scholarship related to play, such as the works of William Wells Newell and Lady Alice Bertha Gomme, focused on collecting and categorizing children's sayings and games under the auspices that civilization was progressing and that yesteryear's waning leisure activities—games once played by adults—had been relegated to children. They wanted to capture childhood recollections in order to preserve them. Writing from a Darwinist perspective, Newell argued that American children were the "rustic" vestiges through which these traditions, myths, and songs were kept alive via play.[4] Gomme extended Newell's work, collecting similar items in Britain. Newell and Gomme launched the study of children's folklore, where many of the inquiries exploring play are rooted.

Twentieth-century folklorists, such as Peter and Iona Opie and Brian Sutton-Smith, continued the tradition of collecting children's folklore, but for different purposes. Sutton-Smith and the Opies believed modernization was not diminishing childhood play and folklore but rather intensifying it. In *Children's Games in Street and Playground*, Iona and Peter Opie argue, "The true game, as Locke recognized years ago, is one that arises from the players themselves."[5] They examine the appeal of outdoor games, noting that game types in which children engage evolve over the course of childhood. Furthermore, they agree with Newell's observation that children were the conservators of these games and playful stories. Yet, the Opies, as well as Sutton-Smith, believe that children also creatively modify existing games to reflect their own personal circumstances. The altered nuances are then transferred to other children along with the remaining original texts.

Other scholars expanded the field of play studies and children's folklore by investigating the transmission, power structures, and complexities of play. Today children's folklore contextualizes a variety of play genres—jokes, riddles, games, sports, legends, tales, taunts, pranks, and rituals—under the process of play. Scholars examine adherence to rules, spaces (e.g., indoor or outdoor), institutions (e.g., Boy Scouts or summer camps), and the material culture of the lore and the play that formed the activity. Their research emphasizes play as, rather than a onetime game, a process that reflects social and cultural values and maps changes to these viewpoints over time. Scholars of play studies also examine the reconfigurations of historically specific rules for certain forms of play—something children may do in order to have the particular activity meet the needs of those participating (e.g., altering the rules of an impromptu baseball game when one does not have the required number of players).[6] The work of these folklorists influenced scholars studying play from the perspectives of anthropology, psychology, education, material culture, history, and sociology and has shifted the focus from play as a window into child development to play as a reflection on human condition and strategy.

As play studies emerged as a field, scholars grappled with research that underscores what Brian Sutton-Smith described as the "temporal as well as spatial diversity" of play. As a subject, play can incorporate multiple meanings depending on the designers of the activity, the participants, and the dynamics associated with the specific type of play.[7] More important, however, Sutton-Smith's analysis has moved play beyond its association with childhood. He argues that while important to childhood, play does not end when adulthood emerges. In *The Ambiguity of Play* (1997), Sutton-Smith explores seven "rhetorics" of play—progress, fate, power, identity, imaginary, self, and frivolity—and the context of each rhetoric in order to highlight scholars' multidisciplinary approach to the subject. Throughout his work several themes emerge: (1) play is by definition broad and includes active and passive participant forms; (2) play has its own language and communications that vary within the performative frame; (3) that play provides a clear evolutionary link as progress is challenging to prove since not all play is educational and future oriented; and (4) the author finds difficulty in applying both adults' and children's play to each of the rhetorics examined, furthering Sutton-Smith's argument that play exists across the life span.[8] Sutton-Smith argues that play is adaptable and ever-changing to meet the needs of society and participants. He describes how his own view on play evolved, ultimately drawing on a sociobiological theory, and compares play to evolution, thereby making play adaptability one of the most important cognitive functions for human beings. Along with Sutton-Smith, most contemporary play scholars agree that, aside from its direct health benefits, play allows individuals to navigate change, anxiety, and sociocultural constraints. Play is also a way to connect with the past, present, and future in a realistic or fanciful way.

Recent psychologists, sociologists, and educators have promoted play that fosters development, socialization, and creativity. Education professor Joe L. Frost, for example, warns of the long-term consequences facing society because of the decline of free play and recess during childhood. Exploring the decline of free play because of changing political viewpoints on education, decreased recess time, and parental intrusion into children's daily routines, Frost has called for placing more emphasis on play in natural and built environments to promote innovative thinking among children and to combat social ills such as obesity.[9] Psychologist Peter Gray correlates a decrease in free play with an increase in psychopathology, particularly anxiety, depression, and suicide among children and teens.[10] Other scholars, such as Carroll Pursell, explore new forms of play, specifically the interactions between play and technology. In *From Playgrounds to PlayStation* (2015), Pursell reviews the use of objects in play, noting that toys have always been part of play technology, have been historically gendered, and have been increasingly devoted to learning and development. While Pursell devotes particular attention to recent technology, he also argues that all play objects (even those associated with adult hobbies) emerged because of changes in play as an activity as well as a social construct.[11] Play scholars have clearly moved beyond the accumulation of material objects to meaningful interpretations of play as it relates to multiple life stages. Folklorists, in particular, have challenged the notion that play is something that ceases once a person moves beyond childhood, and they analyze the ways in which folklore collections and performances reveal cultural beliefs in fanciful ways.

THE CHILDREN'S MUSEUM MOVEMENT AND PLAY

If scholarship about play places value on it as a necessity for human existence, why have many of the institutional manifestations around play connected it primarily to childhood? As changing perceptions regarding childhood as a distinct period of life development evolved, so too did the notion of play as an activity of children. While adults have long recognized developmental variances between infants, children, and themselves, the discernments associated with these differences have developed over time. Society's contemporary view of childhood is largely a nineteenth-century construct. Prior to the nineteenth century, views on children placed more emphasis on their roles within a family's economy. When time did allow for recreational activities, children and adults enjoyed them together, particularly in rural, agrarian locales where work and leisure commingled within the family structure. In the nineteenth century, as industrialization gained a prominent foothold in the US economy, urban growth and industrial development separated families, particularly males, who left homes in order work in factories, largely removing work life from the domestic sphere. While nineteenth-century market and industrial revolutions further delineated work and play, eighteenth-century Enlightenment philosophies, such as Locke's viewpoint that children were not born evil but could be shaped by their environment, softened perspectives toward children, recognizing childhood as a distinct phase within the life cycle. Nineteenth-century educational initiatives, such as the public school movement and Friedrich Froebel's kindergarten movement, lent credence to play as something children did as part of their development. Social reform movements, particularly the playground movement and advocacy for child-labor laws, further solidified the concept of play and children in an institutional setting. The concept of the children's museum was a natural result of the reasoning around play as a tool that facilitated children's growth.

Current children's museums have a number of interactive exhibits that emulate shopping experiences, nineteenth-century home life, classrooms, or modes of transportation. These institutions often also contain interactive theaters, dress-up areas, and exhibit elements designed just for toddlers. But when the first children's museum, the Brooklyn Children's Museum, opened in 1899 (as a separate building of the Brooklyn Institute of Arts and Science), the focus was to allow participants a hands-on learning experience that would enhance their understanding of science and the natural world. Anna Billings Gallup was the driving force behind the creation of an engaging learning space where children (mostly ages ten and older) could touch, examine, and otherwise interact with natural history artifacts as a way to supplement their textbook learning. While primarily object-based, her methodology soon expanded to include child-friendly discussions and lectures related to other topics such as the origins of Christmas celebrations and Thanksgiving traditions.[12] As her museum's programs expanded to include Americanization programs geared toward immigrants, the ideas she espoused influenced the development of other institutions. In 1913, the Boston Children's Museum opened with a science collection; in 1917, the Detroit Children's Museum opened as a partnership between the Detroit Museum of Art and the local school board. In 1926, the Indianapolis Children's Museum opened with a hodge-podge collection accumulated through donations from children and adults in the surrounding area. All of these institutions were established to engage children through collections of adult-made artifacts. Museum directors believed that allowing children to touch, see, and smell objects learned about in school would enhance their overall educational experience. Gallup's efforts also prompted some museums to create separate gallery spaces for children within their existing institutions. Samuel Pierpont Langley, Smithsonian secretary from 1887 to 1906, opened the first children's gallery at the Smithsonian. In 1941, the Metropolitan Museum of Art created the Junior Museum, designed to highlight its collection in ways that would be more inviting to children.[13] In 1943, the New York State Historical Association opened a separate children's museum on its grounds to provide a place for "visual education and recreational inspiration in the arts" for more rural, central New York families affected by World War II.[14] While the museum was described as a free-standing building, the location was two rooms in the association's Central Quarters building. The goal was to create an area within the museum to provide children hope that their war-impacted family life would one day be restored and to foster early learning in the museum with the hope of cultivating the audience into adult members.[15] Most of the museum's collection consisted of Native American relics, and programming connected these objects to the state's burgeoning social studies curriculum. Science centers and other museums, such as the Newark Museum, also began incorporating theatrical skits, art, and games around their holdings as ways to educate their younger audiences.[16]

As time progressed, however, children's museums moved away from a strict adherence to object-centered educational efforts to self-directed exploration through activity. The Boston Children's Museum claims the development of the first hands-on exhibit for children, "What's Inside," in the 1960s. This exhibit did more than just allow children to hold or draw an object. It illustrated to them how things worked. For example, children could see a toilet cut in half, fostering an understanding of plumbing.[17] By the 1970s, most children's museums began to focus on play exploration as a way to enhance learning in science, art, and history. In the last twenty years, many children's museums, such as the Boston Children's Museum, have openly examined play as a "vital activity that children use to learn about and interact with their world, and gain the mental, physical, and social skills necessary to succeed in adult lives."[18] Curators developed exhibits allowing audiences to look inside the body, pretend to live in the 1800s, work as a carpenter, make artful creations out of found objects, walk through a Japanese tea house, learn how to tell stories through dress-up play, and perform music using indigenous instruments.

The Association of Children's Museums was established in 1962. As of today, there are over five hundred children's museums in the world, over half of which are in the United States.[19] Sixty-five percent are located in urban areas; thirty-five percent of them opened as part of downtown revitalization projects.[20] While their mission statements vary, most all of them espouse the importance of fostering learning through play, broadly defined. Although less object-focused (some have no artifact collection), they all utilize play to help audiences make sense of the world around them. Because many of these institutions serve urban areas with diverse audiences and populations, they also began to incorporate play from a folklore perspective. They utilize play, both intentionally and sometimes organically, to transmit folklore to foster an understanding of other cultures and traditions of the past.

At present, beyond activities used to teach mathematical or scientific principles, children's museums incorporate folklore in two main ways: by providing a hands-on education about the past or contemporary traditions and by recording and highlighting play as a framework for understanding childhood folklore and history. The most common reason these institutions have integrated play is to teach about the traditions of a particular culture, primarily one represented in their surrounding area or region. In 1979, the Boston Children's Museum acquired a Japanese house as a gift from Kyoto, Japan, and through audience participation, staff utilize the space to highlight Japanese life, ritual, art customs, and ceremonies. Another exhibit, "Boston Black: A City Connects," uses play as a way to delve into community folklife and offer an understanding of multiple ethnic perspectives. Children can imagine shopping along a street in a predominantly African American neighborhood and learn, through play, the importance of hair styles and traditions of African American women. They can also pretend to work in Cuban restaurants and participate in other ethnic traditions found in the local area. Play is utilized as a cultural broker and folklife teaching methodology about social and cultural differences through a common, joyful experience.[21]

The Brooklyn Children's Museum's "World Brooklyn" exhibit accomplishes a similar goal. Children explore, through play, the different ethnic traditions that can be found in the community.[22] The Indianapolis Children's Museum exhibit "Take Me There China" allows opportunities for children to play instruments and wear traditional Chinese ritual costumes. "Stories from Our Community" is another exhibit at the museum that looks at how storytelling "preserves our history, tradition, and ideas" and gives opportunities for children to connect with both the past and present community by evaluating artifacts and tales that inspired storyteller authors.[23] These institutions have developed ways to utilize play in an engaging manner, thus allowing children to connect and understand the rituals, games, and lives of members of nearby communities.

Play has also been incorporated in children's museums as a way to underscore the importance of childhood and its own folkloric patterns. Leading the charge in this initiative was the staff at Portland Children's Museum, which, in 1986, videoed play at three area playgrounds over the course of a summer in order to develop prototypes of games they could utilize in an upcoming exhibit. Inspired by the collecting work of William Wells Newell and the performative analyses of Iona and Peter Opie and Brian Sutton-Smith, museum curators and exhibit designers wanted to underscore the multiple meaning of playground games and the cultural nuances they revealed. The goal was to develop a playground exhibit that highlighted the social demographics of the playground, including gendered play, and create a space where multigenerational participation would occur among audience members. While collected games became part of their archive collection, the museum developed an exhibit in which people could learn the games and engage in play.[24] This exhibit was one of the first to depict play as a reflection of cultural inferences and exhibit the transference of folklore related to childhood games.

As these institutions underscore the importance of learning through play, they are increasingly categorized as for children only, creating an audience challenge for museum administrators. Some museum professionals also argue that these institutions are not "museums" in the true sense of the word because they focus less on interpreting objects and more on activity as an educational methodology. Former Boston Children's Museum exhibits director

Elaine Heumann Gurian once noted, "I do not like *museum* because we are more than a museum, and I do not like *children's* because we are not a museum for children only."[25] While some institutions such as the Please Touch Museum in Philadelphia have removed the phrase "children's museum," such challenges have led to questions about why play is relegated to an institution devoted to children at a time when there is a contemporary focus on the concept being used throughout an individual's lifetime. Play with a folk concept could be an activity incorporated in any museum as a means of connecting the past with the present for generations. One museum, The Strong, has begun this initiative and merits detailed analysis.

THE STRONG: A CASE STUDY FOR PLAY

While play is foregrounded as the learning methodology for most children's museums, The Strong has devoted its mission to play as an overarching interpretive theme that drives its collecting habits, exhibits, educational programs, and community outreach. Located in Rochester, New York, The Strong "explores play and the ways in which it encourages learning, creativity, and discovery and illuminates cultural history."[26] Since The Strong looks at play, broadly defined, from a variety of perspectives, it does not position itself as a children's museum but rather as a "highly interactive, collections-based museum devoted to the history and exploration of play."[27] The Strong serves families and a broader community, underscoring its existence in both the children's museum and the history museum camps. The museum interprets the world's largest collection of toys, games, dolls, video games, and research about play for its diverse audience of adults, children, scholars, teachers, and collectors. The Strong emphasizes play as a portal for understanding history, culture, social and psychological development, behavior, and creativity.

While elements related to play existed at the museum's founding, The Strong's focus on play as an interpretive frame has developed over time. In 1968 collector Margaret Woodbury Strong acquired a charter for a museum she coined a "Museum of Fascinations." The following year, Strong died, and the board of trustees charged with the care of her collections brought in museum professionals from around the country (Old Sturbridge Village, Smithsonian, Colonial Williamsburg, and others), all of whom noted the objects associated with playful themes but none of whom proposed a museum focused on this subject. In 1982, the museum opened to the public as an institution that focused on everyday life, particularly mass production from 1820 through 1940. One innovative collection initiative of the museum was open storage, with a considerable amount of space devoted to particular penchants of study that had piqued Margaret Woodbury Strong's interests—paperweights, windmills, miniature toy furniture, and especially dolls. The museum produced some particularly well-known exhibits that explored African American life, mourning rituals, and the Victorian parlor.[28]

In an effort to sustain and grow its audience in the 1990s, the museum dropped the 1940 end date and moved into more contemporary collecting. Before this change, however, The Strong designed a small, hands-on exhibit, "One History Place," in 1987. "One History Place" allowed children to explore parlor, kitchen, and transportation habits of the nineteenth-century middle class and pretend to live as people of that era. Additional market research in 1992 and 1994, respectively, revealed that 70 percent of the museum audience consisted of families with children twelve and under, even though there was no specific set of exhibits for them beyond "One History Place."[29]

Refashioning the museum's mission to include the present allowed the museum to develop exhibits that would appeal to the institution's audience. In 1997, the museum opened "Can You Tell Me How to Get to Sesame Street?," an exhibit designed in conjunction with Sesame Workshop. Visitors to this exhibit could explore Elmo's house, sit on the stoops of a mock Sesame Street set, pretend to be a street food vendor, and play hopscotch or checkers on an urban playground. Other exhibits, such as "When Barbie Dated G.I. Joe: American's Romance with Cold War Toys" (1994), "Small Wonders: A Fantastic Voyage into the Miniature World" (1995), and "Kid to Kid" (1996) all examined toy artifacts as reflections of contemporary culture. While the "Small Wonders" and "Barbie" exhibits, in particular, looked at the playthings from a more historic rather than folkloric perspective, these exhibits nonetheless represent an interpretive shift prior to The Strong's mission change.[30] Around this same time, museum administration began to reexamine the early documents related to the scholars who originally surveyed Margaret Strong's collection, recognizing that much of what she collected was about play. Further reflection led to a new scholarly emphasis on play as a way of fostering physical, intellectual, and social growth in all individuals, especially children.

Internally, staff began discussions on ways to best interpret The Strong's massive collection (over five hundred thousand objects) in ways that would both highlight the original intentions and artifacts belonging to Margaret Strong and attract a wide audience, including those families. Exploration of play was a natural fit. In 2003, the museum changed its mission to interpret play as a window to explore imagination, creativity, and discovery, as well as a way of examining the past and its connection to the present. The institution changed its name to Strong National Museum of Play (currently The Strong) and in 2006 opened a $37 million expansion that nearly doubled its square footage to 285,000 square feet. The Strong's staff positioned the museum as the only one in the world dedicated solely to understanding the importance of play. Seeing themselves as having a stake in both the history museum and the children's museum fields, the staff launched other initiatives that transformed the institution into an authority on the subject of play. When the museum expanded in 2006, it opened the Woodbury School, a Reggio Emilia–inspired preschool for three- and four-year-old children. Shortly after the museum's expansion, the organization renamed its library and archives the Brian Sutton-Smith Library and Archives of Play, after one of the preeminent play scholars of the twentieth century, and began expanding its already massive collection of play scholars' papers, toy advertisements, books, and related materials. In 2008 the museum launched the *American Journal of Play*, a scholarly journal dedicated to exploring the subject from a variety of interdisciplinary perspectives, and in 2009 staff launched the International Center for the History of Electronic Games (ICHEG), which focuses on collecting and interpreting electronic games. Regarding the former, the journal's advisory board includes play scholars from a variety of perspectives, including folklore. All of these entities within The Strong further solidified the institution's commitment to play studies.[31]

From a collections perspective, the museum continued to devote itself to acquisitions related to this topic. In 2002, ahead of the change in mission and focus, the museum purchased the National Toy Hall of Fame from the A. C. Gilbert Discovery Museum in Salem, Oregon (in 2015 this exhibit changed to the Toy Halls of Fame, since the exhibit features both toys and industry innovators as inductees). Over fifty toys are currently in the hall, with new ones named each fall. The museum receives nominations each year based on specific criteria—toys must have longevity, achieve iconic status, promote learning, creating, or discovery through play, and represent innovation in toy type or the method of play.[32] While the majority of inductees are mass-produced objects—Lionel trains, the Slinky, and *Star Wars* action figures, to name a few—others are rooted in folklore. The cardboard box (inducted 2005), the stick (inducted 2008), the ball (inducted 2009), the blanket (inducted 2011), and the puppet (inducted 2015) are objects that are not subject to mass commercial production or toys that include set rules and instructions to specify how participants play. Furthermore, even in the museum's interpretative discussions and presentations of other objects in the hall, such as the baby doll, Etch A Sketch, and Play-Doh, curators and exhibit designers emphasized that players, not adults or designers, guide much of the play related to these objects.[33] The inclusion of noncommercially produced and branded toys illustrates the institution's commitment to collect objects broadly related to the subject matter, rather than those that highlight only modern-day consumerism.

In addition to collecting hall of fame–worthy artifacts, the museum sought to expand its collection of historical and contemporary play objects. Margaret Woodbury Strong herself had accumulated thousands of dolls, doll accessories, and miniature toy objects (including doll houses), but museum staff wanted to develop targeted collecting areas that further highlighted the play-related artifacts and filled gaps where needed. The Strong received an Institute of Museum and Library Services grant that funded a multiyear exploration of the museum's collections (to recognize gaps) and brought in visiting scholars to learn how to better interpret play. Folklorists, historians, and education scholars from across the nation worked with curators to identify gaps and to develop goals for future acquisitions. The Strong's staff utilized the study to broaden the concepts related to its collection, including an expansion of noncommercialized objects associated with play across the lifespan. Staff developed collecting goals around hobbies, crafts, other non-mass-produced objects.

While original play-related artifacts largely represented mass-produced toys, the museum also acquired artifacts that analyzed play beyond consumer culture. The museum has a wide array of homemade, folk-related childhood play artifacts, including dolls, skateboards, scooters, amateur art projects, and miniature objects. In 2006, the museum received a donation from the Historical Society of Pennsylvania. This collection, which the historical society had received from the Balch Institute for Ethnic Studies, included over three hundred dolls, action figures, puppets, and other toys representing various culture groups. Many of the objects were homemade and in ethnic dress.[34] The museum also continues to acquire homemade objects from the nineteenth century to the present.

Aside from a focus on play as a collections component of its mission, what makes The Strong unique is how staff incorporates artifacts and interactives as a way both to highlight play as culture and to foster multigenerational conversations and create broad appeal around the subject. While folklorists are not permanent members of the museum's staff, the ways in which staff interpretively approach the subject and the exhibit components and programming they use definitely lend credence to a folkloristic viewpoint on play. A significant interpretive guide that mapped how the institution would, through exhibits, explore play in a cultural context was the museum's *A Framework for Interpreting Play* (2002). Scott Eberle, vice president for play studies, notes that the *Framework* argues that play can be explained through six main lenses (he refers to them as "elements"): play as anticipation, surprise, pleasure, understanding, strength, and poise. These elements are best highlighted in the "Field of Play" exhibit, which opened with the museum's expansion and renovation in 2006. "Field of Play" is a highly interactive, artifact-infused exhibit that explores how these elements of play relate to development, socialization, and individualism, all basic components of human culture. Visitors explore each element through playful interactions—navigating a ball through a large structure, exploring a slanted house, climbing a rock wall, competing with friends in a simulation drag race or a game of Dance Dance Revolution, tossing computer-generated bubbles or soccer balls, and walking through a kaleidoscope.[35] Visitors also encounter toys and other leisure-related artifacts that represent each element, further connecting the concept of play "texts" to the behavior and skills play enforces.

While many of The Strong's exhibits afford the same opportunities as other children's museums, such as mimicking shopping experiences, sailing a ship, flying a helicopter, or playing dress-up, other exhibit components utilize play as a way of understanding the activity itself and the groups it includes. For example, the "Time Lab" (1999) exhibit includes a section in which adults and children can record recollections about their favorite toys and games and how they played with them. "Play Pals" (2014) explores the history of toys but allows participants to learn about that history through play. Visitors (both adults and children) can explore the evolution of action figures, dolls, and plush toys and then engage with imagination stations allowing for pretend play, "superhero" reflex testing, and story creation. "Reading Adventureland" (2006), an exhibit that allows participants to step into stories representing five different components of children's literature, has a nonsense section with a machine that allows a person to tell either a well-known or made-up story, and then jumbles it up before repeating it in a "mash-up" fashion, thus allowing participants to explore wordplay in a folkloristic manner.

From a scholarly perspective, the institution also incorporates the use of folklore to better understand play participation. In the late 1980s, the institution began the Doll Oral History Project, which, although it records memories of doll play from a middle-class, white, adult-female perspective, has been an invaluable resource for scholars analyzing doll play in the early twentieth century. The museum also continues to engage in collecting present-day play folklore through the ICHEG initiative to video-record contemporary game play, as a way not only to capture historical data about particular games but also to better understand the structure and development of online communities associated with play.[36] Additionally, the museum partners with relevant organizations, such as the Association for the Study of Play, the New York Folklore Society, and the Eastern American Studies Association, and connects with leading free-play advocates, such as Joe L. Frost, to further highlight the mental, physical, and spiritual benefits of play. Museum staff also work with the Toy Industry Association, video game software companies, and collectors to explore the intersections between commercialism and play for both children and adults. Their connections with these individuals and organizations have advanced their archival collections and allowed them to host conferences and to develop publications and exhibits that interpret play as a lifelong phenomenon.

While The Strong portrays itself as an interactive museum looking at history through the cultural lens of play, public perception and audience demographics place it in a family-centered museum category. Since its expansion in 2006, The Strong has worked to broaden the age demographic of its audience by producing adult-oriented exhibits around themes related to board games, electronic games, and superheroes. In terms of programming, the museum offers a range of activities from toddler-specific ones each Tuesday to the annual "Play Ball" gala that raises funds for the museum and is geared primarily toward adults. The Rochester community has embraced the institution because of its inclusivity related to programs and initiatives for all community demographics and its focus on play. Thanks to The Strong's fellowship program, scholars utilize the space, the artifacts, and the archival materials to further research in the field of play studies. And museums from all over the world benchmark The Strong's design and programming initiatives.

What makes The Strong particularly innovative about its use of play is its institutional commitment to the study of the subject. Unlike museums that explore learning through engaging interactive exhibits on a variety of topics, all of The Strong's topics provide highly interactive exhibits that focus solely on play with the activity proving the play point. For example, in an exhibit titled "American Comic Book Heroes: The Battle for Good vs. Evil," the museum staff provide a historical interpretation on the role of comic books and their appeal while encouraging audience members to engage in activities that allow them to take on the characteristics of their favorite heroes. The exhibit inspires fantasy play and frames the type of play associated with these popular cultural influences. Other exhibits, such as "Time Lab," interpret play from the perspective of popular trends that made their way into toy designs, emphasizing the constructs of play and the intersections between popular culture and historical events as well as designer and manufacturer preferences. The artifacts in The Strong's video and board game exhibits encourage audience reflection on the ways in which toys that may seem distasteful today (e.g., board games that depict insensitive stereotypes of African Americans or Native Americans) can be better understood in the context of their times. The museum's approach to its subject matter provides opportunities to explain a toy in its historical context and discuss the objects' cultural relativism.

The Strong also highlights how history museums can combine interactive and teachable moments that underscore play as a lifelong process that exists beyond childhood. By creating engaging exhibits covering all ages, the museum emphasizes the role of play in everyone's lives and the way the activity under investigation can help people understand more about identity, power, and socialization. The Strong's broad-audience approach with play creates intergenerational conversations and interactions, which scholar Anna Beresin refers to as "deep sustained play," meaning learning and engagement between both adults and children. Beresin argues that children's museums can utilize play to create connections between young and old while underscoring play narratives associated with the past. The Strong's use of play as a lens onto culture facilitates this dialog.[37]

FIGURE 20.2
"Deep sustained play" can be found in exhibits where both adults and children play together. It can provide intergenerational transmission of ideas and traditions based on play. In The Strong's "Wegmans Super Kids Market" exhibit, children and adults can learn about family traditions and rituals around food and consumerism. (Photo: Simon J. Bronner.)

In addition to offering a site for deep sustained play among all audience members, The Strong is continuing to develop itself as an authority on the subject of play. Through its active collections acquisition program (which includes both three-dimensional and documentary artifacts), the museum is establishing itself as the research center for play. For example, the National Toy Hall of Fame selection committee includes leading psychologists, educators, and advocates for play. Its partnerships with the Association for the Study of Play, as well as its archival collection of play scholars, such as Joe L. Frost, Brian Sutton-Smith, Anthony Pellegrini, Doris Bergen, and Lella Gandini's early childhood and folklore collection, have also positioned the museum as an advocate emphasizing the importance of play across the lifespan.

Appealing to a wide audience through a variety of topics, collecting and interpreting in interactive ways, and becoming an authority on the subject matter also creates challenges. While play is the theme of the museum, the museum is not an open playground. The Strong still has galleries with physical boundaries, themes, and directional means of navigating the space. The challenge of an enclosed space creates a need to tell a finite story, when play has many aspects that do not fit within a confined area. In conjunction with the challenge associated with play in a gallery-type space, the connection to outdoor play proves to be a difficult task in a museum setting as well. The Strong does highlight outdoor activities as forms of play with both its Dancing Wings Butterfly Garden and outdoor Discovery Garden. Exploration of playground play, however, is not as evident in the interpretation. While the institution fills this gap with *American Journal of Play* articles and as a depository for some of the papers of Joe L. Frost, a leading advocate of recess, these materials are not typically used by the general museum audience.

The museum's audience of families with children also affects the degree to which deviant and dangerous play can be explored in The Strong's exhibits. The museum does delve into discussions about this play type, however, with articles in the *American Journal of Play*. For example, Jay Mechling's article "Gun Play" explores biological and cultural perspectives related to deviant play among boys. Utilizing Gregory Bateson's "Theory of Fantasy Play," Mechling argues that biological makeup and gun imagery expressed in frontier myths and popular culture lend credence to a fascination with toy guns and that gun play allows boys to explore issues related to power, pretend, and reality through the lens of socialization.[38] These ideas are difficult to explore in an exhibit space. While The Strong does mention certain controversial subjects related to play, particularly violence in electronic games and the dangers of some once popular games (e.g., Jarts), violent or dangerous play examples are not widely utilized.

Finally, the intersections between the material culture of play and the activity of play create an interpretational concern in a museum setting around the voice or authority that guides the storyline. How manufacturers or game designers want people to play with their products may differ greatly from how participants engage with these objects. Determining whose perspective will be heard then becomes an interpretive task that may lead to exclusion. The Strong acknowledges that interactions with objects vary in a variety of ways. For example, as noted earlier, the museum collects and interprets how homemade artifacts of play have been utilized by people from all over the world.

Children and adults can also leave messages about what playing with a certain toy means to them. The ICHEG's project of capturing video game play within the moment in order to understand online gaming structure and context allows for the voice of the play to lead in driving the interpretation. Yet, for the most part, the interpretive story is woven through a white, middle-class perspective on play, both for children and adults. The perspectives of younger children can be even more muted when developing an exhibit aimed at them. A challenge then becomes how to shed light on play, broadly defined by demographic factors and deviations from the original rules for engagement with the material culture of the activity. Despite such challenges, The Strong nonetheless sets a high bar with respect to how museums, particularly children's museums, can utilize folklore methodologies and other scholarly methods to move beyond play as learning interpretation to helping audiences understand what play reflects about society and culture.

FOLKLORE, PLAY, AND FUTURE IMPLICATIONS FOR CHILDREN'S MUSEUMS

Folklorists emphasize play as a repeated activity or practice shaped by traditions. Although most folklorists view play as an aspect of everyday life at all ages, they note the special enactments and contexts of play in childhood as an adaptive response to rapid physical, social, and cognitive changes. While The Strong could still do more to examine play through the lens of folklore, the museum has nevertheless adopted many folkloristic ideas of tradition and cultural context in its interpretation of play. The Strong's model has both practical and theoretical implications. From a practical standpoint, children's museums can utilize folkloristic methodologies and scholarship to inform the use of play behavior for enhanced learning. Ironically, children's museums are rarely about children; rather they are about how children negotiate space provided for them by adults. To be sure, children's museums, such as those in Boston and Indianapolis, have already featured play techniques to teach traditional rituals and to underscore cultural nuances of both past and contemporary cultures as lived by adults. I suggest, however, that these institutions can move beyond this interpretive method by utilizing play as a historical and folkloristic tool to interpret childhood. For example, rather than have children explore a streetscape in a culturally diverse neighborhood through play, children could also explore play through youth cultures that define that neighborhood. Recordings of street games developed by children, as well as other pretend play that takes place in a community, can further reveal how play is transmitted from children to children across generations. Adult connections to this type of play could also be facilitated by encouraging both parents and children to play with adult games, such as card games or horseshoes. Incorporating play across multiple generations in a diverse-neighborhood simulation emphasizes this lifelong playing concept while fostering learning about diverse cultural traditions related to community.

Another way children's museums could frame play in a larger context would be to provide a space that facilitates group activity. Many folklorists, such as Gary Alan Fine and Anna Beresin, have penned ethnographies on group function in play. The former studies small group culture and the creation of subcultures that arise from a play framework around competition. The latter looks for patterns associated with group socialization (in terms of numbers and gender composition) and cultural transmission associated with free play in the context of recess on school playgrounds.[39] In a museum setting, however, emphasizing points about group play is difficult as the primary interactives promote artistic expression or pretend play and often elicit solitary play, as children are attending a museum with an adult who may or may not feel invited to engage in the child's play. If children's museums provide an outdoor space or an indoor space that mimics a playground in order to explore more activity related to free play, then those museums could effectively highlight the importance of everyday games and free play among children. This is not to say that museums would replace school recess but that museums could utilize a simulated environment in the same fashion as an open-air museum by emphasizing the traditional and contemporary varieties of this genre of play. While children's museums would likely have to position staff within these areas to initiate or monitor such types of play, devoting space to said endeavors could further an understanding of playground dynamics, contemporary variations of playground games, and other social constructs of play.[40]

Folklorists can also assist all museums in the transition from a traditionally staid approach to a more playful one by including both adult and childhood perspectives on play in their interpretational narratives. Since many folklorists have collected play-related texts, these can be used as conversation starters about the types of jokes, legends, and word play used by children.

Such scripts can be contextually analyzed to provide examples of the varied meanings behind such sayings, incorporating how children utilize words and stories to navigate through various tensions or life circumstances. Activity centers within these spaces could also provide participants an opportunity to create expressions of their play that museums could then add to their collections. For example, visitors could be given the opportunity to record their own joke and explain where they learned it, why they find it funny, and what it means to them. Furthermore, folklorists could assist museums in capturing play traditions through ethnographic approaches that would allow audience members to collect and explore their own family, neighborhood, or school play traditions, thus empowering audience members to discover both personal meanings around the activity of play (such as why children engage in fantasy play) as well as broader meanings of play beyond games. Utilizing methodologies developed by folklorists can provide meaningful connections between the activity and objects used in play.

Aside from the aforementioned practical implications related to understanding play as folklore concept, The Strong has challenged the cognitive perceptions of play and moved the discussion beyond childhood, exploring some of the same themes emphasized by folklorists and other scholars who study the subject. When we look at play as a lifelong endeavor, two theoretical considerations arise: the effect on age-based institutions when play is portrayed as a "cradle-to-grave" concept and children's museums' ability to pitch full experiences of play in a museum setting.

The Strong has successfully been able to combine the object-driven focus of history museums with the interactivity of children's museums in a way that attracts a broad audience and creates a multigenerational dialog around play as a subject of inquiry. If other children's museums embrace folkloristic viewpoints that expand on this notion that play does not end with childhood—or if museums traditionally for adults integrate "commotion" in the form of incorporating youthful activities, rituals, and play "performance" behaviors into their current interpretation and gallery spaces—will the role of children's museums be undermined? As noted earlier, one reason that children's museums evolved was the belief that play only occurs in childhood. Children's museums arose, in part, because of an educational movement that emphasized learning about adult subjects through play and engagement with pretend scenarios and objects. Children's museums and age-based exhibits within traditional museums (e.g., children's galleries within the prescribed "adult galleries" of a museum) have perpetuated a division between children and grown-ups. In 1979, Peter Marzio underscored this concern at the Conference on Children in Museums by arguing, "When a children's museum seemed to be really working, it was also a great museum for adults; and if that were true, why couldn't a great adult museum be also very great for children. . . . [T]he thing I detested about the idea of children's zones and children's museums is that they could become simply another block being added to the elements that tend to split families apart rather than being a place where families could be kept together."[41] Marzio's comments highlight the difficulty of keeping play solely in a children's museum. Museums often form silos between the children and the adults bringing them. If children's museums adopt the folklore perspective that play continues beyond childhood, and if other types of museums more fully integrate children into their institutions, then the successful concepts of hands-on learning that have been celebrated by the children's museum movement may also undercut their purpose and function.

In addition to discerning whether or not play, broadly interpreted, may mitigate the need for separate museums for children, the use of play as the driving experience at a museum has an additional ramification. All museums, including children's museums, market the uniqueness of their institutions to their respective audiences. If children's museums incorporate play as a folkloristic concept into their interpretive frameworks, then those same museums must emphasize the distinctive educational quality of their play as something that children, and maybe adults, cannot find elsewhere. If most museums discuss how they bring history or concepts to life in ways not found in books or on television, how will museums do the same with play? From a play perspective, folklore scholars can bring their expertise to bear on the importance of play as an adaptive process, one that reflects cultural undercurrents among activities that appear delightful and fun as well as crude or dangerous. Museums will then have the opportunity to provide the interactivity and educational planning that allows for their audience members to have a "playful" experience that focuses on what the engagement reveals in the context of self-expression, socialization, and identity formation. Folklorists thus have an opportunity to play a role in the changing twentieth-century concepts of "folk" within museums from ideas that are attuned to an agrarian past to twenty-first-century notions that make museums vibrant and culturally conscious in new ways.

Play is not the only theme that can be conceptualized according to folkloristic ideas of cradle-to-grave practice orientations. Subjects such as the body, fantasy, language, and rituals relate to play as folklore concepts through which scholars have made connections to repeated actions within these subject areas based on traditions, yet have emphasized the adaptive functions of these themes as reflections of cultural changes. Although the particulars related to those subjects are beyond the scope of this study, children's museums, as well as other cultural institutions, could be poised to emphasize these concepts in engaging ways.

While challenges to the integration of folklore and play in children's museums related to spatial constraints, sensitive subject matter, and target audience exist, folklore theory can provide a framework that fosters a greater sense of the role of play across cultures, traditions, and life spans. Children's museums have the opportunity to lead the charge for expanding the views of a museum beyond the traditional temple perceptions (e.g., a place where one looks at important "stuff") to a forum-based approach that allows for multiple voices and understandings on play to be heard. Folklorists have much to offer the museum field and can help museum professionals continue to explore both planned and more organic ways in which to study play from an ethnographic perspective as well as as a method for teaching both about the past and other cultures. Specifically, they can help children's museum staff revolutionize their exhibitions and programming by embracing folklore as a way to approach learning and community engagement. Play creates a framework through which museums can widen their interpretive narratives and their audiences and, perhaps, as the opening scenario suggested, eventually provide more natural, and less surprising, interpretive streams in traditional museums and outdoor living history centers.

NOTES

1. James E. Johnson et al., *The Handbook of the Study of Play* (New York: Rowman & Littlefield, 2015), 42.

2. John Locke, *Some Thoughts Concerning Education*, ed. F. W. Garforth. Abr. ed. (Woodbury, NY: Barrons Educational Series, 1964), 164–66.

3. Ibid., 186.

4. Iona and Peter Opie, *Children's Games in Street and Playground* (Oxford: Clarendon Press, 1969), 1.

5. Ibid., 1.

6. For a lengthier discussion on the types of children's folklore studied as well as the history and future implications of this research, see Brian Sutton-Smith et al., eds., *Children's Folklore: A Source Book* (Logan: Utah State University Press, 1999) and Elizabeth Tucker's *Children's Folklore: A Handbook* (Westport, CT: Greenwood Press, 2008). Both works provide a thorough overview of the settings, activities, methodologies, and concerns related to studying children's folklore.

7. Brian Sutton-Smith, *The Ambiguity of Play* (Cambridge, MA: Harvard University Press, 1997), 6.

8. Ibid., 118–19.

9. Joe L. Frost, *A History of Children's Play and Play Environments: Toward a Contemporary Child-Saving Movement* (New York: Taylor and Francis, 2010), 1–7.

10. Peter Gray, "The Decline of Play and the Rise of Psychopathology in Children and Adolescents," *American Journal of Play* 3, no. 4 (Spring 2011): 457.

11. Carroll W. Pursell, *From Playgrounds to PlayStation: The Interaction of Technology and Play* (Baltimore: Johns Hopkins University Press, 2015), 162–65.

12. Edward P. Alexander, *The Museum in America: Innovators and Pioneers* (Walnut Creek, CA: AltaMira Press, 1997), 136.

13. Edward P. Alexander, *Museums in Motion: An Introduction to the History and Functions of Museums*, 2nd ed. (Walnut Creek, CA: AltaMira Press, 2008), 168–69.

14. Mary E. Cunningham, "The Children's Museum," *New York History* 24, no. 1 (January 1943): 68.

15. Ibid., 69.

16. Eleanor M. Moore, *Youth in Museums* (Philadelphia: University of Pennsylvania Press, 1941), 85; Cassandra Zervos, *Children's Museums: A Case Study of the Foundations of Model Institutions in the United States* (thesis, Pennsylvania State University, 1990), 94.

17. Alexander, *Museums in Motion*, 173.

18. "Power of Play," Boston Children's Museum, http://www.bostonchildrens museum.org/power-of-play.

19. Alexander, *Museums in Motion*, 167–68.

20. Association of Children's Museums (http://www.childrensmuseums.org/childrens-museums/about-childrens-museums, accessed October 18, 2015).

21. Boston Children's Museum (http://www.bostonchildrensmuseum.org, accessed October 11, 2015).

22. Brooklyn Children's Museum (http://www.brooklynkids.org, accessed October 25, 2015).

23. Children's Museum of Indianapolis (http://www.childrensmuseum.org, accessed October 25, 2015).

24. Peter G. Christenson, "Collecting and Interpreting Playground Games: A Children's Museum Project," *Children's Environments Quarterly* 4, no. 1 (Spring 1987): 51–53.

25. Elaine Heumann Gurian, "Adult Learning at Children's Museum of Boston," in *Museums, Adults and Humanities*, ed. Zipporah Collins (Washington, DC: American Association of Museums, 1981), 275, quoted in Alexander, *Museums in Motion*, 180.

26. "Mission," The Strong, http://www.museumofplay.org/about/mission.

27. Ibid.

28. G. Rollie Adams, "Ready, Set, Go! Finally a Museum of Play," *History News* 61, no. 3 (Spring 2006): 7–8.

29. Ibid., 8–9.

30. Scott G. Eberle, "How a Museum Discovered the Transforming Power of Play," *Journal of Museum Education* 33, no. 3 (Fall 2008): 269.

31. The Strong (http://www.museumofplay.org, accessed November 8, 2015).

32. "About the National Toy Hall of Fame," The Strong, http://www.museumofplay.org/press/fact-sheets/about-national-toy-hall-fame (accessed November 17, 2015).

33. The Strong (http://www.museumofplay.org, accessed November 2, 2015).

34. E-mail correspondence from the author to Patricia Hogan, curator, The Strong, November 11, 2015.

35. Eberle, "How a Museum Discovered the Transforming Power of Play," 271.

36. Ibid.

37. Anna Beresin, "Children's Museums of Children's Bodies," in *Children under Construction: Critical Essays on Play as Curriculum*, ed. Drew Chappell (New York: Peter Lang, 2010), 137, 144.

38. Jay Mechling, "Gun Play," *American Journal of Play* 1, no. 2 (Fall 2008): 192–209.

39. For further information regarding the transfer of preadolescent cultural nuances through a group setting of Little League baseball, see Gary Alan Fine, *With the Boys: Little League Baseball and Preadolescent Culture* (Chicago: University of Chicago Press, 1987). Anna Beresin examines recess play in two books: *Recess Battles: Playing, Fighting, and Story Telling* (Jackson: University of Mississippi Press, 2010) and *The Art of Play: Recess and the Practice of Invention* (Philadelphia: Temple University, 2014). Her work underscores that adult and childhood perceptions differ regarding free play and that children utilize this time for socialization, creative development, and cultural transmission.

40. A space devoted to continuing the research around free play and group dynamics would further the scholarship of Anna Beresin, Steve Zeitlin, Steve Roud, and Iona and Peter Opie.

41. *Proceedings of the Children in Museums International Symposium* (Washington, DC: Office of Museum Programs, Smithsonian Institution, 1979), 168, quoted in Alexander, *Museums in Motion*, 180.

21

Folk Arts in Education and Museums

LISA RATHJE AND PADDY BOWMAN

Museum educators and practitioners of folklore in education share methods, goals, and challenges. In this chapter, Lisa Rathje and Paddy Bowman examine the intersections of folklore and museum education. They note that practices and curricula that use the tools of folklore and ethnography to connect classrooms and communities with museums, as well as with museum objects or collections, provide a rich praxis for learning. Through the lens of folklore, they consider best practices for learning and engagement, including museum outreach. They offer a case study from the Vermilionville Living History Museum and Folklife Park in Lafayette, Louisiana, as one aspect of doing this work and explore how the core methodology of folklore—ethnography—may inform museum education.

Folk arts in education (FAIE) works in the crossroads of disciplines, partnerships, and innovative processes. Folklorists doing FAIE have become adept at using the content, skill sets, and creativity of folklore and ethnography to their fullest to inform their work with K–16 educators and students and navigate changes in education policy and practice imposed by national education standards, high-stakes testing, and reduced school budgets.[1] Museum education is a specific field that includes a wide variety of organized formal learning opportunities (docent-led student visits, curriculum guides, teacher training) as well as informal learning features for the casual visitor, from exhibit-based activities and techniques (hands-on, multimedia, accessibility) to programming (lectures, workshops, and other adult programs; family days; festivals; intergenerational programs; child-friendly guides; discovery carts) and other creative endeavors. In the 1960s, museum education began emerging as a distinct field situated within schools of education or museum studies programs. Many museum educators have also come from other fields, including folklore, and many folklorists have worked in museums in noneducation positions (curators, administrators, archivists) or in conjunction with museums to develop exhibits and programs. The practices and curricula that use the tools of folklore and ethnography to connect classrooms and communities with museums, as well as museum objects or collections, provide a rich praxis for learning.

A study of museum education through the lens of folklore includes a consideration of best practices for museum strategies for learning and engagement that connect meaningfully with communities, prepare students to visit museums, offer professional development for teachers, provide critical reflections on visual literacy and object-centered lessons, and develop lessons that explore curating exhibits in the classroom. This chapter looks at a case study from the Vermilionville Living History Museum and Folklife Park as one aspect of doing this work, as well explores how the core methodology of folklore—ethnography—may inform museum education.

AN ETHNOGRAPHIC APPROACH TO WORKING WITH LEARNERS IN A MUSEUM SETTING

Folklore and its sister fields of cultural anthropology, oral history, and cultural sustainability all rely upon ethnography as core to their practice and bring a theoretical framework that is well suited for discussions of exhibiting culture, the art of display, and ethical concerns of appropriation and representation. Beginning with a definition, ethnography, simply and literally, can be described as "writing culture."[2] Ethnographic methodologies quickly become more complex, creating an organized system for gathering documentation of living people and cultures in the field, as well as analytical frameworks for assessing and using these materials. The intersection of folklore and educa-

FIGURE 21.1
Many types of museums include items and images of clothing and adornment in their collections. Local Learning invited distinguished museum educators to create online learning modules in conjunction with our first volume of the *Journal of Folklore and Education* to expand on the theme "Dress to Express: Exploring Culture and Identity."[3] Because dress and adornment carry such deep, complex meaning, they present exciting opportunities for learning across disciplines and age groups. Using these modules, users may also call upon local museums and historical societies to help students encounter artifacts of dress and adornment firsthand.

tion with museum education is fluid and complementary. Best practices for both value critical literacy skills (including visual literacy), inquiry toolkits, and thinking strategies that make connections across disciplines. This section considers the ways in which ethnography can inform educational programming and praxis in the museum setting.

Although some of these points may seem obvious, the power of engaging ethnography as a skill set in museum education needs to be unpacked. We have identified four tenets of ethnography with potential significance for museum education. We begin with the foundation of ethnography, observation, and its signature tool, one's field notes. Recording the concrete details of what one sees when observing a space or group of visitors and then thoughtfully considering one's response to these notes and what they suggest creates a place for new insights to emerge.[4] Examining this first tenet further reveals that ethnography provides a mandate for better knowing visitors or audiences. Many museums are good at gathering demographic information about visitors, and a deeper knowledge may provide deeper benefits, especially in light of educational programming. Just as visitors come to a museum with assumptions, so do museum staff assume or take for granted what they "see" in their galleries or public spaces. Over time, details may come out from such close observation that reveal new characteristics of those engaging with the museum or exhibit.

Likewise, ethnography uses interviewing to learn more about the specific people of an identified group. Some questions that could potentially inform the protocol for this kind of study include:

> *What assumptions do visitors bring to their experience of an institution?* Do they hold certain beliefs about what can be exhibited? What does a "good" museum visit mean? Are there ways that museum exhibits are supposed to look or feel?
>
> *What places in the museum feel most comfortable? Which are most challenging?* And while this question could relate to physical structures or staffing-related concerns, we are just as interested in cultural and experiential responses. In other words, what can visitors most relate to in the institution? Are there exhibits/areas that they do not prefer? What informs these feelings? Do exhibits challenge what they know; political beliefs;

feelings about what they think should be on display or not; existing ideas about "authenticity," or, again, what makes a "real" or "good" collection?

Quickly these questions start to suggest one of the points that informs this work: all visitors bring their cultural conceptions of what makes a "good" museum experience, and a museum, in learning more about its visitors, can either work to meet these expectations or use museum education and outreach departments to engage more directly with these expectations and create a space for growth and learning.

The inquiry mind-set that many docents and museum educators bring to their work dovetails nicely with the interview protocol of ethnography. What an FAIE approach overlays with these strong tools is an appreciation of and sensitivity to culture. In what ways are responses to an exhibit or item in a collection informed by culture? Conversely, what is assumed about museum culture or an exhibit that a new visitor who is not acculturated would need aids for interpreting?

Additionally, many museums already use some tools of ethnography in evaluation protocols as they observe visitors—documenting their use of interactive exhibit stations or the time a visitor spends reading labels or other exhibit signage. Some museums may also have story booths as a part of their programming. While these may be for education, evaluation, or both, the collection of visitor stories directly related to the exhibits or their immediate experience at the museum is also directly related to the work of ethnography.

The second aspect of ethnography that we wish to unpack relates to critical ethnography frameworks that mandate that this work be dialogic at best, or at least take into account how authority asserts itself in both the delivery of educational content and the collection of information about a particular population. To understand the significance of this relative to museum education, we start with the assertion that the same troubling tenets of colonial perspectives that inform early ethnography, of course, may be on display in the museum. Museums are becoming more aware of the ways that traditional exhibition has upheld white privilege.[5] Likewise, academic writing on "re/presentation" has worked to trouble the colonial impulses inherent in the work (see Barbara Kirshenblatt-Gimblett, Maribel Alvarez, Nina Simon, and others).

The move toward reflexive and reciprocal ethnography as a part of a critical protocol of ethnography decenters the authority from the historically (mostly) white, academic, male author writing about cultures other than his own. Reflexive ethnography takes the researcher's positionality and subjectivity into account. Clearly this speaks not only to the realization that one's presence will change and influence the site of research but also to the fact that one's own cultural perspective will change and inform the initial observations, as well as the analysis of the ethnographic material gathered. Reciprocal ethnography grew out of the realization that reflexive ethnography did not yet address the need for a sincere dialogical commitment between researchers and those they interviewed. As Elaine Lawless writes, she sees reciprocal ethnography as an opportunity to take ethnographic studies into a "more multilayered, polyphonic dimension of dialog and exchange."[6] This emphasis on seeing fieldwork as more collaborative and the sharing of knowledge as more dialogic has created opportunities for new ways of learning and sharing in the field. It also signaled a new ethics of representational practice that decentered authority, resisting the impulse to find it solely residing with the "academic" voice in the field. The implications for museum education are myriad and include a need to create opportunities for dialog within the museum space and using educational programs to facilitate ways for knowledge to be collaborative rather than one-directional.

The third aspect that we unpack regards how ethnography asks us to be mindful of the value of materials and knowledge collected from the visitor or audience. The field researcher carefully documents the field experience, often using audio, videos, and photos that not only advance their own research goals but are also suitable for archiving. Ethnographers see their work as potentially having importance to later generations and find ways to ensure that the voices and images of the community they document are not only properly represented but properly saved and, accordingly, properly valued by people who do not culturally or otherwise identify with the documented group.

The narratives and knowledge of the community defined as "local" to the museum and/or the visitors whom an institution is trying to serve better are important. While some museums have found ways to implement robust community-centered programs (see, for example, the Wing Luke Museum of the Asian Pacific American Experience under the leadership of Ron Chew, as described in his address to the British Columbia Museums Association Conference[7]), all museums may consider the ways that valuing visitor narratives can enhance the museum experience. Rather than experiencing the museum as a passive consumer, in this model the visitor would also be a producer of meaning and content within the space of the institution.

The fourth tenet of ethnography that we acknowledge here is that this methodology provides a cultural lens through which the museum educator may better understand the institution and its outreach. When the educator sees an educational opportunity both as content delivery and as an initiative that may reach across and between potentially diverse cultural perspectives, a new, rich arena for developing appropriate and meaningful educational platforms arrives. This final tenet actually encompasses all three above but reminds the reader that the information gathered through an ethnographic process is also cultural. To read and analyze the data through a cultural lens means that larger master narratives that may inform our analysis must be examined. It also reminds us that the institution of the museum itself is a culture. Too often "culture" is relegated to narrow conversations about ethnic diversity. To see the work of museum education as engaging with and between different cultural perspectives provides additional sensitivity that may enhance the programming.

Significantly, all four characteristics of ethnography that we have "unpacked" can directly apply to the design of museum education curricula and practice. We briefly outline below what this may mean relative to each characteristic. Designing an educational experience that asks the visitor to become an ethnographer employs

1. *Observation and interviews:* Asking visitors to take note of the concrete facts that they can observe and then asking them to respond to these facts creates a space for learning. It also encourages visitors to begin to look at the context for an artifact or collection, ask questions about the assumptions they may have brought to the experience, and help monitor what other questions they may have.
2. *Dialogic communication:* Creating a space where the visitor can actively construct meaning about an artifact or display allows for a cocreation of knowledge that brings diverse viewpoints and ways of knowing into a museum. This may prove particularly helpful when creating museum education programs that touch upon controversial topics or issues that may touch upon sensitive or political issues.
3. *Local knowledge:* Using interviews or other narrative devices, visitors can feel empowered to call upon and share their knowledge and history, know-

ing they can contribute a valuable aspect of the larger story invited by the museum exhibit.

4. *Cultural awareness:* Helping museum visitors see that they, too, have culture begins to wear down the tired dichotomy that suggests museums are for displaying the cultural artifacts and heritage of an "other" or the "elite" class. Educational programs that encourage self-discovery of a visitor's culture create an opportunity for greater reflexive understanding of what is represented through the artifacts in a gallery.

LOCAL LEARNING @ VERMILIONVILLE: A FOLKLORE AND MUSEUM EDUCATION CASE STUDY

In spring 2012 the Vermilionville Living History Museum and Folklife Park in Lafayette, Louisiana, began planning a Folklife Education Initiative, led by the Vermilionville Living History Museum Foundation Board. Based upon the track record of success that the Acadiana Center for the Arts (AcA) and Lafayette Parish School System (LPSS) had experienced with bringing folk arts into arts-integrated projects with Local Learning: The National Network for Folk Arts in Education, the Vermilionville Foundation invited Local Learning director Paddy Bowman to discuss directions that Vermilionville might take to deepen educational offerings and student connections; develop partnerships, especially with local schools; and invigorate artisans' engagement.

Thousands of students from across Louisiana visit Vermilionville annually. The foundation wanted to create strategies and resources to prepare teachers and students for these field trips so that students would get more than an excursion, teachers would connect the visit to the curriculum, and students would relate folklife to their lives and communities—not only to the historical past. Another goal was to increase overall attendance and develop a relationship with local educators. Four years later, Vermilionville points to successes that include standards-based online lesson plans, ongoing partnerships, a dynamic summer camp, annual professional development institutes, a full-time education coordinator, and National Endowment for the Arts funding. This case study outlines the project and how a folklorist influenced process and products.

Vermilionville opened in 1990 with a mission to preserve and represent the Acadian, Creole, and Native American cultures in the Attakapas region from 1765 to 1890. It is the cultural division of the Lafayette Parish Bayou

Vermilion District, established in 1984 to beautify, conserve, and manage sites on the Vermilion, ensuring preservation and enhancement of natural and cultural resources. More than fifty thousand people from around the world visit each year. The twenty-three-acre site includes a village of historic traditional homes and buildings, a restaurant serving Cajun and Creole food, a gift shop, and a busy performance center where frequent events such as music jams, concerts, dances, films, and lectures highlight regional and Francophone culture. Many artisans who work at Vermilionville learned their crafts at an early age from family and community members. Skills include spinning, weaving, instrument making, net making, Cajun and Creole music, blacksmithing, healing arts, needlework, rosary making, and wood carving.

Despite this concentration of traditional artisans and the involvement of folklorists, ethnomusicologists, and historians in creating the organization and serving on the board, education programming mostly involved scheduling school field trips. When the staff and the foundation board decided to expand and deepen education outreach, Local Learning joined the planning committee. Our expertise included professional development training for teachers and artists, curriculum writing, knowledge of national trends and issues in public education, and our partnership with the AcA and LPSS through the three-year Local Learning @ Lafayette model project that had just concluded. We began by inventorying assets: Vermilionville's historic village, artisans, performance center, and lively schedule of folklife events, plus the environmental education potential of Bayou Vermilion. A new education coordinator invited two University of Louisiana (UL) College of Education faculty members to use Vermilionville as a laboratory for students to create lesson plans relating to the village and regional culture and addressing state education standards. Local Learning worked with selected artisans to write artist statements to introduce them to teachers and students and hone their public presentation skills. Thus began the Vermilionville Folklife Education Initiative.

Enthusiastic about the success of these first steps in bringing folklife education practices to bear on education and outreach, the initiative expanded to adapt the Local Learning @ Lafayette model, which pairs a folk artist, a teaching artist, and a teacher for residencies that inspire folklife-infused arts-integration projects. Participating classes' field trips to Vermilionville rounded out the model. This model was appealing to the museum because it provided a point of entry for its artisans to be in local classrooms and make their arts relevant in a contemporary context, not just a historical one, and brought students to the museum. It appealed to teachers who could gain tools for connecting students' personal and family traditions to a larger regional story and core curriculum. Now field trips to Vermilionville were more meaningful, and students, as well as teachers, saw opportunities to connect the museum campus to their own learning.[8]

Project teachers are paid for institute participation, quarterly workshops, and planning time outside the school day. They work in public and private elementary, middle, and high schools in Lafayette and Iberia parishes. Subject areas include English language arts, social studies, French, visual art, chemistry, and math. Several French Immersion teachers participate. Folk artists are paid for two classroom visits, one to introduce their art form and another for student interviews. Teaching artists observe the folk artist residencies to document what students are most interested in, which informs the art projects that they plan with the teachers to incorporate a core curriculum topic and student interviews with family members about folklife topics. Teaching artists work with students during six class periods and are paid for class visits, planning time, and curating an exhibition for the annual citywide student arts expo that serves as a culminating project.

Local Learning provides ongoing support, pointing teachers to lesson plans, interview guides, and other resources and helping the Vermilionville education coordinator plan and conduct quarterly workshops to share new strategies and address teams' progress. Support has also been cultivated locally through the schools, a regional folklife center, and UL education students' lesson plans.[9] Project teachers and teaching artists use resources introduced in institutes and workshops, such as Louisiana Voices[10] and documentaries featuring South Louisiana on Folkstreams.net. They receive a thumb drive loaded with publications such as *The Teacher's Guide to Local Culture* and *The Kids' Guide to Local Culture*[11] and excerpts from *Fieldworking: Reading and Writing Research*,[12] worksheets and rubrics for folklife topics, and observation and documentation tools to prepare students to visit Vermilionville.

How has the involvement of a folklorist specializing in FAIE influenced the Vermilionville Folklife Education Initiative and this museum? Veteran project teachers say that it is not the funding that inspires them to stay involved; it is the folklife content and what students learn through the interview process and interaction with folk artists and family members. They note that this project better prepares students for field trips to Vermilionville, where students are asked to observe closely; document artifacts, buildings, and artisans; and interview artisans. Teachers also report that teaching and using the interview process has exciting benefits. Students listen more closely, craft thoughtful questions, and discover commonalities with those they interview—artisans and family members—as well as one another. For example, when asked why he was so intrigued by his interview with an artisan of the Avogel tribe at Vermilionville, a student replied that he had only read of American Indian history in books. Learning in person, "It was the truth, not history book truth." About interviewing, another student said, "I think there is something very special about being able to walk into a room with a stranger and by the time you leave, having them trust you enough to tell you their life story, where they came from, and how they ended up where they are. And I think that's something that an older generation appreciates a lot more than we do because we don't get it on a daily basis. We have social media, and we have everything immediately, constantly. We very rarely take time to sit with one person."[13]

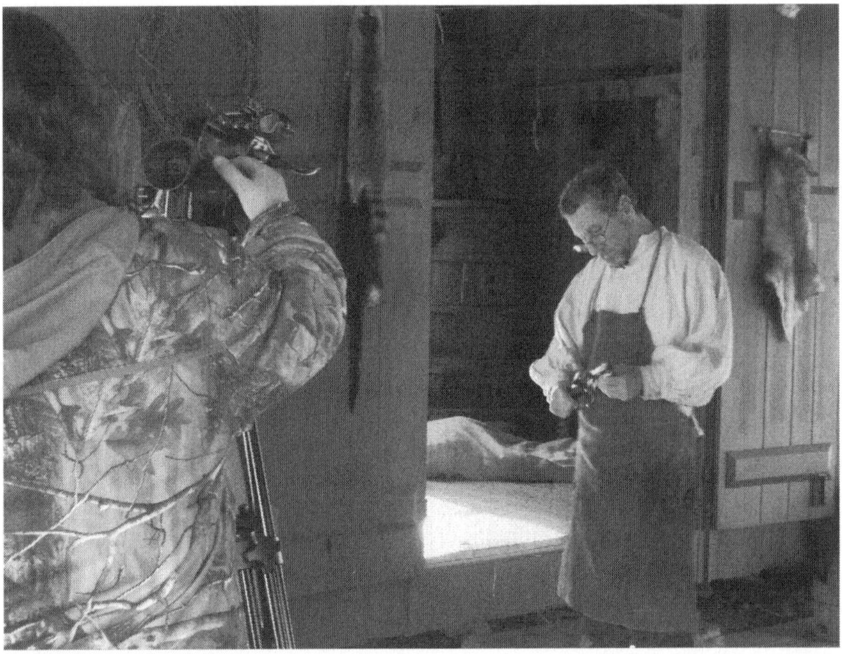

FIGURE 21.2
Lafayette High School students produced a documentary on Vermilionville artisans during year three of the Local Learning @ Vermilionville project. (Photo: Melanie Harrington.)

Teachers are also excited about uncovering contemporary folklife, their own and their students' traditions and are more cognizant that connecting classroom and curriculum to the local and students' lives engages them meaningfully. For example, one student said, "Being in French Immersion, I remember when I was younger coming on field trips almost every year [to Vermilionville]. Being able to revisit and reevaluate it now that I am older, now I appreciate the culture." Learning from a Cajun accordionist at Vermilionville that he was forbidden to speak French in school, a student expressed newfound appreciation. "French Immersion is cool . . . trying to correct the wrongs of back then. We are helping to preserve the culture." Finally, a high school student realized, "Through my work with this project, I think I know more French than I thought I did. I interacted as a social being. . . . [T]his encouraged me to minor in French."[14] At Local Learning, we believe that relating folklife to teachers' and students' lives and personal traditions has made the biggest difference for the Vermilionville Folklife Education Initiative. Artisans are now viewed not in terms of long-ago traditions; how they learned and how they are sharing their skill takes precedence. Emphasis on the question "Where is this kind of tradition or skill in your life?" means that family members' and students' personal traditions are uncovered and seen in the context of regional culture and history. In addition to lessons about naming traditions, family folklore, games and play, and interviewing, students' culminating art projects have incorporated the whole experience: folk artist interview, family interview, museum field trip, a curricular connection, and visual art. Several projects used natural materials that students gathered at Vermilionville. They made dyes from plants and sculptures from fallen branches and bamboo. A high school history residency with a Creole musician was tied to studying Supreme Court cases related to racial segregation, from the *Dred Scott* decision to today. Students made a sculpture of Amédé Ardoin's hat, coat, and fiddle and installed it on the ferry at Vermilionville to represent the connection of the past to the present. Another high school history class studied the Industrial Revolution through the crafts of Vermilionville artisans and made a quilt with squares depicting artifacts such as a spinning wheel and an anvil. Through such immersive experiences at this museum, students have seen themselves as part of history and contributors to local culture. They are excited to bring their families to Vermilionville to see their artwork and meet the artisans whom they have gotten to know and respect.

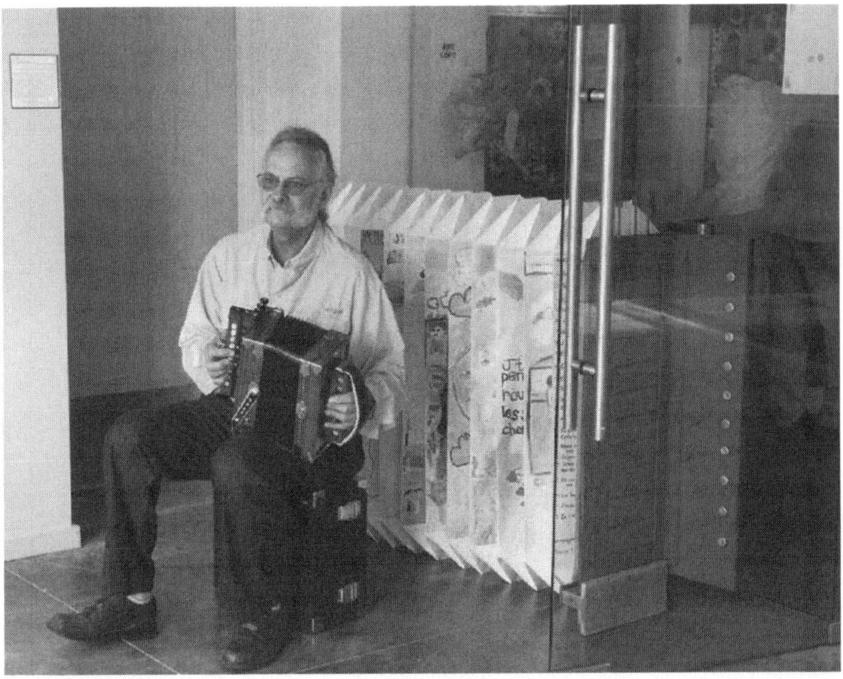

FIGURE 21.3
Elementary French Immersion students chose lyrics from favorite Cajun songs and illustrated watercolor panels for a large accordion sculpture as part of a Local Learning @ Vermilionville residency with Cajun musician Nonc Jules Guidry. He was impressed and moved by students' fluency in French, which he was forbidden to speak in school. (Photo: Paddy Bowman.)

The museum artisans find that students who have prepared for their residencies by reading their artist statements and inventorying their assumptions about the artist and the art form are excited and ask relevant questions. Students develop rapport with the artists and connect to their passion for their art. Teaching artists report that by the time they start working with students to create artwork inspired by their field trips and interviews with the folk artists and family members, their creativity is bubbling over. They make sophisticated, multilayered connections and metaphors.

A three-year project teacher, Harriet Maher, summarized her experience:

> A 30-year teaching veteran, this first year of Common Core has been challenging. Nonfiction plays a more prominent role, and using primary source activities

has helped me to "put a face" on nonfiction. The real Godsend, though, were the opportunities afforded by Local Learning at Vermilionville. Brigitte and I (and our students) have worked together all year because we were given the rich gift of time with a folklorist, fine artists, native craft artists, and other practicing teachers for ongoing support and collaboration throughout the year. That kind of gift is priceless—and rare.

NOTES

1. See Bowman and Hamer 2011.

2. See Clifford and Marcus 1986; Behar and Gordon 1995.

3. Bowman and Rathje 2014.

4. See Sunstein and Chiseri-Strater 2002 for more on writing and teaching with field notes.

5. See the *Museum 2.0* blog (Simon, n.d.) for more on this.

6. Lawless 1991, 38.

7. Chew 2005.

8. See the *Local Learning Folk Arts Integration Handbook*, found at http://locallearningnetwork.org/journal-of-folklore-and-education/current-and-past-issues/volume-one-2014.

9. See "Lesson Plans," Bayou Vermilion District, http://www.bayouvermiliondistrict.org/vermilionville/educate/lesson-plans.

10. See Louisiana Voices, http://www.louisianavoices.org.

11. Wagler, Olson, and Pryor 2004.

12. Sunstein and Chiseri-Strater 2002.

13. Personal correspondence from the education coordinator to the authors based upon student evaluations.

14. Personal correspondence from the education coordinator to the author based upon student evaluations.

WORKS CITED

Alvarez, Maribel. N.d. *Arts in a Changing America.* http://artsinachangingamerica.org/author/alvarez.

Behar, Ruth, and Deborah A. Gordon, eds. 1995. *Women Writing Culture*. Berkeley: University of California Press.

Bowman, Paddy. 2012. *Local Learning Folk Arts Integration Handbook*. Local Learning Network. http://locallearningnetwork.org/education-resources/library.

Bowman, Paddy, and Lynne Hamer, eds. 2011. *Through the Schoolhouse Door: Folklore, Community, Curriculum*. Logan: Utah State University Press.

Bowman, Paddy, and Lisa Rathje, eds. 2014. "Dress to Express: Exploring Culture and Identity." *Journal of Folklore and Education*. http://locallearningnetwork.org/journal-of-folklore-and-education/current-and-past-issues/volume-one-2014.

Chew, Ron. 2005. "Five Keys to Growing a Healthy Community-Connected Museum." Community Arts Network, Reading Room. http://wayback.archive-it.org/2077/20100906203155/http:/www.communityarts.net/readingroom/archive files/2005/02/five_keys_to_gr.php.

Clifford, James, and George E. Marcus. 1986. *Writing Culture*. Berkeley: University of California Press.

Kirshenblatt-Gimblett, Barbara. 1998. *Destination Culture: Tourism, Museums, and Heritage*. Berkeley: University of California Press.

Lawless, Elaine J. 1991. "Women's Life Stories and Reciprocal Ethnography as Feminist and Emergent." *Journal of Folklore Research* 28, no. 1: 35–60, http://www.jstor.org/stable/3814539 (accessed March 26, 2016).

Louisiana Voices. 1999–2012. http://www.louisianavoices.org.

Simon, Nina. N.d. *Museum 2.0*. http://museumtwo.blogspot.com.

Sunstein, Bonnie Stone, and Elizabeth Chiseri-Strater. 2002. *Fieldworking: Reading and Writing Research*. 2nd ed. New York: Bedford/St. Martin's.

Vermilionville. N.d. "Lesson Plans." Vermilionville. http://www.vermilionville.org/vermilionville/educate/lesson-plans.

Wagler, Mark, Ruth Olson, and Anne Pryor. 2004. *The Teacher's Guide to Local Culture* and *The Kid's Guide to Local Culture*. Madison Children's Museum. http://artsboard.wisconsin.gov/docview.asp?docid=18875&locid=171.

Resources

The following are some notable national and international resources for those interested in learning more about folklife theory and practice related to museums. This is not an inclusive list of the extensive resources available on museum work from museum, historic preservation, and other professional associations. The selected resources are actively engaged with folklife and museums as part of their mission or programming. They also reflect some emerging twenty-first-century progressive museum practice that incorporates folklore in their services and work. There are numerous local museum and culturally specific museums that are dedicated to the documentation, collection, and presentation of the traditional culture of their communities that are not listed here.

The contributors to this volume identify (and often use as case studies) historical and innovative international museum practice that draws upon the field of folklore—from the early open-air museums in Nordic countries and Europe to the new ethnically specific and topical museums of today. These museums are also valuable resources for understanding the relationship between folklife and museums. While not listed here, they are cited in the individual chapters.

Many continents, nations, states, and regions have professional associations devoted to the study of folklore, intangible cultural heritage, and museums. They can be valuable resources for scholarly inquiry and professional practice.

National Folklife Organizations

American Folklife Center, Library of Congress: https://www.loc.gov/folklife

American Folklore Society Section on Folklore and Museums: http://www.afsnet.org/?page=MuseumSection

American Folklore Society: http://www.afsnet.org

Center for Folklife and Cultural Heritage, Smithsonian Institution: http://www.folklife.si.edu/contact/smithsonian

Local Learning: The National Network for Folk Arts in Education: http://www.locallearningnetwork.org

National Council for the Traditional Arts: http://ncta-usa.org

National Endowment for the Arts: Folk and Traditional Arts Program: https://www.arts.gov/artistic-fields/folk-traditional-arts

Society for Ethnomusicology: http://www.ethnomusicology.org

State Folklife Programs

Most states have a state folk and traditional arts program. Many are housed in state arts or humanities agencies. A growing number are now based at major state universities. Others are separate, free-standing folklife cultural centers. These programs are accessible through Folk and Traditional Arts, National Endowment for the Arts.

Museum Professional Organizations with a Folklife Focus

African Museum Council: http://www.culturalheritageconnections.org/wiki/International_Council_of_African_Museums

American Anthropological Association: http://www.americananthro.org

American Association for State and Local History: http://www.aaslh.org

Association of African American Museums: http://www.blackmuseums.org

Association of Living History, Farm, and Agricultural Museums: http://www.alhfam.org

Center for Folklife and Cultural Heritage, Smithsonian Institution: http://www.folklife.si.edu

International Coalition of Sites of Conscience: http://www.sitesofconscience.org

International Council of Museums: http://icom.museum

Museum Educators Roundtable: http://museumeducation.info

National Council for the Traditional Arts: http://ncta-usa.org

National Park Service (United States): http://www.nps.gov

UNESCO: Museums in Safeguarding Intangible Cultural Heritage: http://icom.museum/programmes/intangible-heritage

Museums/Centers

Center for Southern Folklore: http://www.southernfolklore.com

Center for the Study of Upper Midwest Culture, Madison, Wisconsin: http://csumc.wisc.edu

CityLore, New York City, New York: http://citylore.org

Kentucky Museum, Western Kentucky University, Bowling Green, Kentucky: http://www.wku.edu/kentuckymuseum

McKissick Museum, University of South Carolina, Columbia, South Carolina: http://artsandsciences.sc.edu/mckissickmuseum/mckissick-museum

Michigan State University Museum/Folk and Traditional Art Program, East Lansing, Michigan: http://museum.msu.edu/s-program/mtap

Philadelphia Folklore Center, Philadelphia, Pennsylvania: http://www.folkloreproject.org

Vermillionville Living History Museum and Folklife Part, Lafayette, Louisiana: http://vermillionville.org

Vermont Folklife Center, Middlebury, Vermont: http://www.vermontfolklifecenter.org

Western Folklife Center, Elko, Nevada: http://www.westernfolklife.org

American Museums with Major Focus on Folklife

Abby Aldrich Rockefeller Folk Art Museum, Williamsburg, Virginia: http://www.history.org/history/museums/abby_art.cfm

American Folk Art Museum, New York, New York: http://folkartmuseum.org

Blue Ridge Institute and Museum, Ferrum College, Virginia: http://www.blueridgeinstitute.org

Colonial Williamsburg, Williamsburg, Virginia: http://www.history.org

Conner Prairie Interactive History Park, Fishers, Indiana: http://www.connerprairie.org

Fenimore Art Museum, Cooperstown, New York: http://www.fenimoreartmuseum.org

Living History Farms, Urbandale, Iowa: http://www.lhf.org

Museum of International Folk Art, Santa Fe, New Mexico: http://www.internationalfolkart.org

Old Sturbridge Village, Sturbridge, Massachusetts: https://www.osv.org

Plimoth Plantation, Plymouth, Massachusetts: http://www.plimoth.org

Shaker Village of Pleasant Hill, Harrodsburg, Kentucky: http://shakervillageky.org/about-us

Shelburne Museum, Shelburne, Vermont: https://shelburnemuseum.org

Smithsonian Institution (Museum of American History, Museum of African American History and Culture, Museum of African Art, National Museum of the American Indian, Museum of American Art, and Museum of Natural History), Washington, DC: https://www.si.edu

The Henry Ford, Dearborn, Michigan: https://www.thehenryford.org

Acknowledgments

We want to begin by thanking all of our contributors to this book. It has been rewarding to interact with these groundbreaking colleagues who are passionate about their training and convey so powerfully how it has enriched their museums. We are pleased to be able to share their diverse experiences and the lessons they have learned in their essays. We want to add that we have learned a great deal from our other professional colleagues, including our current and past museum colleagues, as well as our colleagues from the fields of folklore, history, anthropology, American studies, ethnography, ethnomusicology, and museum studies. We want to extend special thanks to the American Folklore Society (AFS), the American Association for State and Local History (AASLH), and the American Alliance of Museums, as they have been especially supportive and valuable in the preparation of this book. Thanks are due Donna Engdahl for assistance converting articles from the 1987 book to digitized format. Finally, we want to thank Charles Harmon, executive editor, and his colleagues at Rowman & Littlefield Publishing Group. Charles Harmon has provided us with valued professional guidance, encouragement, and support through the editorial process and throughout the production of this book.

Index

Page references for figures are *italicized*.

About the Editors

C. Kurt Dewhurst, PhD, serves as director of arts and cultural initiatives and senior fellow, university outreach and engagement; curator of folklife and cultural heritage at the Michigan State University; and professor of English at MSU. He is also director emeritus of the MSU Museum. His research interests include folk arts, material culture, ethnicity, occupational folk culture, cultural economic development, and cultural heritage policy. He has curated more than sixty exhibitions and many festival programs during his career and has an extensive publication record. He teaches courses in folklife, material culture, and museum studies. He currently serves as chairperson of the board of trustees for the American Folklife Center at the Library of Congress; he is past president of the American Folklore Society; chair of the Advisory Council, Smithsonian Center for Folklife and Culture; chair of the Michigan Council for the Arts and Cultural Affairs; vice chair of the Michigan Humanities Council; and president of the Michigan Museums Association. He is also an advisor to the Nelson Mandela Museum in Mthatha, South Africa, and an advisor for the development of the new Ahmed Kathrada Foundation Museum Center on Non-Racialism in Johannesburg, South Africa. He has served as an advisor to the development of the Nokomis Learning Center, Okemos,

Michigan; the National Cultural Center in Bangkok, Thailand; and the National Heritage Center at the University of Fort Hare, Alice, South Africa.

Patricia Hall is an independent folklorist and museum consultant living and working in San Diego, California. Previously, she served as director of education for the American Association for State and Local History (AASLH), where she designed and led museum seminars, oversaw the association's Consultant Service, published and produced written and audiovisual materials (*So You've Chosen to Be a History Professional* and *Now That You've Chosen History: Here's How to Get the Job*), and presented papers and published numerous articles on the relationship of folklore and history. She has produced and annotated historical albums of folk and country music for the Franklin Mint, Time-Life, and Rounder Records. In 1987, she coedited *Folklife and Museums: Selected Readings*. In 1993, she published the illustrated biography *Johnny Gruelle, Creator of Raggedy Ann and Andy*. In 1990, she envisioned and curated a major exhibition on artist/author Johnny Gruelle at the Indiana Museum of History. Several years later, she served as chief historical consultant and board member of the Johnny Gruelle Raggedy Ann & Andy Museum in Arcola, Illinois. She has also served on the boards of the Tennessee Association of Museums and the Inter-Museum Council of Nashville. She holds an MA in folklore from the University of California, Los Angeles, and a BS in psychology from the University of California, Santa Cruz.

Charlie Seemann is executive director emeritus of the Western Folklife Center in Elko, Nevada. He holds a BA in political science from San Francisco State University and an MA in folklife studies from the University of California, Los Angeles. He was deputy director for collections and research at the Country Music Foundation/Country Music Hall of Fame for twelve years, then program director at the Fund for Folk Culture in Santa Fe, New Mexico, before coming to the Western Folklife Center in 1998. He retired from that position in July 2014. He is coeditor of *Folklife and Museums: Selected Readings* (1987). He has produced and/or annotated more than thirty documentary albums of folk, country, and cowboy music. In 1983 he received a Wrangler Award from the National Cowboy Hall of Fame and Western Heritage Museum as well as a Grammy nomination for the New World Records anthology *Back in the Saddle Again: American Cowboy Songs* (1983). He received a second Wrangler Award in 2003 for producing *Buck Ramsey: Hittin' the Trail*, a joint project of the Western Folklife Center and Smithsonian Folkways Recordings. He has written numerous articles on Western culture and cowboy music. He is past president (founding president) and still a board member of the Alliance for California Traditional Arts, was a congressional appointee to the board of the American Folklife Center at the Library of Congress, and is a member of the board of the Washington, DC–based National Council for the Traditional Arts. In 2014 he edited the poetry anthology for the National Cowboy Poetry Gathering's thirtieth anniversary, *The Anthology: Celebrating 30 Years of Wrangling Words*, and in 2016 he edited a second version of *The Hell-Bound Train: A Cowboy Songbook* by Glenn Ohrlin.

About the Contributors

Susan Asbury is a PhD candidate in American studies at Pennsylvania State University, Harrisburg, and is director of student rights and responsibilities at Elizabethtown College (Pennsylvania). She holds an MA in public history from the University of South Carolina. Asbury has worked at the South Carolina State Museum, Berry College, and The Strong. Most of her scholarship relates to the material culture of play, and she has delivered presentations on princess play, frontier imagery in board games, and the intersections of history, memory, and culture in nineteenth-century board games. Her most recent publication is "The Checkered Game of Life: Depictions of the Life Cycle in Board Games," *Midwestern Folklore* 41, no. 2 (Fall 2015).

Robert Baron is the founding director of the Folk Arts Program of the New York State Council on the Arts (NYSCA). Baron previously served as director of NYSCA's Museum Program, currently also directs its Music Program, and is on the faculty of the master's program in cultural sustainability at Goucher College. He has also served as folklore administrator of the National Endowment for the Humanities, senior research specialist in the Education Division of the Brooklyn Museum, a Fulbright senior specialist in Finland and the Philippines, a Smithsonian museum practice fellow, and nonresident fellow of the W. E. B. Du Bois Research Institute at Harvard University. He is a fellow of the American Folklore Society (AFS) and received the Benjamin A. Botkin Prize from the AFS for significant lifetime achievement in public folklore. Baron's research interests include public folklore, cultural policy, the history of folklore studies, creolization, and museum studies. His publications include *Public Folklore* (edited with Nick Spitzer), *Creolization as Cultural Creativity* (edited with Ana Cara), and articles in *Curator, International Journal of Heritage Studies, Journal of American Folklore, Journal of Folklore Research, Western Folklore,* and *Children's Folklore Review.* Baron received a PhD in folklore and folklife from the University of Pennsylvania.

Marsha C. Bol, PhD, is director emeritus of the Museum of International Folk Art in Santa Fe, New Mexico. Over the past thirty-four years she has worked as a director or curator in four museums—the Museum of International Folk Art (twice), the New Mexico Museum of Art, the Carnegie Museum of Natural History, and the Maxwell Museum of Anthropology—and as associate professor at the University of Texas, San Antonio. She has a PhD in art history from the University of New Mexico and is a specialist in Native American art and architecture and Spanish colonial art and architecture.

At the Carnegie Museum, she was curator of the Alcoa Foundation Hall of American Indians, producing two books on the topic of American Indians and the natural world. She is author of numerous articles and is currently working on a book/exhibition project about "beadwork adorns the world."

Paddy Bowman is director of Local Learning: The National Network for Folk Arts in Education and coeditor of the *Journal of Folklore and Education.* She received an MA in folklore from the University of North Carolina and was awarded the 2013 American Folklore Society Benjamin A. Botkin Prize for lifetime achievement in public folklore, and is a member of the society's fellows.

Simon J. Bronner, PhD, is distinguished professor of American studies and folklore and chair of the American Studies Program at the Pennsylvania State University, Harrisburg, where he also directs the Center for Pennsylvania Culture Studies and coordinates the graduate certificate programs in folklore and ethnography and in heritage and museum practice. He is author or editor of over thirty-five books on folklife, material culture, and heritage studies, including *Explaining Traditions: Folk Behavior in Modern Culture* (2011), *Encyclopedia of American Folklife* (2006), and *American Material Culture and Folklife* (1985).

Aleia Brown, PhD candidate, is a visiting curator at the Michigan State University Museum where she primarily works on a joint exhibition with the MSU Museum and the Desmond and Leah Tutu Legacy Foundation in South Africa. Brown is also a public history doctoral candidate in Middle Tennessee State University's Department of History. She is particularly interested in how museums navigate issues of race and gender from 1968 to the present. As cofounder of the Twitter chat #museumsrespondtoferguson, she is engaged with the current dialog on museums responding to racialized violence and police brutality. Her publications include "On Race and Museums: Starting Conversations, Embracing Action," *Museums and Social Issues: A Journal of Reflective Discourse* 10, no. 2 (October 2015): 109–12, and, with Adrianne Russell, "Museums and #BlackLivesMatter," in *Code | Words: Technology and Theory in the Museum*, ed. Ed Rodley, Robert J. Stein, and Suse Cairns (2015).

Meg Glaser is artistic director for the Western Folklife Center (WFC). She has served as a director of Western Folklife Center programs since 1990, conducting and overseeing research and fieldwork, producing exhibitions, performance tours, and other WFC events. She is a founder of the National Cowboy Poetry Gathering, assisting in the production of this event since its inception in 1985. Prior to working at the Western Folklife Center, she was program director (five years) and associate director (two years) at the National Council for the Traditional Arts in Washington, DC, producing national performing arts tours, the National Folk Festival, and other events for the National Park Service, Library of Congress, and National Endowment for the Arts (NEA). She was an arts management fellow at the NEA (1982–1983) and a program coordinator for the Smithsonian's Festival of American Folklife (1983). She has served as a grants panelist and site visitor for the NEA; a grants panelist for the Fund for Folk Culture, Bush Foundation, Idaho Commission on the Arts, WESTAF/Forest Service, and Nevada Arts Council; and a consultant for the Northumberland National Park and Centrum Foundation. She served as a trustee for Nevada Citizens for the Arts (2001–2005). In 2004 she was honored with the Nevada Governor's Award in the Arts. She received her BA in music education at the University of Utah and did graduate studies in ethnomusicology at the University of Washington. While living in Seattle she performed with the Mazel Tov Klezmer band. One of her special interests is brass band music from around the world, and while living in Washington, DC, she spent many hours recording shout bands (gospel trombone bands) of the United House for Prayer for All People.

Jo Farb Hernández is a professor and director of the Thompson Art Gallery at San José State University (California). She has worked in the museum field for over forty years, including service as president of the California Association of Museums and director of the Monterey Peninsula (California) Museum of Art. Hernández also directs SPACES (Saving and Preserving Arts and Cultural Environments; www.spacesarchives.org), a global nonprofit archive documenting art environments and self-taught arts. She holds an MA in folklore (with a concentration in folk art) from the University of California, Los Angeles, and is author of over thirty books and exhibition catalogs, from the English-language study *The Day of the Dead: Tradition and Change in Contemporary Mexico* (1979) to more recent volumes, including *Forms of Tradition in Contemporary Spain* (2005), winner of the Chicago Folklore Prize, and *Singular Spaces: From the Eccentric to the Extraordinary in Spanish Art Environments* (2013), which has been described as the "most impressive single volume of research ever published in the field of self-taught art." A Fulbright Scholar, Hernández is a well-known lecturer and exhibition juror and serves on the editorial or advisory boards of several international art journals and art environments.

Carrie Hertz, PhD, is curator of textiles and dress at the Museum of International Folk Art in Santa Fe, where she also serves as a core member of the Gallery of Conscience curatorial team. Previously, Hertz directed a community-based folk arts program as the curator of folk arts at the Castellani Art Museum of Niagara University and taught classes on curatorship, material culture, and folklore in the art history with museum studies degree program. From 2013 to 2015 she served as an advisory member of the American Folklore Society's Folklore and Museum Policy and Practice Working Group, contributing to a coauthored white paper. She is also cofounder, with Suzy

Seriff, of the Experiments in Exhibition professional development series, held in conjunction with the annual gathering of the American Folklore Society. Hertz received her PhD in folklore from Indiana University.

Bill Ivey is former chairman of the National Endowment for the Arts and served as team leader for arts and humanities in the Barack Obama presidential transition. From 1971 through 1997 he was director of the Country Music Hall of Fame and Museum; he is currently a visiting research associate at the Indiana University Department of Folklore and Ethnomusicology. His new book, *Folklore: Politics and Public Policy*, is forthcoming in 2017.

Jason Baird Jackson, PhD, is director of the Mathers Museum of World Cultures and professor of folklore in the Department of Folklore and Ethnomusicology at Indiana University, where he is also editor of *Museum Anthropology Review* and the Material Vernaculars book series. His own scholarship has focused on the ethnography, ethnohistory, and ethnology of the American South, with a special concern for this region's indigenous peoples. He is author of *Yuchi Ceremonial Life: Performance, Meaning, and Tradition in a Contemporary American Indian Community* (2003) and *Yuchi Folklore: Cultural Expression in a Southeastern Native American Community* (2013). He has edited several scholarly volumes, including *Material Vernaculars: Objects, Images, and Their Social Worlds*. His recent museum work has included collaborative projects focused on folklife in southwestern China. Jackson is convener of the Folklore and Museums Section of the American Folklore Society.

Barbara Kirshenblatt-Gimblett is chief curator of the core exhibition at the POLIN Museum of the History of Polish Jews and university professor emerita and professor emerita of performance studies at New York University. Her books include *Image before My Eyes: A Photographic History of Jewish Life in Poland, 1864–1939* (with Lucjan Dobroszycki, 1977); *Destination Culture: Tourism, Museums, and Heritage* (1998); *They Called Me Mayer July: Painted Memories of a Jewish Childhood in Poland before the Holocaust* (with Mayer Kirshenblatt, 2007), *The Art of Being Jewish in Modern Times* (with Jonathan Karp, 2008), and *Anne Frank Unbound: Media, Imagination, Memory* (with Jeffrey Shandler, 2012), among others. She was decorated with the Officer's

Cross of the Order of Merit of the Republic of Poland by the president of Poland for her contribution to the POLIN Museum.

Richard Kurin is the Smithsonian's acting provost and undersecretary for museums and research responsible for all its national museums and scholarly and scientific research centers. For decades he directed the Center for Folklife and Cultural Heritage, overseeing the Smithsonian Folklife Festival and Smithsonian Folkways Recordings. Kurin served on the US Commission for UNESCO, helping draft the international treaty on safeguarding the world's living cultural heritage, now ratified by more than 160 nations. He led a US and international project to successfully rescue Haiti's cultural heritage following the devastating 2010 earthquake and oversees similar efforts in other nations. As liaison to the President's Committee on the Arts and the Humanities, he's been honored by the International Council of Museums, Harvard University's Peabody Museum, the American Folklore Society, and the American Anthropological Association; he is also a fellow of the American Academy of Arts and Sciences. Kurin earned his doctorate in anthropology from the University of Chicago, taught at Johns Hopkins University's Nitze School of Advanced International Studies, and is the author of several books, most recently *The Smithsonian's History of America in 101 Objects* (2013).

Marsha MacDowell, PhD, is curator of folk arts, Michigan State University Museum; professor, Department of Art, Art History, and Design, Michigan State University; coordinator, Michigan Traditional Arts Program (a statewide program of the MSU Museum in partnership with the Michigan Council for Arts and Cultural Affairs); and director of the Quilt Index, an international digital repository of stories and images related to quilts, their makers, and their users. She has served as director or team member of numerous local, national, and international traditional arts–focused exhibitions, festival programs, documentation projects, digital humanities projects, and curriculum development initiatives. In addition to many studies of quilting traditions, MacDowell has published on women's folk arts, Native American weaving traditions, museums and folklore, folklife and education, digital repositories of thematic material culture, and many aspects of Michigan folklife. She has served as an elected member of the board of the

American Folklore Society, is a member of the society's fellows, and was a member of the AFS folklore and museum task force.

Howard Wight Marshall, PhD, is professor and chairman emeritus of art history and archaeology and former director of the Missouri Cultural Heritage Center at the University of Missouri, Columbia. Marshall took his BA in English at the University of Missouri and his MA and PhD in folklore and anthropology at Indiana University under Henry Glassie. Marshall worked at museums and consulted for the Smithsonian Institution, worked for several years at the American Folklife Center in the Library of Congress, and taught at George Washington University and Kansas State University. In 1982, he returned to Columbia to establish the Missouri Cultural Heritage Center at the University of Missouri Graduate School and to teach material culture, vernacular architecture, and historic preservation in the Department of Art History and Archaeology.

Marshall's books include *Folk Architecture in Little Dixie: A Regional Culture in Missouri* (1981), *Buckaroos in Paradise: Cowboy Life in Northern Nevada* (with Richard Ahlborn, 1981), *Missouri Artist Jesse Howard* (1983), *The German-American Experience in Missouri* (with James Goodrich, 1983), *Vernacular Architecture in Rural and Small Town Missouri* (1984), *Paradise Valley, Nevada: People and Buildings of an American Place* (1995), *Barns of Missouri: Storehouses of History* (2003), *"Play Me Something Quick and Devilish": Old-Time Fiddlers in Missouri* (2012), and *Fiddler's Dream: Old-Time, Swing, and Bluegrass Fiddling in Missouri* (forthcoming).

John F. Moe, PhD, is senior lecturer in the Department of English at the Ohio State University, where he is also affiliated with the Program in Folklore Studies and the Narratology Project. He taught as Fulbright professor of American studies at the University of Bergen, Norway (1990–1991), the University of Tampere, Finland (1995–1996), and the University of Tartu, Estonia (2003–2004). From 2008 to 2009 he served as the Norwegian Marshall Scholar in residence at the Norwegian Emigrant Museum in Hamar, Norway. His publications are primarily in American studies and folklore, with a focus on American ethnic folk traditions and material culture. His publications include *Amazing Grace: The Life and Art Work of Elijah Pierce*, "Edenic Philosophy and the Indian Reservation: Membership, Citizenship,

Identity and the Dilemma of Belonging (with Special Reference to the Writing of Louise Erdrich)" (2013), and "Artistic Expression and the Struggle for Justice: African American Folk Art and Literacy Narrative in Post–World War II America," *in Deferred Dreams, Defiant Struggles: Critical Perspectives on Blackness, Belonging and Civil Rights* (forthcoming). He has initiated and assisted in the development of a range of exhibitions on African American folk art, traditional textiles, human rights, contemporary Turkish art, and Norwegian migration to the United States.

He holds a BA in English and American civilization from the University of Iowa, an MA in history from Indiana University, an MA in folklore from the Folklore Institute at Indiana University, and a PhD in history and American studies from Indiana University (1978).

Diana Baird N'Diaye, PhD, is a cultural heritage specialist and curator at the Smithsonian's Center for Folklife and Cultural Heritage. She developed and leads "The Will to Adorn: African American Dress and the Aesthetics of Identity," a pan-institutional, multisited research project that was a featured program of the 2013 Smithsonian Folklife Festival. Her training in anthropology, folklore, and visual studies and her experience as an anthropologist and studio craft artist support over thirty years of fieldwork, exhibitions, programs, and publications focusing on expressive culture and community-based cultural industries in Africa, the Caribbean, and their diasporas in the United States; children's play and performance; and dress traditions and fashion in Oman, Mali, Kyrgyzstan, Uzbekistan, and Japan. She is a research associate at Michigan State University (MSU) Museum and the University of Iowa's first interdisciplinary writer in residence. She holds a PhD in anthropology and visual studies from the Union Institute. She is currently coeditor of a volume of essays titled *Curatorial Conversations*, on curators' perspectives on the Smithsonian Folklife Festival. N'Diaye's forthcoming book on "The Will to Adorn" is scheduled to be part of the Mellon Foundation–sponsored series Folklore Studies in a Multicultural World.

Lisa Rathje, PhD, is assistant director of Local Learning: The National Network for Folk Arts in Education and coeditor of the *Journal of Folklore and Education*. She also teaches courses on research methods and cultural partnerships in the Goucher College master's program in cultural sustainability.

Suzanne Seriff, PhD, is director of the Gallery of Conscience, an experimental exhibition lab within the Museum of International Folk Art in Santa Fe, New Mexico, which draws on the power of folk and traditional arts to catalyze dialog, engagement, and action around social justice and human rights issues both at home and abroad. She is a founder and the principal coordinator of the Global Folk Art Network, an international consortium of folk artists, markets, and museums dedicated to building capacity, sharing resources, and catalyzing action around positive social change through the traditional arts. Seriff received her PhD in folklore from the University of Texas, Austin, where she currently holds a position as senior lecturer in anthropology, teaching courses on folklife, museum studies, immigration, Jewish material culture, and arts-based activism for social change. As an independent museum curator, Seriff has directed and guest-curated a number of nationally traveling exhibition projects (and publications), including *Recycled, Re-seen: Folk Arts from the Global Scrap Heap*, for the Museum of International Folk Art (coedited with Charlene Cerny, 1996), *Forgotten Gateway: Coming to America through Galveston Island* (for the Bullock Texas State History Museum in Austin, Texas), and the Gallery of Conscience's inaugural exhibition in 2010, *Empowering Women: Artisan Cooperatives That Transform Communities.* The Gallery of Conscience's seminal engagement with the National Dialogues on Immigration Project of the International Coalition of Sites of Conscience is depicted in Seriff's chapter of the forthcoming publication *Interpreting Immigration: Connecting Past and Present at Museums.*

Daniel Sheehy, PhD, is director and curator emeritus of Smithsonian Folkways Recordings. His four-decade career in public-sector service includes work as Smithsonian Folkways (2000–2016), director of the Smithsonian Center for Folklife and Cultural Heritage (2009–2013), director of folk and traditional arts at the National Endowment for the Arts (1992–2000), and NEA staff ethnomusicologist and assistant director (1978–1992). A Fulbright-Hays scholar in Veracruz, Mexico (1977–1978), he earned his PhD in ethnomusicology from the University of California, Los Angeles (1979). His publications include the *South America, Mexico, Central America, and the Caribbean* volume of the *Garland Encyclopedia of World Music* (coeditor, 1999) and *Mariachi Music in America: Experiencing Music, Expressing Culture* (2006). Under his leadership, Smithsonian Folkways published more than 225 recordings, earning five Grammy awards, one Latin Grammy, and twenty Grammy nominations. In 2015, the National Endowment for the Arts awarded him a Bess Lomax Hawes National Heritage Fellowship.

Virginia Siegel is a folklife specialist for the Kentucky Folklife Program, located at Western Kentucky University (WKU), in Bowling Green. Siegel holds an MA in folk studies with a concentration in historic preservation from WKU, as well as a BFA in historic preservation with a minor in architectural history from the Savannah College of Art and Design. Her background has included experience in museum, archive, and preservation nonprofit settings. While a graduate student at WKU, Siegel received a research fellowship from the university for her thesis work on New York City Puerto Rican casitas, completed in cooperation with the American Folklore Society's Working Group on Folklore and Preservation Policy.

Candace Tangorra Matelic, PhD, president of CTM Professional Services, teaches museums about community engagement and organizational transformation through professional workshops and courses, including the University of Victoria, Johns Hopkins University, and state and provincial museum associations. Her consulting work focuses on helping cultural organizations engage their communities and then fundamentally transform their visions, assumptions, organizational cultures, and work patterns. In her forty-year career, she directed a center for contemporary arts and a children's museum (both in Santa Fe) and two National Historic Landmark sites (Mission Houses Museum in Hawaii and Historic St. Mary's City in Maryland); she also served as a programming department head at the Henry Ford Museum (now known as the Henry Ford) and Iowa Living History Farms. For ten years she directed the Cooperstown Graduate Program. She holds a PhD in organizational studies, an MA in museum studies, and a BFA in fine arts, American studies. She has presented at more than one hundred conferences in the United States, Canada, and Europe, over thirty-five times as a keynote speaker or invited guest. Her publications include two coauthored books and thirty-two articles or chapters. She is based in Fort Worth, Texas.

John Michael Vlach was born in Honolulu, Hawaii, and raised in Berkeley, California; he currently resides in Washington, DC. He attended the University of California, Davis, where he majored in English, taking a year abroad at the University of Ghana as attendant to anthropologist Daniel Crowley, who dissuaded him from attending law school in favor of folklore. He obtained a PhD in folklore at Indiana University, where Henry Glassie directed his explorations of material culture. His dissertation about the dissemination of African American construction techniques, especially the shotgun house, continues to influence studies of vernacular architecture. His teaching career spanned more than thirty years at the University of Maryland, College Park, the University of Texas, Austin, and the George Washington University (GWU), from which he retired in 2013. He was an inspiring mentor and teacher. He also published, coauthored, edited, or coedited ten books and numerous articles; curated several important museum and library exhibitions; served on the boards of numerous distinguished academic and professional organizations; and chaired the American Studies Department at GWU for several years. He is a fellow of the American Folklore Society.

Michael Ann Williams, PhD, is professor of folk studies and department head of folk studies and anthropology at Western Kentucky University. She holds a BA in anthropology from Franklin and Marshall College and a PhD in folklore and folklife from the University of Pennsylvania. A university distinguished professor, she has been teaching folklore at WKU since 1986. She teaches courses in vernacular architecture, museum procedures and preservation techniques, cultural conservation, folk art, and folklore theory. Her research interests include social and symbolic use of space in vernacular architecture, national and international heritage policy, and cultural representation and the staging of tradition. She served as chair of the Kentucky Historic Preservation Review Board from 1993 to 2005 and is an advisor to the Kentucky Oral History Commission. She has also been an active member of the Vernacular Architecture Forum, formerly serving as the newsletter editor and as a vice-president and board member. Most recently she served as president of the American Folklore Society (2014–2015). Her publications include *Great Smoky Mountains Folklife* (1995), *Homeplace: The Social Use and Meaning of the Folk Dwelling in Southwestern North Carolina* (2004), and *Staging Tradition: John Lair and Sarah Gertrude Knott* (2006).